<u>FRONT SLEEVE SYNOPSIS</u>

EVERI MANN's Guide To Governing OUR Un-Governable Government.................

This Job May Be An Adventure, But It's Not About "Hitting The Lottery", or for "The PERKS!"...........
....Hey: "<u>Just Do Your Duty, Then Go Home!</u>"

   I got so tired of listening to Beck, Hannity and Rush eternally complaining without some kind of tangible strategy for any real retaliatory Game Plan to reverse this "alternative-reality" our ever-evolving United States has been suffering for these decades now, that I finally started hearing echoes, but around the periphery of some of the same points, suggestions and ideas I'd written myself with some frequency, days or weeks earlier on my little obscure Blog. Now finally on the same wave length, I immediately realized that I just might have something important to contribute, and I needed to quickly write this comprehensive counterrevolutionary book because these guys, as superb as they all are at what they do, weren't really offering any "Plans For A Counter-Attack," or for that matter "an actual Solution" in any form to stop this growing madness, this malignancy on the backside of our Country's God-given Liberty and Freedom!

   So, this is kind of a Cook Book, a Psychology Book, a Point/Counterpoint History Book, a "Surviving-Liberalism" manual; Advice to the besieged, the depressed, the seething silent-majority in need of a Pep-Talk, a booster, for not just "fighting back", but to once and for all "defeat this eternal enemy", this relentless-foe and to finally WIN!

   Speak-up and serve but one Master! I will never hold back and never give an inch, and to that end I endeavor to illustrate through My series of 100+ consecutive, rather glib, occasionally caustic satirical vignettes, recollections and examinations, dissertations and rants; each pounding home the simple axiom: "<u>To Be Silent = They Always WIN!</u>"

~ <u>Love Letters To The "Spinners", The "Sycophants", The Professional "B/S'ers"</u>~

And To You Professionals We've All Got Your Numbers NOW, Finally Thank God. Nobody Believes Your "Shhh,..*Spin*" Anymore! No longer skulking in the dim shadows, <u>*WE ALL SEE YOU NOW*</u>!

Well, perhaps our children still believe your Shhh...<u>*spin*</u>, and some of our grandchildren, and maybe a few of our great-grandchildren yet, since You have controlled their minds for decades now, from the impressionable ages of 4, up to the incurably-infected 34, from PS-69, up to Columbia U. and the citadel of autocratic Liberalism: Harvard Graduate School since 1636.
I wonder, what with Red Lining, forgive the pun, but still your "minority preferences", inclusion-quotas, and anti-discrimination lawsuits, if any of the native-Americans had ever matriculated to that prestiged "alma mater" <u>*way back when, in those good-old lazy-dayz of the 1600's Indian summers*</u>?

Prior to The PODs on The QUADs taking-over "total control" of Academia with their reeducation institutions, mind-meld lab-oratories where every good little obedient Eloi are supposed to all be the S.A.M.E., advancing on to Law, Journalism, and especially the Publishing Houses, re-writing our true American history, now in their own images for the New GREEN Utopia, many of us on that "time-line" barely escaped those very long tentacles of "The Movement" back in the 60s! That was before the Morlocks got their tenured-claws into all those sweet young nubile, sopho-moronic minds, who would unfortunately be following us into the greater ultra-enlightened, liberal "liberation-generation" years to come; <u>*Pie-in-the-sky & Free-Lunch!*</u>

<u>You want a Utopia?</u> Travel to another planet because America is as close as You're ever going to get, and You're now about to ruin that for everyone else.

<u>You want a Utopia?</u> Just let people have the God-given Freedoms all fellow human beings deserve and never impose "another's will" upon any Person or People! Just allow our new Democracy, and that old "Golden Rule" to be your compass, whether You believe in any Higher Power or not, but never the Occupy-Mobs, or the elite's Chosen-Ones dispensing-out True Justice!

<u>You want America to be unconditionally Socialist?</u> OK, here's 3 Wishes; PROTECT the borders, NOT (1) child ever goes to bed hungry, and ALL Research on Children's Diseases is entirely funded by OUR Government Taxes! .... <u>That's It! - All you get!</u> .... <u>That's UTOPIA!</u> ....
That's   UTOPIA!   Pg. 1

IN GOD WE TRUST

Thank you to the American patriots, to all those independent free-thinkers, and to those Crusaders waiting to be freed around the world, still in chains behind cyber-curtains, who brave the demons to inform us and the world with their valuable Videos, Websites and Blogs of crucial events, issues and information each day, all helping to keep American FREE; unfiltered by governments, or our own compromised national Press and Media pawns!

And a special thanks to that Lady, North To Alaska, (the Duke would be proud a' yah), and to all the Bloggers that answered, contributed and challenged my Blog Posts, all helping me jump-start and gel my thoughts to get my points of view across during the wee hours of so many of those mornings.
…. (I have changed all Blogger's IDs to shield them.)

"Keep the Internet FREE"…Remember "Fahrenheit 451"…the "next shoe"!
(Some controversial video links listed in my book exposing corruption, graft and skullduggery in politics may be removed from the Net over time! …..Be vigilant!)

I will endeavor to find current "live" web-addresses for those "same" expose' videos, featured in this book, that are "continually blocked" following this publication, and to post "SAME" on my web-site: www.SENTRYMAN.org and with continual BLOGs *to keep the "harsh light of truth" shining on crimes, institutions of hatred, and rampant hypocrisy!*

As the Government, and exactly who is the Government???_____
As your Government scans your Emails for "Hate Speech", listens-in to your Cell Phone for "Whatever", watches you and monitors your every movement from many GPS vantage-points; how many stories and tales, books and movies have foretold of this astounding inevitability, and all You do is "passively relax", buy some over-priced popcorn and enjoy the show!

This is NO movie, and "You are the Star" in your very own Reality Show, but YOU are not even paying any attention……!

DEM Attorneys donate to DEM candidates = Rewarded with a Judgeship?_____
DEM controlled Senate ENDs the "US Constitutional Filibuster" = Stack the Courts?_____
DEMs quietly NIX Electoral College, State by State = Coronate DEM President by an Urban Popular Vote?_____

"LIBERTY for ALL?", or the 3 fastest ways to keep America progressively Democrat? ………Hail Caesar!

Your State Legislators usurp the last vestiges of your "State's Sovereignty" all for the National "Collective's" Eminent Domain and new World Order: your "Handlers" are selling YOU "Short" as THEY all bet "*Long*"!

You think actor Nicholas Cage, for instance, got a raw deal, or deserved his fate because he wasn't paying attention with his own $100 Million dollars, or so? You've been bought with "promises" and "play money", sold-right-down-their-officially sanctioned "polluted"- river with your own Tax dollars, but yet on-CREDIT no less.

You still owe that $17 TRILLION+ (and growing daily), THEY've all borrowed in Your name, with Your forged signature!………..Be-warned, wake-up and *"SMILE": You're on Candid Camera*, but no one's laughing anymore!

LIBERTY Circumvented = FREEDOM Deigned   A REALITY THAT "PROP-86" CAN PREVENT!
You still have a very small "window of opportunity" if you ONLY OPEN YOUR EYES!

Ever wonder why, when it's in the 30's in Orlando, FL on December 7th, 2010, (20 degrees lower than normal for this time of the year in America), we don't hear anyone in our journalistically-pure investigative "Media" ever mentioning former Veep Al Gore's "Grand Illusion" to Save-Our-Planet cash-cow:
"Man Created" Global Warming? ………..hmmm!

**Extra thank-yous to my patient wife and my family when posting my Blogs, and while writing this book!
(I apologize for redundancies, while expressing passions during 3 years of Blogs to different patriots, included in this Book!...There are still a lot of gems, golden kernels, and fertile seeds in here for those "needing some nourishment, some help with weeding our garden, or for a new direction with a straight path", and even some bright-ideas that may need repeating with our society's *light-speed* attention span!) ………*So, Go Get 'em Kid!*

FOR MOM

It Was Never About The Black Guy,
...... It Was About "That Guy" !

AND <u>WASHINGTON's PYRATEs AND SNAKESss</u>

THE FINAL SOLUTION
<u>FIRE THEM ALL??</u>

<u>PART 1</u>

YOUR Absolute Last Chance To
$ave America For Your Children!

<u>TIME HAS RUN OUT !</u> ~~~ <u>THE ONLY HOPE: PROP. 86</u>

SENTRYMAN
Self-Published
USA

*Many of these chronologically-listed Chapters are verbatum, and reprinted formerly-posted conversational debate-streams, and my personal "disertations to the wind" & "shouting at the dark" rants posing "questions never asked, and solutions never debated"; as my (4) small self-employed successful businesses, with their solid 30 year customer-base, all similtaineously started to fail as Americans fatefully began to-listen to the chicken-little DEMs across this great nation leading up the the '06 mid-term elections, then becoming even more intense as the 2008 election approached.

Understandably, now SPOOKED, overly-cautious families were gradually succumbing yet once again to the sycophantic Doomsayer's drumbeat-diatribe touting "the sky is falling, the planet-nears-incineration, and Bush destroyed the universe", yadda, yadda, (which, if you remember, happened long after the DEM's 1970's Warning of an impending long "global-winter" predictions, but: "give the DEMs more tax dollars and we'll heal the sick and end hunger" mantra.)

Now by 2009 with the arrival of a new savior, everyone's customers promptly "snapped-shut their purses & closed their wallets" in a grand self-fulfilling prophesy that only the DEMs could really appreciate, fully ensconced with their 100% foolproof diabolic Game-Plan manuel with the same 50 year's worth of Bugaboos and Strawmen; "always the mean, corrupt, racist opposing team's fault", any of which THEY've never solved during as many years with a much greater times-at-bat average in the U.S. Congress, but who's counting, obviously not the Voters.
Well, if your spouse always believes the same lies whose fault is it?......That's non-secular humor!

Of hearing the specific "topic-du jour" hitting Media Outlets during my day, I'd start fuming, asking myself: "why didn't the Media ask this, or how stupid do THEY think we are?" I'm sure everyone does that. But with my life's work directly impacted each day, I became compelled to try and do more to effect the outcome than just flailing around in the current, and reverse the Tides,…yah sure!

The ideas and retorts started to pour-out on notes scribbled onto any shread of paper, all over my truck, jambed into my pockets as I'd pause with a tool in hand to keep that thought and my blood pressure in-check. Then by the end of long workdays I'd be all primed and ready to respond in-kind, typing hot-lead on my PC non-stop after dinner during a single session, usually until very late at night, then "post" it late that same evening, or I'd "auto-post" for the following morning.

Raw, passionate, un-edited, I didn't care; just "get it out" time/stamped and dated for the morning's consumption over coffee with other Cyber-warriors to spar with when I returned back home. So please, forgive my punctuation and grammer, I was public school educated!….ha, ha, ha,…ahhh haa.

It has been a cathardic process and served its purpose, but I soon began to feel that perhaps my personal expresssions of old sage advice and somewhat private dialogues might be of some value to a wider audience, especially those with only the government's "controlled network" liberal media sourced "leftist points of view"; NYT's, NBC, CNN, MSNBC, Daily Kos, Letterman, the Comedy Channel and SNL, etc., so the idea for a "Point/Counterpoint Primer" sprang eternal, and also too, just maybe my great-grandchildren might not think I'd done nothing about the incredibly disasterous -fix they may all find themselves in someday, when I had the chance to speak-up, way back when! ....Like: Benghazi, "they knew and allowed our men to be murdered"!

.........And, "Ft. Hood attack" was flagrantly and factually an "Act of War", premeditated by a radical Islamic terrorist aggressor, and as such, all US Military personnel involved deserve "War Zone" pay, Purple Hearts, and accordingly their rightful benefits due for spouses; You cheap, scared weasel politicians obstructing these awards! …You're administrators, NOT our omnipotent rulers. You work for us! Unless the mitigating circumstances disallowing just remunerations by all said, US Officials is that they're sympathetic to the Jihadist, and are in fact traitors to these United States, they then should be replaced immediately to join the Assassin in the docket!........(For instance.)
What I asked, what I advised, take your pick, an every-man's view: that's what this book is all about!
~ Award Sergeant Rafael Peralta the "Medal of Honor" - semper fi ~   Pg. 4

CHAPTER CONTENT

*A Challenge:
Instead of voicing: "*the government gave*",
I want You to try and remember to start responding:
"*Obama didn't give you that,
me & your neighbors, and your grandchildren PAID for that!*"

Government doesn't create anything, and pays for nothing!
See if your perspective doesn't start to change a little Pal...

TIME IS UP!

TIME IS UP! ™©

NO, YOU CAN'T BORROW IT...WRITE ME, WE'LL TALK, OR
YOU'LL SEE ME OFF YOUR STARBOARD! ....ARRRGGG!

PREFACE

"Love Letters to The Left"

Connecting the Dots between Liberals,……… Progressives……..
………and RHINOs, ..……...sanctimonious Republicans,………..

and; The Apathetic,…......The Uninvolved,…......The Uninterested:
those Patriots only engaged and conscious for two weeks every
four years prior to Election Day,……. The Usual Suspects – The
"Independents"! Save Our Country With A Citizen Government!

By SENTRYMAN

Want to take the "Bull" and "Pork" by the horns and ears, and
finally corral, hogtie and leash these wild Beasts & Burdens?

Want to finally solve all these problems yourself, once and for all
to save the Republic, *that great COUNTRY you once loved*?

Want to guarantee yourself a better chance at the polls, that
your Vote will matter this time, and will actually change the tide
before we're all washed-out to sea toward JAPAN and CHINA?

Don't rely on an A.C.O.R.N. to organize the US 2010 & 2012
Elections to honestly "represent, or count" what America really
wants their elected Representatives to accomplish in Congress!

<u>Don't rely on "dyed-in-the-wool" moderate-Democrats</u> who change their
Spots during any campaign, sounding all "conservative" to get re-elected;
<u>they're lying as usual to hide their Real Agendas!</u>

And don't rely on the GOP either to finally show some character,
or have the guts & hutzpah to call those Democrats on every
deceptive trick, maneuver and lie that they will create & repeat to
UNJUSTLY INFLUENCE the uninvolved, the uninformed, the
uninitiated, the uneducated, and disenfranchised: NOW (49%) =
"Interdependent On The Dole, On The Take, On The Wrong Side"

<u>YOU'VE GOT ONE LAST CHANCE & IT'S ALL UP TO YOU KID!!!</u>

Chapter 16

Inspiring Inauguration Benediction: When Blacks not asked to "Get in Back"?

Posted by SENTRYMAN on January 22, 2009 at 6:00pm

With the inspiring Inauguration benediction of 1/20/09
that asked The Lord;

"We ask you to help us work for that day;
when Black will not be asked to get back,
when Brown can stick around,
when Yellow will be mellow,
when the Red man can get ahead, man,
and when White will embrace what is right!"

Well, we all do await that day to finally come, perhaps in 2016, or 2025 or 2051,
**(Wait a minute),
hasn't the United States of America already accomplished all of this???

Haven't we passed umpteen Laws to benefit "All" Minorities for decades now, and to the
detriment of the national economy to segment and divide our citizens, "for decades now",

and, speaking in terms that are only politically acceptable when used by "The Left",
using "COLOR" of a human being's skin as the defining determining factor;

don't Native-American's, (that would be the Red Men?), instead of immersing themselves
into society and taking full advantage of all that America provides to everyone, and
making a success of their efforts, like the "other Indians" have so capably accomplished,
they've parceled themselves off from their countrymen to concentrate their attentions on
running their Casinos with "their singular" Federal Tax-Free exemption, with State Taxes
at a special-rate, and sell their Tax Free Ciggies, plus pay "No personal" Income Taxes to
those invaders, the White Man; well, isn't that ahead man,

and then there's the Asian-American's, (that would be the Yellow Men?)
whose many ancestors were enemies of the USA not too long ago, but now virtually thrive
within every category and aspect of American society, and have earned it quite capably on
their own,

and then there's the Latino-American's, (I guess they'd be the Brown Men?)
that have illegally flooded-across the US southern border like locusts,
with approx. estimates up to 40 million un-checked aliens, taking full advantage of the free
Health Care system that their American neighbors provide them and pay for, swamping
and closing hospital Emergency Rooms across the southwest, and have been a major
contributor in Bankrupting the State of California,
while sending much of their "untaxed" earnings, and healthcare savings, back to their
home countries in Central and South America,

and then, finally of course, the favorite cash-cow of the Democrat's big tent, the:
"Black-would-not-be-asked-to-get-back", (the Black Men?),   Pg. 13

(that would be the percentage of the American population who label themselves: "African-Americans" & "slave-descendants"),
that have probably been here in the America's far longer, in terms of centuries than most (White Man) European-descendants here today utilizing the label "American", only when it's applicable,…..those guys?

Excuse me but, isn't there a MAN, an AMERICAN Man,
that calls himself an "African"-American, and Black Man in the White House?……. A poor, poor unfortunate guy of alien ancestry who attended 3 U.S. colleges, one being about the most prestigious and expensive University in America, who worked his way up the ladder in "Light-Speed" to become the most powerful person on the planet EARTH, while taking full-advantage of what America has offered to anyone who lives here,
including to "those" who would lie, cheat and steal, and even murder to come here?

And yes,
this thesis exemplifies that one time in America when rich "White Men" for personal gain, (using "Liberal's terminology"), had turned their backs on their President who had spent His last 8 years working for (1) goal: "to protect the American citizens" and also thankfully for those unfortunate souls living on the other side of the earth, set-upon by their savage Dictatorial Rulers,
these same complicit white Fat Cats assisted in making His life a Double-Edged living-hell without defense; criticized, lampooned and ridiculed "daily", and that unlucky President while besieged in his Oval Office 24/7 nonetheless kept "his country of whiners and complainers" all safe as bugs-in-a-rug from future attack having sacrificed HIS own personal SELF and reputation, tossed on the Media's Barbeque Spit for the sake of His nation, without reward, respect, appreciation or acknowledgment for the magnificent Herculean-feat for 7 long years…….A 100% successful "<u>mission accomplished</u>"!

That same man who prioritized, allocated and donated, on behalf of the most generous people on the earth by 10 to 1, the American Taxpayer, more Foreign Aid in order to help AIDs victims in Africa, that's a continent for those with a public school education, and this is the Guy that the all-caring LEFT hates?

"Kick-him on the way out-the-door", which was the "Inaugural celeb" mantra singers sang into the wee hours of the celebration festivities, all unaware of what perils may lay ahead. That stellar behavior always shows a lot-of-class and personal decorum and integrity!

Perhaps Bush should have concentrated his motivations for personal-gain and had ignored the perceived threats, and played while Rome burned, allowing a (9/11 Part-TWO) in the subsequent years to allow a Washington, or a Chicago or an LA take the 2nd hits?

I don't think that would make the RICHHHH shoppers on Rodeo Drive very happy,
or even sit-well with Susan Sarandon & Tim Robbins, thus finding Bush a-bit remise,
(you should really get married for your children's sake someday while it's still available to heterosexuals),

or sit-well with these fellow patriots either;
Ted Danson, Robin Williams, Will Ferrel, Chevy Chase, Steve Martin, Mike Meyers, Dan Ackroyd, Tom Hanks, Dustin Hoffman, M/M Warren Beatty, Jason Alexander, Kevin Bacon and Kevin Kline, James L. Brooks, Rob Reiner, Jonathan Demme, Don Henley, Bonnie Raitt, Jane Curtain, Cher, Barbar, Michael Moore, Fran Dresser, Garry Trudeau, Lorne Michaels, Tina Fey, Baldwin, Bill Maher, David Geffen, Steven Spielberg, Harrison Ford, Al Franken, Tina Fey, Jessica Alba, JZ, Mr. Clooney, Jay Leno, David Letterman, or heaven knows, 99% of the rest of Hollywood who hate the guy, they wouldn't be very happy with that "Off-Broadway performance" either.

Oh, and the "always patriotic" Music Industry of course rooting for "W", ha, ha, ha, (excluding real "Country"), exceptions for M/M McGraw who crossed to the Dark Side and The Dixie Chickens both in the opposing Camp,
not to forget "The Media"....sorry if I neglected a few million other spoiled Libs, but I'm being too glib!...They've all hated the President and what he's stood for, unless it's saving their bacon, but even then......^.........^.........^_____Flat Line!

* Funny thing is this Rogue's Gallery would be the very "1st people to be exterminated" by Al Qaeda if President Bush had wavered from his duty, or the fight and they had won, thus relegating and installing all females into smart Burkas never to be heard from again!

((Wait a minute, let me think about the second half of that sentence again for Hollywood!))

Nah, nah, nahhh, nah,
nah, nah, nahhh, nah,
hey, hey, ey, gooood bye!.....

Classy Americans lovingly pay homage to their old President who kept them safe, with his 1st Lady on the Capitol steps, Inauguration Day, singing their good-byes with that chant!

Less we forget the "eloquently" fond farewell by the Hip-Hop Artiste's Jay-Z and Jeezy's rapping good-byes on "YouTube"; http://www.youtube.com/watch?v=9NIACFqoHAY

"Good-bye Mr. Bush, You M&%$!#-F^%$&R, etc. etc.,
My President Is M&%$#&F&(%EN Black".
(paraphrased, with respect to the Artiste's copyright, but something's lost in translation!)

Would you like to talk Opportunity, Freedom, Liberty, American Sacrifice?

What I'd like to pray for is to ask the Lord to help
(those people that always notice color "first", or all They see and know is color);
*Liberals, progressives and Democrats,
*the career purveyors of the "Race Industry",
*and the arbiters, "the Media" elites:
 scholarly objective journalists all, to finally stop their sublime repressed discrimination dividing Americans into groups, classes and cliques,

*to stop assigning victim status to "the flavor of the month"
in order to gain some attention for whomever they need a favor from in return for a "government funded" Pay-Day,

*and, Lord, to intercede and not allow "the Extreme Left and this Media cabal"
forcing the Obama Administration to govern on "Race". Thank You God!

"Barack Hussein Obama"
is the People's President of the entire United States, not just the Left's!

WHAT, this Reverend never read or heard Martin Luther King speak the words in 1963:
"not be judged by the color of their skin but by the content of their character"?

Well, again, this is 2009 and it's about time to develop some character,
 and not use or notice color anymore!

How about everyone using only this label, if and when appropriate: *"I'm an American"*,
for a change like MOST Americans do, even those that came last week?

That will go a lot further to lessen any division we create for ourselves,
 and still resides in the mind of this Reverend!

Get Over It.......Move-On......Quit Whining!!

We've all pretty much traveled the same journey in some fashion or another over the
millennia.

In the immortal words of the Mafioso: *"it's nothing personal, it's only business!"*
More to the point: "it's only Human Nature"!

We "all" started in African a 1000 millennia ago;
crawling from the ooze, or maybe hitched a ride on an asteroid from Mars, who knows,
or Even Beamed-Down-Here In 6 Days From Wherever, Scotty,
I don't care.

After that, whichever is your preference, it's all;
The Fellowship of Man.......
The Survival of the Fittest...
The Tyranny of Men...........
The Law of the Jungle........
To The Victor Goes The Spoils......we're all in the same boat here!

It's nothing personal...... it's only Human Nature!

OK, all you out there griping and whining,
you got a problem with the current state of affairs,
and want to be constant complainers living your lives in the past with hate, regret and
despair?

Well then, take it up with Alexander, or Caesar, or Genghis, or the Conquistadors....
(Now there's a nice bunch of guys who decimated an entire continent and a quarter of
another), and their descendants in Mexico now want California back.....please!
Good grief.....have we learned nothing from history?
.... Some people have short memories and are delusional!

Getting back to Western Civilization, now there's an oxymoron. Again, if You have a
problem with the current state of affairs take it up with the Pharaohs and the Princes,
Queens, Captains & Kings, the Potentates, Monarchs, Rulers, Czars, Leaders, Fuhrers,
Sheiks, Shahs, Sheikhs and Ayatollahs alike,

from Chinese Emperors and Empresses, to the Black Hills' Chieftains with the 7th Calvary
Surprise Party, to Montezuma's conquer and absorb,
Mayans and Aztec offerings to the Sun, El' Presidente dictators, to Easter Island Idols,
we're back to the Vikings, Ulysses, Hannibal and Ali Baba,
Heralds and Nobility All, all buying and selling their brethren and sisters into Slavery along
the way,
no matter the color, ending with the Patriots & Proletariat's guillotine blade.

Lest We forget those scurrilous and terrible Presidents of those United States of America, ruling with their mighty hand of shared-Democracy, only relinquishing their heavenly authority, but for every 4 years by paper slips placed intp a box. Those evil doers, ooooo!

Enough!...........
............Enough!...........
.......................Enough All Ready!

Hey, geniuses;
It's always been the guys with the sharpest swords, the biggest catapult, the greatest armies, or now the quickest minds, and that's the way it's going to stay down here until we're all grousing next about franchising Outer Space.

You want to bitch about something actually relevant: Nigeria, US southern border, China.

Real Slavery Exists Today
more than ever and more insidious,
as we collectively sit-on-our-hands and watch real-time pyrates on TV off the coast of Africa, and on the High Seas of Indo-China, bandits and bad guys aplenty from the our Gold Coast all the way around to the East Coast in Manhattan sweat shoppes. It's real and it's everywhere, and all you want to bitch about is 1860?
The more things change, the more they stay the same!!!

A nation of whiners and One Man stands up......ALONE
to Terrorism and Tyranny ....and This Man You Hate?

Enough!...........
............Enough!...........
.......................Enough All Ready!

Just as in Rome, yet to convert to "Christianity",
some of My Ancestors might have fallen prey to the "Lions" in the Coliseum..."Gulp,"
we were on the menu in those days, and they ate Slaves back then, and they weren't Black,

and,

if my later Ancestors hadn't migrated from Western Europe to Eastern Europe, they may have fallen prey to the "Inquisition",

and,

my Ancestors on my other-side would have fallen prey to Nazi Germany if not emigrating to the United States in the 20s,

and I wouldn't be here writing this right now.

So, is it Fate, is it Destiny?.......God's Plan or Dumb Luck?
Funny how things work out, we play the hand we're dealt!

What's important now in 2009 at this very moment isn't where we've been, or where we've come from, or even the journey we've all made to get here, nor that some of our Ancestor's fought for the UNION Army from Ohio to "End Slavery",
and other's from Virginia were forced to fight for the Confederacy to "Keep Slavery",

but where we are going tomorrow.
And hopefully that's NOT back to some Feudal System of Collectivism.

Liberty, Individual Freedom and the Pursuit of Happiness for All Men, that is all that has ever been really important here, and
Socialism or Communism has never, and will never give You that or Keep YOU FREE!

"CAPITALISM" Got Us Here and You Dance With The One You Came With.

No matter the journey, we're all just lucky to be alive right here today, and tomorrow, and for the rest of our lives it is our own responsibility, alone with whatever we want to do with it, Reverend.
That will always remain possible in a land where all men are created equal: "America".

Now, go back out there, You *new* 500,000 Americans and find another job. You can do it, I have. I know it isn't easy. Put your hands back in your pockets and don't join the professional unemployed. We all know: "There's No Free Lunch!"

Do your best and buy something "American Made" whenever possible to give a fellow American, maybe even your neighbor, some work and it will always come back to you.

That Day Has Come,
that day is here,
and that time is RIGHT NOW Reverend!

SENTRYMAN

---

4 Comments

Comment by Ava on January 22, 2009 at 7:01pm

This, and the Jay Z "song", it all was not just offensive, it is defamatory and it is an outright racist attack. Didn't the people who voted for him read up on Michelle Obama and the Black Liberation theology, what did they expect would happen? You know, this man BHO is trying to start a civil war here.
He is crazy.

We really have to form a White Anti-Defamation League. I am totally serious about this. The Jews did it and we also have to do it now. Our black conservative friends will back us up with this.

Your rant is very expressive and true but I feel the same and where is it getting us. This man is evil and there will be NO END to the repercussions. The hatred has been unleashed, and it's going to be bash whitey all the way by everybody. Fighting back will label you a racist, but I say we must fight back. It has already gone TOO far and something has to be done. What do you say?

I'm telling you, it's going to get WORSE.

Comment by G-Ma on January 22, 2009 at 6:58pm

This poor old man is lost in the world of 50 and 60 years ago.
We are no longer racist, we have a black President.

Comment by Cowgirl Losi on January 22, 2009 at 6:19pm

It is amazing to me that he even had the audacity to say that. Oh well, some will always want more no matter what they are given. Victimization is a liberal disease.

Comment by SENTRYMAN on January 23, 2009 at 2:49am

It doesn't matter to be Right, or In The Right, or Just, or even Hopeful anymore, it's all out of our hands.
The Genie's Out Of The Closet and The Man Behind the Curtain is One of Us.

A Tax Cheat as Head of the IRS,

a Terrorist's best friend as Attorney General,

a little southern attorney and Big League Wannabe and some nepotism gets You a "Senator-ship" and "Sec. of State", when a Ph.D. is a deficit and big-bucks from Arabian sands pays-off big time,

a Dove is our Super 007,

a Socialist is spun to acceptability,

a Has-been is a quid pro quo,

with an array of Retreads and Sharks are statuesque,

the formula for "Real Change"

and that's all everyone will have left in their pockets
with this Merry Band Of Robbing Hoods,

and our "American Idol" (Rookie at the Helm)
with his pack of groupies that call him The "N" Word with pride.
Isn't that S-p-e-c-i-a-l!

All these same President's Men that Bankrupted the Nation,
who couldn't pick-up on a Bernie Madoff for 30 years, and only then
when he ran out of pocket money,
and these are the same guys running the show from Now on and will solve all of
our problems?

His 1st at bat; "Gitmo's closing" and the Terrorists are in our midst.
Don't You all feel safer now
and You think forming another Group or gang or Guide is the most effective way to
foil these rapscallions?

Keep think'n hard though because it's just starting to get Real,
but starting another "Interest Group" will just add your names to another very long
list of gangs, like;
Bloods & Crips, Hell's Angels, Daily Kos'ites and Huffington Post'rs

and The White Anti-Defamation Leaguers......,
Might as well be "The League of Extraordinary Disappearing American Patriot
Living Fossils "!

OR,

We might try using a more righteous superior intellect
"being smarter than the average Bear", Boo Boo,
with a 1-2-3 Punch, followed by a 100 smart jabs after that.
Just be creative and keep the pressure on, nothing violent.

Keep the pressure on, it's all local and Is Up To The Individuals!!

#1- Start from the very bottom-up
Kindergarten: that's where Hitler got them from and unless we get our kids away
from the NEA that's what they'll grow up to be.

Take your children back. Get them out of Public Schools and pound your
Representatives for Choice & Vouchers.
Pre-read they're Text Books.
Put up a fuss, shine a Light on Hypocrisy, and watch the weasels scatter.

#2- Then, a salvo across the bow: fight for Secret Union Voting, and
do whatever you can to nominate and elect Conservative Superintendents of Schools.

I realize that's like finding a Jew hiding at a Nazi Rally but You must start with the fundamentals.

#3- Then, a Shot to the Head: get your local conservative officials elected and keep on their case to protect them from governmental Peer Pressure.

Vote For Conservatives, not necessarily Republicans. Look at Schwarzenegger, Bloomberg, Crist, McCain and the official Lobster Trap RINOs!

Press your neighbors and your relatives,
whether you alienate them or not with logical debate, backed-up by facts to give You confidence.

<u>No yelling, all smiles, these are POD PEOPLE you're talking to.</u>

Read and listen to Newt, Rush and Shawn and Levin, O'Reilly and Morris, Coulter and Goldberg, Ingraham and Beck, Lowry, Rove and Malkin......Take an AM Headset to work….. Watch FOX-News daily and nightly.

Read their books, give them to friends and our uninformed family. O'Reilly's books to kids, great.
Get the newest economics book by Thomas Sowell, Ph.D., to see how it all should really work.

Dig your heels in and don't compromise, don't placate, don't cooperate. Agitate like an organizer.
Be a Fly in the Ointment!

With Hillary demanding on her first day, giving fair warning that everyone must fall into line for "the Program."
This is Code for; shut-up, sit-down, get-out-of-my-way, and let me pass our agenda or I'll eat your face.

Was that Goring or Goebbels??........Ah yes, Lady Himmler!

<u>This is a War people!   Take prisoners and educate them back to sanity!</u>

*Beating "The Enemy" Is Paramount From Now On. OUR opponents will not cease till they own everything that you hold dear, including your Soul!

<u>SENTRYMAN</u>

Chapter 1

A Conservative debates his friend, a LIB,
"Old Buddies chat about Dinosaurs & Afrika"

Posted by SENTRYMAN on November 8, 2008 at 6:30pm

This back and forth conversation, (sniping) with my friend;

(I'm pointing to the< Right in Black, "your left") and

(my good friend, a "confirmed Lib" is pointing >>> Left in Blue)
 "your right";

who absolutely HATES Sarah Palin and for what?

For being a mother that didn't kill her 5th child,
for being a woman that won't stay home and tend to her brood,
for being a woman living on the backside of the Boondocks,
for being a woman that kills animals,
for being a woman out of touch with reality,
for being a woman that spends money like water,
for being a woman that bans books,
for being a woman that doesn't read books, and,
for just being a woman I think,
who I think,
just might remind him of his Ex-wife?

==

He states:>>>" I'm getting vibes that your too stressed out about Obama,"

< true, congratulations.
You still lost that $10.00 from me and I gave you odds too. You should have bet.
You may need it after Obama's economic policies.

>>>"and stress is not healthy."

< true

>>>"Last I heard; the election is over and he won by
a huge margin."

< untrue,

< 53M votes to 48M votes isn't huge,   **Pg. 22**

especially considering ACORN signed-ups;
"Underage" people and "illegal" people,
 (live people and imaginary people) 10 to 20 times, even up to 70 times each.

< Where's that recount now, huh?.....But that's for another day.

< The Highest to Lowest "LANDSLIDE" Presidential Ranking Stats below illustrate the
definition of the word "HUGE"!
==

<<<<<<<<<<<<<<<<<<<<<<<<<<<<<<<<<<<<<<<<<<<<<<<<<<<<<<<<<<<<<<
#25th 2008 Barack Obama 67.66%

#7th 2004 George W. Bush 53.16%

#48th 1980 Ronald Reagan 90.89%
#49th 1864 Abraham Lincoln 90.99%
#50th 1792 George Washington 100%
#51th 1804 Thomas Jefferson 92.05%
#52th 1972 Richard Nixon 96.65%
#53th 1984 Ronald Reagan 97.58%
#54th 1936 Franklin D. Roosevelt 98.49%
#55th 1820 James Monroe 99.57%
#56th 1789 George Washington 100%
==

>>>"Now it's time for the "small minority" to stop the bashing and let him do the job we
elected him to do; .....I don't envy that job at all."

< If the DEMs don't have the necessary 60 votes out of the 100 Senators,
We "ain't a Small" Minority!
Be my guest and do his job
but first tell that to the Stock Market.

>>> "Like your McCain said, "now he's my President and I will support him.""

< He's a good old soldier but I told you He was a Lib.
McCain would have been the smarter bet for the Dems as their President.

< Now instead of "a pig in a poke",
you've let the "Cat out of the Bag" and the DEMs
have got a "Tiger by the Tail."
....Did You watch that pompous gentleman Tuesday night scoot his family off the stage
and start preaching to the faithful?

< Did you watch Biden's face and then OBAMA'S face when Biden came out to share some
of the glory? Obama never smiled, probably knowing He had this Dead Wood he'd now
have to drag around.
Think Cheney was locked in a bunker for his safety?
Now Barack's asking for those vault keys for Biden, for Barack's safety!

< No other Winner has ever acted less gracious on stage and when He told the throng that they may not like some of the decisions He will make and that "they too" will have to sacrifice with skin in the game,
the crowd went silent.
Surprise, surprise, they're still waiting for Clinton's Tax Cut.

< You've got no idea who this guy is!
You didn't read anything I've been sending to you, did you?

< WATCH THIS and WEEP! This is why he won!

http://www.youtube.com/watch?v=P36x8rTb3jl

>>> *"Did you see all the trouble (ding bat) palin got herself into up in the cold land..... I think we've heard about the last of her. Still shaking my head with her most recent.... she thought Africa was a Country and not a Continent."*

< Are you still drinking that Kool Aid?....Try some Green Tea for its therapeutic properties.
You know, in some ways it's true about Africa.
"They should try Democracy, it works everywhere it's tried.".. Rush!

< Hey, ever ask yourself:
<Why is it that the Republicans are always "the dummies"?
Is that so LIBS won't feel restricted by any standards or feel inferior to their individual lack of accomplishment?

<Please permit Me to enlighten You with some "FACTS". Those are things that are doubted, challenged and "proven" already!

<OK, here's our girl.......Read and learn;

<<<<<<<<<<<<<<<<<<<<<<<<<<<<<<<<<<<<<<<<<<<<<<<<<<<<<<<<<<<<<<<<

Sarah Louise Heath Palin (pronounced /ˈpeɪlɪn/;
born February 11, 1964) is the governor of the U.S. state of Alaska and was the Republican Party's vice-presidential candidate in the 2008 election.

Palin was a member of the Wasilla, Alaska city council from 1992 to 1996 and the city's mayor from 1996 to 2002.

She chaired the Alaska Oil and Gas Conservation Commission from 2003 to 2004.

She was elected governor of Alaska in November 2006 by defeating the incumbent governor in the Republican primary and then defeating a former two-term Democratic governor in the general election.

She is the first female governor of Alaska, and the youngest person elected to the position.

She was also the second woman, as well as the first Alaskan, to run on the national ticket of either major party.

<<<<<<<<<<<<<<<<<<<<<<<<<<<<<<<<<<<<<<<<<<<<<<<<<<<<<<<<<<<

< They've bashed Bush everyday for 8 very long years for being "a dolt",
though,
 he was the only President in history with a Master's degree and for "Business", from Harvard no less!

<And yes, his GPA was higher than Kerry's while at Yale (the presumptive "brilliant" standard bearer for the DEMS),
and Bush was in the 1/10th of 1% of all people capable of flying a military Fighter Jet and logged-in over 500 hrs. as a young man,
while Kerry, in comparison, knew how to steer a boat and away from gunfire)
and now President Bush has successfully kept Your Butt safe for 7 long years, amidst over 100 classified attempts by Terrorists = All Foiled,
and to this day Bush has never been credited for doing "1" single thing right, NOT 1 according to the "LEFT" and from our "Objective" Media.

< Isn't that amazing, don't you think that's odd?
Was that The "BASHING" you were asking me about?
It's extremely hard to perform, much less produce, in a environment of constant criticism like that every day, every month, every single year,
but thankfully your President persevered.

< Even Clinton had some good days like "Welfare Reform", even though it was Newt's baby, but Clinton still signed it, albeit with a gun to his head.
You've got to stop this sexist thing about Palin
and your reading just "Leftist Blogs" and start thinking for yourself.
*Now who's smarter, your father or your mother? ha ha ha

< Behavior like that wouldn't have been tolerated in 1942.
If our Country and Our Media had been only 90% behind the President and OUR Military, the Enemy wouldn't have been so encouraged.

<The Backbone Of This Insurgency Today Would Have Been Broken Much, Much Sooner had the "more timid" Allies gotten on board.
If even the French, Germans and Russians had cooperated, but unfortunately all were (on the take) with Saddam.

< The War would have been successfully won "much sooner" than it finally has now with the Surge, and a great many more of OUR brave sons and daughters & Moms and Dads would have never sacrificed their lives in order to protect us all here at home,
 because of a lack of a proper expeditious action from Washington,
and those brave souls would be in their homes right now with their families.

<That's what everyone in the country and the program understood it was all about in 1942.

< Being with Our Military, Fighting for Your Country, On Board with the Mission
and minimizing the bloodshed of our courageous volunteers, are the Watch Words for a Nation and more should realize that if they weren't taught or understand that. But, who today is teaching that, certainly not Our Teachers.
That's what is called "Being Patriot" Hollywood,
and any people or individuals that did anything to prolong the war,
or didn't help our "volunteer" soldiers be Victorious,
The Blood Of Our Dead and Wounded Soldiers Is On Their Hands,
and it doesn't matter who's occupying the White House!

< I've never quite understood the LIB's and DEM's thinking behind this concept;

<"It's O.K. for OUR soldiers to die in Afghanistan or Darfur or Pakistan or on-board the Cole, but jus Not in Iraq, while OUR soldiers are simultaneously defending all of them back here at home".

< Now, all the sniping will get a little worse for a while I'm sure because they don't want Gov. Palin to cause any power shift within the Republican party in the near future, but it's too late!

< This is one smart lady, hunts, fishes, cooks and with 4 kids and a newborn, whoa, and she Watch-dogged the Gas Company Giants in Alaska and got them to cough up megabucks for the citizens, and, then she kicked "the stuffing" out of the "good OLE corrupt boys network" style of government up on the tundra.

< And even if she didn't know where South Africa was or when dinosaurs roamed the earth she's still one of the sharpest public servants I've ever seen....Hell, Obama thinks there's 57 states or is that steak sauce or maybe Kerry's license plate. Do you know They sent hundreds of investigative reporters and lawyers up to Alaska, (probably spoke to every person and some Caribou and wolves), some on four legs too, and to their amazement and utter disappointment she's as clean as the wind-driven snow and they've just got to get her somehow, (maybe she tried to get triple-back on some coupons one time or something), so they'll keep trying.

< So, the best they can come up with is "Dinosaurs and Geography"!.....Hmmm I wonder if any of those erudite journalists ever read a "Weekly Reader" back in grade school on the subject of Dinosaurs or the continent of Africa?...They probably did in Alaska too since it is one of the states in the union, way up there.

< Oh, what am I thinking? The MEDIA's probably too young for that old information and only received the newer, more intrinsic lessons taught by educators on the proper installation of a condom!

< Be afraid out there, all you; Liberals, Socialists, Communists and AC-TORs. Be very afraid.

< This scuttlebutt about McCain Camp in-fighting I would think is from more politically moderate handler's shedding their own responsibility for losing, (thus, insuring their future employment as "5th Columnists") and that's just cowardice and "sour grape back-biting" talking there. Just like the rumor about dinosaurs living 4000 years ago....A quip becomes a joke, repeated enough becomes fact, lives on as myth: JOURNALISM!

< You should be smart enough to see through all that my friend. Even if it was possible to think something that dumb, Palin does have a 4 year degree, with a major in Journalism, so that might give you a clue if she supposedly, at one time, had a deficiency in rational thought.

< You didn't watch that Rose /Brokaw video did you? Here it is again, WATCH IT THIS TIME and then You & I can have a real discussion.

"Tom Brokaw talks with Charlie Rose," http://www.youtube.com/watch?v=hzMas1bVidw

< These two pundits admit "they" don't even know who Obama is and they helped elect him. Ha ha ha

The emphasis of this whole thing has always been "just about defeating Bush", or the legacy there of, anyway, anyhow.

Why do you think they never opened those (million +) absentee ballots in California in 2000?
Because it would most probably have given the Popular Vote to Bush, as well as the Electoral, and even this time again in November they did the exact same thing with all of the Military absentee ballots!!!

Gee, I really wonder who all those soldiers would have voted for???

< It's so incredibly easy since everyone has 1 name, and 1 SS# and 1 face.
The Voter's authentication card would also has a numerical number from 1 to 320 million, and maybe a fingerprint and You can only vote "ONCE".
That's real tough and You can even use the same card to get Your Obama Check!!
BUT, Nooooo!... That's racist, or undignified or demeaning or immoral or impractical or alien-phobic or Anti-Crooked Democrat Politic...Which one??

< The big mistake the Dems made was they should have picked Mrs. Clinton, because The CURE will be far worse than the perceived illness.
"Be careful what you wish for, You just might get it"!

< Sorry I got off on a tangent…. You usually dominant the ranting in our correspondence.

Talk later Bud.
   S.

===

2 Blog Comments

Comment by Shirley on November 21, 2008 at 1:00pm

> Boy, that was a good one. ESP taking your liberal/leftist friend to task...Keep up the good work and BTW I called CBS and told them to get rid of Letterman for more Palin bashing. Now that they won't be able to bash Pres. Bush much longer, they will transfer that hate to Sarah. Let's give it right back to these B------s.

Comment by Lisa on November 8, 2008 at 11:04pm

> It's funny how people made a big deal about Colin Powell endorsing Obama, did the public not recognize that McCain though he may have vote along with Bush was not hired by Bush, McCain was hired by the people of Arizona. and Powell was actually hired by Bush and he was the one that convince the people and UN that we should go to Iraq. Powell also didn't have a problem staying in Bush's cabinet until the War was being seen as a negative.

> Now that Iraq is looking great Powell wanted back in. I lost all respect for Powell when he abandoned Bush. He has the nerve to say that Sarah was not qualified and never met her but though Obama was qualified. Come on Mr. Colin Powell what's the real reason for your endorsement to Obama. I guess Obama does want more of the same, hiring people from the Clinton administration and possibly hiring someone from the Bush administration like you, who ran when things got tough.

Chapter 2

2 Issues Sank McCain/Palin and neither were Sarah's Call.

Posted by SENTRYMAN on November 11, 2008 at 4:30am

#1. Turning his back on his Commander-In-Chief!

Sort of like: "Being for the troops but not the mission," (a popular DEM idiom and fable).

How can you not credit the one Man responsible for keeping Us all safe for 7 long dangerous years,
along with "His" magnificent military (theirs too, fools) that the LEFT supposedly holds in such high esteem?

A marvelous accomplishment considering the previous 8 years under the former Commander-in-Chief, when selfless valor wasn't a high priority,
especially when a 2nd attack upon our nation would have inevitably accomplished doing to this country in a single day
what it's taken the DEMs a year and a half now to do to America after reseizing power of the Congress.

During the campaign McCain certainly and rightfully could have asked:
"Senator Obama, since you have personally levied an indictment upon the current administration for waging a useless, wasteful and tragic endeavor since the beginning of the War after 9/11",
had we not gone to war to fight THEM over there instead of fighting them over her, a strategy that has achieved 100% success,
exactly which of our cities then, Sir, would You have preferred that we would have lose next; Detroit, Chicago, LA?....Pick on!

"You dance with the one what brung yah!"
 Thank You "W"

#2. "I will get every person responsible for Fannie/Freddie, no matter who there are!": John McCain

*Your futile campaign to have been successful only required those two simple sentences, and in doing so You would have honored your President, Yourself, Your running Mate, 48% of the Voting Public and the entire United States of America.

The way the campaign was organized and run from the Get/Go,
and many felt the Ticket Was Upside/Down since our #2 choice was at least or more qualified to run this Company called the United States of America than their #1 pick, You certainly didn't do yourself, your constituents or your running mate any favors,
and the Crazies are still after Our President's Head, as well as Sarah's.

I received this email today, perhaps some of you have also; "calling for a QUICK   Pg. 28

Impeachment of Bush/Cheney before they escape", and this is how I dealt with it, but glib sarcasm won't deter even one of these "nut cases",
so we all have to be vigilant and unite with an even stronger determination than "the Enemy" next time.

Rush has always maintained: "This is a War and Liberals need to be defeated in the arena of Ideas."

So, do your homework and "Don't Turn The Other Cheek" or
they'll chomp it right off like Hannibal Lecter.

These misguided fellow citizens wish to rob You of all that You hold dear,
specifically your;
*Liberty,
*Religion,
*Security,
*Freedom of Speech,
*Firearms,
*the Unborn,
*Unassisted Natural Death,
*Willing the Family Farm,
*the Family Farm free from calculated Eminent Domain,
*No Inheritance Tax,
*Safe Borders,
*Secure IRAs,
*Your Own SS Savings Account,
*the Fruits of Your Own Labor,
*an Official English Language,
*Your Marriage's Sanctity,
*Christmas,
*A Responsive and Responsible Government,
*Banning Lobbyists,
*Term Limits for elected government officials,
*Flat Tax, consumption Tax or combo, but not bleeding the public forever,
*Eating a Hamburger or Selling Bake Sale cupcakes in school,
*Keeping government out of private health Insurance & keeping your doctor,
*Freedom to Choose how you wish to Live Your Own Life,
*Our American Heritage History unaltered, unadulterated, unchanged,
*Our Children's Minds unaltered, unadulterated, untainted and off-limits by sinister forces,

*A Uniform (politic-free / ideology-free / NEA-free) rudimentary education,
   with testing and standards for students, as well as teachers,
*with Freedom to build character, instill independent thought & free expression in our own children as a parent sees fit without governmental interference,
*to teach them exceptionalism and strive to excellence of mind, body and spirit as was the norm prior to the 70s,
when they taught Civics and the 3Rs and Intramurals, which included playing Tag, Kick ball and Dodge ball, Archery and Dance, Home Ec., Metal shop & Wood shop, Arts and Health class, inc. those old films on manners, personal hygiene and abstinence,
(NOT How To Install A Condom in grade school), nor sex class for pre-teens,
 or social networking with computers that they're starting.

And,
*Revamp the Prison System with better programs to reduce recidivism and keep the prisons from filling-up to overflow with "old children" that never received the lessons or training above,

especially now with clogged courts, filled jails and lack of new prison construction, with
*Court Reform for Constitutional Speedy Trials, with consistent "Just" sentencing without pleading down or any early release due to over-crowding,

And,
*Enacting "3 Strikes" nationally and "Jessica's Law" nationally.

If Federal Income Tax can be shared nationally, so can uniformly protecting the public and our children federally, and finally the 3rd leg of the Justice Stool:
*Tort Reform with strict adherence and obedience to "The Constitution of the United states" by our Judges.

And if those aren't what You hold dear Senator McCain, Senator Clinton, Senator Obama then you're probably not the candidates for the job anyway!

***How simple, or should I say: "How difficult could it possibly be for a wise and faithful man or woman to rally around these simple goals,
once much valued and appreciated, to accomplish and instill them once again and most expeditiously, post-haste??

That's what America used to be all about, a dream to work for and die for, before many in this country decided to stop working for their dream, their families and even themselves, because our Government Leaders made it so easy for them not to fail, not to risk, not to try, and at the same time coerced the US taxpayer to finance the folly for the less than motivated, along with every other social experiment the LEFT can author and conger up in return for their votes and limitless power over them, forever.

No better illustrated and symbolized by "Welfare Babies", enslaving young girls, destroying young lives with multiple births, incentivized by escalating checks, like a Washington Ponzi Scheme and disintegrating the family unit with deadbeat Dads and fatherless children. An unending cycle for young women, saved only by one champion: Gingrich's "Contract With America."

But the die was cast, the cat out of the bag, Pandora's Box opened to the world, a smorgasbord of riches and all for just voting Democrat and Your Wish is Their Demand; of complacency and compliance, with of course full cooperation by the American Taxpayer. Capitulation but for a good cause, a just and fair reason that you Ugly Americans, with your wealth and your excess, you owe it to the world, you owe it to humanity; you owe it to the IRS and - the bill - is in - the mail!

Then, finally the other shoe drops for all those other babies. Wow, all of the sudden government's worried about babies. Certainly Not for their breathing little brains getting scrambled with a physician's scalpel for an Abortionist's $5000.00 omelet, but for those trapped within an unfair immigration system stag mire. Seized upon for partisan propaganda.

But now The Issue less urgent, made irrelevant by un-manned borders, unsupervised student visas, free healthcare for illegal aliens, Sanctuary Cities and Don't Ask-Don't Tell for migrant workers; now turned Drug-mules and Sweat-Shop Slaves, with Human Trafficking and Child Sex Rings booming, Black Marketeering every drug and weapon and human organ.

Then the thankless unwashed, the professional Poor get really greedy and understandably impatient for their riches, their Pay-Offs, their piece of the American Pie, so the drug king-pins, foreign criminals, religious terrorists and extreme radicals (foreign & domestic) unanimously decide it was easier to just kill us all and just take our country from us or if need be, just destroy the country in the process, while blind-mice judges with complicit attorneys hand-cuffed law enforcement with a revolving door welcome mat.

And the smiling patient politicians on either LEFT Coast watch and wait for their moment to ride to the rescue like ambulance chasing Attorneys, once frowned upon, but the new morality has freed them of guilt, shame or inhabitation to collect their 1/3rd, No ONE-HALF, No, a greater portion of the Bounty,
and the simple litigation process with court fees should aptly consume the rest of the Pie.

After all, "how much is a human life worth"?
Especially when they knowingly smoked themselves into an oxygen tented early grave with 30 or 40 or 59 years worth of cancer-sticks, they never knew were harmful to their health, so since they smoked away their wife's insurance at $3 or $4 or $5 bucks a pack, illness and medical, let's make it an inheritance and
let's get the little lady "who cleaned all the ashtrays" $79,500,000.00 dollars, shall we?........Sounds fair to me, how 'bout you?

The American Justice System At Work folks, no wonder the Muslims hate us!
But I digress!

==

Re: The Final Abuse Of Power: "The Planned Bush Self-Pardon"

>((("*According to Seymour Hersh there is a conga line of insiders waiting until January 20th to spill the beans on the gross criminality of the Bush/Cheney administration."*)))

** SENTRYMAN commented to *Seymour Hersh's Blog*;.......

Gees, why wait?
We know the war was just about Oil,
even though we haven't gotten any oil for free yet or have even received a discounted rate yet,
and we were still paying above $4 @gal. a month or two ago.

There's still time to stop Bush from protecting us all so well since 9/11;
though having foiled over 100+ classified "terrorist plot" attempts against the United States doesn't hardly seem important enough, so
we can still get him before He leaves office.

Especially after all of the times US interests and personnel were attacked during the Clinton administration
and America did nothing to stop the Terrorists or retaliate for their efforts,
since that president was far too busy playing hide-the-cigar or under his desk,
while on "the Taxpayer's Time Clock" or we couldn't care less, but
(that's "during business hours, work time" and We're paying Him for those shenanigans)?.... Is that a dereliction of duty or grand theft?.. No, fraud for impersonating a President, but the DEMs love him and the college kids think he's relevant.

But when Clinton frees and pardons Terrorists, Thugs and Thieves,
and Twin Tower bombers the 1st time around to return on 9/11 to finish the job, We Should have A Problem As A People And The Courts,

not slough it off on a messy dress and give him a pass,
especially since Nixon did what, personally, exactly that compares to this Ship of Fools?
… At least Nixon had the class to Get Out & Go Home!

http://en.wikipedia.org/wiki/Bill_Clinton_pardons_controversy

http://en.wikipedia.org/wiki/1993_World_Trade_Center_bombing

http://www.freerepublic.com/focus/news/1697884/posts

We provide all these Dudes with our own Taxpayer paid Attorneys under our fair and
equitable civilian Justice System and now armed with their sharp lawyers we can't afford
in our civilian courts, instead of our "already paid for" military courts of justice as in
Guantanamo, they get-out, get-off, get-going
and can return as consultant engineers for 9/11 some eight years later
and correct their mistakes they screwed-up with their first effort.
What a country!?

But now Pres. Obama is going to do exactly what with the Guantanamo Terrorist?
Maybe he can acquit them too so they can come here and blend into American society and
disappear once again. Perhaps to a Cab Stand or a 7/11 near You and plan a 9/11 #2 from
the inside this time with the freedom and opportunity to plot future terror activities with
impunity, like all those released Detainees that returned to the battlefields of Iraq,
Afghanistan and Pakistan and have been recaptured again or killed,
while attempting to kill our boys all over again but doubly determined.

The next time Terrorists can be free to destroy and this time take-out maybe; Hollywood,
or Chicago, San Francisco, Boston, Las Vegas or finish off New York
or
anywhere there are concentrations of Bush haters that never realized or appreciated
anything that man tried to do in protecting us all
or
to correct the economy after the DEMs took over 1-1/2 years ago;
like stemming the collapse of Fannie and Freddie that was blocked by the DEMs so they
could milk-it for themselves of million$ of our tax dollars,
so,
there is still time for Bush to pull-back on his radical behavior
and we can kick him out!

Too bad there wasn't even a single Republican to hang that Fannie/Freddie Rap on or we
would have had Senate hearings and
a public scandal and a debacle to blame Republicans with before the Election.
Oh well!

I wonder why (no one's) head ever rolled for bilking the government and
bankrupting the American Taxpayer?.......S-T-R-A-N-G-E!

Maybe we'll get to the bottom of who's at blame for that when Obama takes office,
because two of his advisors who had made over $100 million dollars while they worked
there during that very time,
maybe they can give Obama some incite as to who might have been responsible for the
greatest debacle in American history. But, who's counting?

I sure hope so before we run out of "Treasury Dept. Printing Press Ink".

>(((*Seymour Hersh: "Waiting . . . because if they did it now
the two of them would be tarred and feathered on the way out the
door*."*)))

Tarred and feathered? Ahhh

How about just wasting some more time for the government to have more hearings,
they're not doing anything productive in Washington anyway,
besides bailing out every bank, Insurance Co. and business in the US and
now The Auto Industry is next
and with their Unionized Heath Plans,
will get a special bailout with more of our money too,
so then we can be charged $30,000. for an overpriced $20k "Green Car"
that we can plug into our own electric, (that's powered by coal), at home that we also pay
for again.

Then, since Bush and Cheney go home in 2 months anyway to their own multimillion
dollars lives,
 that they had before they went to Washington,
since they didn't even need the job, unlike the Clintons that only became millionaires after
they went to Washington,
Bush and Cheney can just, aaah, Go Home since their 8 years are over and
then we can go fight crazy Warlords in Darfur or Nut Jobs in Iran,
or tackle Putin in Russia since he decided last week to move missiles into the Baltic's
states All pointed at the West,
or
we can still try to find Bin Laden hiding in (somewhere like the Rocky Mountains),
also protected by millions of other crazies.

No Problem! Can't wait!

>(((*Seymour Hersh: "But we the people do not have to wait. We can and must demand the
immediate impeachment of both Bush and Cheney for what is already known*."*))))

What was that again?

>(((*Seymour Hersh: "At the very least the defiance of congressional subpoenas at
the behest of the White House is an open and shut case for
accountability now*."*)))

Well, that's a problem because no administration has to comply with those and never will,
no matter who's living in the White House,
unless you maybe have some tapes, or recordings, or a stained dress,
or
a President lies Under Oath, for instance.

Maybe we can get Jeb Bush if he runs as her VP with Gov. Palin in 2012 or 2016?

>(((*Seymour Hersh: "obvious that Bush is planning the most wholesale and wrongful
pardon
of the worst political criminals in American history*,"*)))

You mean like pardoning those 2 Hispanic/American US Border Guards,

while protecting our country from terrorists sneaking-in and protecting our children from drugs,
that shot that "Drug Runner" transporting his 800 lb. of "MaryJane",
 in the butt and
then they were sentenced to 10 years in prison? Equal justice under the law??

Or, like Marc Rich hiding in Europe, who's wife had visited the President at the White House
over 25 times when Hillary wasn't there and arranged her husband's Pardon.
She had visited Clinton, alone in the Oval Office, more times than any high level security advisors had ever visited the President in his 8 years of office? ......Hmmmmm.

They must have been discussing the socio-political ramifications of jamming foreign entities into places like ole Burma!

[note: MARC RICH, 2001
In 1983, financier Rich was indicted for evading more than $48 million in taxes, and charged with 51 counts of tax fraud, as well as running illegal oil deals with Iran during the 1979-1980 hostage crisis. During his last week in office, President Bill Clinton pardoned Rich, who had fled the U.S. during his prosecution and was residing in Switzerland. Clinton's eleventh-hour move, along with pardons of his half-brother, Roger, and former business partner Susan McDougal, outraged Republicans and Democrats alike. The Rich pardon sparked an investigation into whether it was bought by the hefty donations Rich's ex-wife, Denise, had given to the Clintons and the Democrats. In the end, investigators did not find enough evidence to indict Clinton.]

Oh wait, my mistake, that was a Clinton pardon! Ha ha ha......Hmmmmm, how fortuitist!

Let's get'em with a Citizen's arrest, while we are still allowed to own guns.

Thanks for the tip.

SENTRYMAN

 **Chapter 3**

"Folks, Government Creates Nothing, Government Produces Nothing. It's your country!"

Posted by **SENTRYMAN** on <u>November 28, 2008</u> at 5:00pm

Dear Mr. President and Governor Palin;

You both are the only individuals I believe have the strength of character, with the least to lose,
that can rap the American Taxpayer right up-side-the-head with a good dose of proactive reality.

All any "real" Leader has to do to re-program this bogus economic crisis is go before the American public,
catch the their attention by waving something shiny like a coin,
look them straight in the eye and say;

"Folks,
Government Creates Nothing, Government Produces Nothing!
It's your money we're talking about,
It's your government,
It's your country!"

"All we do here in Washington is find ways to spend your money
and usually NOT the way You want or need,
and if this current erratic superstitious economy doesn't turn itself around
that is exactly what Washington will continue to do!"

"The last 2 months have been totally orchestrated by unpatriotic devious forces and also
manufactured by self-serving market "Speculators" (betting the Market up or down, and
usually DOWN at everyone's expense,
while reaping (raping) tremendous sums of money in the interim). We can't say "profits"
because they risk nothing, contribute nothing and with a corrupt system, don't even have
to put-up their own money, while subverting and capitalizing on consumer's irrational fear
that's finally catching up with the unholy decisions previously made by your
"unrepresentative" Congress after the '06 Dem. election wins,

and more specifically,
these Carpetbaggers seized upon that incredibly illogical lack of confidence that the
uninformed and the uninvolved always manifest in themselves; an un-American lack of
faith in our heritage, our history, our country and in oneself,
and for no other reason. Pg. 35

This self-manifested and self-fulfilling prophecy, purposely designed by a certain segment of our government is very calculated, capitalizing on ignorance and fear,
which produces the greater need and the misconception that only a drastically expanded Government is THE "ONLY" ANSWER to save one's bacon and this sinking ship.

But, it's that very Government drilling all the holes in the hull that will scuttle Our ship and drive it onto the rocks to be scavenged & salvaged by these very Government, taxpayer subsidized and salaried, Pirates,
because the true reality is "The Only" Answer lies within the American psyche;
The American Citizen, The America Taxpayer, The American, some of who have lost faith in themselves and others that realize our government has lost faith in the American Way, The Constitution of the United States of America and all of US! .... The rest are part of the problem!

It is really now up to you fellow Americans to turn this foundering Ship of Fools around before it hits bottom
and each of You has it within your power to accomplish it, if only tried!

Stop cowering in your homes watching reality shows, playing videos games and hoarding gold as a possible hedge while thinking it's all going to miraculously work itself out on it's own, because it can't and it won't.
"Not without courage, dedication, cooperation and sacrifice!"

There are sinister forces at work here and they want to destroy Capitalism, Free Enterprise, our free economy and our free country, along with our Democratic system form of government, not only from the outside but from within as well.

All we need to do is just stop shivering with panicked emotions,
go back outside into the light and live your lives once again like normal thinking, believing human beings..... It's really just that simple folks!...

It's like changing one's demeanor on a cloudy day with some PMA. Just a little different perspective and a positive outlook can make all the difference with illness, in Life, and even in that stupid Stock Market where an inkling, a figment, a wisp of air or a rumor can bring suspicion and panic to an otherwise calm and beautiful day, but that's another kind of lack of faith addiction.

It will be a brand new day tomorrow. The sun is going to come-up as usual. You're still going to have to cut your grass or shovel snow,
stop on the way home to buy some milk and groceries, feed your children and your pets and life will most assuredly go on as usual, but if you really want your life to improve and be more fulfilling, happier and retain your Free-Choice,
by not handing over your entire existence to Your Taxpayer Paid Government Handlers that will make all of your decisions for You from now on the Time Is Now!

This is the time to go out and buy that new car or
buy that home or buy that income investment property,
because these prices have never been lower and this is the time to take full advantage of the great silver-lining opportunities during these dark times!
Go give your family a nice little Christmas.

Smarter People Than We Are Doing Just That At This Very Moment
and they're NOT saying anything about it while you hide and hoard your gold, and They will reap all the benefits and rewards from your fear and indecision.

YES, Now is the time to Stand Up with the courageousness of being an American,

walk straight out your front door and live your lives again and
that is precisely what will solve these problems.

Problems that We here in Washington cannot, nor ever could or ever will.

It's now all up to You, unless of course
You just want Washington to keep chiseling away at your freedoms, to keep printing
money, mortgaging your futures with foreign countries around the world and borrowing
another 7 trillion dollars, which They're perfectly willing to do,

permanently placing your children, your grandchildren and even your great grandchildren
into Servitude with Lifelong DEBT, and just because you wouldn't take your destiny into
your own hands for a better tomorrow. Would You?....Will You?

Now, get out there and "win this one for the Gipper and for Yourselves!"

We are being conditioned "By Design" to No Longer be proud of our country and
ourselves with an illusion, a delusion that the only thing we can have faith in anymore is
"The Government."………and Not in God or in your neighbors or in yourselves!

Then ask yourself this extremely important question;
"What is it that Government does well?"

Or, let me rephrase:
"What is it that Government has done so well in the past that you want to repeat it?"

All Government does is reinvent the wheel and Itself every 4 years just to get reelected.

Our Constitution delegates, virtually loans the powers and has charged your United States
Government with a single mandate that is quite simple and that is to:
"protect our backs from enemies foreign and domestic
and leave the Citizenry alone to pursue our own happiness
and protect us from those that would endanger it".

Meanwhile, Government has enough trouble just trying to successfully protect the borders
and keep us from being attacked again, (come-on, watching a fence for rabbits, how
difficult can that be?...

We pushed back Fascism, Nazism, Imperialism, Communism) and these guys can't keep
the scum sneaking over through the neighbor's yard,
much less having to worry about the Wardens being Coconspirators in taking our own
freedoms away!!!........Geeeezzzzz!!

So, tell OUR Government to leave our freak'n Freedoms alone
and just try to protect the United States of America. That should be a full time job, try
doing it while we go about living Our lives freely in the greatest country, in the history of
man on Earth!

That is something very sacred to remember, to be proud of everyday and to be thankful
for. For all those that came before, who believed and died and didn't come back, to secure
that Right for their families, their neighbors, their countrymen and for you.

Just like those still out there right this minute in the breathless HEAT, the hard COLD, at
the bottom of a thousand fathoms, and the vacuum's edge of our atmosphere in the silent
Darkness, protecting each and every one of us minute by minute.

Only A Free People Can Create and Protect This For Themselves
***Something like that is really all someone like You both that We believe in, has to say
 Mr. President and Governor!

....No Spin, No BS, No Lies!...
Leveling with the American people with the old fashioned TRUTH for a change!

So take that Sen. O.,
keep your hands off our money, just stand back and watch what Americans can do for themselves
and have always done by themselves when Freedom is allowed to work unencumbered,
then Liberty flourishes!

Merry Christmas and
God Bless the United States of America.

Preserve The Constitution Above All!"

SENTRYMAN

Ps, President Bush:
You better pardon those two US Border Guards ASAP,
their families are waiting!

Pps, Governor Palin:
We are behind You if you want that thankless job in 2012 or '16.

---

2 Comments

Comment by Diane T on December 1, 2008 at 4:17pm

   BEAUTIFULLY SAID!

Comment by SENTRYMAN on December 1, 2008 at 10:11pm

Thank you. ....Like minds.

Chapter 4

"Xmas Sale$ Will Be Poor"!   Didn't Your Mother Teach You?:
"If You Have Nothing Good To Say, etc".

Posted by SENTRYMAN on December 1, 2008 at 10:00pm

Who Does It Serve To Predict Only Disaster?

Who Does It Serve To Predict Only Defeat?

Who Does It Serve To Be A Doom & Gloom'r?

Who Does It Serve To Be Pessimistic, ALL The Time?

Who Does It Serve To Shot Yourself In The Foot?
It's Your Own Foot Idiot!

It's Also Your Own Country, You Idiots!

Well, all of the Experts and Pundits and Soothsayers, Prognosticators and Wall Street Talking Heads, ALL said;
Black Friday will be Bad, a Disappointment, Lower than expected and Can't have a positive effect on one of the Worst economies in US history.
Blah, Blah, Blah ! ! !

Gee, I wonder, if anyone had been the least bit positive and enthusiastic with an e.g. "will be better than average" prediction,
that the final tally to date might have been 2x or 5x better than the SURPRISE "Up 7%" actual improvement over last year's numbers at this point,
that the professional jeer-leaders DIDN'T anticipate we could ever achieve?
Couldn't Hurt and could ONLY HELP!...... jerks!!

I'm certain that the shopkeepers, the buying public, and the US Economy would have appreciated a rosier outlook, because I'm 100% positive the figures would have been much, much higher!

NOW again, those same experts are starting to predict that the same "good" showing after Thanksgiving will never hold-up throughout the Christmas Holiday Buying Season.

Who are these people, enemies of the State? That is certain! Why not just say we'll probably all die from a meteor impacting the planet, which is about as accurate and likely to occur from these prognosticating geniuses.

Pg. 39

My God people, what's wrong with You, listening to this gibberish bilge?
Negative…Negative…Negative…How can you live your lives believing this stuff?

If your date spoke like that, you'd drop'm.
If your kids talked like that, you'd slap them.
If your wife talked like that, you'd start drinking.
If your husband talked like that, you'd divorce him.
So Just STOP it!

Same goes for that stupid ridiculous-gamble, crap-shoot Stock Market….
It's no better than Jimmy-the-Greek betting the line in Vegas. Get a life!
I'm just amazed serious people participate with their life savings with these horse
track touts. Blue Chip, Conservative funds, Aggressive funds, you'll still crap-out!

And Just Like Your Mom Told You, (In Case You've Forgotten):
"If You Don't Have Anything Good To Say"……WHAT?????...YES!
"Keep Your Mouth Shut!!"…
"Keep It To Yourself!"...
"Bite Your Tongue!"……Familiar?

Hey, How About A Moratorium On Anyone "In This Country At Least" Not
Spouting One Negative Opinion About Anything For The Next 12 Months?
...........Wow, then watch production and profits soar!

NO ONE KNOWS WHAT TOMORROW WILL BRING,
SO STOP TRYING TO MAKE IT HAPPEN, YOU %&*%#@%&*&,
BECAUSE IT'S COUNTER-PRODUCTIVE, IT NEVER HELPS & IT's ALWAYS BAD!

Here's YOUR counter to THEIR predictions, your Silver bullet for these wolves:
"Turn-off the TV, turn-off the Radio, and your Internet for 30 straight days,
ignore them all. Keep getting the paper but only read the coupon ads and job
classifieds, and just live your lives as normal as You'd really like it to be"!
What do you think would happen?........Will the world end, or will things improve?

And this warning goes for the geniuses at Treasury and The FED also,
who finally announced that We are officially in a Recession....Shut-the-%&$#-Up!

Wow, what a surprise, since the Media has been telling us that for 7-3/4 years that
a calamity was about to happen under President Bush, they finally got what they
"preyed" for.....yah, PREY…

Actually, it only started downhill after the '06 Democrat election-takeover, January
2007, and THEY finally got just what they'd been wanting and hoped for, *Surprise.*

You know what a Recess-ion is, a momentary pause before We get back to work?

Ps, "Drill here, Drill now ! …….. Let them eat Oil ! ……… Problem Solved !"

SENTRYMAN

2 Comments

Comment by Karen C on December 1, 2008

THANK YOU, My husband and I were just discussing AGAIN this absolute
BULL of this election cycle and how ludicrous it is that a man so
un-qualified to be our president could get elected and such an INEPT
Congress that pass bail-out bills that we still don't think were needed...let the
market take care of itself, go through whatever pain might be necessary and
come out stronger on the other side...I think we better start having some
pretty darn specific tests of basic skills before anyone is even allowed to run
for public office!!

 ### Comment by SENTRYMAN on December 2, 2008

It's become an emotion driven American Idol nation
where usually the #2 guy or gal is the more qualified superior choice,
and
 for either Party.

This last election exemplifies my theory.
Carrie Underwood, the exception! ha ha

Chapter 5

FOX NEWS Asks: "Is Caroline Kennedy qualified to be a US Senator?"
....................................Celeb always trumps expertise!

Posted by SENTRYMAN on December 16, 2008 at 3:30pm

Current QUESTIONs:
Is Caroline Kennedy qualified to be a US Senator?

Who is actually qualified for government service anymore?

A novice junior Senator is elected President and
each of our elected government Officials are either very inept for being "asleep at the switch", or
criminally complicitous for "bankrupting and bringing down our country."

Our employees did it while we were at work.... They write the laws, they enforce the laws, they collect our money, they spend our money, and they watch each other's backs.
Well, the slumber party's over, they've trashed the house, emptied the frig, stolen our stuff and corrupted our kids when we weren't looking, so now they're hooked on tripe and freebees....So what are we going to do about it? .....Send them back to Washington!

An Alaskan, who earned her positions and worked her way up the ladder, isn't qualified, but Caroline, who is basically a celebrity, (and that always trumps experience or expertise),
wants to fill the N.Y. Senator's post that is currently held by another
(Celeb / southern Carpet Bagger with no practical executive experience, who started at the top and went sideways,
who also ran a campaign on nepotism, quid-pro-quos and favors, called-in or promised by a fairy-Godfather / hubby),
so gee, what's the problem with Caroline?

At least she's rich, so she doesn't have to steal from us.
Oops, forgot she's a Democrat and can rob the Taxpayers blind with impunity if given the opportunity!

SIDE NOTE: a mandatory (2) "Term Limit" for all elected government Officials would solve most of our problems right away, thus culling-out the self-serving bribable Statesmen, since they rarely represent their constituent's best interests en-masse anyway, except for Bringing-Home-The-Bacon, (bribes & pay-offs) for their "business Sponsors specifically".

Unfortunately that cannot and will not ever happen,
because this is No longer a representative-government, and We Americans are now totally boxed-out, and many of us don't even realize it and little will change. Certainly not without blood in the streets and a repeat of the "1776 Revolution" all over again.

Pg. 42

We Feed and Protect the World and We are the Bad Guys?
Talk about a bad PR management!
We're more interested in Camelot, than the reality of our brave soldier returning home and bestowing the respect and honor they so richly deserve.

"Camelot": a masterpiece PR concept created and designed by Caroline's mom to preserve The Legacy.

America's greatness, generosity and goodness constantly defamed, as Bush's resolve and courage all bashed-in-the-head on the nightly news, e-v-e-r-y-n-i-g-h-t, constantly replaying and re-living denounced condemnations of the US Military's savagery from Viet Nam to Baghdad,
and unforgivably dismissing "our ever-continuing missions to Free Peoples" across-time and across the globe.

Do we remember which President sent all those US soldiers over to the jungles of south-east Asia, or His Party affiliation?....... I remember it was pretty unpopular.... Hmmmm!

We're never reminded of who ENDED the Viet Nam War, or what His Party affiliation was!

I never hear of that echoed or mentioned in the mystical "Halls of Camelot"!

But, we are exposed ad nauseam to the mis-characterized folly, with daily vicious guttural ridicule and vitriol for a Commander-in-Chief and his Military of a thankless nation, greeting his returning warriors from the greatest, most successful, lowest-fatality, shortest battle ever unequaled in history,
with the War yet to complete, and the Peace yet to win,
this "Mission Accomplished" was still indeed very successfully finished,
but regrettably Crapped-On by a petulant partisan Press and their lapdog groupies.

An embarrassment of riches to the thankful parents and to Liberty-Loving Free People in a dangerous world that so many returned,
made bearable only by the reminder that the United States Military is always there for You, fighting for Peace in Europe, in Africa, in the Pacific, fighting Communists in Indo-China, fighting Communists in the Caribbean, fighting Communists in Central America, fighting "For The Muslims" October 23, 1983 in Beirut, Lebanon, fighting for the Muslims in Kuwait, fighting for the Muslims in old Yugoslavia, (with their thousand years of feuding), fighting for the Muslims in Somalia, fighting for the Muslims aboard the USS Cole, fighting for the Muslims in Afghanistan, fighting for the Muslims in Iraq, and dying, and dying!

Don't ever forget how many soldiers died to FREE Peoples on distant shores, while protecting their own, at home.

Today, a revolutionary appreciation of America and the US combat soldier is the only ""Real Change"" in Man's thinking we all hope comes about someday that will replace the anger and the envy that their-own centuries-old ancient forms of governments have never fulfilled, or ever achieved for themselves.

That understanding we would welcome, and have yet to see from old allies and former foes, but it can never be attainable through weakness, appeasement, capitulation, or "Camelot", and Certainly Not By President Obama!

Let me ask you something theoretically;
Does anyone ever think about all the years of wasted time, wasted man power, wasted money, the tragic waste of human life and resources on both sides of the Cold War, all based on a false premise, a suspicion, a fear by the Russian hierarchy and people? that

supposedly the United States wanted to invade eastern Europe and conquer the USSR, but when the Russian Bear collapsed under its own communist weight as the utter failure of a system of government it really was, what did the USA do?.......Did they attack, colonize, imperialize? I think we befriended all 15 pieces, but with a jaded eye on just 1 in particular!

Did the great Satan seize the moment and consume them?....?

Did the Imperialists spread their disease across the globe as other ancient Empires and Dynasties have repeatedly done throughout time?

Did anyone congratulate President Reagan for his resolve, steadfastness, and.. Star Wars?

Did anyone chastise and castigate the old Soviets, those war-mongering dinosaurs?

Has anyone in this country from the "opposing Party" thanked the great man for having that courage, that integrity, that vision to guide us through those tenuous dark times?

I hear enough lately about Gorbachev's gracious gifts to humanity, and of the virtues of the Cuban Health System, and that Bush is a "worthless draft-dodging idiot",
and that Obama as the brilliant savior will solve all of our problems,
and that Kennedy was a God, (of course, when not in the company of a any Starlets),
and that Hamas and Hezbollah, and Ahmadinejad and CHAVEZ aren't all that bad,
but Vice President of the United States, Dick Cheney is a conspiring war-mongering tool of Halliburton, (though evil Halliburton is "for-sale" because their 6% profit margin is so low that no one else wants to buy them up, plus, they're the only guys that can do those particular jobs, as compared to Congress which makes a far, far greater profit off Gas Taxes "for doing nothing", and they don't even do their job as well, or at all!

Kind of like the USA, the dupes, the dolts, the destroyers of men- the world loves to hate, unless there's a volcano, or an earthquake, or tsunami, or an invading army that shows-up and once again the Americans are badly needed, again, and again!

Do I think Caroline Kennedy is suited, is capable, is qualified to be a U S Senator?
What do you think?

SENTRYMAN

--- ---

4 Comments

Comment by Ava P on December 16, 2008 at 5:28pm

I think it's a plan. I'm going to post a discussion on this, too.
I think she will run for POTUS maybe with Powell.

Comment by Cheryl S on December 16, 2008 at 4:36pm

If her last name was Smith would she even be considered?

Comment by Bard on December 16, 2008 at 4:22pm

In a word ... NO!

Comment by Ray on December 16, 2008 at 3:52pm
I have seen this. The Kennedy bought this seat for Caroline. NY is the same as IL

 ## Chapter 6

Ever Hold Something You Love So Tight You Crush It?

Posted by SENTRYMAN on <u>December 20, 2008</u> at 3:30am

You know friends, I watched these 2 videos last night on "Team Sarah"
and when I got through, and I wiped my eyes and thought:
<u>Sarah Palin is too good for the Lowly 48!</u>

In fact, she should stay right where she is, safe with her people of Alaska
that love and appreciate her,
close to her family who need their Dad and Mom,
like those two gentle souls.

We can envy what they have from afar but we don't need to share it, or
spoil it......We can all just work real hard on our own lives and problems,
and try to emulate their pure happiness and successes for ourselves
without trying to take away some of theirs.

And that especially goes for us talking her into risking everything she has
just to come down here to be our Champion, and make us happy trying to
solve all of our problems that we apparently can't manage on our own.

Ever hold something that you love so much, so tightly that it's smothered,
like a toy or a flower, or a relationship and You destroy it?...You spoil it for
everyone, especially the very thing that was so important.

The problems are within ourselves, but so too are the solutions.
It doesn't really matter who lives at 1600 Pennsylvania Ave.,
it's those 535 Rapscallions in Washington that have continually ruined our
lives, and THEY all need our (UNDIVIDED) attention, council and
monitoring, not the other way around to put things RIGHT!

Let's make this Palin site a little refuge shielded from Secularism,
Liberalism, Progressivism, ISMism, and all the other Insan/isms outside,
preserving this Fan Club of mutual appreciation with safety in numbers as
a role model, but,
let's leave the Palin's alone!

We all just might need someplace decent and clean to escape to someday
Pg. 45

and She'll be there waiting for us with open arms,
a wink of an eye, that incredible smile, and a;
"Howdy stranger, You escape from the lower 48?"

Let's Not Ruin A Good Thing and Leave Well Enough Alone!
(my original video selections were removed. I guess they were too positive.
Here's a few nice substitutes)

1. Sarah without the got'cha.
http://www.youtube.com/watch?v=63xWXvOdGNM&feature=related

2. A plainspoken woman is called upon to serve
http://www.youtube.com/watch?v=kZ6EByJUx48&NR=1

http://www.youtube.com/watch?v=BAsgJR5lm5c&list=PLC4874CA55F0EE2F0&index=4&playnext=2

http://www.youtube.com/watch?v=BAsgJR5lm5c&list=PLC4874CA55F0EE2F0&index=4&playnext=2

SENTRYMAN

----

1 Comment

Comment by Susan W on December 20, 2008 at 1:11pm

> Well said.
> I think that's why it's so important for us to keep sending her letters
> of encouragement and coming to this site and keeping it energized
> with activity and inspiration. This site is like a haven for me. It always
> makes me feel so good to come here...it reminds me that not
> everyone in our country is mean-spirited and vicious.
>
> There is a very good chance that Sarah or someone close in her
> family does visit this site.
>
> When she's having a bad day and it feels like the whole world is
> crashing down upon her, I hope that she knows that she can come to
> Team Sarah and get our love.

Chapter 7

We Can Bail-Out Every Inept Thief, BUT, We Can't Afford To Fund Our Troops?
.....Who's Money Is It Anyway??

Posted by SENTRYMAN on <u>December 20, 2008</u> at 12:30pm

"Hey Senators, Ladies & Gentlemen, US Representatives;

We can <u>bailout</u> the Financial Corps. that take advantage of us,

we <u>bailout</u> the Insurance Corps. that take advantage of us,

we <u>bailout</u> independent Corps. that take advantage of us,

we <u>bailout</u> Companies that give themselves "salt in our wounds" Bonuses,

we <u>bailout</u> Foreign Governments that hate and disrespect us,

we <u>buy</u> from Foreign Countries that cheat and poison us,

we <u>buy</u> Foreign Oil from Countries that rob-us and want to kill-us,

we <u>bailout</u> Our own self-indulgent government officials with reward for
their incompetent failures and largess to themselves;
they, elected and salaried to represent Our interests, not their own,
take advantage of us quietly with 3:00 AM "Pay RAISEs",
(because They're so proud of the fine work they haven't accomplished),

but, We Can't Afford To Give Our Troops every single thing that they need
to protect themselves while defending all of America,
and the/Our government stabs them in the back as their legs are blown off?

<u>But, We Do Have The Money To Fund "Planned-Parenthood",</u>
Who Plots and Plans To "Kill Born & Unborn" Baby Children Forever?

<u>"Is that what You're telling the American Taxpayer, boys and girls???"</u>

<u>SENTRYMAN</u>

Pg. 47

Participate in Democracy, sign the petition Form Letter

I am writing to urge you to oppose any legislation that provides or increases taxpayer funding of abortion.

It's a crime that taxpayers are forced to subsidize the abortion industry, particularly when it is against our own personal morals and beliefs. I strongly urge you to respect my beliefs and those of millions of pro-life Americans across the country. We do not wish to subsidize an industry that damages women's lives and destroys innocent human life.

Many Senators have expressed a desire to reduce abortions. Retaining restrictions on federal taxpayer funding is the best way to accomplish this in the short term. Even abortion advocacy groups have admitted that restrictions like the Hyde Amendment have contributed to a national decline in abortions.

Please respect the rights of taxpayers and ensure a decline in abortions by maintaining current federal funding restrictions.

I would appreciate a response to my letter.

Susan B. Anthony List Activist

Stop the Bailout for Planned Parenthood & the Abortion Industry!

Susan B. Anthony List President Announces Launch of Grassroots Campaign Opposing a $1.5 Billion in Federal Taxpayer Funds for the Abortion Industry

Sign the petition at:
http://www.youtube.com/watch?v=znS0kuTDrW0&feature=player_embedded#!

Washington, DC
December 2008

Chapter 8

"What's Wrong With Being A RINO?"

A "Supposed" Fellow Conservative Laments On A Blog,
So I Took Him On. With No Rebuttal = I Ate His Lunch!

Posted by SENTRYMAN on December 20, 2008 at 4:00pm

"What's a RINO to You?", he asks!

I set down my knife and fork, and consider his quandary for a moment;
Well, (thinking off the top of my head here)........."What's in a name?"
"A Rose by any other name!"...... "A Tiger can't change its stripes!," etc., etc....hmmmmm

We all live our lives today with some kind of "Label": No uniforms, No flags, No white hats anymore, can't tell friend from foe. Who are the good-guys and who are the bad? Political correctness dictates: No judgments allowed in this politically charged universe!!!

No more black & white, or more good VS evil! Thank you, just shades of grey Secularism in Technicolor with your all-inclusive progressive liberal society!
Not so long ago we were all just "Americans". Now, we're members of the greater world, so want happened?

The individualism of Man!.......Once an Inherent Right to be a FREE human being on this planet in a mythical place called: America,
but now we're just holding on to this big spinning ball in the outer cosmos of the infinite for dear life.

"Can't we all just get along", boo hoo. Can we, can we huh, pretty please?...Yah, RIGHT!
If we all did that there wouldn't be a need for Liberalism....ha ha ha, yea
Socialism feeds on strife, friction, heat, fear, disparity, greed, elitism, ...human nature.

("I need......I want......I want even more.....I want what you've got.....I want it all.")
Sound familiar?.........We don't have to work anymore, government will provide it for us,
but at what expense? ....Our government has "its most control" over us right now, but,
it's our labor, it's our money, it's our stuff, and we worked for it: shouldn't we own it?
It's now being incrementally re-distributed to all those who refuse to work for it,
and recipients have just about out-numbered us.....What happened?.....What changed?

That inherent "Right to be Free" I mentioned, to be one's own person, un-shackled, to be different that sets one apart, free will, free thought, the individual, a little or to extreme;
American!....Anything goes?....Pierced flesh, tattooed sleeves, chartreuse Mohawk, smoke Weed!...OK, fair enough, free country! *Nothing new there, seen it all,* but, You know what?
...Smoke ciggies or cigars, salt, cheeseburgers & fries, soda pop, cupcakes?
...Now you're really getting carried away. Still fair enough...well, but, ahh?
Just don't be so liberal Jackstraw, that you take freedoms away from others, not in your preferred commune.   Pg. 49

You want to be an idiot, your choice!...
You want to be un-original, follow lock-step and boring?...No problem, your choice....
But, just stop the feigned-outrage for those that follow their own hearts, join-up to "complete the mission", do the heavy lifting like those that protect you, who pay the price for your freedom so you can look or act like an imitation of what we already invented, and created in the 50s and 60s, & 70s.....same old, same old...nothing new under the sun!
No Judgments, No Rules, No Laws, Me-Me-Me!.....Love the one your with, right Stephen!

You're late to the party guys, and your mentors never grew-up either, and they still can't face reality, or responsibility. They couldn't destroy us back then, and you're not going to destroy us today, or tomorrow. Coo-Coo-Ca-Choo Peter Pan.

<u>Want to be "really" different today? Avant-garde? Try being normal. Now that's different!!</u>
And don't give me: "What's normal?".....That's getting real old too!

<u>Exactly what does this tirade, my tangent, have to do with "LABELs" and "RINOs"?</u>

What ever happened to Innovation, Excellence and Accomplishment?
Does anybody learn anything today at home, or in church, or at school?
What happened to simple polite common decency? Lost to the Essenes at Qumram?

Or, is it; "Let's just get along", in lock step, same uniform and mind-think,
Liberalism, Socialism, Fascism, Nazism, Communism, Imperialism, Ismism?
Insanity VS Chaos....Are those our only choices today?

Which is it Hollywood?   Which is it Capitol Hill?   Which is it World Bank?
Guns, Bombs, Terror, IEDs, Somali Pyrates, Slaves, Slaughter VS my neighbor Ed's lawn!

Can't have it both ways! You're either for personal freedoms, or it's the New World Order.
You know that ole' saying: One way for the Masses and another way for the Bosses?

"Do as I say, Not as I do"! ....The masses VS the Masters!.....Slave VS Massa, "Yessa Massa" wasn't invented in the Pre-Civil War southern states you know.
There is more Human Trafficking, Sex Slavery and Depravity Feeding Upon Children across the globe today than ever before, and exactly;
What Does Civilized Man Do To Stop It, Or Even Notice and Address It? For cripe-sake!

Do We Care About Anything, Really??

I want to be left alone to worry about Ed's crabgrass creeping over into my lawn. I don't want to be thinking about some maniac creeping across the border, visiting, residing, or being here at the Imperious discretion of sanctuary city Liberals, driving on our roads without insurance or documentation, doing elicit things, driving hopped-up on something or looking over their shoulder and just happen to cross the center line and kill two coeds driving in the opposite direction, while on their way to the basketball game Friday night....."Why is HE here at all, at that point in time?"...Ask Washington, ask Democrats, ask Liberals, ask ourselves, because we tolerate this insanity, this malaise!.....We've all crossed the line, because there are no Lines anymore, there is no center!

Maybe we're only thinking about Elvis, Madonna or Princess Di?............Are we all RINOs?
Can we think about something greater than ourselves. Can we see beyond our rhinoplasty noses? Can we see the hand in front of our face, or are we all Texting?...See the bigger picture people! There are a great many enemies and very bad things out there, and our government is not doing their job to protect us with all the money they confiscate. They cannot give us freedom, but just take it away!
They apparently can't stop others from taking our freedoms away either, which "is their

primary job"! They only look inward, seeing us as the problem, not searching outward defending our rights and freedoms. Pride, lust, envy, greed, sloth, geez…morons!

Hey, all "Di" had to do was wear her darn seat-belt, duhhh, like the only guy that lived in the destroyed car that night. Self-responsibility, Self-reliance, Self-initiative, Self-respect…that's your real lesson for the day children; "Wear Your Frigg'n Seat Belt", Not About Land Mines!... Are there no lessons to be learned anymore? Is everything viewed through a filtered-lens in some Reality Show gossamer fog?

Nancy Reagan was repeatedly mocked for "Just Say No", ha-ha-ha. Well, it is that easy! She should have made it: "Tell'm To F-Off!", then maybe someone might have listened. The stupidity and the coarsening of society has now become rudimentary and mainstream, but a simple campaign to tell everyone to:
"Buckle-Up Or You'll End-Up Like Di",
is beyond the common sense, brain power of Madison Ave sycophants, but just might have saved 1000s of lives, maybe millions of humans over time. Though to be fair, I personally haven't stepped on any Land Mines lately. …..Thanks!.....

The utter waste of grey-matter is society's inheritance, thanks to Liberalism. Can we ever address the root causes of anything to solve (1) damn problem for good, Fini, The End, without the Spin? Those mindless Rock Concerts to feed a nation 1 cold meal, those Rocker-Celebrity garage-sales for Dictators…brilliant! ….could I have mooore, please Sir? The Botoxed-Body-politic, you would think that the useless, hapless United Nations could at least all agree to abolish S-L-A-V-E-R-Y TODAY! …..Wouldn't You Think???

Who are they, this League of Nations? ……………Man's Sin – Man's Stain!
A Pox on Civilization, feeding upon our own brothers and sisters…Corporate Cannibalism!

WE give the United Nations cheap Rent, and WE Pay the most Tribute to this House of RINOs, this House of Cards.
I.e. IRAQ's tainted "Food-For-Oil Program", foreign governments and the UN all in bed together with Saddam, all prostitute themselves to circumvent the sanctions with a Whore-Master, while American must do all the Heavy Lifting. Now there's a formula for success.

Does the MEDIA take their teeth out of Bush's hide for a second and ask:
"Is Anyone On The Take Here So War Can Be Averted, and Saddam's People Can Finally Be Fed and Saved Before This Devil Eats Them, After He Built His 51st Palace, of course, and also Builds A Nuclear Bomb With All That Money He's Stealing From His People?", nahhh!..... http://www.slate.com/id/2071905/

Do We Kick The UN Out Of New York For Their Total Uselessness In Stopping Crimes Against Humanity? Hoo-rah!...As they point fingers at America, while filling their pockets and their bellies with their Diplomatic Immunities.

This isn't news folks and it isn't new. The USA "paying for it all" is getting very, very old! It's been the same since the beginning of time, the guy with the biggest club rules the cave, or those with the longest Knives in the Roman Senate on the Ides of March..
But today; Whomever has the most Supreme Court Justices, makes his own reality!

"Can't we all just get along?"…NO!......Why must we always compromise? We compromise our values in order to get along, and it's always the Right side-of-the-isle compromising!

*You want a Foot Bath in your Airport on Taxpayer's dollars? ..No problem!

*You want a Prayer Rug in school? …No problem, but Jesus Is Out, No Jesus!

*You want to dismantle thousand years-old marriage tradition to give a child a name?... No problem, but No "Old Testament", No "New Testament"…Sharia Law in America applies!

*You want to Vote without proving Who You are?....No Problem!
Or, how many times You've Voted already, or even if You're a citizen?... No problem!
But No Photo I.D. to guarantee the sanctity of the US Electoral System! Oooo, nooo!
 I object on religious rights: A photo might steal my soul. yadda, yadda…. (well, at least that worked for native-Americans)!....Is everything and everybody Crazy, or is it just Me?

It's hard enough to keep the government from raping the public, now you want equity?
After 200+ years we're still working on equality! "A Shining Beacon On A Hill."
How many times are we going to Start-up that Hill without any permanent advancement?
(1 step forward, and 3 steps back: Administration after Administration)

We can't even agree; "No New Taxes" or "the Lower the Tax = the more revenue is generated into government coffers for the Public Good!"...Got to be one's RIGHT, idiots!

Nor can We even "try" a simple FLAT-TAX, or a Combination there of, after years of half-hearted debate; *Oooh, …that would mean We'd relinquish our power and our authority, and our hold on the great unwashed taxpayer.*

BUT, We Sure Can Pass A National "Golden Fleece" of $700 Billion Dollar$ In A Single Week!...... Amazing work, diligent Legislators ALL!

Can't our Government ever agree to get anything done that's meaningful for the Taxpayer, their employers, with any significant value to benefit the entire nation, much less doing it expeditiously?...Try anything simple, just to see what it would be like. It might work!....Oh, like, protecting the Southern Borders from Lost Raiders With An Empty Ark, that they're looking to fill-up with cash, and pay no taxes, and stop by our hospitals, then split!

How about passing 1800 Gun Laws, so "nothing works"....Oh, there's good ideas!

What the heck?….. They're all Lawyers down there in Washingtonville. Shouldn't be a problem, unless someone's a "slacker" & dragging their feet! That should take an entire week to chop those 1800 useless laws down to 3 strikes = done deal………Just saved 25 million victims from suffering future crimes, billion$ of dollar$, and imminent deaths. Now -What's -On -The -Agenda -For -This -Afternoon?....HELLO?...HealthCare? The debt?

With Our Current Government, It's Always; "re-inventing the wheel" and "fiddling with something that ain't broke"….But, They Always Seem To Break-IT, Again, and Again.
But I digress, back to the issue at hand.

His question was: "What's a RINO to You?"………...Hmmm?

My Simplest Answer: A sheep in wolves' clothing) = R.I.N.O.
"Symbolism Over Substance!"
That's all we ever get, and that's precisely what we don't want, anymore, that's it.

How about for some "Real Change"; every man and woman in politics just admitting what they'll really do, meaning it, and actually doing what they said, then standing behind their words with honest conviction, no matter which way the cards fall = NOT being a R.I.N.O.

All we expect is just some simple HONESTY! All we want is just some simple Honor!
All we voted for is just simply your Integrity..... Is that so freak'n hard?

What ever happened to "Practice What You Preach"? …….. CrCrCrCrooks!

Why do all DEMs have to run to the Right in order to win?
Why do all REPs have to govern to the Left in order to survive?
Why does the Public fall for that election after election?

Hey, here's a thought: Do what the @%^# You say you're gonna do!…that's "change"!

What's a RINO?…….If You don't know by now you're part of the problem!

A Conservative Is A Conservative,
and A Republican, for the most part today is a modern RINO,

R I N O = Respectability In Name Only
R I N O = Representative In Name Only
R I N O = Right Is Now Optional

<u>RINO Synonyms</u>: Fraudulent, Double-Dealer, Charlatan, Snake, Side-winder, Impostor, Treacherous, Skunk, Sleeper Agent, Turncoat, Benedict, Usurper, B/S'er, Graham, McCain, Snow, Chafee, Snow, Spector; you know, Progressives, LIARS!

*As John Wayne would have said: <u>You're either with us or agin' us pilgrim!</u>
Or was that Walter Brennen?….No, Duke!

It's Right VS Left…That's Your Choice…That's the Game…This side of the field, or that side of the NET.
Make a your choice, you can't play both sides! What do you think you are, a RINO?

There are No Independents, they are but Democrats without courage! You know who you are, and if you don't, you shouldn't waste a vote, or your countrymen's dignity!
Just pick a side…..If You're a Liberal be a proud liberal, and run-on-it to get elected.

Have the conviction of your own beliefs. Be honest with yourself and your constituents to whom you owe your job and allegiance!…..

It's OK, this is America….. Have the courage to be who you are and what you believe.
That is the "pursuit of happiness".

Don't raise your Right hand and pick my pocket with your LEFT!

<u>Don't ever be a RINO!</u>

<u>**SENTRYMAN**</u>

Chapter 9

Think; "al Qaeda", Domestic Terrorism, DRUGS, 1 World Order, Russia or Atheism threatens the US?.......REALITY CHECK!!!

Posted by SENTRYMAN on <u>December 24, 2008</u> at 2:30am

http://www.democrats.com/

ALL ABOARD FOR THE "Comet Hale-Bopp 2"

<u>SENTRYMAN</u>

Chapter 10

What is "SPIN"? ....
Your Mother would have said: "You're Lying"!

Posted by SENTRYMAN on December 24, 2008 at 3:26pm

What is "Spin"?

My Mom would have called it "Lying",
unlike Politicians and today's almighty Media Press, striving for their (accuracy in Journalism); SPIN,
"an oxymoron".

**Kind of like voting 10 or 20 times for "The Winner" of, let's say;
American Idol, a certain Minn. Senator, or even a President for instance,**

Or for "GLOBAL WARMING!"

Webster's

*Spin:
Definition: circular motion
11.
Slang. to cause to have a particular bias; influence in a certain direction: *His assignment was to spin the reporters after the president's speech.*

Slang:
spin one's wheels
spin doctor

Synonyms: circuit, gyration, revolution, roll, rotation, spiral, turn, twist, whirl

**Lie:
Definition: untruth
Synonyms: bear false witness, break promise, BS*, bull*, con*, concoct*, deceive*, delude*, distort*, dupe*, canard, cock-and-bull story*, couch*, falsehood*, falsity*, fib*, fiction*, misrepresentation*, misstatement, prevarication*, story*, stretch*, tale*, untruth*.   **Pg. 55**

OK, now you would really think with today's ever-evolving Lexicon that the word "SPIN", and the word "LIE", would be interchangeable Synonyms!...But, we'll settle for the SLANG: B/S...

But again, who's writing the books? Who are the "Gate Keepers"?

So much for the unchallenged Liberal Academia, with a Socialist Agenda, regurgitating Revisionist-History as fact with their total monopoly to influence our children's minds.

Take *"GLOBAL WARMING"* for instance ....but,
2008 WILL BE COOLEST YEAR OF THE DECADE! .....Ooops.

*"Global average for 2008 should come in close to 14.3C,
but cooler temperature is not evidence that global warming is slowing, say climate
scientists".* ......guffaw, guffaw

HALF-TRUTH = SPIN......SPIN......SPIN......SPIN......and more SPIN, etc!!!!!!

"Scientist admits that in as much he presently is Not affiliated with any University or Project or Applying for any Grant, he can stand with those fellow scientists that think Climate Change is a constant, with present extremely diminished activity on the surface of our Sun, and that Global Warning Is Not Man-made".

Finally, TRUTH raises its ugly head when money is Not Involved!

http://www.dailytech.com/Sun+Makes+History+First+Spotless+Month+in+a+Century/article12823.htm

"Drop in solar activity has potential effect for climate on earth.

The sun has reached a milestone not seen for nearly 100 years: an entire month has passed without a single visible sunspot being noted.

The event is significant as many climatologists now believe solar magnetic activity – which determines the number of sunspots -- is an influencing factor for climate on earth.

According to data from Mount Wilson Observatory, UCLA, more than an entire month has passed without a spot. The last time such an event occurred was June of 1913. Sunspot data has been collected since 1749.

When the sun is active, it's not uncommon to see sunspot numbers of 100 or more in a single month. Every 11 years, activity slows, and numbers briefly drop to near zero. Normally sunspots return very quickly, as a new cycle begins."

http://www.telegraph.co.uk/earth/wildlife/3761269/Spider-as-big-as-a-plate-among-scores-of-new-species-found-in-Greater-Mekong.html

The Sun (AggManUK)
http://www.youtube.com/watch?v=mrC0Wog16oo

Universe - How Big Are You?
http://www.youtube.com/watch?v=AT8T54w_jYM&feature=related

HALF-TRUTH = SPIN = STRETCH = LIE = Journalistic & Scientific integrity

So much for Truth or Honor in the scientific community anymore;

Today's Reality = "SPIN"

SENTRYMAN

 ## Chapter 11

The Rallying Cry for all of us is to:
"Vote With Our Dollars for Homeland Security".

Posted by SENTRYMAN on December 27, 2008 at 9:43pm

A friend, who's a "Homeland Security" officer writes his blog, that says
"The Rallying Cry" for all of us is to: "Vote With Our Dollars",
which is "Mightier than the Pen" or the "Sword".
==
He Writes;
I was finally cleared for my Top Security Clearance and drilled with a group equally cleared. By mid-2002, we had been informed of how many different terrorism plots we had "dodged the bullet" on!

In a pre-election CNN report - they revealed that "dozens" of plots have been foiled due to our Fantastic "Department of Homeland Security".

In a matter of months, George W. Bush and Dick Cheney formed one of our most amazing organizations - the "Home Land Security" -

Americans unfortunately just don't understand or appreciate just what this is all about and how important it is. In September of 2002, while attending The National Defense University in DC - rather than writing war games, as was planned - I was invited to help with the first "Joint Homeland Security Symposium"

*Drafted by a two star general, Gen.*********, to work with his group at the Pentagon the following week. Once again with my clearance, I was able to sit in on the vital discussions.*

*In a nutshell folks, our imperative efforts to protect this great nation are unnecessarily impeded, since the rest of the world isn't too hot on patriots working for the defense of this country AND much of this is due to OUR OWN MEDIA,
and how they have reported all of these events since 9/11. Had OUR MEDIA been supportive of the Bush administration, we would be in an entirely different position around the world.
Once again, the reason the McCain/Palin ticket didn't win was totally due to the MEDIA selecting exactly what the Americans, along with the world, heard and choosing how it was reported -*

Here's our mission folks - we've got to join hands across this country and the world and let the MEDIA know how we feel about their coverage, and then not doing any business with the sponsors on their NEWS or TV Programs that depict the USA in any unfavorable light, since it's OUR advertising dollars, the Life Blood, that helps keep programs like "The View" on the air. We have the power - what say all of you?   Pg. 58

He expresses:
the rest of the world isn't too hot on us in this country. Much of this is due to OUR media and how they report.

My comment:
Much of it is due??..............How about: All of it!!

I just watched; (Mike Wallace-"Lite"), Chris Wallace interrogate VP Cheney on FOX-News. Try to catch the re-run.

Chris didn't "water-board" the Vice President, but he wished he could I'm sure, and Chris asked questions, but wasn't listening to any of the answers.

Chris noticeably learned nothing as He plowed through his list, or he would have changed his tone and inferences, just as one learns or realizes something new.

There was so much information to be proud of and thankful for, that the Bush administration had considered and accomplished in order to keep us all safe since 9/11, and, on behalf of an ungrateful nation.

Chris' and The Media's primary objective, and their usual strategy is to phrase a question with a false premise to set-up a "misspeak" or a "slip of the tongue", and to also ferret-out any admission and self-condemnation while responding, but not in order to discover anything unknown to inform the listener, their paying customer.

"Chris Wallace questions Cheney" and I paraphrase;
i.e. Since the Bush administration ""failed"" to capture bin Laden, and must "pass" that problem onto the Obama Administration, don't you consider that as a: "total failure"?

e.g. The Bush administration made: "never allowing Iran to have a nuclear weapon", the centerpiece of their administration, don't you see that as "another total failure"?

He expresses:
Had OUR media been supportive with the Bush administration, we would be in an entirely different position around the world.

My comment:
I have recently written about this subject on my own Blog also. Please check it out.

I contend that had "The Media" been "on-board" with the President from the beginning, just like all Americans were in 1942, putting their personal animus aside, (and hadn't encouraged or sympathized with the Terrorists, like today), today's MEDIA would have been "brought along and been on-board" to justly influence our short-attention-spanned, indifferent, petulant, celebrity-crazed nation to be with "The Program", and then too, the World would have followed right behind, still shaking its head and wagging its tail of course, but ultimately this War would have already ended" years ago!

1000's of heroic troops wouldn't have needed to sacrifice their limbs, and their lives to protect all of us, and those patriots would in fact, be home with their families right now.

And, I further maintain that: With Our Media Not Doing So As They Did Back In 1942, This Media "has the blood of every soldier on their hands"!

These very "pseudo-patriots" would be the first despicable individuals to "call for the impeachment and the public hanging" of President George W. Bush, had Bush "done nothing" and Los Angeles had been the second 9/11, with Chicago 9/12, but, by the grace of God = "W"!

He expresses:
Here's our mission folks - we've got to join hands across this country and the world and let the media know how we feel about their coverage,
wrote down the sponsors and then blogged about not doing business with these sponsors since it is their advertising dollars that kept the View on the air.
We have the power - what say all of you?

My comment:
Go for it, try anything.

But that doesn't influence networks like NBC, or the NY TIMES, that (would, will, and have) gone down in flames and taken all their sycophantic employees and followers with them.

Nor does it affect movie and TV personalities who our kids emulate, and not to exclude the majority of the Music Performers again, that the youth are hard-wired into, and then of course, there's the Internet.

We are in a War here too at home, in case no one realizes it.

This fight is much bigger and more pervasive than we wish to realize or accept.
The LEFT touts and pats themselves on the back for their "Grass Roots" efforts, except it is really how they corral and influence our young, kind of like the Hitler-Youth movement.

My POINT:

You want to break the cycle,
start being more "hands-on" with your kids in grade schools, in high school, and then with their liberal colleges that you're sending them to, that you are going into debt, and footing the bill for.

It's getting even harder and more time consuming with your younger children I'm certain, with jobs and a lack of "choices or alternatives" available to parents today, plus an institutional-reluctance for "teacher monitoring and testing", even in Private Schools, than it would be with your capability to influence your adolescents where it may already be too late.

Though, it is finally getting a bit easier to select a "Conservative" alternative College like "Hillsdale", since you're primarily consumed with the financial aspects of the last phase in educating your children, there has been a very short list of schools that wouldn't reverse everything you've imparted to your kids for the last 13 years, since Liberalism has a strangle hold death-grip on all Academia for decades and it's going to get much worse very soon, since the frost is off the jack-o-lantern, or is it: the bloom is off the rose!

Ever hear of ACORN?
Well, it's going to be the "Children of the Corn" if you don't watch out!
http://www.hillsdale.edu/

Other extremely important tasks that everyone needs to employ is to sit down and review all of your children's, and/or your grandchildren's text books; that's if their liberal parents will let you, grandma and grandpa.

When Lincoln and Washington, for instance, are synopsized and relegated to "a single page or two" in many current textbooks, we don't really stand a chance anymore people.

We've handed our children's brains, quite literary, over to the enemy's subtle propagandists! ....So what do you expect when celebrating Earth Day and Winter Holiday, bye-bye Christmas vacation? I used to like those days-off from school too on Feb. 11th and the 22nd. So much for that murdering- barbarian Columbus and his Day either.

Be vigilant because it means "all of our futures" now with "Death Initiatives" on the ballot. "Soylent Green" could be a reality someday in your future!

You think I jest?
Where do you think Mad-Cow disease actually came from??...Look it up!

SENTRYMAN

==

1 Blog Comment:

Comment by Life & Liberty on December 28, 2008 at 1:20am

I agree that DHS (Department of Homeland Security) is a fantastic organization, I work under their umbrella too and it is amazing how much this organization has done to protect, investigate and thwart those who wish to do us harm.

Our history of patriotism is our future and the generations to come MUST be taught that.

Chapter 12

Top 10 quotes of 2008...................WOW,
7 out of 10 are Republicans.......Big Surprise!

Posted by SENTRYMAN on December 29, 2008 at 11:00pm

AP: Top ten quotes of 2008
Monday, December 15th 2008, 9:48 AM

with SENTRYMAN Critiques, *A and **B

Lester/AP,
as compiled by the editor of the Yale Book of Quotations:
----

1. "I can see Russia from my house!" — Comedian Tina Fey,
while impersonating Alaska Gov. Sarah Palin on the TV comedy show
"Saturday Night Live," Broadcast Sept. 13.

*A - What Sarah should have stated, instead of "Sarah's accurate quote",
paraphrased: (*You can actually see Russia from the coast of Alaska!)

**B - She should have stated:

"I'm standing strong here in Alaska guarding our backdoor, watching those
Russkies' as usual, just so they don't try anything funny, like in Georgia!

And that's "Not Georgia, USA", either Tina!"

----

2. "All of them, any of them that have been in front of me over all these
years." — Palin, responding to a request by CBS anchor Katie Couric to
name the newspapers or magazines she reads, Broadcast Oct. 1.

Pg. 62

*A - What Sarah should have stated, instead of the expanded quote, as she explained to Greta Van Susteren,
paraphrased:
(*I was taken aback at that foolish question, since Katie must feel we, up here in Alaska are so removed that we don't get the same press and magazines as the lower 48, I didn't want to be rude.)

**B - She should have stated:

"Well, I really try not to read those "Yellow-journalism" news rags too often, and especially not the "NY TIMES, Washington Post, US News, TIME Mag. etc., really most of them, including AP, UPI,
nor listen to; CBC, BBC, CNN, MSNBC, CNBC and NBC, CBS and ABC of course,

Opting for truth & accuracy, I prefer FOX-NEWS and government communiqués, and also RUSH and HANNITY and O'REILLY, of course!"

----

3. "We have sort of become a nation of whiners." — Former Sen. Phil Gramm, an economic adviser to Republican presidential candidate Sen. John McCain, quoted in The Washington Times, July 10.

*A - TRUE - TRUE –TRUE

**B - He should have said;

"We are a nation of whiners; So, GIVE US OUR NATIONAL WELFARE CHECKS "....."Boooo Hoooo,
and pull your heads out of the trough, wipe the cream off your chins and GROW UP PEOPLE, THERE'S NO FREE LUNCH!"

----

4. "It's not based on any particular data point, we just wanted to choose a really large number." — a Treasury Department spokeswoman explaining how the $700 billion number was chosen for the initial bailout, quoted on Forbes.com Sept. 23.

*A - Are these people paid by our tax dollars?

**B - What is this, a divorce attorney, or a "defense attorney" adding up their bill?

What Poor, Poor Fools Are We, That We Hired These People To Lord Over Us!

---

5. "The fundamentals of America's economy are strong." — McCain, in an interview with Bloomberg TV, April 17.

*A - TRUE - TRUE -TRUE

**B - At that time, what with Barney Frank lying through his teeth about Fannie and Freddie, it was true and probably still is,
but unfortunately that's why "our misplaced priorities" will continue to afford;
-sports stadium prices,
-rock concert prices,
-$12. @ gal. bottled water,
-designer jeans,
-Wii,
-the newest Boysenberry phone,

though, we really will work our way out of this mess sooner than any "foreign government" will ever appreciate. ha ha ha

***C - Oh, I forgot:
we should all grab our picket signs and march "for higher pay" for those "Saturday Night Live" show-writers....ya, sure!

None of us could live on their meager salaries, especially in Democrat NYC!!....awe....

---

6. *"Decisions by the Secretary pursuant to the authority of this Act are non-reviewable and committed to agency discretion, and may not be reviewed by any court of law*
or any administrative agency." — the Treasury Department's proposed Emergency Economic Stabilization Act, September 2008.

*A - What is this; a Coup d'état, or a Junta'?

**B - We Poor, Poor, Poor Fools!!

----

7. *"Maybe 100." — McCain,*
discussing in a town hall meeting in Derry, New Hampshire,
how "many years" U.S. troops could remain in Iraq, Jan. 3.

*A - The World knows He didn't say that, but that doesn't matter.

**B - But, since we're still stationed around the globe, post W.W.II,
I can easily imagine we could be in IRAQ in 100 years,
especially if IRAN hasn't turned the globe to a cinder in the interim, or
we haven't made Arabic the official language of the USA.

But even with that eventuality, we'll still be in IRAQ....We're in IRAQ!

Better ask Phil Donahue!

Perception is Reality,
Truth lost forever, is Anyone's Opinion Today,

"Journalism is dead in 2008"; quoting Shawn Hannity

----

8. *"I'll see you at the debates, b------."* — *Paris Hilton*
in a video responding to a McCain television campaign ad, August 2008.

*A - No, You stay in Los Angeles honey.

**B - Caroline will take your place and "represent" New Yorkers just as adeptly!

----

9. *"Barack, he's talking down to black people. ... I want to cut his ... off."* — *Rev. Jesse Jackson,*
overheard over a live microphone before a Fox News interview, July 6.

*A - Nooooo, did I really hear him say that?

http://www.youtube.com/watch?v=8Wf6LnwRZXA&feature=related

**B - Nooooo, must have been taken out of context or misquoted.
Jesse would have said: *"I have a minor disagreement I wish to discuss with our President at his earliest convenience"*!

http://www.youtube.com/watch?v=TQI_6buUggM
----

10. (tie) *"There are no atheists in foxholes and there are no libertarians in financial crises."* — *Krugman,*
in an interview with Bill Maher on HBO's "Real Time," broadcast Sept. 19.

*A - Who cares what either of them have to say!

The Associated Press's list of the Top 10 Quotes of 2008 featured two from Nobel-winning economist Paul Krugman.

But Krugman, it turns out,
was not actually quotable-enough to merit credit for either.

HOLD -THE – PRESSES, Obama Batman!!

11. How Could We Forget This Great Sen. Barack Obama Quote Out On The Stump:

*A - "I've now been in 57 states....I think 1 left to go"......

   "1 left to go, Alaska and Hawaii, I wasn't allowed to go!"
- Barack Obama, 2008

**B - Freudian Slips?

("57 States")
http://www.youtube.com/watch?v=aMBSYBvpBv8&feature=related

("my Muslim Faith")
http://www.youtube.com/watch?v=XKGdkqfBlCw&feature=related

(who's a Moslem?)
http://www.youtube.com/watch?v=qOu-3dDQuac

"In God We Trust"

SENTRYMAN

Chapter 13

AOL Survey Asked;
Obama to Lunch With Ex-Presidents: *"What Would You Ask?"*

Posted by SENTRYMAN on <u>January 8, 2009</u> at 4:44pm

What Would I Ask The Presidents?
If you could put one question to Pres. Bush, Pres-elect Obama and the ex-presidents at their White House lunch, what would it be?

I Wrote on the AOL Blog;

"As Our current President, George W. Bush stated that He wished the President Elect Obama "Success and Goodwill",
and ex-Pres. Clinton stated: *"I Love This Rug"!*............(I'll bet he did!)"

I Would have asked;

"Would it be correct to say; if President Bush had done nothing after 9/11, and then when LA, and Chicago, and Washington were destroyed, he'd actually deserve the public opinion polls, and ratings he has erroneously earned on AOL and within The Media,
he now enjoys? ....Yes or no?"

Wake-up people!

"The hatred for Bush, like this poll today, serves No Purpose, is totally manufactured and symbolically if not literally is "traitorous".

The 535 legislators with the "purse-strings" are the problem,
just as a negative Media has helped shape and influence the uninformed popular culture, who's own fear has as much contributed to the "over night" destruction of the economy, as has Barney Frank and Chris Dodd."

"Forget about watching TV, or the Stock Exchange, or listening to anyone in the Media,
 and just live your lives as normal as possible for 30 days and the whole

Pg. 68

thing will probably turn itself around before Obama starts spending another Trillion Dollar$ or 2 in his worthless, and I do mean "worth-less" efforts, spending "our money" out of this mess."

"Government Creates Nothing", "Government Produces Nothing",
"they only spend our money the way they wish, and ultimately this will be totally up to us, not our surrogate handler: "Overseers in Washington", to figure all this out and tell them what to do.

"Want to solve some real problems very quickly to send a message to those great-lawyers who do all our thinking for us, those same lawyers who continually let this scenario keep happening, "the Half" that must have been asleep, while the "other Half" were doing their worst!"

"Demand it of Obama! ---------- Demand it of our Legislators"!
Hell, let's just vote-it-in ourselves with a "Citizen's Revolution", or it'll never get out of "some committee":

a National Referendum Petition Vote, any way we can make that happen!

No Committees or Debate, We, The People, Vote-It-In-For-Ourselves=

__2 Term Limits,__ for all elected officials, except the President = only (1), "do your duty and Go Home", as the forefather's envisioned.

NEXT;
__Tort Reform__, that certainly will never see the light with these vampires,

__Outlaw all "Lobbyists"__, we didn't elect and hire these "Representatives" to travel to Washington to be bribed, coerced, bullied, or made millionaires.

__Give the President the "Line-Item Veto"__ or, "__No Bundling Bills__",
  and
  __All Bills Will Be Voted On Separately__, equaling = No Ear Marks = No Pork,

__No Pay Raises__, unless and until We the People vote them one, if deserved,

__freeze all new spending__, and tell Government to go home until they are actually needed to solve a problem, a dilemma or some pressing issue. No "Idle Hands"!....They're not serving us anyway….. i.e. "The Bail-Out",

__FLAT TAX__, steal back our own Money, and then they'll stay home,

* __NO withholding taxes for 6 month, citizen's-free,__ ,

* __Don't "gift-money" to the Banks__, only "loan" our freak'n tax-money to

banks and insurance companies NOT a single dime without "interest & collateral", and we want it back!
(we all know by-the-way, they already own this country, and that's another story, but NOT-MONEY-FOR-FREE-TOO!)

And finally,

* _Don't Buy Any More Foreign Oil_... Drill Our Own Oil... Drill Here, Drill Now and Totally Utilize Our Own Wonderfully Plentiful Clean Natural Gas, and then World, watch what happens when capitalism raises all boats.

SENTRYMAN

==

So, "citizen Patti" comments on my AOL Blog entry:

#1- _"Will we ever get out of the mess we are in?"_

#2- _"Will we ever be respected again in this world?"_

==

and I answered her #1 question;

"Hi Patti,

You asked me: _"Will we ever get out of this mess, and will America ever be respected again?"_

The simple answer to #1 is without repeating myself:
Yes, of course, We Are Americans!

But, not while the future administration is thinking;
(as quoted today by Pres. Elec. O-bam-as':

"Only government can solve this problem"!..........&
"there will be many Trillion dollar deficits in the future"!
- Barack Obama

THERE IT IS! THE RE-DISTRIBUTION OF WEALTH!!! ...."SOCIALISM"!!

Hey everybody, we haven't been attacked since 9/11, and things were going along pretty good till the DEMs in the 2006 Election touted; "everything was crap", and only THEY could "CHANGE" things.

So the great un-informed believed them, and WAH'LA: "Change"....Happy?

It became "$1-Trillion" times worse, and it's going to get another $Trillion times worse in 2009! duhhhhh

Can anyone anywhere connect-the-dots?

Can anyone understand the concept of Cause=and=Effect?

Again, FEAR got us into this mess, and FEAR will continue to permit government's death-grip on our minds, and our wallets, to continue.

Only WE citizens finally becoming rational and realistic enough to recognize our fate without having the faith in our country's Constitution, our great democracy and in capitalism, our salvation,
we will end up like every other great civilization throughout history: Uncivil to its own people, decayed, and destroy itself from within!

People: "Earn your day's pay & go spend some money on American stuff."

How many times must We be told to actually listen and heeeear this:
"There - Is - No - Free - Lunch."...................It-Really-Is-That-Simple!

Tell your guys in Washington to stop taxing-us into our great, great grandchildren's enslaved future. Do what we say and Leave Us Alone!

**** (If) Sam Walton, God Love Him, had a Division that had 535 executives that were all culpable, and responsible for screwing-up as badly as OUR stellar elected-officials have performed over the last 12 months for their employer, the American taxpayer,
that Wal-Mart Division, that Section, and that Building would be destroyed, leveled, and become a ancient footnote at management seminars on:
"How to screw-up a "good thing" and screw-yourself out of a job!....
NOT following established "standard business practices and ethics" in the real world, all those 535 Execs. would be home on-the-couch with their Pink-Slips in hand, before Katie Couric smiled on their TVs spewing the evening's serving of liberal Propaganda Pablum for that day!

So, why do these guys still have their jobs, Americans?...HELLO?

***Ask yourselves 1 simple question:

"What does government do well"?,

besides protect us from foreign shores…but ONLY when we give our soldiers the necessary issue of proper equipment to perform their tasks?

The government announced today "the date" to switch to Digital-TV will be extended because they can't even get that organized right, and "We Want To Give These Guys The Authority To Run Our Health-Care, To Be Healthy?

Heck, even mandating Digital-TV "ALONE" is a ridiculously "stupid idea", and is designed to TAX, REGULATE and CONTROL the Populous of Free Speech, and Free Will; you new Socialists!

These Guys Can't Even Run The Veteran's Health Administration With Pride Or Competence After 60 Years. You'd think these 535 EXPERTs would have all the flies-out-of-all-that-ointment by now! They use that Vaseline for us!

Are we all asleep, crazy, or just stupid???...............Hell, maybe ALL 3!

#2 Patti asks Me: *"Will we be respected again?"*

Patti, don't ever believe the Media, just believe in your our heart and mind. We build fences to keep THEM-OUT, not to keep THEM-IN!

I've got an idea Patti;
How about we really make the entire World MAD at Us,
We tend to our Own House 1st instead, for a change;

A. *We Stop Feeding The World For One Year*
   Since We're Supposedly So Hated Anyway,

and then;

B. *We Don't Buy Another Barrel Of Foreign Oil from A-N-Y-B-O-D-Y,*
   and then We Only **"Drill-Here and Drill-Now!**

Our Problems Are ALL Solved With A Stroke Of The Pen, (half-hour, tops), but then we'll have to build a 40' foot-high wall instead
to keep E-V-E-R-Y-B-O-D-Y out!" ....Oooops!

<u>SENTRYMAN</u>

 **Chapter 14**

The 20 Demandments of the United States of AMERICA.

Posted by SENTRYMAN on __January 8, 2009__

"A Peaceful Citizen's REVOLUTION"

"Our" government has its Own self-satisfying, self-indulgent, *self-aggrandizing* Death-grip wrapped around Our collective necks,
and their Own greed will never serve or protect US, their employers!

Demand of OUR Government with a Citizen's National Referendum
by a (PEACEFUL) Non-Violent Ultimatum For:

"The 20 Demandments"

No GOVT. Committees,
No blue ribbon Sub-Committees,
and without any idle Legislative Debate,

We must demand of "OUR" elected, non-representative, government employees.
(since they'll never comply or permit any reduction of their power or authority,
that We their employers, The America Taxpayer have granted and entrusted to them,
nor would they ever Vote-It "Out Of Committee" to make these viable as any of OUR LAWs,
with the following provisions;

#1- (2 Term) Limits for all elected officials, & Presidents only (1),
This Civic Duty Is Not a Career, nor an Annuity, and certainly not a Life appointment.
It's a Calling, a Service, a Sacrifice and then Go Home as OUR Forefather's envisioned.
"THE MOST IMPORTANT and IMPERATIVE of the 20"

#2- Tort Reform,

#3- Outlaw all "Lobbyists",
we didn't elect, hire or pay these representatives to travel to Washington
 to be professionally bribed, or made millionaires.

#4- Give the President the "Line Item Veto"
or, "No Bundling Bills."
All Bills Voted On Separately, equaling = No Ear Marks = No Pork, unless
voted upon its own merits, with a majority approval for the general good!

Pg. 73

#5- No Pay Raises for Government Officials
unless and until "we, the people" vote them one, when it's deserved,

#6- Freeze All New Spending,
and tell Government to go home until they are actually needed to solve a problem, dilemma or pressing issue.
No Idle Hands!....They're not serving us anyway.....
i.e. "TRILLIONS In-Debt, with Bailouts to friends and past associates",

#7- 12 months Freeze: NO INCOME TAX.
No More Bailouts,
Keep Our Own Trillions Of Dollars In Our Pockets and That Will Solve The Problems Immediately,
(that's "RIGHT NOW", for you Washingtonians),

#8- FLAT TAX, or Consumption TAX,
or a combination there of, and Dismantle the IRS from going after citizens or businesses for political retribution, then the Congress will stay home till needed.
.....On second thought, Dismantle the IRS,

#9- "Don't Buy Any Foreign Oil,
Drill Here, Drill NOW, and use Natural Gas!"
Continue to research, experiment, invent and design all the Wind Mills, Solar Panels, Geothermal, etc., etc., that private Industry wishes to create, but in the mean time, break the yoke of our oppressive pseudo-green government and,

#10- No More Eminent Domain,
or Reconciliation for Corporations or Private Business,

#11- Election Funds Limit,

i.e. a FLAT $100 Million (for all contenders) to divide!
(NOT McCain's $140 million Vs Obama $700 million),

#12- "3 Strike" GUN LAW
The confused police shoot'm or lock'm-up, and the Courts let'm out.
Do You really think the 18,000 guns laws on the books are working?

And who runs the Government? .....LAWYERS!
And who teaches the Lawyers? ......LIBERALS!
And who wants to charge the Taxpayers $400. @ hr.
for anything and everything? ....LIBERAL LAWYERS!

Hey, Geniuses, this is how to "make a Law in 1 minute":
A - Carry a Firearm in the commission of a felony = 10 Years

B - Fire a Firearm in the commission of a felony = 25 Years

C - Kill someone in the commission of a felony = Life!

Do you know how many trees I just saved, or how many court dockets I just
cleared???.......(that's real "Green" Government)

and how many lame-brained villains and felons just decided not to "Carry"
Firearms in the commission of their chosen professions = ?
but hey, a lot more than 1 minute ago!

**So why must this be a lifelong debate while lives are ruined and people
die??

***Now we can start working on their compunction and propensity for
committing Felonies in the 1st place!

And while we're discussing the psychological, philosophical and
sociological ramifications,
who runs and ruined their Education in the first place???.......GUESS!

#13- ENGLISH, the official language of The United States of America!

#14- Military on the Border and Finish The Fence,
Train new recruits with duty-guarding our country's 4 sides with our
already paid Military. It's FREE!

#15- Legalize all Non-Criminal Illegal Aliens with a <u>5-year Green Card,</u> & immediate citizenship by joining the US Military.

#16- Every Citizen has a national Voter Registration, (Thumb Print - Photo ID) card or "YOU Can't Vote".

No more calamities like:
I.e. (More people voting for Obama than even lived in the town!)

#17- No one leaves Prison without a GED and a professional skill, which means; teaching inmates what they never learned in our Liberal Public Schools that We Paid For, That As Children They Didn't Receive,

#18- Returning Military will be employed by Our government of 1 year stateside, to insure a safe-integration back into civilian-society, this for all our valiant former warriors and volunteer protectors.

#19- Give the Military and active Troops whatever they need to properly Defend OUR Country, with Full Health Benefits for our returning Military.

#20- "<u>Marriage</u>" is between a Man and a Woman!
(If you can't make babies, you don't need this ancient ceremonial rite!
A religious precept & custom based on rightful-heritage for the "<u>offspring</u>")

<u>SENTRYMAN</u>

(A) An Immediate "Works" Project:

Put Men To Work Tomorrow On An
<u>Across-America FLOOD Diversion - Interstate Irrigation Network;</u>

to PIPE flooded rivers & streams away from communities, capturing flooding and Run-off with a series of Pumps & Filters to pipe & redirect waters to any region of the country with any drought to stabilize top soil wind erosion, to quiet areas threatened by imminent fires, and irrigate feed-grasses for starving livestock and suffering crops.

Pg. 76

We can filter-out when necessary and replenish the Reservoirs, Sink holes, irrigate the deserts of the Southwest and Southeast Texas, dry-ponds and drained lakes and restore reserves for fighting brush and forest fires, and perhaps even make Death Valley bloom with the excess run-off.

***How do we accomplish this and solve most of the other problems too??**

We Could Pass This Stuff, And Any Innovations In An Afternoon,

while these ineffectual, dilettantes that sit around wasting 6 months debating about sending "imminently needed" supplies, protective equipment and ammunition to the battlefield, for those very Troops Protecting Their Pampered Jobs, Salaries, Purloined Perks and Silly Butts back in the stale, vacuous Halls of Congress: House and Senate included, who don't deserve the pompous positions of power we've all granted them!

But wait, "the sky is falling - the sky is falling", oh sure,
They Can Pass A $700,000,000,000 - Bill In Only 5 Days,
and WITHOUT-EVEN-READING-IT!!! …..WHAT???

*THAT ALONE SHOULD BE GROUNDS FOR US, WE THE PEOPLE, TO "FIRE -EVERY-ONE-OF-THESE -DECADENT -THIEVES", WHO AGAIN ARE ONLY JUST "PAID-EMPLOYEES" OF THE AMERICAN PEOPLE, THE AMERICAN CITIZEN, THE AMERICAN TAXPAYER!

THOSE SAME PEOPLE, THESE WASHINGTON-GUYS CHEAT AND FLEECE FROM ACROSS THE FRUITED, EVERY - SINGLE - DAY!

This is what "We, The People",
We Freedom Loving Citizens must figure out and very soon,
or our children's, children's children will still be paying for this disastrous boondoggle-mess, and be trying to figure it out in 3009!

If We Can All Figure This Out In Time, And Make This Happen,
We'll Bring Our Country Back From The Brink,
and save the United States of AMERICA for OURSELVEs,
for OUR KIDs, and for THEIRs TOO!

SENTRYMAN

In CONGRESS, July 4, 1776

The unanimous Declaration of the thirteen United States of America

When in the Course of human events it becomes necessary for one people to dissolve the political bands which have connected them with another and to assume among the powers of the earth, the separate and equal station to which the Laws of Nature and of Nature's God entitle them, a decent respect to the opinions of mankind requires that they should declare the causes which impel them to the separation.

We hold these truths to be self-evident, that all men are created equal, that they are endowed by their Creator with certain unalienable Rights, that among these are Life, Liberty and the pursuit of Happiness. —

The Constitution of the United States

Preamble Note
We the People of the United States, in Order to form a more perfect Union, establish Justice, insure domestic Tranquility, provide for the common defence, promote the general Welfare, and secure the Blessings of Liberty to ourselves and our Posterity, do ordain and establish this Constitution for the United States of America.

**YouTube Videos will continue to be blocked, for whatever politically-correct excuse, but I will endeavor to find copies and reestablish them at:
http://www.sentryman.org/id8.html

Chapter 15

<u>Sonia Asks SENTRYMAN: *"Who is going to stop the Media"?*</u>

Posted by SENTRYMAN on <u>January 11, 2009</u> at 5:30pm

"Hello "SENTRYMAN",

Who is going to stop the media? They are dangerous. Not only do they outright lie and ignore the truth, they put our national security at risk. Who is going to do something about this?"
......from Sonia

"Hello "SENTRYMAN",

The goal of a newspaper is to sell papers, and they don't care how they go about it. Many Journalists do not care what they say, their only purpose is to get numbers.

Our courts, under the guise of freedom of speech, have allowed the media a free reign to abuse the Freedom of Speech Laws, and the Ethics of the Media, and all of this comes under the power of Congress, who makes the laws.
As I mentioned before, our Congress lacks the morals and values of the traditional years. If our country has liberal lawmakers, our country leans liberal.
What Can We Do?"
......from Lois

==

OK Ladies, hold on to your Manolo Blahniks, it's going to be a bumpy sprint,
and SENTRYMAN is going to make it into a clear cut strategy;

You have a real grasp of the problem and You asked me:
"What can we do about it"?

Change the Laws?
Change the Congress?
Change the Media?
Change the Ethics?

<u>Girls, There Are No Ethics Anymore; in Politics, in Business and with much of Religion!</u>

In a world today run for the most part by half-educated ideologues once cradled and tutored by (Academia's Elite-Establishment); themselves weaned on 60's liberal-babel propaganda from ex-Hippies, Yippies, Yuppies and Guppies,
that would qualify one for a Ph.D. in Feminists: Burn-ur-bra, U-PIG studies, by today's standards, each without the basic common sense of any 18 year old Eagle Scout, much less, that of a 16 year old Boy Scout, these Media elites with their monstrous death-grip
Pg. 79

on young minds centered in popular culture today, in which we all must unfortunately reside: There Are No More Standards, or a simple yardstick to measure differences between Ideologies.

i.e. Rampant unchecked pedophilia from the Berkshires to the White Mountains, the Atlantic to the Pacific.

ALL of which could be unanimously-eliminated tomorrow with the fledgling "Jessica's Law", continually postponed, or cowardly rejected by so many state legislators that stalwart men with firmer resolve would totally-eliminate this predator-pestilence with a much simpler FINAL-Solution: A National Castration Law to snip the problem in the Butt.

Instead of diluting the problems and mixing the message, distraction, sleights-of-hand, shiny objects, changing the subject and the rules, or the usual: stirring up dissention between races, ethnicities and class envy....but I digress;
We hear what They want us to hear-We know only what They let us see-They fool no one!

Every issue is framed the way they want. The Judgementalism of Religions as being Bad, but the Stalinistic-Judgementalism of Yellow-Journalism is Righteous and Sacrosanct. Never sanctimonious or hypocritical, because "they are doing the judging."....That's good!

Remember this dichotomy; "Practice What You Preach": a religious slam,
and "Do As I Say, Not As I Do," a liberal tenet? .....Which is the more hypocritical?

Here is two sides of the same coin as seen through a myopic lens of a Progressive Liberal Media, and the Democrat Party. Each complicit co-conspirators are jockeying for control of our minds......Judgmental prigs, or Keepers of the flame?

i.e.
A. "Bush created 10 million New Jobs".....so what, big deal, they're all at McDonald's"!!
....The Liberal mantra.

B. "Obama wants to "create, or keep" 3 million (new or old) jobs.".....Oooooo, shiny!
**A flurry of cheers and fanfare, applause, congratulations and bows all around
 for just the mention, the intention, the warm fuzzy feeel'n.
(No credible result or measured accomplishment required, or necessary in a liberal world)

Seriously, do we see any difference between A vs B? .....Anyone admit it?

Definition of: "create", and this isn't Webster's, it's "only mine",

"Creating" is making something new and original from whole cloth.
 NOT using someone else's table cloth as a tarp, anew.... That's called "re-cycling",
 like brown stationery, or green toilet paper with cute little speckles."

In Mr. Obama's case: Any new cloth will be the material that the Treasury Dept. prints new money onto, that hasn't been backed-up by any tangible assets, or even "paid for" yet!

On one hand, we now have rising-unemployment for the last 12 months in a row, and Mr. Obama tells us, ("But it's Bush's fault!"),
though Bush didn't get any credit for the first 6 years with the creation of "10 million new jobs", when the Democrats were in the minority, and weren't in total control of the government,
unlike the last 2 years when the DEMs took-over control of Congress & jobs turned south!

Ever wonder why the hundreds and thousands of job offers that fill the Employment Section in hundreds of city's newspapers across this nation are never filled and always listed there, available and unfilled?
You would think all these "employment classified" section columns would be empty, except for: <u>Wanted: Kosovo Land Mine Defuser</u>, travel, room and board included, health benefit: subject to new administration rules.

<u>*a Paul Harvey moment:</u>
Ever notice that Paul, the glass half-full kind'a guy, always says;
"*our Employment rate today is 94% for 300 million Americans*"?

So seriously, why aren't these "job offers" filled from across the fruited plain?
……..Why?.......100s to 1000s in every city, I thought there was going to be unemployment, the likes we haven't seen since the Great Depression?

Do you think the DEMs called-it the "Great Depression" because that's the result they were looking for, because I think that's what it's about today.

Come-on!.......Think hard!......What?……People don't have the <u>"education"</u>?

….<u>And who runs our education?</u>.....You're doing better!

And why are the jails and prisons to overflowing,
 so our Liberal Judges can utilize a "Revolving Door" policy for those poor victims of misfortune, those unfortunate criminals lacking all that proper education?...Hmmmm!
….**<u>And who runs our education?</u>**

Gooood, a rhythm is forming.

And why is the majority-population in the prisons <u>primarily minorities</u>? Lack of education?
….**<u>And who runs our education?</u>**

And who do the minorities overwhelmingly vote for in each election, with their lack of proper education, because of a lack of an education?
….**<u>And who runs our education?</u>**

And now, who does the liberal Democratic Party want to be "allowed the Vote" while residing in, or once released from, prison with their lack of an education?
….**<u>And who runs our education?</u>**

And WHO doesn't want the American Taxpayer to have School "Choice",
or government mandated Teacher "proficiency" Standards,
or eliminating Tenure,
or creating any Student Testing Standards either?
…..**<u>And who runs our education?</u>**

This is called: "c.o.n.n.e.c.t.i.n.g.t.h.e.d.o.t.s" journalism students, and you don't need to be Columbo, or Doctors Lee, Wecht or Baden.

It's called Accountability!...We little people have to do it every day, if not in a UNION to hide behind to defend your weaknesses and screw-ups!! Fantastic, You're doing great and now you're on a roll!!

Remember the old Democrat controlled government who was supposedly asleep in 2007, and also the first-half of 2008 when that (lame duck) dumb-@$$ Bush was forced to step-up and think outside the box, during his Swan Song just before his retirement, in order to save the United States once again from the brink?
(Really, what was in it for him on the way out the door to make the extraordinarily difficult decisions, and make himself a "goat again" for an unfriendly, unappreciative populous, duty, love of country!)

And He proposed a $700 Billion Dollar Bailout to stabilize the nation's markets, the banks and the Insurance Industry, the crucial financial underpinnings of a once strong nation. Surprise, surprise, all of the Democrats loved the idea, and 3/4's of the Congress jumped on-board,
even though 80% of American public saw it as the "last straw" for a vilified president.

Of course, not being privy to the desperateness of the situation to fully understand the gravity of a pending 2nd disaster, with public trust fractured for a marginalized president, specifically crafted by a deceptive Media, America uniformly disagreed, but unexpectedly ignored, and really got upset at the government, but (Bush got 100% of the blame) again.

Fortunately for all of us, and more so for the culprits involved, it actually stopped the financial slide and a certain collapse of the nation's monetary system, when said Speculators were selling-out their mother's retirement funds, along with their country for a lark, or greed, or some more sinister clandestine conspiracy that we'll never be apprised of;
"Bush Saved The Day", "Bush saved 100 million jobs", "Bush Saved the USA", Again!

And, might I remind YOU, with only ½ of the allotted monies that Bush thought might be needed: ($350 Billion) of the $700 Billion purposed, but
No One Said "Thanks Mr. President". (President Bush got ZERO credit for his gutsy move), and (Bush got 100% of the blame) again. The DEMs would have spent every cent!

Today's group-think realizes that this risky stop-gap "strategery" did nothing to stimulate the Economy tomorrow, and everyone is now scratching their heads with what to do next.

But NOW, with the "All New" Totally Democrat Government soon to be in place, that wants that 2nd half, the $350 Billion that Barney Frank's got his sweaty, sticky fingered vice-grip around, formerly known-as, in pejorative terms: the "Bush Bailout", it will now be renamed with a "bright bow" & a proud smile, the official: "Bush/Obama BAILOUT" going forward!

(Don't Forget and Remember: Connecting-The-Dots and Accountability)

AND NOW, trumpets blare: "Hail To The Chieftain"; another $$TRILLION dollar$$ to spend anew, (that would be the: 2nd "OBAMA" BAILOUT, right?

O.K., now those with a current public high school education I'm sure can follow along;
..... "And - who - runs - our - education?"

Now, this is No longer a campaign to Stabilize, or to Stop a Crash, but to "CREATE"!
(Remember that term: Create?)

The Program; to "**save or create**" 3 million New or Current Jobs,
(((a dichotomy, or an oxymoron, or just totally Obama Bull$#!% ?))), and
maybe blow a smidgen of cash on some minor stuff that our President deems necessary.

Do ya think, maybe, huh, maybe?

HALLALEUYA Brothers & Sisters......NOW A "Bail-Out" IS OK, Mr. Obama?....BRILLIANT
SUCH AN INNOVATIVE IDEA WITH NO DETRACTORS, and THE MEDIA's ON-BOARD,
<u>& still isn't reporting on any of those 80% of American Taxpayers thinking it's still CRAP!</u>

Wonder how many million Jobs Bush SAVED with his brainstorm Bail-Out?
...Nahhh, he's still considered an idiot, but you're worried about Ethics ladies?

.... <u>And who runs our education?</u>.................But I digress again.

Everyone wanted change this year, Change, Change! .....Jingl'n in our pockets.

Well, you hit on it,
but you need to connect-the-dots, as they say, because George W. Bush really did.

When we were repeatedly attacked so many times all during the Clinton years, with the
finale' on 9/11 when a brand new, and real Commander-in-Chief came On-Board, and
emphatically connected-the-dots, he took Terrorists by their turbans and returned the
favor, taking the fight to the enemy and we haven't been hit since!
I didn't hear any applause, or feel the love, or appreciation or gratitude!.......Hmmmmm!

I wonder if the 9/11 Terrorists had chosen to wipeout, oh, I don't know,
maybe the "Trans-America" building, along with a few collateral GAYS in San Francisco,
instead of the "Twin Towers" in Manhattan,
or maybe Grauman's Chinese as Ground Zero, or Universal and MGM studios, if certain
people's priorities in "The Media, and in The Congress, and in the movie industry, the 9th
Circuit, Code Pink and The Color Purple", would have been any different? ...Whoa!...Hmm

Oops, how insensitive, I forgot PETA, and left out "The GREENS". I'm sure a Chihuahua or
two and a Lhasa Apso would have been sacrificed in the dust and smoke clouds that
would make some seals and walrus' cough, and contaminated ALCATRAZ.

**Phew, a moment for some levity, an original Joke, "just off the top":

"Hey, all you San Franciscan's and Californian's rooting for Hesbalah and
Hamas; Do ya know, what is the difference between "Gun Loving Conservatives"
and "Gun Loving-Radical Muslim Terrorists"?

Answer:
"The Conservatives are at home sitting on the couch with their guns, watching
football,
and the Islamic Terrorists may soon be in your home, with their guns to your head,
watching soccer"!".......................*SENTRYMAN '09*

Change?.....You want Change?......Try Changing "Your Attitude", for today, and for the rest of your life.

Try fighting for what you think, speak-out. You don't have to be rude like Bill Maher or David Letterman, nor politically correct like Sen. Obama.

Stop being the "Quiet American" and "The Ugly American."
Stop letting today's Hollywood Movies redefine the old America, our soldiers and our citizens ....People are watching this tripe, and are being falsely influenced and jaded toward we Americans as badly as the old propaganda films in Nazi Germany.

You think the thought of Guantánamo insights rage, and spurs-on terrorist training camps? It's nothing compared to stimulating terrorist enlistments when Hollywood defiles our military with their brand of mind speak, Free-Speak!

You want to garner "warm & fuzzy" feelings for the depraved, and about the deprived? Shift the blame, blame the other guy, take no responsibility, solve nothing, be Liberal. That's EASY, just give your money and your soul to the Democrat Party, and they'll take care of you and everything will be just fine, and you won't need to think or worry anymore.

Yeah, you Democrats, you Liberals, you progressives have done a bang-up job over the last 50 years when you've been in power 92% of that time, maybe 99% with our RINOs holding your hair above the community trough......Aren't things just great!

.....And who runs our education?

The system corrupt?
The Government corrupt??
Are We CORRUPT ???.....................YUP!........................YUP!........................YUP!...................

Either we're in it up to our necks, or we're just too self-absorbed to notice, and we're in it up to our necks.
We're finally all now in the same slimy pit, and thank-you Bernie Madoff...
That's Hollywood's KARMA. Feeling the sting Steven?

While Bush's, and McCain's efforts to reign in those guys at Fred's/Fannie, that was while Barney and Chris Dodd ran interference with Sarbain/Oxley, you are all feeling the sting now!... What does it feel like to get nailed by a compatriot democrat?...That "Indiana" came right into your temple and stole your golden Idol. How come that scenario wasn't on the story board? ....You should have listened much closer to the Pitch?

We all know what it feels like!
We've all been dumbed-down to where Socialism doesn't look half-bad anymore, and Communism couldn't be as bad as those evil Conservatives say, either... Isn't that the plan? .....Right Mr. Penn?...Right Mr. Moore?...Right Mr. Glover?...Right Mr. Turner?

Take a look in the mirror, unless you're Michael Jackson, and what do you see:
 The Enemy Is Me!

The confused police shoot'm or lock'm up, and the Courts push'm-out & set'm FREE!
You'd think those 18,000 congressional attorney's guns laws would be work'n for yeah?
.....And who runs our government: LAWYERS.

.....And who taught those Lawyers?

Hey, geniuses,

Carry a Firearm in the commission of a felony = 10 Years
Fire a Firearm in the commission of a felony = 25 Years
Kill someone in the commission of a felony = Life!

How hard can that be??
Do you know how many trees I just saved,
or how many court dockets I just cleared, and how many gangsters, gangstas, and
all those without a GED, just decided not to carry Firearms anymore?

**And now let's really start working on the greater problem to solve their
necessity for committing Felonies!**
…..And who runs our Education?

You are really connecting dots now!.........We'll never get a Flat Tax!....Period!
Our Government will never, never, never relinquish the Power of "OUR" Purse!

We can't stop them from giving themselves Pay-Raises,
and we can't stop them from voting with their cronies for whatever they want.
You think Journalism is dead, well, then so is your Liberty.

Oh ya, but "are we still anything" as a country, a people, a person, if powerless?

Maybe some of our less enlightened fellow Americans who have fallen prey to the Big Lie
would have us think or believe this fateful misconception, but We Are Americans, and
what we all still possess is something our forefathers, ancestors and patriot soldiers
fought and died to give every American for all time: "Freewill and the Vote". And every
American, including the 2/3rd's of us Non-Voters that ignore that Right possesses that Gift!

Then how unforgivable it would be if that Vote was being compromised; sold and bought
on the cheap. Very soon, more people will be voting in this country, who are permanently
"on the Dole" and NOT paying taxes at all, than those "who are working" to pay for all the
rest. Not to forget those very few who still volunteer to fight, and perhaps die, daily to
secure that RIGHT for each and every one of us!

The very instant when that precarious scale-tips "Socialist", that's when we all must start
to worry. The same formula that supported solvency in Social Security for decades, (16)
paying-in for the (1) receiving benefits, is the basic theorem, inverted, to balance and
support our security. A few fight so many remain free, when compromised, now "on the
edge", (2 workers are paying-in for the 1 receiving benefits). This mathematical, symbiotic
relationship reciprocates your Vote and someone to safeguard your Right to Free-Will, as
convoluted as any intertwined Ponzi, is now desperately in jeopardy!

When there are more Takers than Givers, fewer and fewer will feel the need to work, so
too, those to Hear the Call to Fight to Support those Rights, each interdependent upon the
other, the Ponzi finally unravels and so does the faith required to protect our Liberty,
we all fail as ONE. ......One For All, and All for One!... Your future hangs in the balance!
That's not just for the Three Musketeers, it's also for the Three Mouseketeers!
Their future hangs in the balance too, with what we as Americans decide to do next!

Until then, what we still have and what it is that we can still do, is paramount!....

They want us to buy their newspapers, buy and read their magazines, buy & read their books, buy & listen to their music, buy & watch their movies, to keep donating to their minions more and more of OUR Tax dollars, then to just stay home glued to the screens, while THEY run the country for us, along with the all-to-important "Voter precincts".

By the way, the next time you hear an idiot actor, or comic, or celebrity, or so-called Journalist mention that Bush stole the election in West Palm Beach, don't just sit there politely silent....Speak up and remind those idiots that those "3 specific-precincts" that caused all the trouble have always, and continually been totally run by Democrats, and those same terrible "Chad riddled" machines had previously, and successfully elected Bill Clinton 2x, and without any problems!.... Hmmmmm,.....Or Did They Really Elect Clinton?

That's "two fingers" for those with a public education!..... (2 times)
.....And who runs our Education?

And if Ted Danson and Robin Williams and Chevy Chase and Steve Martin and Mike Meyers and Dan Ackroyd, Tom Hanks, Jason Alexander, Kevin Bacon and Kevin Kline; producer James L. Brooks; directors Rob Reiner and Jonathan Demme; singers Don Henley and Bonnie Raitt and actress Jane Curtain, cartoonist Garry Trudeau, Saturday Night Live creator Lorne Michaels, Bill Maher, Dream Works Studios CEO David Geffen, etc., etc., etc., all want to contribute to Al Franken's campaign in Minnesota,
(and I had no idea Mr. Clooney and so many Hollywood elites had a 2nd residences in Minnesota too, go figure.)
it's OK. .....It's a Free Country....Just Don't Vote Twice! That's 2 fingers!

And since it's a free country, we can all start noticing those things too, writing them down to remind ourselves and our friends, and when We want to spend Our Money, the little we have left that Washington hasn't stolen or pilfered, we don't spend our money Watching Their Movies or Their DVDs, or do we spend our money reading their books, or listening to their music, or spend our money reading their papers, or even watching their TV shows, and WE turn the channel when a "30 Rock" commercial comes on, and also switch the channel when those individuals appear on LENO. That's Freedom Of Speech & Free Will!

And if LENO makes another "Bush" Joke, "Turn Him Off" too, and don't watch him when he moves to 10 PM. The manufacturers of Tooth Paste and Cover Girl, and Sham-Wow, and Ford Trucks, and the Next Great Drug Rx will all get the message very quickly exactly who we want to spend our leisure time with, and our dollar$ on!

Vote with your Feet,...Vote with your Dollars,...Vote with your Mind!.....
*These Entertainers "entertain" Us....We don't pay them to think for us...
**They act an emotion, and repeat someone else's thoughts, they "imitate"...
***No more, No less....ACTORS, professional story-tellers, are Make-Believers!
****No More - No Less!....

They have no more power than what You give to them, They can't "intimidate" anyone!... Their Opinion Carries No More Weight Than My Opinion Does to Barbara Walters or Diane Sawyer....They are but 1 of 333,000,000 other Americans! ****No More - No Less!....

Vote with your Feet,...Vote with your Dollars,...Vote with your Mind!.....
We still have that, and they'll never take that away, nor have any influence on our kids if we just start paying more attention to this, and less attention to them.

P.s. Simple Question: What has the Democrat party really done for Americans

with African-American ancestry over the last 50 years,
besides promising they will deliver a better-day-tomorrow?

I know Lincoln was a Republican. His men that risked their lives and limbs, and died to Free The Slaves were Republicans,.... and The Plantation Owners were Democrats,

President Eisenhower, a Republican, got things really going again to better the lives of these specific Americans after 2 very long Democrat Presidencies, (hello),

Nixon, a Republican, put teeth into "Affirmative Action",
and Geo. W. Bush, and we all know his affiliation, (even with a high school education), he provided more money and aid for countries in Africa "than any single man in History", and Martin Luther King didn't believe in violence,
 so who exactly do African-American's take their marching orders from?

Now, there's a lesson or two in there somewhere.
Any of you Libs out there that stumble upon this little rant of mine, I'd like You to just consider it for a moment, and answer a question or two for yourself,
and of course one is: And who runs our Education?....ha ha ha

I wonder if anyone with African-American ancestry have ever considered or discussed the symptoms associated with Stockholm-Syndrome?

Wow, now we're getting a Rookie to run the world.....So much for affirmative action!
Personally I would have preferred someone with the grit, common sense, and a track record with tempered experience like a Condoleezza Rice, or Colin Powell, had the Republicans been allowed free-will for their own candidate, for a actually realistic viable chance to snag the top slot choice....   How about;

CONDOLEEZZA and SARAH In 2012! Or *SARAH and CONDOLEEZZA In 2016!*

Wow, how's that one Barack, Hillary?

This NEW Administration is a rehash of Clinton Retreads and Clintonistas,
with a smattering of Chicago mafia-lite, (rookies all), and some ex-Bush financial advisors, (but it was Bush's fault),
and the adults thank God; the disrespected, and always unappreciated Military...

.........That's Change????......No, That's the Carter Administration!

But watch, The Media will now concentrate their attentions on bashing a little obscure, untainted, innocent soul from Alaska for the next 8 years, because honest clarity of purpose, pure vision, and decency, scares the Hell out of them the most.

Judge Not, and Yea Shall Not Be Judged, and "Glass Houses", etc., etc.

KARMA can be a bitch Mr. Franken for anyone who doesn't believe in GOD.
Good luck Stuart!

You can go to sleep now Lois and Sonia, there is a Santa Claus!

SENTRYMAN

P.s. .....And who should run the Education of your children?........YOU!

 **Chapter 17**

**OBAMA Targets Conservatives;
A "Quiet Revolution" against the "Body Snatchers"**

Posted by SENTRYMAN on <u>January 24, 2009</u> at 10:00pm

AVA asks SENTRYMAN<u>:</u>
"what can we do, how about our own Special Interest Group:
"The White Anti-Defamation League"?"

<u>SENTRYMAN answers Ava with a few novel ideas;</u>
"" Since the Pendulum has finally swung to the extreme opposite direction,
it doesn't matter anymore about being "On The Right", most of us are finally there.

It's now just about being "In The Right"! ....So who's the Enemy: We are!

Like a New Commission in the Obama Justice Department, designed for prosecuting
"Bush War Crimes", in order to rein in an Imperial Presidency,
in exchange for an Imperial Congress, where are the Good Guys?
"Et tu, Brute"

OK, a line must be drawn: <u>They Must Not Pass, and We Must Win!</u>

That is now primary and tantamount to Our very Survival as a People Who Value Family,
Religion, the Right to Own Property, Justice, Hard Work, Free Enterprise, Free Trade,
Democracy, No Taxation without Representation,
and The Constitution, with Liberty for the Right to live FREE....Seem reasonable & fair?

We had it once and let it go without realizing it; for we knew not what we'd done.
You've heard that old refrain a thousand times: didn't realize what I had, till it was gone?
How many times must we repeat that until in sinks in? Does the pendulum have to keep
swinging into eternity, or can we finally learn our lesson from history and from our own
mistakes once and for all?

All's not lost yet, but we can never get it back their way, and Not by their rules. We have
the numbers, we have the resolve and the passion, so let's then utilize it and take full
advantage of our God given Rights. We still have time, though short, in knowing our faults
we have the strengths to reclaim the greatness, and majesty of the last best hope for
mankind on this planet.

The time is ripe for the next <u>"Quiet Revolution"</u>, in the vein of a Dr. King or Gandhi,
or better yet another Paul Revere, with our Guns in reserve:
("they're coming....they're coming,...I'm afraid, they're already here"!)

Like the "Pod People" in "Body Snatchers", we are greatly outnumbered,
especially since there is enough "PORK" in this Stimulus Package to "BRIBE" a Pope or
even sane people willing to compromise their values for 30 pieces of Silver,   Pg. 88

so the real fight is just beginning, and our complacency has put us on the defensive, back on our heels on our own 10 Yard Line.

http://www.rushlimbaugh.com/home/daily/site_012309/content/01125113.guest.html

*If supposedly, 90% of all Americans still believe in GOD, a healthy "majority", that's a good start, but 1/2 of those turn the other cheek and their backs on Abortion,
so that cuts our team to 45%, now the "minority"..........
How quickly the Tides Change when self-interest is involved.

President Obama becomes the 1st President of many benchmarks. Of one, 1st ever to reference and acknowledge "Atheists" as a tangible political-entity of consequence in an inaugural address; Quote:
"[We are a nation of Christians and Muslims, Jews and Hindus — and non-believers.]"

WOW, how Politically Correct and inclusive,
but our Constitution and our country was founded, in fact, built on the historical Judeo-Christian values and tenants, and
on the foundation of Greek Democracy that those 300 Spartans defended, fought, and died to preserve, well,
here we are again almost 2500 years later fighting the same foes for those same Liberties.

As for the President's quote, it's amazing to me how the Jews got knocked down from 1st to 3rd position, when it all started with them. Of course in all fairness,
President Obama was? Muslim before he supposedly became "a Christian"?

Actual US numbers,

Christians 78.4%, Jews *1.7% and "Muslims 0.6%",
Hindus 0.4% —
and non-believers 1.6%)

(*Jews would have been higher had the NAZIs not put their ancestors in-to ovens!)
I think Germans tried that with Hansel and Gretel a number of years earlier.

Oh, and the Hollywood Scientologists = (500 thousand), lest we forget Tom and John!

----

other Freudian OBAMA quotes:

"our schools fail too many",

"a nagging fear that America's decline is inevitable,
and that the next generation must lower its sights."

How uplifting and encouraging Mr. President!.......What-a-Guy!
So, Who's Responsible Then, President Obama?

Well?   Who Is Teaching All These Kids Who Can't Read, Or Succeed Anymore?
The LIBERALS,
....the DEMs,
......the ATHEISTS,
........the Defeatists,

.........the Traitors,
...........the 5th Columnists,
.............the Hollywood Elite,
...............the Media, and the NEA???..............."all the usual suspects"!!

****[ALL WE EVER HEAR ABOUT: IS HOW STUPID OUR KIDS ARE!....

WHY DON'T WE EVER HEAR FROM THE N.Y. TIMES, ETC., ETC, DECRYING

"WHO EXACTLY IS TEACHING" ALL OF THESE KIDS THAT REMAIN SO STUPID???

AND, WHILE WE ARE AT IT,

WHY ARE THE PRISONS FILLING-UP SO QUICKLY NOW WITH THESE "STUPID" PEOPLE,

and "WHO" WERE ALL OF THESE "STUPID" PEOPLE EDUCATED BY,
.......Hmmmmmmmm.......STUPID TEACHERS ?]

How about putting some Stupid Bankers, or Stupid Insurance Execs. from The Wharton,
OR A FEW STUPID POLITICIANS WHO HELPED DESTROY THE AMERICAN ECONOMY
INTO PRISON FOR A WHILE,
and then we might not get as many "stupid alumni" running the country anymore?

"BERNARD MADOFF......WHO"? ..... HELLO???

How did all You brilliant guys; the brightest bulbs, the sharpest pencils, blah, blah,
miss this "invisible" guy flying below the radar in a golden C-130,
UNLESS ALL YOUR "COLLECTIVE GREY-MATTER" WAS SO-DEEP IN THE TROUGH
YOU COULDN'T SEE BEYOND YOUR DRIPPING SNOOTs?....Or is it SNOUTS?

**There used to be an army of civilian crusaders, known as "Journalists" in America,
who ferreted-out all this stuff for the "public good", while Americans, busily preoccupied
working, toil, sweat, fingers bleeding on worn hands; were keeping this country bold and
running for the benefit of one and all. But now I guess Oaths are passé, and just another
stupid tradition becoming obsolete in a new Green enlightened secular-progressive world!

Another brilliant OBAMA quote, Jan 21, 2009:
 "a nagging fear that America's decline is inevitable!".....Says who, President Obama?
.......President Hussein Obama?

*NOTE:
One of the first most urgent and pressing things that our "super-intelligent",
(we are told and reminded regularly), President OBAMA has done to help OUR Nation, and
OUR Economy is to "Reverse-the-Ban" on the Federal Funding on all Abortions Overseas,
(what'tha #@(&), so now every American taxpayer can help "Pick up the TAB" paying for
continuing "Abortions" around the world now too!
How charitable, an inspirational debut, and that's gonna save lots of US jobs!
O.K., Now That's "Our Government At Work, Spending Our Tax Dollars Wisely On Behalf
Of The Sleeping American Taxpayer,"
and they said "Bush was Guilty of Social Engineering?"

NOTE, the second time President Obama took his "oath of office" that day (in private, and without His trusty teleprompter), was also "without" putting his hand on the Bible a second time. …..Hmmm!

*No Birth Certificate,
**Muslim,
***Personal Records Sealed,
****No Flag Pin,
*****No Hand-Over-Heart salute,
******No TelePrompTer to instruct how to respond,
*******No Bible?............Hmmmmm!

NOW, a "Line Has Been Drawn in the Sky", as well as "In The Sand"
…Ahmadinejad!............Do We Get A Do-Over Too?

My daughter once said to me when she turned sweet 16: "it's my body Dad, and I can make my own decisions."

Whoa, "where'd You hear that", I said? …..
Quickly followed by: "Hey, It's Not Your Body Till You're 18 Kid"!

But, who's going to back me up here, certainly Not society, much less OUR Government, so what can a father do?....Well?

I.e. Islamic Law states:
I can strangle her, or there's the "Public Stoning" option,

or the insensitive Way:
yell, and watch her run away,

or the affluent Way:
bribe her,

or the Catholic Way:
welcome my new grandchild,

or the Liberal Way:
watch her body wither from drugs, or HIV, or both,

or the Women's Lib Way:
smash the baby's head and drag it out of the womb,

or their Mother's Way: hope for the best!....thanks dear!

or then there's a Dad's Way:
then Social Services takes her out of the home so she can do what-ever, and I can be sent to jail for 30 days, and do 6 months of anger management,

or a Democrat's Way:
get as many voters as one can manufacture and collect your government stipend.
Wasn't that a "Mother's for Hitler" award program?

(I know what you're saying Dads: but Moms always side with their daughters.)

Oh yeah, that $5000 per year Catholic school education didn't get me the result I'd expected to help shield her from outside influences,
but again, there aren't any imperative Nuns helping-out anymore anyway, moth-balled in dormitories, relegated to their oath of poverty, the obsoletes trash-heap!

(Holy Smoke, thank goodness for Nuns, the cheapest, most valuable asset on the planet that any religion has ever enjoyed, yet squandered away),
for a newly prioritized Church that underpays teachers, cuts healthcare for support staff, and can now only afford bookoo property, Tribute to Rome, and their Priest's lodging, board, and a retirement parachute.....hmmm!

Along with that unfortunate and unnecessary legal-financing of more than an occasional "Alter Boy" Law-Suit, because of a good-old-boy mentality that should have opened marriage to Priests a hundred years ago, instead a 1000 years ago eunuchs and a chauvinist geek pseudo-political Council, who amazingly thought celibacy might be a preferable self-sacrifice to the Deity, rather than self-flagellations, but that Inquisition thing worked out real well for them instead!

How'd that Goodwill & Hope, Changing Hearts & Minds work-out for ya' over the years?
.......**It created the Protestants and their copy-cat associates!**

I repeatedly told "Father" over tea during theological discussions that: The Church was "shooting itself in the foot",
and that: #1 - educating our children should be the primary objective of the Church because "That's" where the future of the Church lay, but apparently "Lay" teachers, who are increasingly "Liberal", with a tolerant Church's blessing, are what our kids are left with, instead of those once-indispensable, all-caring, tough-as-nails conservative Nuns and Jesuit Scholars, today traded-in for that irrepressible All-Mighty "Plate"!

But, look-out, there's always that unintended consequence...KARMA!

 (and thank you Pope for "not" backing BUSH)......
No, we don't need anyone actually standing-up against the REAL-EVIL-ON-THIS-EARTH, or defending LIBERTY, that's an abstract.....What.....Only Angels need carry swords!

**But, Thank God For President Bush............ ("7" Undefeated Seasons.)
Well, You Have A Real Tough Act To Follow There, President Obama!**

Now, getting back to the discussion with my daughter:
My first impression upon hearing those increasing-numbers of HIV and AIDs figures across the US, and also decimating the Continent of Africa at large,
was to say, well, so then;

Keep your legs closed girls..................done.
Use a condom Charlie...........................done.
Be faithful to ONE partner, Biff.............done.
Stay married, jerk……………….................done.
Obey your vows, pal.............................done.
Love your spouse, fool..........................done.
Rape demands mandatory castration, done.

<u>DONE. DONE, DONE = NO ABORTIONs NECESSARY!</u>
<u>Gee, that was tough!</u>

I know what you're saying now:........"Chauvinist Pig"!... "How insensitive"!
So, big deal!.......Sticks and stones, then go bury your good friend Charlie!

But I digress, and why do I use this as an example?

Because nothing makes any sense anymore, it's all "out of our hands" today.
Common-sense....gone, archaic!.......
It's that age-ole' battle once again: You VS The World!......So what can You do?

How about a Peter Finch anguished "scream out the window"?
And strangely enough, it was just before He auspiciously disappeared from this earth.
Was that really "just acting"?

"I'M FED-UP WITH THIS CRAP and
I'M JUST NOT GOING TO TAKE THIS ANYMORE" !!!!

<u>"GOT ANGER?" ….. GET ANGRY….GET REALLY, REALLY ANGRY!</u>

The Genie's Out Of The Closet, and
The Man Behind The Curtain Is One Of Us.

A Tax Cheat as "Head of the IRS" that can't do his own taxes,

a Terrorist's best friend as "Attorney General", touting: "adopt a killer",

a little southern attorney'esss, Big-League wannabe, where nepotism raises its ugly head
and gets You a "Senator-ship", and big-bucks from Arabian Sands pays-off big time with a
"Sec. of State" consolation prize,
but, who's keeping track, a Ph.D. is now a deficit,

a Dove is our #1 Super "007",

a "Socialist" is spun into acceptability,

a "Has-been" is a quid-pro-quo,

and an array of "Retreads and Sharks" as pristine, statuesque symbols of US authority,

<u>the formula for "Real Change"?</u>

and that's all everyone will have left in their pockets, (just some change...$3.44),
a couple tin Dimes, a few wooden Nickels, 9 zinc Pennies, a $3 Dollar bill,
and a big I.O.YOU,
with this Merry Band of Robbing Hoods,

and an "American Idol" Rookie is at the Helm,
with his pack of groupies that call him The "N" Word, with pride.
http://www.youtube.com/watch?v=HZS88qRu4eA

Isn't that Special!........and his first "Up-At-Bat";
"Gitmo's Closing" and the Terrorists are NOW in our midst!
Don't You All Feel Much Safer Now With That: Oh So, Benevolent Gesture?

I sure do,
but I have Dogs, and Guns, and Fences, and "DELIVERANCE" playing a loop on my TIVO, and You think forming another Group, or Gang, or Guild is the most effective way to foil these rapscallions in Washington?

These Same Men That Bankrupted This Nation,
who couldn't pick-up on Bernie Madoff for 30 long years, and then only when ole' Bern ran out of pocket-change for a few days thanks to Barney Frank and Chris Dodd,
and these are the Same Guys that are running the whole show from now on to solve all of our problems? REALLY?....Hmmmmm..........*"THEY" ARE THE PROBLEM!*

I'm still waiting for Chris Dodd to come up with those "sweet-deal" mortgage papers he promised gov't. investigators 6 months ago.......*"cricket-chirp, cricket-chirp"*

Had Dodd been a Republican he'd be jumping out of a plane over a Georgian swamp for a little R&R get-away,
but as a Democrat, well, you keep your US Senate Seat...Sounds Fair Enough To Me!

Or, as a Democrat you can make a deal with an Illinois Prosecutor, and save your butt.

Or, as a Democrat, especially if you're high-enough up on the Food Chain, no one will remember anything tomorrow, thanks to the NY Times, NBC, MSNBC and CNN!

By the way, if you want to see the 1st wave of insurgents in action, just go to
www.rushlimbaugh.com

Liberals Plan to Separate Elected Republicans from Their Voters
January 23, 2009
http://www.rushlimbaugh.com/home/daily/site_012309/content/01125113.guest.html

"If the conservatives walk away from the base, the base would be about 30 million people, maybe -- yeah, around 30, 'cause what did McCain get, 55 million votes?
And the people we're talking about, the 24 to 30 million people in the evangelical, pro-life, southern, it's not necessarily geographic here,
but that's about how many votes they represent if they show up is 24 to 30 million people in a presidential race.

So you'd figure if they bolted McCain would have gotten 30 million votes, not 55 or 58. But that's what they want."

" And these cultural issues, you know what Obama had to do to wrap up all this? He had to move to the center during his campaign. He had to go right. Look, all the Blue Dogs, look at how Paterson just appointed this Blue Dog Democrat who wins in a Republican district 'cause she's more of a conservative than the Republicans in her district in New York are."

"We need to hire lobbyists. I'm dead serious. No, I'm dead serious. I'm trying to also make a point. But, look, I think what's coming is going to be a concerted effort by the Obama administration to separate our elected officials from us on the Republican side."

"And Colin Powell says, "You gotta stop listening to Rush Limbaugh." Trust me, General Powell, they had years ago, and now they're just being honest about it. "We don't like these supporters we have in the South, we don't like them, they're too white, too homogenous, all they care about is guns and taxes."

Rush continues;
http://www.rushlimbaugh.com/home/daily/site_012309/content/01125113.guest.html

----

SENTRYMAN weighs-in;
"*Here, I take one exception to Rush's idea on "Our Own Lobbyist.

Again, it's playing by their rules.
It shouldn't be a "Bidding War" and The Guys with the Best Perks!

I think we must play by the Original rules of Engagement,
from "My BLOG of Jan. 8, 09"

"AOL Survey Asked: Obama to Lunch With Ex-Presidents,
What Would You Ask?"......................

Demand of Obama with a Citizen's Revolution, No Committees or debate,
The American People want;

#1- *Two Term Limits for all elected officials
then return to your shoppes and farms, you've done your duty
as the founding fathers envisioned, not a Life-long Career

#2- *Tort Reform, take the Vampires out of Justice,

#3- *Outlaw all "Lobbyists", we didn't elect and hire these Representatives
to travel to Washington to be bribed, or to work in the Cabinet,

#4- *Give the President the "Line Item Veto" or, "No Bundling Bills",
All Bills Voted On Separately equals = No Pork, No Ear Marks,

#5- *No Pay Raises at 3AM,
we, the people, vote them one if they earn it,

#6- *freeze all "new" spending,
and tell government to go home till they're needed,
they're not serving us anyway, i.e. "The Bail-Out",

#7- *FLAT TAX, steal back our own Money, then they'll stay home,

#8- *Close the IRS, no explanation required,

#9- *6 month citizen-tax free, NO withholding taxes,

#10- * "Bail-Out" means "LOAN", don't give away,
only loan to the banks and to the insurance companies,
(since, by-the-way, they already own this country),
and not a single dime without interest & collateral,

#11- * "Don't Buy Any Foreign Oil, Drill Our Own Oil and use Natural Gas!"
and finally,

#12- *Election Funds Limits,
i.e. $100 Million for all contenders!
NOT another McCain $140 million Vs Obama $700 million!

But, #1- MOST OF ALL "TERM LIMITS" …..(2) max.

(* For all <u>20 Demandments to the Constitution</u>, refer back to Chapter 14)

<u>***So how do we accomplish this to solve most of the problems??</u>

We Could Pass This Stuff In An Afternoon On Election Day With PROP-86,
and these ineffectual, dilettantes who take 6 months debating if to send desperately
needed supplies to the very Troops Protecting Their Silly Jobs, their Salaries,
and silly Butts.
<u>But Remember, They Can Pass A $700,000,000,000. Bill In ONLY 5 Days If Desired! WHAT?</u>

This is what "We", Freedom Loving Citizens must figure out,
or our children's, children's, children's children will still be trying
to figure this out in 3009! ""

<u>SENTRYMAN</u>
==

<u>1 Comment</u>

<u>Comment by Ava P on January 26, 2009 at 7:27pm</u>
      I agree. What can I say …..

Chapter 18

"The Night Of The Long Knives" or "KristallNacht" looks like a training exercise.

Posted by SENTRYMAN on January 25, 2009 at 4:30pm

OBAMA approval rating is now 68% across the fruited plain after almost 1 week, but who's counting,
unless you're paying attention, and caught this on "Huckabee" Saturday evening alerting America to the pending legislation to make "us all" FELONs if we even object to Obama's radical anti-Life, anti-Marriage Agenda;

**(Liberty Alert, January 23, 2009
Mat Staver is Weekend Guest on "Huckabee" Show on FOX-News to Discuss the Obama Administration's: Liberal Social Policies posted-up on the White House's WebSite minutes after President Obama took The Oath Of Office.)

http://www.lc.org/index.cfm?PID=14102&AlertID=949

[[the new administration has launched its liberal social policies. In just a few minutes after the inauguration, http://www.whitehouse.gov/
unveiled Obama's agenda that includes "radical anti-life, anti-marriage plans"]]

Go to: www.whitehouse.gov
click "Agenda",
click "Civil Right",
scroll 1/2 way down to: "Support for the LGBT Community",
and read how Your old America will no longer exist,
or be recognizable in 4 years because GOD is about to be vanquished!

I guess Senator Obama neglected to tell all The Faithful about these little Gems over the last 2 years! Just his "lee-tol frenz", as Al Pacino would say.
Isn't that what Journalists used to report until they were in the same crowd, jumping and screaming like Beatlemaniacs? ....Apologies to Ringo,

OBAM-MANIACS: O-BA-MA... O-BA-MA... O-BA-MA...

I thought in a Democracy, the majority rules?....Well, not in The Obama Democracy!
That Idiom referred to the "People's Majority Rules"...Not, his Party's Majority taking-over.

Of course, in an academic argument, a pure Democracy is The Coliseum's Mob Rule,
but our representative Democratic Republic tempers that strident anvil, so the little guy doesn't get squashed in the mix,
but still the 1% population Group, or even the 0.1% Group doesn't get to "call the shots" or force the other 99.9% of the American people to bow at the ankles, conceding to radical demands and do back flips either,
unless it's the ""LGBT"" Group bank-rolling Obama's Campaign.

http://www.whitehouse.gov/agenda/civil_rights/

Pg. 97

Why can't our (supposedly) most articulate President (Teleprompter-at-the-ready) identify this (individually Lesbian and Gay coalition) openly and plainly, if President Obama's so proud of the quid pro que?
Not just slipped-in like another dripping Pork Chop, inserted into the fine print in the back section of a Congressional Bill, where-in that future NON-GAY Americans can be arrested and put in Prison for just holding a sign on public streets that reads:
Marriage = Man & Woman!
*Free expression and Free Speech will now be (Hate Speech), and a Felony…Cute trick!

Where You can be arrested if You even laugh at a "male" co-worker who decides to come to work in a flower-print dress and a pink balloon on his head, and (even if He isn't Gay) but just a "Cross-dresser" who just decided to wear that to work today…..
Must be "Cross-Gender Thursday"...ha..ha…OOPS, get the cuffs, oh boy,
……..just committed 3 Felonies…..HA..HA..HA!
*This will now be (Hate Speech) and a Felony!

----
*WHITE HOUSE WEB SITE:
"President Obama supports the Employment Non-Discrimination Act, and believes that our anti-discrimination employment laws should be expanded to include sexual orientation and ((gender identity))."
*This will now be (Hate Speech) and a Felony!

Where "Same Sex" Marriage will be Federally Mandated, circumventing any and all State's Constitutions.

*This is where "The Freedom Of Choice Act (FOCA), the most radical and divisive pro-abortion bill ever introduced to Congress, would create a "Fundamental Right" to Abortion that Government could not limit, but would have to support,
and the "American Taxpayer would have to "Pay the Bill", of course…..
….Write your Congressman……(***This, from a card handed out at church this morning)

Now that's your Representative Democracy at work?

Yeah, in Nazi Germany, or in any Islamic State.
No, I correct myself, they BOTH just Kill Gays There!

I should have said: Ancient ROME where Nero and Caligula let it all hang out Dudes, or maybe DeSade, to be Historically correct!

America used to stand for truth, natural, normal, rational, conforming, sane, established standards: "THE CONSTITUTION"!

But, Never To Ideological Extremes; Far Right, Or Far Left, Or especially the Far, Far Left!....So why do we continually have to reinvent the democracy wheel, year after year, Administration after Administration?…

Don't we have more important things to worry about and concentrate on, like Al-Qaeda as an example?
Can you possibly imagine of The Congress of the United States and President Roosevelt interrupting their daily concerns for the nation's safety dealing with Hitler advancing in Europe, or The Japanese Imperial Fleet encroaching on Australia, but instead considering legislation defending: Men in Bolder, Colorado and across the nation, who wanted to wear a pretty Moo-Moo, or a Sari, or a nice pleated skirt with matching shoes down the boulevard, and arresting anyone that might laugh or jest?.........Well, can you?

<u>(The Thought Police have arrived my friends!)</u>
YES, Elections do have consequences, for all You Moderates, you Independents and the Uninvolved.

Well, you're in it now, up to the waistband on your Panty Hose, whether You like it or not, and also up to your silly little: "I Don't Vote" necks, too!

You think America is despised by the rest of the world now?
Think very carefully people......Europe hates the US because we are successful and supposedly always right, and according to the European-socialists: we're "too far Right". But They, on the other hand, have become TOOTH-LESS Leftists in this recent century; Because, They Enjoy The Luxury And Savings, Since We Fight Their Wars For Them!!!

But strangely, Islam hates America the most, because we are "too far Left", indulgent soft and decadent, and They Are Anything But TOOTH-LESS, and very soon we will be viewed by Them as such a "stain on the earth", with our ever increasingly "Progressive Ideologies", that They will come for us with all their strength, their minions and their bombs, that will make "The Night Of The Long Knives", "Kristallnacht" look like a training exercise.

You Think History Doesn't Repeat Itself?....This Fight's Been Coming Since 700 AD, When They Were But, Scattered Tribes Across The Sands In Search Of Their Identity.

<u>Now They Reach Across The Globe AND THEY're COMING FOR US!</u>

Thank you Obama for fulfilling their prophecy! Where is Rudy when We need him?

<u>FROM THE WHITE HOUSE WEBSITE:</u>

"Support for the LGBT Community -- Barack Obama, June 1, 2007"
http://www.whitehouse.gov/agenda/civil_rights/

http://search.whitehouse.gov/search?affiliate=wh&query=LGBT&form_id=usasearch_box&submit.x=34&submit.y=18

***Expand Hate Crimes Statutes:* Support for the LGBT Community....**

<u>QUOTE;</u>
"While we have come a long way since the Stonewall riots in 1969, we still have a lot of work to do. Too often, the issue of LGBT rights is exploited by those seeking to divide us. But at its core, this issue is about who we are as Americans. It's about whether this nation is going to live up to its founding promise of equality by treating all its citizens with dignity and respect."
-- *Barack Obama, June 1, 2007*

<u>SENTRYMAN</u>

Chapter 19

Let Free Markets and Free Enterprise Set The Price,,,,,
Not Robber Barons!

Posted by SENTRYMAN on <u>January 31, 2009</u> at 8:30pm

<u>*Hey Sentryman, Frank here.*</u>
(paraphrased);

Appreciate the jest, but having been a farm kid so I know the difference between a farm subsidy and a bailout.

Bailouts are giveaway moneys that are spent on Wall Street firms.

A farm subsidy is a Department of Agriculture program meant to rescue farmers who have busted their tails on the CHANCE that that S.O.B. in the previous paragraph won't jack with the raw price of the commodity ("my crop"), he or she happens to be WORKING THEIR FAMILIES AND THEMSELVES into an early grave to grow, harvest and deliver to market, that can fail or thrive, LITERALLY as the wind blow.

On Wall Street, commodities prices are toys to be played with all day - every day, and their playing dictates with whether the farmer can or cannot only feed his farm animals (with the crop or for the crop) or plant a new crop, but whether his children get fed and clothed and educated today, tomorrow and next year.

Those farm subsidies are a farmers insurance because State Farm, Farmer's Mutual, Nationwide, Allstate and GEICO, just don't insure cows, pigs, corn, chickens, beans and peas against loss (against the actual damages of drought, hail, flood, rain, wind, tornados, pests, rustlers) oh . . . and the Wall Street Willie's gamesmanship too.

Now Sentryman, do you understand why strong leadership is needed and why we're tossing the ideas/thoughts?

===

Hey Frank, SENTRYMAN here;

[["And those crops or as they're called on Wall Street, commodities are toys to played with by the suits."]]...Frank...

Frank, You're preaching to the choir.

My Joke was a metaphor for a far greater indictment upon us, as consumers, and as a People all buying into "a Deal", "Price Fixing", "Isolationism", "Tariffs and Socialism", as long as it profits: "Me, Me, Me"!

<u>Service and quality, (honor) are things of the past.</u>

I caught the end of Glenn Beck yesterday talking to a famous
(Inventor - Entrepreneur - Industrialist),
that echoed a story about a meeting of young and old Wall Street Traders,
and a young Wall Street Turk stands up and stated that: *"today we all Lie, Cheat and Steal;
To and From our Customers, and that's Standard Practice now"*,
to which the Old Timers clutched their colostomy bags, and were shocked and appalled at this brazen, blatant unholy trinity of today's "Businessman's work ethic",
but, We all know it's not just on Wall Street!

i.e., How about the "BIG Dig" in Boston, a State & Fed governmental boondoggle, what was it supposed to take: 5 years, and it took 20+ years to finish?
…….And now the bridges are breaking apart and dropping-down onto the taxpayer's automobiles who paid for it all!

That's American workmanship, American pride, or Democrat's graft?

<u>So, Vote Democrat and get a check in the mail!</u> Sounds good to people with no gumption.

Unless you're one of those cruel, mean Republicans, who work and pay for everything, <u>and who'll get a bill in the mail!</u>

Who cares who's blood is used as ink, and upon who's backs the entitlements rest, and who must now work even harder and longer, and for even less money now to pay for it all. With ever increasing costs till it seems eternity, certainly NOT Mr. Congressman need worry for his constituents, but We and our great-grandchildren footing the Bills…NUTZ!?

The system has made us all "Kept Women", and so to, they; the "Wall Street'ers", Politicians and Executive Robber Barons, "All",
 do nothing in the chain of ideas; conception, R&D, finance, construction, organization, administration, manufacturing, finance, creation, more R&D, distribution, installation, litigation, and the April 15th quarterly, with a PIMP government all along for its CUT, or We'll Cut Your Throat,
and for now "Wall Street'ers" get to move the chess pieces around, and (Set the Price).

What happened to Supply and Demand, or free-markets, or any aspect of Reality, but Hillary can buy a "Senate Seat", or Chris Dodd can get a $75,000. discount-break on his mortgage without any scrutiny, or a hint of impropriety…..Cool !

That's OK, but where's mine, mine, mine? Well, I don't work for the government, or the Unions!

If it were an equitably even playing field, which OUR Founders envisioned, the fee for a man's labors, or products and goods, would be set by his own choice, sweat,
 and God help us, supply & demand,
along with the help and luck of good weather,
and not predetermined or manipulated by the Devils-On-The-Dow.

We lost our farm.

Americans have lost the farm, as it was no longer sacrosanct or important, "Just Price."

The Market, The Managers, The Middlemen, The Wholesalers, The Distributors, all take their pound-of-flesh to set the price for the common good, and just for today.
The common conglomerate's profits for offering "Low Price" is no longer shared by American Farmers, but China, on the backs of their $5.00 a week Farmers,
 and the Hell with safety or quality for consumers or that farmer.

Profit margin by any means! - Isn't that what's now really important?........ "Price"?
Not the Free Market, Not Supply and Demand, Not choice, quality vs price.....It's all crap!

But, with all things, there's always a twist, a sacrifice, a chink in the armor that inevitably cheats us all = to bite us in the butt, but it's never explained or exposed up-front.

Whether it's our Soldier's Body Armor = Failing!
or
Auto or Airplane Parts = Failing!
or
Milk, Baby Toys, Baby Foods, Baby Furniture = Failing!
or
clothes, heaters, candles, jewelry, paint, seafood, toothpaste, recliners, etc., = All Failing!
.............But who's counting?..............

Obviously No one, and no more "Made In America", it's just about PRICE......Idiots!
"You Get What You Pay For", gee, never heard that before!. Did you attend public school?

*NEVER UNDERSTOOD THIS, EVEN AS A YOUNG MAN;
if the government gets bids as they are required, they always take the "Lowest estimate", and then that contractor or supplying manufacture with that lowest price, always cuts corners & quality to make-up the disparity with deception, to attain the necessary profit margin, falsifying Docs., cheating with cost over-runs, and if he's well-enough connected with a politician, those Over-Budget/Over-Runs added-up are invariably more than the legitimate, highest-quality, rejected Bidder originally had estimated,
and, the disreputable low-Bidder races his way to-the-bank to cash-the-check ASAP, because his sub-standard, faulty, dangerous, poor quality product endangers Americans.

*Here's a Novel Idea Mr. & Ms. United State's Government Representatives:
"Always Take The Middle Bid"!
That'll keep everyone more honest and on their toes, instead of:
the Lowest "Stab Americans In The Back" Bidder Always Wins!

How hard can that be?.....Maybe a $Million Dollar Study, good money after bad, and some Congressional Committee hearings and conferences can come to the same conclusion?

Tell You what,
send me a check for $1000, since I just saved myself and American Taxpayers a minimum of $1 Trillion dollars in kick-backs, graft, bribes & theft, and You can keep the idea!

Maybe we're fooled, maybe we want to be fooled, maybe we just don't have time to think about how badly we know we'll be fooled, maybe you don't know we know, we're not fools, but, if Brand-B orange juice is cheaper than Brand-A, that's usually the one For Us. But it's our choice, we're paying for it. Since Brand-B comes from a foreign country that uses near slave-labor, unsafe work practices, sub-standard or No quality controls, and also uses lethal pesticides, all to lower costs & increase output, we don't care because we can't read anymore anyway, ignorance is bliss. So what if we get cancer one day, we $aved today!

It's cheap, that's all we want to know about! But Not a government choice!

If there's Poisons added to the Baby Formula,
or Lead in the Toys,
or frozen Hamburger is combined with 20 other sources from 8 different countries, and continually frozen/thawed/frozen again, and if not incinerated properly by the school Lunch Ladies before serving it to your children, they'll all Go Crazy, or Brain-Dead, or get gastritis PANCREATITIS, or just Die quickly if they're lucky, this is the primary responsibility of your US Federal Government: protecting US for enemies foreign and domestic! "Your Government at work for You".

Protect our equal "Rights", the borders, the food supply, public safety, no one cheats us, and leave the rest to your employers. If in doubt, refer to the US Constitution, which doesn't include most of the shenanigans you Government employees have concentrated on the last 30 to 50 years.....You can't even stop spending money we don't have!
In theory, a step in the right direction, it just losses something in the Translation!

You want to pay $1.00 for a McDonald's burger,
or pay $5.50 for a 100% superior cut of ground beef at Smokey Bones, that's Free Choice, Free Market, Free Will, Supply & Demand that Governs the Market place
with Free Enterprise in Capitalism.

Liberalism, Socialism, and Communism gets You government inspectors making appointments with Meat-Packer Processing Plants for the unscheduled? Spot-check Inspections, and bad-meat in schools, and gets you Dead!
Let Free Enterprise set the price, and government can guard the quality if not too busy.

In the 60's, as I'm watching farmers destroy their milk on TV, when everyone whined that we might have to pay an extra $.25 for milk or bread, and the farmers were pouring their life's-blood profits down the drain to make the point,
I thought to myself, (shut-up, are you kidding me here?)
If the Farmers wanted $0.25 extra, probably just so they could at least break even, or they'd just as well pour their milk down the street,
<u>let the Farmer's set their price at a $1.00 extra,</u> so them they could pay some bills, buy a new tractor, or fix the 2 broken ones, build another Silo, plant a new field, buy some more cows and another bull,
 so as a result the increased production would lower the price itself for all,
but the Farmer would still make more money in the end on the volume consumed.

Isn't that what Henry Ford and Ray Kroc had in mind from their inception?

Hey, back then, while the price of a Corvette went from $3500 to the bargain $100,000 for a Vette in 2009, we're still moaning about the price of groceries, and that Peanuts are now poison,
and that's probably only because some poor deluded farmer was trying to make a couple extra pennies on every pound of Peanuts so he could pay his mandated employee's Workman's Comp. premiums for next month, and so "We All Suffer."

How about thinking outside the box for a change,
and somehow Government stopping its own Gambler's speculations betting on Oranges or Pork Belly Futures, (long or short), and let the real market set the prices?

If we can pay $4.00 for a gallon of gas, and afford $12.00 @ gal. for designer-water,
we can pay a $1.00 extra for a Florida orange that's "not poison",
if that's what the market will bear with a little more of an educated consuming public.

But, with Government "fixing the price", and annually bribing Farmers for decades, along with the (Gentleman/Farmer/Politicians, and Wall-Street Land Owners), of which there are a few in Congress today Who Perpetually Get a PAYDAY For "Not" Growing A "Specific Crop", (that's a sweet deal), just never seemed quite right to me,
and we're just gonna have to agree to disagree on this one, I'm afraid FRANK.
What do really think?

Not to mention, do we even have cotton anymore?
Because every garment comes from outside the United States, a long, long, long way away. Doesn't that little trip add enough cost to the cotton products to make those Indian-cotton or Egyptian-cotton bed-sheets, that only last months, compared to the quality American-percale sheets that last you for years, making a little subtle ad-campaign, while keeping our American workers employed, worth the effort and more profitable in the end?

You know those hefty tariff taxes Washington enjoys, along with our fascination for nice imported exotic wood furniture from the Southern-Pacific Rim, and supposedly cheaper steel and housing lumber, etc., etc., from old adversaries to our own country's detriment with loss of jobs and unnecessary expense, that coin doesn't seem to trickle-down and benefit their employers, they just blow that too!
...So why bother, who really benefits?
Environmentalists, politicians, foreign politicians, Japan; do we?
I wonder sometimes what we have a government for, other than keeping us safe from without and within, and lately THEY don't do a very efficient or good job with that either!

Oh, here's a Good One Signed into Law last week: "Equal Pay"!
OK, fair enough, no problem from this chauvinist,
but in the "Fine Print" one reads that; "She" can now sue her past employers from back to 10 years!.....WOW, (sweet for Attorneys', funny how that got in there),
how would You like that hanging over your head Mr. Chauvinist businessman as you figure out your next year's budget?

"Equal Pay" or "Eternal Employment For Attorneys"?
(There's the RUB!>>>>>>>>>>>>Follow the Money!), are there any barristers in Congress?

So then, let's recap;
*Reduction in market forces,
*Price fixing,
*Subsidies, and losing the Family Farm,
*Gays will soon be protected by a new "Hate Crimes" Bill,
*Equal=Pay, or I'll sue your butt,
*Unnecessarily high food, water & UNFORTUNATE gas prices,
*Tainted Food,
*Sweet Deals with Low Bids,
*Dangerous Imports, and
*No Help STOPPING Speculators manipulating 'The Dow', betting on the failure of the United State's economy,

((May 3, 2007 ... M/M Chung are being sued for $65 million over a lost pair of pants belonging to a contentious local Judge)),
Hurray for the Attorneys once again and Tort Reform is un-American?

God Bless the real United States of America, "the old America"!

SENTRYMAN

Chapter 20

SENTRYMAN.... "can you tell me WHY people are hypnotized over Obama?"

Posted by SENTRYMAN on February 2, 2009 at 12:30am

"SENTRYMAN... I am mystified. Can you tell me WHY people are hypnotized over Obama, with these questions below?"

by Sharon,
questioning one of SENTRYMAN Blog posts on January 26, 2009

And SENTRYMAN answering Sharon's questions on February 2, 2009

*O.K. Sharon, I'll give it a shot since I've avoided the Kool-Aid!

She asks;

Why would someone want universal abortion?...............................
Anti-Religion / Anti-Standards / Anti-Christ / follow the money.

Why would someone want to ban parental-control over children?...
Communists / It takes a village!!

Why would someone want to force average Americans to observe agendas that are against their beliefs?...
Anti-Religion / Communists / Fascism / follow the money.

Why would someone want to continue bankrupting America?....
Anti-Capitalism / Communists / follow the money.

Why would someone want to take away Conservative Talk Radio?....
Anti-Free Speech / Communists / Anti-Constitution.

Why would someone want to take away our guns?.........................
Anti-Constitution / Communists / Anti-America / 5th Columnists.

Pg. 105

Why would someone want to make people more dependent on the government
for their health insurance, food, income?...
Liberals / Progressives / Socialists / Communists / follow the money

Why would people walk around looking actually hypnotized over the man,
Obama?...
*Sun Myung Moon / Jim Jones / David Koresh / Heaven's Gate / Mao / Lenin / Soros / Chez /
public education system*

Where did something as evil as Pelosi..Reid..Franks & the others come from?
Untalented wannabes / 60's Hippies / Yippies / Yuppies / Guppies!

Why are many Republicans looking goofy over this man?.............
RINOs / permissive parents / 60's Hippies / Yippies / Yuppies

----

SENTRYMAN *continues with some questions & answers of his Own;*

Well Sharon,
a wonderful encapsulation of some vital questions we're all scratching our heads over,
and concerns we all have today, *not only to the individual and our country,
but for humanity.*

Of course, my answers are purposely glib-opinion in my incredulousness' of having to
even voice an opinion on these matters involving a government official, much less a
President of a new 3rd world country: Americabad,
including his cronies in crime, co-conspirators and dysfunctionaries ALL, who have been
running the Congress for the last 2 years, trailed by our own lapdogs,
hoping to pick-off a stray more like hyenas, than tigers that stalk their prey,
because these predators lack the courage to attack any close-knit herd.

**But, I too have some questions of my own Sharon,
and some skeptical speculations.**

So, "where have all the journalists gone", (ala, Joan Baez)
and the caustic philosophers, honest economists, truthful scientists, rational
climatologists, and where have all the deep-thinkers gone;
 not trolling for government grants?....nahh Challenging the status quo?....naaahh

**If everyone else is in on the game, or "on the take", then probably them too!*
We are alone in the dark woods with a flintlock and damp powder.

Yeah!....Where is the Representation "We Paid For" In The Congress with centuries of pain
and blood?
Why has the Congress been totally ignoring their employers for years now
until this last stand, last week?
***Hmmm?*

We elect bright young faces and send them off to Congress, with a note pinned to their coats and a shiny new lunchbox. Still wet behind the ears, they're 1st congressional assignment, baited and corrupted every time, follow the money, and they return home weak of character, peer-pressure riddled: compromised damaged goods, a second term already beckoning before the 1st one is earned,
and we wonder WHY the process yields such little result for all our effort.

**We continue to hope that integrity and honor will stave off temptation, but like a parent's love turns anger into self-guilt, we'll settle, just happy for any attention, Always Forgetting After The Exhausting Campaigns, As Life Settles Back To Normal, That These People Are "Our Employees" and We Aren't Their Parents,
And We Should Have Greater Expectations For Our Own Intentions, And Demand Results.
....This Is What We Are Paying For, Or You Are Fired.....Or,
you're really gonna get a talking-to when you get home, and be grounded if you don't call home more often!!......Oh Lord!*

Where was the freak'n "common sense" from the Body-Politic and the Media for the last 8 long, long years,

or for any Public Outrage from someone, anyone speaking-out against the incomprehensible-hypocrisy surrounding those stupid dumb Voting machines in those 3 Democrat precincts in South Florida, that could, and had, and did successfully elect President Clinton, (not once, but in 2 consecutive elections), (4 yrs. apart), including successfully completed and sanctioned mid-term, and the primary elections "electing DEMs" every two years to boot, HELLO?,
but then incredibly, almost miraculously, those very "same machines" became incapable of correctly tabulating votes with those "same cards" to deliver another Democrat Victory,

and then just as strangely and incomprehensibly they delivered a Republican President?...
…..... I-M-P-O-S-S-I-B-L-E,....HOW TERRIBLE ……..
unless those same machines were "pre-rigged" every-time over the previous 8 years and someone forgot to re-synchronized them, like in Minnesota?
**Oops!!......Oh Lord!.....HELLO?*

Where was the Journalistic "Hippocratic Oath" when we elected an "American Idol"
 for the highest position on the planet,
who is still a stranger, and a mystery to most Americans,
with vast gaps of his life, blocked, hidden, sheltered, banned, off-limits,
that NO ONE is allowed to investigate?
**No Comment?....Hmmmm

I.E. What courses did the young Community-Organizer select to learn at his 3 colleges?
(Intrusive?...wouldn't you really like to know that?...We do of every previous President!)

What, "if anything", had He ever written (to deserve) to be editor of the Law Review,
and at Harvard no less?....wouldn't you really like to know that?...

Bush enjoyed "No Kudos" for being the only MBA-President and from Harvard, the Idiot, with only Liberal jeers.
So how did Barrack "earn" such a lofty position at this most prestigious university??????
..........(That He Couldn't Afford To Attend)!

How and what did He instruct, and who did He mentor as a professor,
and Who did He read, (a'la Sarah Palin, we needed to know),
who were His mentors, and His friends in school and on the mean-streets of NYC,
before all His newly BFF-great buds in Chicago started to befriend Him,
like: You Know Who! ....???......tick, tock.....*really*: unrepentant 60's urban-terrorist
Prof. William (Bill) Ayers, a founder of the radical liberal's "Weather Underground".
**But Barack's still a blank canvas just like an Actor. Give him the "right script" and
He becomes that character. But in this case, I guess it's a "LEFT" script.*

Are these even His words uttered today?
Why is He never asked to prove or substantiate literally anything?
Could He even qualify for any "top security" clearances as a citizen?
*Fortunate that He doesn't need one, but forget The Media or The Press "Vetting" this guy,
and where was the FBI in the VETTING-PROCESS, for the most powerful human on earth?

Why does "Junk Science" trump "Reason" today, and "counters" recorded-historical-fact?
***Hmmmm!*

*I don't want to think that Scientists are just as corruptible as Sociology, or English
Professors, but?...We'll just give them a break and consider them entrepreneurs, rather
than Leftists who accept government Grants as bribes.*

Why is "Palm Reading" and mysticism making a resurgence in 2009?
***Are You Freak'n Kid'n Me?....Because Religion is dead, man!...
"Power to the people", Dude!*

*The Hollywood Elite and The Media, all stricken with "SNL Group-Think" all KNOW,
in comparison to a proven commodity they've labeled an idiot, George W. Bush, the only
President in presidential history with a Master's Degree, in comparison to this Man of
Mystery; this Hope, this Wish, this Dream that can only speak with "cue cards and a
teleprompter", and
still can't pony-up an impromptu, recorded "independent" thought without visual aids.*

***Wasn't That the premise for the movie: "The Candidate", with Robert Redford?
Or, Maybe that was "Superman 4", but He ain't what stops another 9/11,
that was a George W. Bush!*

Why don't they teach civics in Jr. high schools anymore, or even in senior high schools
for that matter?
**Showing my age, sorry... That is the study of the interaction between the responsibilities
we have as human beings to each other, and as American citizens, as well as the powers
that we, the people delegate, that we loan to selected regional representatives, and THEY
to carry-out those mutual duties upon our behalves, to each other on a day-to-day basis,
for the common good,
while we, their employers, work very hard at home earning the money to pay these
representatives, who, it apparently seems do so little to earn their daily-bread, except sit
around dreaming up ways to extract, and collect more of our monies for their own mutual
personal agendas and benefit,
instead of performing their responsibility to us with their utmost honor and integrity,
in serving their bosses, We, the People......Did you get that?

(It's what all those old dudes do in Washington. Not the state, the city!)

Why does Detroit have a 49% illiteracy rate in 2009, when the entire state is a Democrat
stronghold and more money was being spent on education in the last 8 years than at any
time in history, and by the terribly insensitive George W. Bush?

**That's more money than the entire US Budget of the Reagan's Administration, and it's still never enough for the Teacher's Union, to enable teachers to properly teach their students to read: their own diplomas or their arrest warrants, whichever comes first, oh, but wasting 6% of the US government's budget today to protect ourselves, and in Iraq and around the world, is some kind of travesty and futile expenditure, according to those Academics and Comrades on Capitol Hill?

Why do teachers hate standards and testing, and choice and vouchers?
**Why do Vampires hate the bright light of day?

Why are kids so sedentary and overweight with the onset of adult diabetes today?
... Don't they have Gym and intramurals anymore?
**Law Suits?....Don't have any balls left? (those are sports-balls)

How many boys today own a baseball mitt, instead of a Wii?
**I know it's against humanity to run and jump, or play Tag, Kick-ball and Dodge-Ball in schools anymore.
Thank God, someone might get hurt or have fun???...Think Carpal-tunnel syndrome is prevalent playing with your Wii,
or covered under government health insurance, or a pre-existing condition?

For that matter;
Where were the intellectual, independent thinking, teachers and professors, scholars and Priests, as the Nazis slowly accumulated their power in Germany over a 10 year period?
**You know about Liberals and fighting!

Why didn't anyone ask what's that weird smell,
or what all the black smoke billowing out of those chimneys is from in those early concentration-camps days?......

**In fairness perhaps, maybe in the beginning someone did and then joined the attendees, but, they unanimously acquiesced", maybe that "snappy" uniform You get to wear, or der Führer would kill You!
No one on the LEFT in America gave a hoot about Saddam either, and to this day it's still argued, like rejecting the Ship of Fools!......At the time, I believe those were Democrats too.

Where were the sane patriotic Iraqis before Saddam gained power, and also right after?
**Oh yeah, I forgot, he killed them all!

Where were the civilized Iranians when the Shah was deposed?
**"They acquiesced"!

But, there was No odor from gas ovens, must have been "fear of the Scimitar" and the Ayatollah, who would kill them!
Around and around we go, and where it stops, no Socialist knows!

Where was the outrage when Castro didn't deliver on "The Dream"?
**"They acquiesced", or he killed them all; Michael Moore!

Where were the Senators that didn't dip their knives into Caesar's blood?
**Out to LUNCH at Caesar's?

Why didn't sanity intervene when the French Guillotine was Slice'n and Dice'n, 24 hours a day?
**"They acquiesced"!
I know who was running the government, but where were the conservatives?.........Elba?

Where were the English when the Spanish were decimating an entire continent?
**"Follow the Money"!

Always the Opportunists, They hired Top-Guns of the day; The Privateers were All just waiting offshore to steal the other guy's South American contraband. ....
Oops, sorry: Treasure!

*QUESTION:
How is it "Treasure" when it wasn't FOUND, in the 3rd place,

and it wasn't even LOST, in the 2nd place,

but it was STOLEN, in the 1st place???

I think it was Glenn Ford in so many western films of the '50s, that created that quiet-American hero persona; simple common man, defiant, a resolute character, the symbol of American honor, strength and resolved reverence.
Where are they today?

Unlike a contemporary actor today, that tries to decimate faith, and dissect a 2000 year old religion, a micromanaged autopsy for the money.
I have the 30 pieces of Silver for You.

Karma comes in many forms in LA, Mr. Gump, like:
Floods, Mud Slides, Brush Fires, Blizzards, Earthquakes, Volcano, even Hemorrhoids, Ulcers, Arthritis, Gout!..........Better say your prayers, just in case!

Why is it that Faith Hill, that can sing the most moving rendition of the National Anthem, and America, doesn't have a clue?
but, Jennifer Hudson accepted, she was great.

All puzzling questions in deed, wish I had the answers.

If I did have the answers I'd be very rich, or get assassinated
 since <u>Truth</u> isn't very popular in our "popular culture",
nor is <u>Truth</u> very profitable, and can confuse the paying customer,
    for <u>Truth</u> rarely raises its head in any movies made today!

God Bless America....and.....In God We Trust!

"The true danger is when Liberty is nibbled away, for expedients, and by parts.... Edmund Burke

<u>**The only thing necessary for evil to triumph is for good men do nothing."**</u>
Edmund Burke

<u>**SENTRYMAN**</u>

----

2 Comments

Comment by Del on February 2, 2009 at 4:20am

Wow!!! Sentryman and Sharon!

That post certainly lays it all out, I don't know if its hypnotism or not but it certainly follows the cult of El Duche (sic) and Hitler and Perron,

It is--- I don't know what it is but it is of great concern.
It is the mob gimme, gimme, gimme now, you promised!! You are the greatest. The trouble comes when the attempt comes to pat more than lip service.

Maybe the believers will become impatient -- we can hope!

Comment by usfrog on February 2, 2009 at 5:02am

> Try reading: <u>"An Examination of Obama's use of Hidden Hypnosis Techniques in his Speeches".</u>
> (pdf version, about 60 pages)
>
> This document has been on several Blog sites, sorry I do not have the link.
>
> Pretty hard reading if you are not a professional but worthwhile all the same.

Chapter 21

"Create a crisis that only you can solve:
DESTROY THE ECONOMY!"

Posted by SENTRYMAN on February 2, 2009 at 10:00pm

#1- Twilight Zone: The sound of a roar and a flash of light,
"The Monsters Are Due on Maple Street" is an episode of the American television anthology series to teach kids about the dangers of prejudice and hysteria.

The question of whether the monsters of the title are the suspected aliens, or the prejudiced residents of Maple Street is open to interpretation.
March 4, 1960, Wikipedia

#2- Ever play the game "Rumor," by assorted names, is when the Teacher tells a student a story or secret, and each subsequent student repeats the same story, naturally colored by their own feelings, experiences, social morays, prejudices and expressions, and by the time this simple story is relayed through the 30 impressionistic student's minds it has morphed into something that can be quite frightening?

#3- "A Vote for Me will get You?"; a chicken in every pot and a car in every garage.

During the presidential campaign of 1928, a circular published by the Republican Party claimed that if Herbert Hoover won there would be "a chicken in every pot and a car in every garage." Infoplease

All of this sounding familiar now?

***What do these 3 innocuous; ideas, promises and perceptions
have to do with each other, and how are they interrelated
when causing, or solving our current Financial Crisis of 2008-09?***

"It's the Economy Stupid"!
Sound even more familiar?

*(the phrase used so aptly during Bill Clinton's successful 1992 presidential campaign, in order to demean, undermine and destroy George H. W. Bush with four simple words, and to unduly influence the uninformed, gullible American-Idol mentality of an all too impressionable voting public, "strategically minimizing" an incredible body of experience, and life's service to one's country,
where prerequisites are no longer germane, and are foreign to the debate.)
One slogan, one idea, one perception that challenged, countered, and swept aside
a tall man in the saddle, no, in a cockpit... and swept aside integrity and honor,

Pg. 112

a life time of judgment and experience, a successful businessman, a self-made millionaire, a decorated naval flyer, a member of the House of Rep., a UN Ambassador, Chairman of the RNC, Chief Liaison to China in the early years, Director of the CIA, Vice President, and the President of the United States of America.

Not a bad resume,
but President Bush, Sr. was defeated by a Rookie, and also by an "off-hand remark";
(1) Accusation,

(1)One Sound bite, One line: "It's the Economy Stupid"!

(1-a) But certainly not Alone, that doesn't happen, but WHY?

············· "It's the Economy Stupid"! ··················
QUESTION: WHO WAS IT THAT WAS STUPID AGAIN?

Monumental Question for DEMs:
How do we get back the White House in '08 with another Rookie,
especially when the only weapon we've had is: "There were No WMDs,
and now things are turning around in Iraq?....Wonders the DNC Jan. 2007

Their Problem:
Everything's going along pretty good in the USA;
best unemployment rate in 40+ years,
(more people working then have ever been employed,
including the 40 million uninvited illegal aliens,)
low, low interest rates,
GDP is up,
Stock Markets are going through the roof,
we've reversed the pending Recession of 2000-01,
Bush brought back the entire nation's business collapse after 9/11,
US military had turned a corner in Iraq,
America freed 28 million oppressed people in the Middle East, 1st time
        Voting, little girls attending schools and allowed to learn,
our evil President's unkind anti-terror techniques decimated Al Qaeda,
Bush kept our country safe 6 tough years with new rules and safeguards,
finally starting to build The Fence across our Democrat sponsored borders,
and,
Bush finally secured the Prescription Drugs for the Seniors that everyone wanted,
(AT THE TIME), except for the YOUNG Conservative!

Their Dilemma:
What Do We Do About It??? ....Wondered the DNC, Jan. 2007

"Well, It *Worked Once, or Twice, and Every Election Cycle Since*",
they can't be that stupid every time but,
maybe we've made them dumb enough and it'll work again!!........
What else have we got to SPIN?....ZERO!....But that's never stopped-us before!

Ref: "DNC-Answer Book"
"Ole' Political Dirty Tricks: Hand Book For Dummies, by DNC":
Chap. III,
Pg. 32,
Sec. 2,
Par. 1;
"It's The Economy STUPID".....

Right!....There it is!!.........Oh yahhhh....I forgot that!

The DEM's Solution

#1 – Undermine and smear your opponent: "LIE"
Create a crisis that only you can solve.
(A) DESTROY THE ECONOMY!

The RESULT

*Nov. 2007, The DEMs took control of the Congress, and the Country quickly went to Hell-in-a-hand-Basket, preparing the way for the 2008 Presidential Campaign.....SUCCESS!

Reality Check: WHY?

This un-credible "Financial Crisis" in our United States is the direct consequence of a self-fulfilling prophecy; based upon a false premise, a Rumor, a bogus scenario, and predicated on the assumption that if you tell a lie often enough, people will begin to believe it, and the greater the lie the faster it spreads.

Additionally propagated by a willing and complicit 4th Estate, for 665 day straight, it's subconscious slow-water-drip, wearing away even solid-rock conviction;
this "Chinesesque Water Torture" technique had tortured the "American psyche" till the "skewed daily" falling economic figures began to reflect the DEM's calculated and desired result, and a robust American economy finally started to plummet;

"We Liberals can feel your pain, and know You are hurting, hurting very badly and only WE, The Democrats can bring You through this dark time, to protect You and solve all your problems";

and Behind Curtain #2

"We'll put 2 cars in every garage, and a booklet of KFC coupons in the glove compartment, and pay your house payment and your Electric bill, and provide (all that you deserve), including "Free" HealthCare, and additionally send You and anyone in your household, legal citizen or not, "a CHECK", and even a chance to attend college for "Free", and All This Can Be Yours M/M America for the simple task of Voting in November,
(forget we never taught you to read in the first 13 years we had You as students),
You don't need that anyway, just remember us, your DEMs and don't forget to
<u>Vote Obama</u>,
and often!

Or,
We, the People, can remain FREE,
beholden to no one, self-reliant independent thinkers; living our own lives, earning our own way, and finally rejecting any further government spending our children's, children's MONEY,
creating a 100 years' worth of Interest-ONLY DEBT.

[There is No Crisis, other than the one we've created in our own minds.]

GO TELL THE SMARTANS To Stop Spending Us Into The Poor House,
to leave us alone with a smaller government, and
Stop Eminent Domain, Enact A Flat Tax, and Finally Close The IRS!

"Idle Hands Are The Devil's Workshop"!

Congress, You Don't Pass The Laws We Really Need, And You Create Laws We Don't Want
.............Had You been doing your jobs
things would have never gotten this bad, and would never have let this happen to us,
to us, Your Employers......

So, as any parent dealing with a bad Babysitter, entrusted with care of our child and our better interests, and who allowed our baby to drown in the tub while Texting the DNC, and the RNC, YOU ARE FIRED!...But in reality,
just go home till we have a real problem that we need some bureaucrats to screw-up for us, and if and when think we can finally trust you again, then we'll tell you to return.

*Note:
On TV today, an (unnamed) young Info'ette asked:
"Is the world's economy dependent on the Stimulus Package"?

Huh, Give Me A BREAK!.......Who told her to ask that question?

Then this guy from "Chrysler" comes on and says that we can buy a new vehicle on their "PLUS/PLUS" Plan at the Employee Price with additional rebates to $6000.00,
at 0% interest for 48 months and asks:
"What are you waiting for people?........Cars have never been cheaper!"

Well, that's actually worth repeating: "What are you waiting for people?"........For that matter: *the same applies to Home Purchases, and that's what they all should be telling you every day, and not that things will get worse
 unless you let us spend your money for you!!*

See, that's the simple trick: "You" spend your money the economy SAILS...."They" spend your money the economy FAILS!....HELLO?

Why can't the American Consumer, and Voter figure that out on their own?

"Car Dealerships closing,"............"6,000 Layoffs, 20,000 Layoffs, 50,000 Layoffs."
Do you like reading this every day?

Well, as of last Friday, we're all going to be paying for (Abortions around the world) now!
Thank You, Mr. President!!!!

So, if we don't develop some character and gumption, and go out there and live our lives as normal as possible, and buy a car, or a truck, or a house, or whatever else you would normally be spending money on during the first 5 years of the Bush administration, <u>We will DOOM ourselves</u>!

<u>Reality Check Again:….......WHY?…......... Why do we do this to ourselves?</u>

Do You really think someone else can solve Your problems by spending Your money on Condoms for our school children, but then sponsoring foreign abortions,
or building golf courses with Tax dollars,
or targeting approx. (ONLY 25%) of the $819 BILLION "STIMULUS DOLLAR$" on jobs, and then only after 2011?

*Right now only ($1.00 of every $7.00) Stimulus Dollar is earmarked to create New Job Employment before the middle 2010, and 2011, hmmmm, just in time to be doweled out to DEMs for "Bribes" and "Pork Votes" in the 2010 & 2012 Elections?.....
<u>…….Your Tax Dollars At Work, FEEL GOOD Americans?…….</u>

<u>What'a ya people want, a Hollywood style Rehab?…..</u>

<u>Government Has No Money, It's All Yours!…..</u>

<u>Government Produces Nothing !!…..</u>

<u>Government Creates Nothing !!!…..</u>

<u>Government Does Nothing !!!!…..</u>

<u>There is "No Free Lunch" !!!!!</u>

<u>Government Has No Money, Just Borrows & Spends All Yours</u>

<u>NEVER HEARD THAT ONE BEFORE, RIGHT?</u>

So, Get Out There and Live Your Lives, and Enjoy Your Fleeting Liberties!

<u>"We" Are The Only Ones That Can Make The Economy Rebound</u>

Or, You'll Kick Yourself In The Ass Every Day, Someday SOON!

<u>SENTRYMAN</u>

Chapter 22

ASHLEY JUDD Judges!   The Wolves are circling Sarah Palin!

Posted by SENTRYMAN on <u>February 7, 2009</u> at 12:00am

*Ashley Judd, that gracious lady of the Silver Screen, "movie star",
has an issue with a member of the government of the United States of America.*

*Well, well, stand in line, but does that give her the right, or the authority to make personal
criticisms and JUDGEMENTS about another human being, as her name doth proport?*

*I thought liberals didn't like standards, or any rules, or Judgementalism? Especially about
citizen's private activities outside her own peer group, and beyond her sphere of expertise
and influence.*

<u>Why not? Sure, Freedom of Speech!</u>......... This is America!!

Ms. Ashley Judd: "Role Model";
**mentor to young women everywhere by her stellar choices, and important
selections of different independent women in society to emulate.**

The essence captured within her character roles she doth portray;
*whores, screwballs, crackpots, murderesses, fallen women, thieves, liars,
victims, and the tainted!...whoa.*
*The weakest of feminine depravities so adeptly and inexorably depicted
with such authenticity, one wouldn't think she was even acting, her
portrayals so vivid, genuine and real, apparently that talented.*

<u>She has now taken up the humble plight of the lowly "set-upon" Wolf</u>,
so unkindly maligned in literature, depicted in stories throughout the ages,
a primitive predator of the first order akin to the tiger and shark.
So misunderstood, if not contained or restricted, could eventually and quite naturally
decimate entire herds of Deer and Caribou, creating an imbalance in the eco-system,
but apparently with Ms. Judd's total blessing!.....go figure?

Ms. Judd decries the senseless and unfeeling thinning-out of the Wolf Packs,
much like I guess she would also think how the mean Allies unfairly performed this regime
during W.W.II to those Wolf Packs, as severe,
when the 3rd Reich U-Boat Wolf Packs would lay in-wait for defenseless Liberty ships, and
Troops ships, and sent them down into the cold depths of the briny deep.

Funny, but I thought hunting, and culling, and thinning in the animal kingdom was all too
natural, and a wise and practiced environmental conservative tenet for the good of the
specie?....The ebb and flow of life.   Pg. 117

Ms. Judd prefers that these packs of wolves be given "free reign & free will",
to conspire and plot, track down, separate-out a calf and her mother Caribou from the main herd,
once isolated, trap and surround the pair and descend upon them,
1st attacking the mother to wound and disable her from defending her baby,
biting into her rear legs, ripping out the muscle and tendons to trip her up and bring her down,
then tearing out the mother's throat,
then collapsing her ribcage, the pack devours her entrails, while her blood still runs hot, pouring out into the snow,
and as her squealing becomes more muffled, and her struggles subside, all the time her frantic fawn, bleating in pure heart pounding terror waiting her turn.

Then, the blood drenched Pack turns their attentions to this frenzied baby,
spinning dizzy from fear, still bleating for her mother's protection now laying dead before her, the baby fawn is eaten in-half.....still alive.

http://www.youtube.com/watch?v=TZlm4OSsiuA

I guess it always depends on who's Ox is getting gored,
or, <u>who's doing the goring, right Ashley?</u>

I can really see why Ms. Judd feels compassion for the poor wolf, of course, if that's her only motivation since we rarely see it in action,
and the raw cruelty and seeming injustice sometimes from a human's perspective of this "Call of the Wild" story, that's played-out millions of times every day on land and sea. A necessary part of the natural world; insect, plant or animal: Eat or be eaten, and that's the harsh reality of real Life as we all know, if we're no longer 8 years old, or a Liberal.

But at the same time, whether it be over-hunting, over-fishing, over-planting, deforestation, over-medicating livestock,
more rational, prudent minds try to monitor things for the good of it all.

Yet humans exploiting and preying upon the animal kingdom like wolves themselves, over-hunting, or hunting endangered species for ivory trinkets, baby seal dresser scarves, eagle feathers, lamp oil, and for the theoretically-imperative aphrodisiacs, or downright eliminating total species, well then,
Sarah Palin would be at the head of the line to defend Animal Rights to stop the atrocities, but I don't remember Ms. Judd coming to the wolves' defense at any time over the years, to petition against this established long-term conservation policy, unless I'm mistaken, before a certain "conservative" woman was risking her own life in the air defending the balance of nature, and the defenseless Caribou…
…maybe Sarah would take Ashley up there sometime, if she asked!

<u>"Babes On Wings With Guns"; sounds like a Friday Drive-In Movie to me!</u>

I'm sure Sarah doesn't enjoy the process as a sport, aside from the necessity.
On the other side of the coin, ruining crop lands, raising food prices, starving farmers and field workers, of their livelihoods, for the sake of a "certain minnow", is also going in the wrong direction to an extreme, helping to raise humans higher-up on that endangered list!

Maybe, if Ms. Judd could take-on another cause, raising money and addressing the issues from both sides, which is more equitable: *"Counseling Caribou" to seek Abortion Clinics for Caribou, or Caribou condoms, now there's a real "seller" for ya.*
Financed by a Grant from a Obama Slush Fund, set-up all along the Pipe Line, so the poor wolf population wouldn't need to be controlled. Even teach Caribou abstinence, oh lord,

never abstinence!...Lots and lots of caribou, and lots and lots of wolves, can't they all just get along?

I wonder if Ms Judd would carry a sign for the Lamb Abortees, or the Wolf Abortioners.

Wait a min-ute,
didn't Hollywood say that the oil pipeline would destroy the Caribou populations?...hmmm

Maybe that was the Polar Bear, or Venezuelan's oil cartel profit margin, can't remember.
We should ask Penn or Gore!

But, how would I know,
I'm not an adult that lives my life playing in make-believe worlds,
or dresses-up in costumes and mimics other peoples original thoughts, emotions
and words during "story-time" every day,
I work for a living!

There has to be a balance in life, as in nature I guess. We all feel for both sides, and for all the animals in the shared spaces on this planet,
and I thank God for "The Hamburger", and Barbecued Chicken.

Haven't had a Caribou steak yet, but I bet it's gangbusters on cholesterol,
and,
(Me Thinks) "the Lady doth protest too much",
and this has less or nothing to do with wolves, and more about fish: the "Red Herring",

other than those Holly-Wolves circling around Sarah, waiting for the KILL!

SENTRYMAN

---

4 Comments

Comment by Frank L on February 7, 2009 at 12:19am

good job Sentryman...spot on....

Comment by Greg H on February 7, 2009 at 12:19am

What I wonder is, how much is the 0bama camp paying Judd and/or Defense of Wildlife to launch this attack, coming as it does right after Gov. Palin has come out forcefully against the massive 0bama spending bill?

I don't think it's a particularly effective attack, most people have grown weary of being lectured to by holier than thou environmentalists, animal rights groups, and Global Warming alarmists.

Check out the ongoing poll on whether you agree with Gov. Palin or Ashley Judd. So far almost a quarter of a million votes have been cast, and 59% support Gov. Palin,

and 41% support Judd.

http://www.youtube.com/watch?v=XcB38vZmYJ8

Although this isn't a "scientific" poll, it is set up in such a way as to accept only one vote per computer, so that people can't engage in multiple voting without going through a rather cumbersome process. Any way you look at it, 223,900 votes is a lot, scientific or not. The poll also shows that 58 percent of people dislike Judd more,
and only 28 percent like her more since she went on the attack.

Whether they know it or not, Gov. Palin will emerge from this fight relatively unscathed and probably strengthened since she has shown a lot of backbone standing up to these people.
..Mere fleas biting at her ankles.

Comment by Ray on February 7, 2009 at 12:24am

She has done that.

Comment by Lauren on February 7, 2009 at 7:50am

I won't say for certain but I think it was on Red Eye, about 4 guys were talking about this. One said Judd was great looking but then they all agreed Sarah was hotter.

Could be reason Judd has it in for her. ..lol

Chapter 23

"I knew Abraham Lincoln
and President Obama, You're no Abraham Lincoln"!

Posted by SENTRYMAN on February 12, 2009 at 3:30pm

The "Media" credits Barack Obama for the renewed teaching of President Lincoln in the nation's schools once again, with his own personal interest of that great President having once inherited a slave nation.

My question would be:
"Why was the teaching about all of our ever presidents ever suspended?
Was there Not enough time in the day after teaching about condoms?"
Sentryman

Rush Limbaugh laments today;
"what is being taught now in schools is that Lincoln might have been Gay, suffered from depression, was in fact a racist and his wife was crazy!"

"well, Thank You President Barack Obama and CNN for once again attacking the traditions of America."
Rush Limbaugh

Rush's patience also wears thin when any politician tries to co-opt and share the greatness, and glory of past great leaders of our nation, as Pres. Obama purposely spoke on the steps of the Lincoln Memorial today,
claiming that Lincoln was also a great Bipartisan President, which coincidentally, he'd also like the Congress to be today with his "100% created and incepted Democrat signature" Stimulus Package.

paraphrased: If this bill is so wonderful and fantastic, and the DEMs can pass it on their own, why do they even need the Republicans onboard to share their glory, or do they need Republicans to (blame-it-on) when it Goes Down In Flames?, especially (since Merrill Lynch can't redecorate their own offices with their own money, [planned and ordered pre-bailout], but the Congress can steal our money to renovate their Congress offices without reproach.)
("Try finding out what Congress does with our Money"), asks Rush. Pg.121

"Lincoln was probably the most partisan of presidents, loved and guided totally by the US Constitution and was never bipartisan.
He arrested enemies and jailed spies and fought 1/2 of his nation that wanted to extend slavery into the US Western Expansion".
Rush Limbaugh

"Lincoln Never Dropped The Charges On Any Enemy Soldier That Had Bombed A US Warship And Had Killed Our Sailors."
SENTRYMAN

In the styled words of Sen. Lloyd Benson, (paraphrased);
"I knew Abraham Lincoln, I learned about Abraham Lincoln in school in the 50s from my "really" non-partisan teachers,
and President Obama, you're no Abraham Lincoln".
SENTRYMAN

Lincoln even thanked God for the gift of Ulysses S. Grant,
as he fired his first 12 generals that couldn't get the job done,
(like another citizen Commander-in-Chief, with little military experience,
some years later that finally found his Grant: "GEN. PETRAEUS"),
while his critics complained that General Grant was drunk all the time,
and Lincoln responded:
"find out what liquor He's drinking and send it to the rest of my generals"!
Rush Limbaugh

SENTRYMAN

Ps, *"If people get the government they deserve,"*
then the citizens in Pennsylvania and Maine, and any other state cursed
with RINO Republicans that are NOT Voted Out and always re-elected,
to stay in office to be allowed to perpetuate this sham once again onto the
next Voting Cycle, then; a pox on You and both your houses, and
You Will Deserve What You Have Sewn. SENTRYMAN

----

1 Comment

Comment by jap on February 12, 2009 at 4:21pm

Yah Obama, also mention how Lincoln would want everyone to be one nation. Wonder what he meant by that?

Chapter 24

AOL: "Experts Rank US Presidents"
& SENTRYMAN weighs-in with "footnotes"

Posted by SENTRYMAN on February 15, 2009 at 6:30pm

[BEST PRESIDENTS]

Abraham Lincoln - Republican
Ranking: 1 - Years served: 1861-1865
This radical Republican freed 4 million slaves while keeping the nation together when it was near collapse.

Footnote:
Radical?
I think that's a "Leftist" description, they mean "Reactionary",
I.e. conservative Republican!
Oh yeah, shot by the opposition, a Slavery loving Democrat!
==

Franklin D. Roosevelt - Democratic
Ranking: 3 - Years served: 1933-1945
Reelected four times, FDR led America out of the Great Depression and through World War II.

Footnote:
His New Deal didn't solve the Great Depression, but only prolonged and deepen it thru "progressive" social engineering,
"Taxing the Rich to Death",
and making everyone-dependent on the Government,
and the effects of his "management theory" linger-on today.
And if continued will make things even worse,
unless of course as in yesteryears,
you're well connected, or (in the government sector) and "part of the problem".
Then you were all set, but NEVER for the benefit of the Taxpayers "paying the Tab".
==

Theodore Roosevelt - Republican
Ranking: 5 - Years served: 1901-1909
The (progressive) Republican's "square deal" policies attacked corporate monopolies and protected consumers through greater regulation.

Footnote:
Obviously they never anticipated a Fannie/Freddie, or Merrill Lynch, GE, Bank of America, Citicorp, or an AIG: ("America" isn't guaranteed)
or

Pg. 123

a Charles Rangel, (who writes Tax Law, but doesn't pay his own fair share),
or the smartest man in America - Timothy Geithner, who can't figure out his own Taxes,
and yet has been placed "In-Charge of 138 million American citizens paying taxes"!

*"Speak softly and carry a big stick"., Teddy wouldn't have left Al Qaeda out there either, without a good clobbering. And Teddy established the US National Monuments Park Service for "all Americans" in perpetuity, "not for the United Nations" to someday co-opt!

After the attempted assassination on Oct, 14, 1912, with the bullet still lodged in his chest, he still gave his 90 minute speech, with the opening line: "Ladies and gentlemen, I don't know whether you fully understand that I have just been shot, but it takes more than that to kill a Bull Moose." ...
He carried the bullet all his days!

The Panama Canal, of course, and given away by Who?....right, a Liberal.

Father of the: Meat Inspection Act, of 1906, and The Pure Food and Drug Act., this patriot Republican was always look'n out for his fellow Americans!

He was an explorer and a hunter, a "real" author, and a Nobel Prize Winner, rightly earned and deserved for negotiating an end of a major War, a naturalist and conservationist, a Warrior-soldier, "Rough Rider" w/ Medal of Honor, Governor, Vice-President,
and his own man!

===

Dwight Eisenhower - Republican
Ranking: 6 - Years served: 1953-1961
The popular World War II commander created the interstate highway system and sent federal troops to Little Rock, Ark., to enforce the desegregation of schools.

Footnote:
Besides the highway construction that so impressed AOL researchers, Ike headed-up the effort to defeat Fascism, Nazism, and Imperialism during W.W.II, so we don't speak German, or Japanese today,

and in later years would once again step-up against tyranny to protect African-Americans from Southern Democrats = another Republican Idiot?

===

Harry Truman - Democratic
Ranking: 7 - Years served: 1945-1953
Truman authorized the use of atomic bombs over Japan and
signed up America to the United Nations and NATO. The Truman Doctrine's anti-Communist policies lasted for decades.

Footnote:
Hated today, for ending the war too soon with "The Bomb" and lessening American casualties,
 by "The Left's" progressive-standards for moral-authority today.

Oops, Democrat!
===

Ronald Reagan - Republican
Ranking: 8 - Years served: 1981-1989
Reagan led the nation to the end of the Cold War and his tax-cutting, budget-slashing "Reaganomics" policies helped revive the US economy.

Footnote:
Probably singularly averted W.W. III,
and brought America back from the Brink of "many" disasters,
who's fiscal policies are totally discredited and ignored today = another Republican Idiot?

==

James Polk - Democratic
Ranking: 9 - Years served: 1845-1849
After leading the nation to victory in the war with Mexico, Polk increased the size of the Union by acquiring California, Nevada and parts of five other Western states.

Footnote:
I thought that was called Stealing Land by Mexicans, and
Killing the defenseless native American, by "The Left"?

Oops, Democrat!
==

Woodrow Wilson - Democratic
Ranking: 10 - Years served: 1913-1921
Wilson established the Federal Reserve in his first term and led America into World War I in his second term. (Source: timesonline.com.uk)

Footnote:
Liberal Pacifist;
His re-election campaign slogan: "he kept us out of the war", until a sneak attack on a ship brought America into the War....how familiar is that?

They forgot the cash-cow IRS,
and the "intended" consequences of the new FED,
that both have helped to almost destroy the monitory system for the World Today,
but America will keep Both of these unjust, arcane relics, and ignore "Reaganomics,"
or even try to incorporate a Flat Tax, or entertain Term Limits For Congress,
so our Government can keep their "ever increasing control" of Free Markets and keep their (Foot on the American Taxpayer's Throat),
and their (Hands in our Pockets)!

And Wilson helped establish "The League of Nations", as bad an idea then,
 as the United Nations is also useless today,
and his nation-building, social-engineering with the Treaty of Versailles: would create the foundation for Germany's reemergence as a super power and Nazism in years to come.

Oh, and Wilson *tolerated expansion of segregation in Federal government.*
Oops, Democrat!!
==

**ROGUE'S GALLERY

===

[WORST PRESIDENTS]

James Buchanan - Democratic
Ranking: 42 (worst overall) - Years served: 1857-1861
A poll by American historians ranked Buchanan's failure to prevent the Civil War as the greatest mistake made by any US president.

Footnotes:
Oops, again a Democrat!

===

William Henry Harrison - Whigs
(the Whigs supported the supremacy of Congress over the executive branch and favored a program of modernization and economic protectionism.)

Ranking: 39 - Years served: 1841
Sworn in at the age of 68, Harrison gave the longest inauguration speech in history on a cold,
wet day without an overcoat or hat. He then got sick and died after just 32 days in office.

Footnote:
This poor guy doesn't deserve "The Worst" category
just because he spoke as long-winded as Barack Obama!
At least he didn't have a teleprompter, but probably why he got pneumonia.

Sounds like a Democrat to me!

===

Martin Van Buren - Democratic
Ranking: 40 - Years served: 1837-1841
Van Buren brutally enforced policies to remove Native Americans from their homeland, resulting in the slaughter of many.

Footnote:
What, that Warmongering terrorist swine, but
we'd never get John Wayne and Roy Rogers, or Hoot Gibson and Tom Mix,
or cheap cigarettes and amoral Casinos.
Oops, Democrat!

===

Franklin Pierce - Democratic

Ranking: 41 - Years served: 1853-1857
Outrage over Pierce's capitulating to pro-slavery states forced the Democratic Party
to abandon him after his first term and helped spawn the Republican Party.

Footnote:
Pierce was a Democrat, and a "doughface" (a Northerner with Southern sympathies)
His reputation was destroyed during the American Civil War when he declared support for
the Confederacy,
Oops, Democrat! "Ofay"!

==

Richard Nixon - Republican

Ranking: 37 (tied) - Years served: 1969-1974
Ending the Vietnam War made Nixon a popular president,
but his cover-up of a break-in at Democratic headquarters in the Watergate Hotel
forced him to resign in disgrace.

Footnote:
Well, fair enough.

But, is that all he did, and then "He quit"?
He should have originally been from Illinois where you never quit.
You have to be staked in the heart like any normal vampire politician, or you'll keep rising
from a grave in Illinois.

He also didn't challenge Kennedy's suspicious victory when all "The Dead" came-out and
voted in Illinois,
thus stealing that election for JFK,
but since Nixon felt it might hurt the nation more, he possessed the personal fortitude and
grace, choosing NOT to make a fuss.
I guess Gore didn't hear about that classy bench-mark gesture!

At least Nixon didn't initiate the project event, (just covering for his boys),
and for President Nixon, "The Buck Stopped With Him",
so He resigned with some semblances of personal Honor,
as not take the country through further embarrassment.
Something Clinton would not so willingly commit, or submit to in later years, but again
Clinton was a Democrat, and lived his life by a different standard held proudly.

Nixon also put teeth in Affirmative Action, created OSHA, EPA,
and opened China to world trade, so the Chinese could buy Obama's debts someday,
 so again = another Republican Idiot?

Side-note:
(and as another unintended consequence in America's future),
also so China could someday contribute to the 1st Clinton presidential-campaign,
and then again contribute even more illegal monie$ for Clinton's 2nd campaign, in
exchange for much needed "missile technology" to correct China's inability to shoot
straight with their weapons-of-mass-destruction, pointed directly at who-do-You-think?

Thanks Bill, now China can reach Hollywood with an ICBM....Hmmmm!
==

George W. Bush - Republican
Ranking: 37 (tied) - Years served: 2001-2009
Bush's "war on terror" was criticized for its mismanagement and his approval ratings sank further during the economic collapse at the end of his second term.

Footnote:
Fortunately he cared more about protecting the country than his reputation,
unlike his predecessor, or successor, Bush kept the nation safe after 9/11.

Some think he should have kept his nose out of the Middle East, but then again,
when, or if a second, third, and fourth wave of Terrorist's attack-strikes came to US shores, as were planned,
it would have eliminated a lot of weak, sycophantic, long-haired, dope-smoking, maggot-infested, good time-rock 'n roll, plastic banana, 9th Circuit, Mahar / Moore Hollywood, FM hippie-types from earthly existence, oh my,
along with possibly millions of average normal Patriotic Americans, all up in smoke,
so most fortunately for them George preferred to protect all Americans,
which again equals = another Republican Idiot?

Yeahhhhh, thank your lucky sweet bottoms, Ms Alba and Tina Fey!
How would you like a nice couture "designer" Burqa, girls?.....3 basic shades, no?

Maybe the American "LEFT", or the America that would be left
would have preferred that scenario, and don't say it couldn't have happened "twice-twits",
no one anticipated a 1st World Trade Center bombing on Feb. 26, 1993, or #2 on 9/11 was even possible on 9/10, (though a popular Video Game existed at that time for a Blue-Print!)

Wake-Up before it's too late,
and before some weak-kneed Democrat gets us deep-in-the-$#!% again, and We need another Republican (according to DEMs) "Idiot", to really bail-us-out and protect America again, as usual!

===

James Garfield - Republican
Ranking: 34 (tied) - Years served: 1881
Garfield served just four months in office before being assassinated by a man he had "overlooked for a position" within his administration.

Footnote:
"overlooked for a position", James apparently had a pretty "good judge of character".

Now, had the assassin had Tenure, he may have been assassinating "young minds" in a university some day.

4 months in office, and AOL has relegated him to the Worst Column?
Geez, "Cheap Shot", forgive the pun?

Why'd He have to go and get shot, that Republican Idiot?
His assassin must have had Liberal tendencies, I don't doubt, you check!

Had Garfield been a Democrat, he'd been deified as some GOD,
like maybe some guy, leaving his troops stranded on the beach at the Bay of Pigs,
  or had taken us to Nam, for instance,

or was popping actresses like M&Ms, which of course,
in a progressive-Liberal non-secular world equals = Sainthood & "Camelot",
only those guys are never like the pure of heart, mythical "Arthur" figure.

<u>We all know King Arthur, and that guy was no Arthur Pendragon</u>!

(sorry for the Church & State reference)

Or maybe if Garfield had <u>stranded his soldiers</u> on the desert in Iran,
or <u>stranded his soldiers</u> in Somalia?

Who knows Who <u>will have stranded his soldiers</u> in the future.

Question: has anyone tallied the number of Republican VS Democrat assassination attempts?

==

Millard Fillmore - Whig
Ranking: 33 - Years served: 1850-1853
Fillmore squandered an opportunity to end slavery, making compromises that empowered some slave states and eventually led to the Civil War.

<u>Footnote:</u>
another crazy Slavery-Loving Whig!
Sounds like another Democrat to me!
==

<u>Oh my goodness,</u> Fanfare, and light-bulb appears in balloon over my head: <u>TAH...DAHHH</u>!

I just realized why teachers don't teach about Presidents anymore,
they are only men with feet of clay!...Good Men to be sure, but still Only Men,
except for the New Guy now, of course,
heeeee's a pre-certified GOD, with all his many years of experience and vast wisdom!

And from the state with the "worst political report card" of any state in the history of this Union!.........That's not "Immaculate", that's just "Incredible", or is it non-credible?

But teachers don't teach any history, or about different religions, unless it's their Ideology;
I.e., Mother Earth, Abortion, Condoms, Weed, Global Warming;
don't cut trees,
  don't eat meat,
    don't burn fossil fuels,
      don't eat cupcakes,
        rely on the government,
          dependency on your Democrat government Leaders can provide everything for you!

Everyone deserves a trophy,
   hate the person that has more than you,
     and liberalism, socialism, progressivism, and communism aren't bad, if you believe,
       no matter what your ancient grandparents have said about it!
"Can't We all just get along?"

Government is only evil (when mean Republicans are in power),

but NOW, a righteous government can solve "all our problems"
with the good Democrat's In-Total-Control, children!

Now let's break for "Meditation" time, playing kick-ball can be dangerous!

==

QUESTION children:

Why is it that when Democrats take us to War = they're the Good Guys, but when Republicans do the same thing, in defense of our nation = they are the Bad Guys?.............tick, tock???......no?

I want 500 words tomorrow on:
"what You can do to stop progress in Brazil with their Indians, oops, Brazilian native-Americans cutting-down their own Rain Forests!

*Good thing the;
Huns, then the Nazis, The Rising Sun, the Reds, Cuban Revolutionaries, the Cong, Iranians, Grenadians, Panamanians, Sandinistas, Soviets, Iraqis, Somalis, Haitians, Slavs and Serbs, the Taliban and Al Qaeda, Jane Fonda and William Aires
all don't hold grudges.....Whew, then we might really have to act someday!

Africa, Get Ready, Here We Come!

SENTRYMAN

*Ps, ONLY KIDDING!
I already knew "why" teachers didn't teach about our Presidents anymore!!!*

---

2 COMMENTS

Comment by Lisa C on February 15, 2009 at 8:00pm

Where did they have "Andrew Jackson"?
Sarah is closer to Andrew Jackson, Abe Lincoln and Teddy Roosevelt than any person our Nation has seen since!

Comment by SENTRYMAN on February 16, 2009 at 2:08am

*Dear Lisa:
I could care less where the readers of AOL positioned Andy Jackson;
A Real "Man For All Seasons",
he really was a man of his time that exhibited the virtues and foibles of all men, great and small.*

*A Hero and a Villain, a Warrior and a Farmer, a Champion and a Husband,
a Father to adopted boys, a Widower, a simple Man of the soil......American*

Andrew Jackson was a Democrat, and a Republican, a Liberal and a Conservative.

Today they would just hang him for "War Crimes",
with a rope he'd confiscated "from the British",
and be hung from a tree he'd seized "from the Spanish"!

According to Wikipedia:
a less than reputable source but adequate for this exercise, capsulated as follows;

Jackson **in 1797 was elected US Senator as a Democratic-Republican.**
He resigned within a year.....In 1798, he was appointed a judge of the Tennessee Supreme Court, serving until 1804.

Besides his legal and political career, Jackson prospered as a planter and merchant.
In 1803 he owned a lot, and built a home and the first general store in Gallatin.

In 1804, he acquired the "Hermitage," a 640-acre plantation in Sumner County, near Nashville. Jackson later added 360 acres to the farm. The primary crop was cotton, grown by enslaved workers.

Jackson started with nine slaves, by 1820 he held as many as 44, and later held up to 150 slaves.

Jackson was appointed Commander of the Tennessee Militia in 1801, with the rank of Colonel.

Jackson defeated the Red Stick Creeks at the Battle of Horseshoe Bend in 1814. Eight hundred "Red Sticks" were killed, but Jackson spared Chief William Weatherford.

Sam Houston and David Crockett served under Jackson in this campaign.

Jackson's service in the War of 1812 against the United Kingdom was conspicuous for bravery and success.
When British forces threatened New Orleans, Jackson now a Major General, he took command of the defenses, including militia from several western states and territories.

It was said he was "tough as old hickory" wood on the battlefield, which gave him his nickname.

Jackson served in the military again during the First Seminole War. He was ordered by President James Monroe in December 1817 to lead a campaign in Georgia against the Seminole and Creek Indians.

Jackson was also charged with preventing Spanish Florida from becoming a refuge for runaway slaves.

The Seminoles attacked Jackson's Tennessee volunteers. The Seminoles' attack, however, left their villages vulnerable, and Jackson burned them and the crops

Jackson believed that the United States would not be secure as long as Spain and the United Kingdom encouraged Indians to fight and argued that his actions were under-taken in self-defense.

The Tennessee legislature nominated Jackson for President in 1822. It also elected him US Senator again.

By 1824, the Democratic-Republican Party had become the only functioning national party.

A Pennsylvanian convention nominated Jackson for President a month later, stating that the irregular caucus ignored the "voice of the people" and was a "vain hope that the American people might be thus deceived into a belief that he [Crawford] was the regular democratic candidate."

Gallatin criticized Jackson as "an honest man and the idol of the worshippers of military glory, but from incapacity, military habits, and habitual disregard of laws and constitutional provisions, altogether unfit for the office of President.

During the election, Jackson's opponents referred to him as a "jackass."

Jackson liked the name and used the jackass as a symbol for a while, but it died out. However, it later became the symbol for the Democratic Party when cartoonist Thomas Nast popularized it.

In 1835, Jackson managed to reduce the federal debt to only $33,733.05, the lowest it had been since the first fiscal year of 1791.

Jackson supported an "agricultural republic" and felt the Bank improved the fortunes of an "elite circle" of commercial and industrial entrepreneurs at the expense of farmers and laborers.

Jackson was a leading advocate of a policy known as "Indian removal", which involved the ethnic cleansing of several Indian tribes.

Prior to his election as president, Jackson had been involved with the issue of Indian removal for over ten years. After his election, he signed the Indian Removal Act into law in 1830.

The first attempt to do bodily harm to a President was against Jackson.
When Jackson was leaving the Capitol Building out of the East Portico after the funeral, Richard Lawrence, an unemployed and deranged housepainter from England, either burst from a crowd or stepped out from hiding behind a column and aimed a pistol at Jackson which misfired.

Jackson attacked Lawrence with his cane, prompting his aides to restrain him. Others present, including David Crockett, restrained and disarmed Lawrence.

After retiring to Nashville, he enjoyed eight years of retirement and died at The Hermitage on June 8, 1845 at the age of 78.

In his will, Jackson left his entire estate to his "adopted" son,
Andrew Jackson Jr.

Wikipedia

I suspect, Sarah does possess many of his strengths and virtues, but little else, other than fiscal responsibility.

Take care.

SENTRYMAN

 **Chapter 25**

"Maybe There Won't Be Any VIRGINs Left When You Get Up There!"

Posted by SENTRYMAN on February 21, 2009 at 12:00am

===

Blogger #1- DeLON366 piles-on 03:09 PM Feb. 20, 2009 and states:

"Clinton Wants Obama to Offer More Hope"

Feb. 20) - Former President Bill Clinton has offered his candid opinion on how he thinks the economic crisis could have been avoided and what needs to be done so that the nation can recover.........but added that Obama should also offer Americans more hope.

"BUSH took what could be described as a, "perfectly waxed, running, well taken care of and fully gassed-up automobile handed to him by an uncle", and picked up his
"HILLBILLIE-DRUG ABUSED-BEER SWILLING-BIBLE THUMPING- NEPHEW F%&KING- FRIENDS
and DROVE IT INTO A DITCH!

And now HE and HIS "FRIENDS" want to say that his "UNCLE" and the "TOW TRUCK DRIVER" are to blame."

===

Blogger #2 -THNDRSHWR34 puts-up his fists 03:11 PM Feb. 20, 2009 states;

"Why is the media continuing to put Clinton this character-less, lying , excuse for a human being in the news.
He blames Bush for this economic turndown when it was his 'Community Re-investment Act,
taken over by Dodd, Rangel, Barney Frank, and the DEMs running of Fannie-Mae and Freddie-Mac into the ground...........What a creep."

Pg. 133
===
===

SENTRYMAN "takes them both" on;

Well Folks, that's America in a "Nut" Shell.

Geez, don't confuse me with the facts; right Joe Piscopo and Tony Danza.

It's always been: Yin & Yang,....Reason Vs Self-Delusion.

SENTRYMAN's response:

WOW, Talk about a Freudian Slips! (2 for 1)!
For the very 1st time Clinton hits 2 nails = right on the head,
of course, the wrong nails but it's a start.

(Clinton states: "if we moved aggressively on this home problem a year and a half ago, even a year ago"),

yes, BRILLIANT,

exactly when the Democrats "took over" the Congress and the Senate in 2007.

YES, the very same People that "Pass - All - The - Laws",
and "Hold - The - Purse - Strings" and stopped Bush right-in-his-tracks from doing "anything they didn't like", or "without their permission or compliance"!

And today: "Obama has single-handedly";
Talked-down Our Economy,
Talked-down the Dow,
Talked-down Real Estate Market,
Talks-down Our ability to affect the dilemma, or any capability to solve our own problems without Government's total involvement and intervention,
and,
Talks-down the seriousness of the "War-on-Terror", as the maniacal (smiling Bomb making terrorists), happily mug-on-camera while assembling their "suicide-bomb jackets" for their legions of eager fanatical minions, all lining-up for their next assignments, and the Super "Bonus" Jackpot-Prizes: 70 Virgins, special Air-mail delivery on the way!

But, hey, what would Clinton know about War, or the Economy?
He was busy barricaded in the Oval Office playing "Groucho Marx"!

(and I apologize to Groucho's memory for the analogy, with all due respect, but you can recognize the visuals. The part of Margaret is played by, well, you know who!)

Clinton did sign: Welfare Reform though, albeit with a gun to his head 3x by Newt Gingrich but Obama has reversed that anyway.

I guess the new President wants poor black American teenagers raising a new generation of fatherless children again, and dropping out of high school, sitting home watching Oprah, never going to college, or creating a life for themselves, or developing their dream.

Didn't the Republicans and Pres. Bill already solve that problem in the 90s?

Oh yah, the DEMs are in-charge now, and they need troops of dependents, new victims, the disenfranchised, and more troops for Acorn!
That's why "The Left" has to be Rude, Crude, Lewd, sanctimonious, sycophantic bullies, and totally in-charge of the US Legal & Court Systems to get their agenda passed,

because the educated, and the more logical & normal silent-majority, would never agree to vote for any of "the Left's" recipes for Utopian tranquility; all living together, singing in harmony on this big planet in your Teepee, in the woods, smoking funny cigarettes, (well, let's just say the majority then),
but, just as long as the DEMs are running the show and making all of the decisions, and making all vital judgments for everyone. *Kum ba yah, my lord, Kum ba yah.*

It's reminiscent of the Russian Soviet Politburo,

and at the same time "The LEFT",
calling for civility and fairness from the Conservatives, to be non-judgmental,
the Republicans just sat there, sitting on their hands with their mouths agape, awestruck, stunned and shocked,
wondering what had just hit them, who must they have offended, oh my,
and what, for heaven's-sakes, had they done wrong! Isn't that right John, Arlen, Olympia?

SENTRYMAN

Again, the Blogger #1: DeLON366,
with his litany of clichés; "Bush doesn't have a clue or an education,
just blathering and seeking out his quarry:"

Blogger #2 -THNDRSHWR34;
"who is utilizing statistical facts, reasoned comparisons and justified outrage,
busily defending Bush and He or She will never bridge the divide."

SENTRYMAN "counters-back";

Correct, neither side can bridge the "fundamental differences", EVER!
It's all Right or Left,
Light and Shade,
Yin and Yang,
Masculine Vs Feminine......Dare I say: Right Vs Wrong?........
What's to agree on when Honor is a stake?.....Compromise = Dishonor!

Compromise what; half-truths, white-lies, kind 'a wrong, make-shift, adjunct, short-shrift, jerry-rigged, sort 'a pregnant?.....................

And that's all we've settled for, again and again for 60 long, too long years; its
 "all - shades - of - grey" , and what has it accomplished in all that time?

...What has it proven?...What have We become??...Shadows of our former selves???

Yes, that's exactly what it is,
as "The Left's" paragons and demagogues "chase Interns" around the Oval Office Desks
Or,
them using Actresses as toilet paper,
Or,
now, when a Man with no Bona-fides, or had been: "proven of under-fire" self- acclaim,
this "impartial" national Media *has doth ordained* today, quote;
 "is bigger than Geo. Washington, and the Presidency is a *step-down*",

I mean, are you freaking serious?....and what journalism school did you attend?

"for the Omnipotent One, trying to change the very foundations of this Judeo-Christian Free Democracy with his: handed-down God given Rights,

and with our freedoms loaned to our Government for safe keeping,
into some kind of quasi-socialist Marxist Commune,
handing-out Kool-aid to its devotees without question or answers,
and now promising to "only take control of the Banks" for a little while"....
(paraphrasing: Rush Limbaugh)

We're still paying Ma Bell taxes on the 1st Marconi telephones, and still have Pay-tolls on some interstate "Freeways",
and all the monies that were created by LOTTO, Mega-Ball, and Power-Ball for our Education systems disappear year, after year,
Horse-balls and hockey-pucks! .....Promises, Promises, Promises.

How many 1/2 cent, or one penny taxes have ever been rescinded,
much less having lowered the Gas Tax last summer for even a few crucial weeks, when we all could have used it, and really, really needed it?....Ha ha ha!....NEVER!

What a bunch of conniving, cheap silly asses Our US Representatives are, and we all sit there steaming, spinning our wheels, and take it, (up-the-tail-pipe, comics say),
again, and again on the chin, while our neighbors, friends and relatives file for bankruptcy,
and still we do nothing for ourselves, or to these dilatants, effete, imperious demons,
these bought-men, these "paid employees"!

We, the Taxpayers always have to sacrifice and tighten our belts, and cutback,
but has government ever (done with less) money, or lowered their own salaries
at 3:00 AM in the dim-lit hours of the morning, when they amazingly all show-up??

They screwed-up Ma Bell and fees went UP.
They screwed-up Cable-TV Fee-restrictions and fees went UP.
They did a great job missing the poisoned Peanut Butter for 2 years,
and can't even control the rampant pedophiles when "mandatory castration" nips that
problem in the butt, tomorrow, and little boys and girls bodies and minds are saved.
Nor can they deter Gangsters from stealing young girls that are disappearing everyday
over the US-Mexican Border, sold for sex-slaves and ransoms.

What the hell are these paid servants good for?

Boy, what if that was your daughter Salma, or Jennifer, or Mr. Spielsberg, or Mr. Hanks?
Oh sure, then there'd be an idle momentary pause in the transaction-traffic, till the
celebrity-factor had subsided, but the pain will never leave those parents from yesterday
and tomorrow when their children disappear!

Hey, Government Officials; Worry about something tangible, more realistic and important
to yourselves, and for the nation for a change!
Make some Real Changes for a change and Not lip-service from a liberal script to be
merely reelected!.........."TERM-LIMITS"
 WOULD SOLVE MUCH OF THIS YESTERDAY, TODAY and FOR TOMORROW!
..........WE NEED BETTER!.......and WE DON'T NEED YOU REPs ANYMORE!

No one can say a prayer in schools any longer, but if you're a Moslem child you can take
over the entire school with impunity. what...What...WHAT?

How about them cause-celeb Columbines, Mr. Moore?...That was a MATRIX Re-enactment
personified, Mr. Director-Goof! ...A HOLLYWOOD Generated Production by imbeciles,
NOT Society's ills, rather social-ilk!
Unless You're referring to Hollywood-High Society, but I digress!

Speaking about "Hick" Presidents, if anyone was the "Hillbilly" it wasn't the rich kid from
Texas. It was the poor kid from Arkansas, who became a multi-millionaire during his
"post"-presidency "Cash-in", filling his pockets currying favor giving special-insight to
literature-loving Arabs, writing plenty of donation checks for his library.

I thought Arkansas was ranked at the bottom, 50th, State in Education when your 1st Lady
packed her bags and left the Governor's mansion for Washington, so
 who's using his library now?.......Roger Clinton or Sandy Berger?

Sandy Berger stole every incriminating "classified" documents already, so it's not him!

Remember Bush was the one that entered the White House, black-haired and rich,
and left with white hair, tattered, torn and unappreciated.
And Thank you again, Mr. President!

Now, while the current occupant in the White House, with his personal posse's distain for
"whitey", and jokes about his Cocaine days, ole Barack closes the prison and exonerates
the Bad Guys.
(Is that Christian Forgiveness, or just Free the Moslem Brotherhood?)

That kind of convoluted logic in a Leader, juxtaposed to an admitted alcoholic with a proven, solid track record, a Leader that kept his nose to the grindstone and kept us all safely protected for the past 7 years, well, I guess we lucked-out with "The Right man at the Right time"!.......... I hope our Luck hasn't run out!

An Excellent Job Well Done,
right on the heels of the previous 8 years with continual attacks, culminating with 9/11, this guy gets saddled with a looming recession, the very worst national catastrophe since Pearl Harbor,
only to bring the country-back from the very edge, stronger, and better than ever to a very secure place for us, and with the lowest unemployment in 40 years,
and with the highest Dow ever,
and the lowest interest rates, and more Americans working than ever before, and all while absorbing an extra 40 million illegals that no one wants to deal with!

I CAN'T SAY IT OFTEN ENOUGH, BECAUSE OUR ELECTED REPUBLICANS CAN'T REMEMBER WHO THEY EVEN REPRESENT,
MUCH LESS REMIND AMERICANS WHO'S THE BEST, & LEAST APPRECIATED PRESIDENT IN THE LAST 100 YEARS, BESIDES TRUMAN!

***freeing 25 million slave-population in Iraq,

***providing more money for Africa than any government, or Rock Star in history,

***appropriating more money for education at large, for unbiased & ideologically-tendentious teachers to educate expectant illiterate charges, than any administration in US history, and it's still never enough,
and where 13 & 15 year-old adolescents are posting "real-time" sex on their Internet cell phones in school, while teachers abandon class-rooms for more important tasks.
The students must be read their diplomas by their parents, maybe why our student's international Science and Math Scores have plummeted.

Nice going teachers, terrific job "ultra-Liberal" NEA members. Are You effetes proud of that feat?....Look for the Union Label, the chant for a job well done in the '70s...no more!

No Conservatives stealing your thunder there. All those "accomplishments and stellar stats" you tenured have all earned on your own. With your very own abilities and professionalism for your craft, as it might as well be touted, no longer a Skill.

Just like the future US Economy and our Wars, they're all Obama's now, Baby!

I noticed Guantanamo isn't closed yet,
and the "Powers" created by Bush; for Wire Tapes & Surveillance, will be kept current in the Oval Office. Ha ha ha , and tee hee, hypocrite-fake!

SENTRYMAN

PS. I've never heard about it, and I apologize if I missed it,
but has any World Leader "ever asked" Moslems en masse, directed at Islam as a whole, with all due respect; if they've ever asked their brethren, or the deluded, radical Islamic minority, Terrorist Killers in their midst;

"Do You really believe there are gifts waiting in Heaven for <u>Taking A Life</u>"?

"Where do you think all these Virgins come from in Heaven?"

"Is there an unlimited supply of Virgins in Heaven?"

"What are you going to do once all 72 are no longer Virgins, and
you're stuck in Heaven with no way to get anymore Virgins?"

"What do you actually do with 72 Virgins?
Do you have to feed them all, get them new clothes all the time, get each a
car?"

"Do you know what it would be like with 72 women just looking to You for
their entire happiness, to solve all their problems,
and if all 72 were angry with you at the same time, what would you do
then?".....Hell might look pretty good after that!

"Did you ever hear the term "Kamikaze"?
Well, there's a good chance that those old World War II Japanese Pilots
beat you guys up there to the goods, when murdering for a God,
and all those Virgins might all speak Japanese by now!"

"Have you actually thought this through, young Mr. Terrorist,
because if you calm down, pray a while, and think on it, get an education,
get a real job,
then you get to buy new cars, and enjoy the newest music, and go dancing,
and laugh and play,
and have a family, and grandchildren for your parents, and all get to go to
Disney World and have a long fulfilling Life, for yourself and your kids.

Or,

Kill Yourself, and never see your parents again,
and just maybe there won't be enough, or even "any Virgins" waiting
when You get up there!!

Or just maybe, they'll only speak Japanese!!"

<u>SENTRYMAN</u>

 # Chapter 26

Barney Demands AIG "Bonus" Names,
Even Though Their Street Mob Wants Exec's Daughter By Her Throat
With Piano Wire!!!

Posted by SENTRYMAN on March 19, 2009 at 5:00pm

*Another On-Going Debate With My "Lib" Buddy;

He Contends:

"Yeah, I saw that live yesterday and agree with him.

We should all know who has "stolen" our money.
Didn't matter what Frank did anyway.... the N.Y. Attorney General already has got subpoenas for their names."

"Death threats, it comes with Public jobs and AIG is a Public company; now it's 80% owned by us."…. (Piano wire)

http://www.youtube.com/watch?v=zEZPSD3Xx_4

"Stop picking on ole Barney.... he's trying to get pot legalized on the Fed level, while several others are trying on the state level in CA.

It will save BILLIONS, plus bring in Billions via tax revenue, just like alcohol."

"Ultimately, that's "how the system works",
everyone in Government just out for their own districts in return for their votes are out for himself."

//

SENTRYMAN's retort;

that's "how the system works?," Shouldn't, it's all a rouse to gain control of private businesses by a certain political party in government,
and that's "Communism", and it's not how our capitalistic, free market, free-enterprise system works in our Free country!

After $11,000,000,000,000., that 11 Trillion buck$,
$PENT by guess whom?

No, it is the "Wa$ted, and $quandered, and mi$appropriated" since 1960, by their solid 33 years, totally in control of Congress, right up until 1994, and all to supposedly "eliminate" one big problem: Poverty!...............Who?

Promises, Promises!!

"The LEFT" of course, but You knew that,
and that's exactly what I think it really accomplished too, with their crocodile-tears, half-hearted, useless effort by just throwing money at the problem for decades = Pee Pee!

After all that time and money, THE Swells didn't solve it!............Did they?

Like a Saddam-For-Food Program, 33 years and $11 Trillion dollars, and the very same percentage of people are "supposedly still" looking for a job, or don't want to work, or can't work because they're homeless, or Bipolar, North Polar, Polar Bear,
or Global blah, blah, blah!

Probably just didn't have the basic skills necessary to obtain or retain any long-term employment ever, or even short-term, because they got a public school, new education?

Government has had one major task, duty, responsibility for 235 years: protect the borders, protect its citizens against all enemies, foreign and domestic, but.......
not run every aspect of our lives for us.....................Where'd that come from?

I don't remember checking that box when you "X" that extra dollar on your tax return to help the "whomever", or was that option on your driver's registration?
...Someone's always reaching into our pockets for something on a government form!!

Government can't do even (1) thing well,
besides, bomb people and break things, of course, (thanks, Rush)
and We aren't even allowed to do that correctly anymore, with this New Gang hold-up on Pennsylvania Ave., like the Clyde Barrow Gang either.

Think Universal Health Care is a "Right" of the American people, under the Constitution, or a gift, or even a necessity?...My wife and I pay $1000 @ mo. With 2x $5000. Deductables and we're healthy, and how many million poor legal citizens, including the 40 million illegals all get it for FREE???..........4T!

Universal Health is a Socialist ploy that will subjugate us, all of us, including health care providers,
and the doctors will now make monetary judgments on everyone's health.
Oh, and along with a Sick Czar, a Government Committee Master judging your health as to whether or NOT you can receive any particular operation,
and even judge whether to save your life; now based on your age, life expectancy,
probably your profession, if you're a LIB, and how many degrees away from Kevin Bacon, if You are over 50 years of age.....Think I saw that movie once?

If that's OK with you, Pal,
because they said You should be happy to save Your country that expense, money better spent on someone younger.....Think I saw that movie too, for the good of the Fatherland:
Deutschland, deutschland uber alles, la, la la!

Just go home and die, Citizen X, for the Fatherland, it's patriotic!
Wasn't that the Movie: Soylent Green?...... Because it wasn't Soy, buddy!

These geniuses, these financial experts, can't even run the Veteran's Administration well, with their dilapidated rat-infested hospitals for our "wonderful wounded veterans" in Washington, DC, and around the country,
nor have they correctly handled Medicare, or Medicaid, or SSI,
so WHY THE HELL is anyone entertaining, and buying into this lunacy, including our "less than insightful" Press, much less debating it for months? .... Incredible insanity!!

And now Obama this week wants our returning soldier's, presently covered under the military insurance, file their "own" personal health insurance to kick-in 1st on claims, if they have any coverage from Mom or Dad's, or from a spouse, in order to save the Government a supposed, or suspected, or a mythical projected $600 million dollars.
....Where do they come-up with this book-keeping malarkey?

Are you freak'n kidding me?
That Goof, Mr. President just gave FREE Tattoo-Removal in LA, and Prostitutes a housing stipend in San Francisco, by American Taxpayer's $300 million Tab last week!...Where do they get this goofy stuff from, and the Media ignores it for the most part. Thank you "Fox"!

Just wait till we're hit again, and the "All-Volunteer" Military doesn't want to volunteer to work for this guy anymore, but, of course they still would under those circumstances.

So let's say, Obama goes to Darfur in Africa like he said he would, to get in between Warring Tribes. Then enlistments-down because no one wants to "pay" for getting shot, on their parent's private health insurance, and, of course, He re-institutes the Draft, so now (government official's children and Hollywood's offspring) can all go defend the United States and the Constitution on foreign shores......"Great!"

I'm sure we won't hear any belly-aching from the "Left" then.
Susan Sarandon will drag her kids right down to the draft board to be 1st in line!

///

My "Lib" Buddy *states:*

"in return for their votes are out for himself"

SENTRYMAN's retort;

There you are 100% correct,

but spending Trillion$ using "markers" doesn't create jobs,
it buys people's souls once government pays us all, no one will ever vote otherwise,
then We're Lost!

I'm personally a bit Libertarian here,
as for legalized drugs and prostitution to brake the backs of drug lord's and gangster's, "bottom-line", "kill crime" for a change, instead of "the innocent",
and prevent young girls from being kidnapped and taken over southern borders as sex slaves, which is ongoing,
but ultimately it would probably destroy the country anyway so it's a toss-up,

and as your driving home late at night with 50% of the drivers coming at You
 in the opposite direction, that are chemically impaired,.......
but you're not worried about the "unintended consequences" I guess?

Few people rarely are today, so we get these overlapping, ever more complex and
compounded issues destroying the government and the nation, all with their good
intentions, and the (unintended consequences)....ENOUGH!

We pay these guys and they don't even bother to "Read the Fine Print", while
spending a Trillion freak'n Dollar$, so what do you expect?

AIG, what a joke!

They sent Billion$ of taxpayer bail-out money to "16 foreign banks", HELLO?
and BILLION$ in Bonuses went to Merrill Lynch, and Bank of America in 2008, HELLO?
and before the new February Cut-Off Line (that no one's worried about),

but Barney wants those Exec's names, right now, with His high and right-eous hand,
all the while he is stabbing Americans in the back with his Left!

I expect NOTHING GOOD from them, and wish we could "FIRE THEM ALL"
and start over with fresh minds and hearts, & "2 Term Limits" to begin with,
 but I digress.

Of course, if you are stoned too, you probably will not care,
because when You get to the hospital they're going to Euthanize You anyway....KARMA

That's what I've never understood about Liberalism, or Democrats for that matter,
They never deliver on any of the promises! ....I almost think that is by design.

The Democrats were the Plantation "Owners" remember,
so "the poor", and "the illegals", and "the disenfranchised",
 and lest we forget: "the downtrodden African-Americans", who've never had a break,
will all continue to buy into "IT",
and take their hand-outs, and the freebies, and keep-on voting for "The Man"!

But as Confucius said, paraphrased;
"give a man a fish he eats for the day,
teach a man to fish he never goes hungry!"

…..(He must have been a Conservative.)

THAT's THE DIFFERENCE BETWEEN Conservatives and Liberals,
but what's even worse is THAT I THINK THEY NOW IT, the same way the Communist
hierarchy knew: "they were taking the People for a Ride", and it was just a matter of time
before they'd figure it out, and the People finally did....Kaput!

I guess you and I will never agree here,
but I appreciate the sparring, keeps me current and sharp.

Talk later

Ps, Hunting down someone's children to extract a pound of flesh for the father's sins isn't justified under any circumstances, in any civilized society,
except for maybe the Mafia, Islamic Extremists, and your basic terrorist pogrom network.
With all due respect!!!

You know, like those stellar individuals that Obama doesn't want to offend, that either;
Bomb women, children, and the elderly,
Slice-Off heads,
Hang Bullet-riddled Incinerated bodies from bridges,
Steal females of all ages,
Steal young boys as work-slaves,

Sell and Manufacture Drugs to enslave the world's populations, just because they're bored with life, or had permissive parents and don't want to get a real job,
or had a Liberal education,

or "GOD told them to do it, or their Dog". Yeah, those Guys!

SENTRYMAN

----

2 COMMENTS

Comment by T M on March 19, 2009 at 8:55pm

Well, you have a few good points going there. . . but let's leave innocent piano wire out of it, OK?

Comment by SENTRYMAN on March 20, 2009 at 12:50am

I didn't make-up the piano wire reference so don't get on my case Pal,
watch this government Official's empathy in action:

Chapter 27

THIS IS HOW IT STARTED IN NAZI GERMANY.

Posted by SENTRYMAN on March 24, 2009 at 2:30am

http://www.nytimes.com/2009/03/22/us/politics/22regulate.html

"Administration Seeks Increase in Oversight of Executive Pay"

By STEPHEN LABATON
Published: New York TIMES, March 21, 2009

"The Obama administration will call for increased oversight of executive pay at all banks, Wall Street firms and possibly other companies
as part of a sweeping plan to overhaul financial regulation, Government officials said."

New York Times 3/21/2009

==

THIS IS HOW IT STARTED IN RUSSIA AND NAZI GERMANY.

[[[[[[[[[[[[---- "possibly other companies"? ----]]]]]]]]]]]]]]

IT'S RIGHT THERE FOLKS!....................ARE YOU LISTENING?

*Barack told (All of You) for 19 straight months, exactly what he was about to do to this country, and no one heard him, or really didn't want to hear
through all the hype of being "a 1st" for this and that,
and refused to LISTEN, nor probably believed this politician would actually be able to pull off what he said he was going to do,
to try and take over total control of every aspect of our lives.
They merely accepted this brash, unrealistic, and irrational "Feel Good" rhetoric,
(all Sugar and nice, and none of the Medicine spice),
as just that, a politician's boast!*

*Who believes politicians anyway, but here it is friends, an honest man!
He believed it, and he said it, and he meant it, and he's doing just what he promised,
so who is at fault?*

*That aside.
the Beginning Of The END Is CLOSE At HAND!!!*

Pg. 145

HIS GOVERNMENT WILL FINALLY RUN EVERYTHING FOR US, BUT AT THE EXPENSE OF TAKING IT ALL AWAY AT THE SAME TIME,

AND UNFORTUNATELY, AS WELL AS THEY'VE ADMINISTERED THE FASTEST
(REVERSAL AND THE COLLAPSE)
OF ANY ECONOMY OR ANY COUNTRY IN HUMAN HISTORY,
THAT A "PEARL HARBOR" AND A "9/11" TRIED TO DO, BUT COULDN'T,
THIS TIME IT'S THE EXCEPTION, A MALIGNANCY FROM WITHIN,
AND YOU CAN SAY GOOD-BYE TO YOUR CAPITALISM, YOUR FREE-ENTERPRISE,
AND YOUR DEMOCRACY....
YOUR FREEDOMS & "THAT" AMERICA, THE WORLD HAS KNOWN AND WE HAVE LOVED FOR 233 YEARS……………………………………GONE!

ELECTIONS CERTAINLY DO HAVE CONSEQUENCES!....HE SAID IT PLAIN: I WON !

Hear that?......Do You Hear That,
all you "Jay-Walkers", brilliant and insightful, pseudo-intellectuals, coolest people in the dorm, who also never heard of:
Karl Marx, or Paul Joseph Goebbels, or Communists, and National Socialists or Progressive Socialists, or even know the name of the current Vice President…..?

No, that (Marx) is not the brand name for a toy company, or one of the funny brothers, nor is (Goebbels) a small furry little rodent named Joey,
that's the VP!

**Today Geithner has called for "additional powers" at the Treasury Dept.,
so He can do a better job, (what's that, a guy on steroids asking for an energy drink)?

"A better job", with what, his own taxes?... Then He'll do "another job" on the American Economy,
and then He'll "take-out a contract" on American Private Business with "Resolution Authority" to intercede into the affairs of Private Company's inner sanctums', and that's even if they never had accepted any Government's Bail-Out Monies!
...That's the American Way, Tovarishch?

"additional powers", Is that an excuse, or a threat?
Sounds like "National Socialism" to me, Herr Geithner!

Pretty soon when inflation, deflation, stagflation, and bureaucratic flagellation hits,
we can use wheel barrel's of money to go buy bread and cheese at the market, like in 1930s Berlin.

Perhaps der Führer should promote Geithner to a "Feld Marshall",
He's already been made an Obergruppenfuhrer.
Sieg Heil B.O.

SENTRYMAN

==
http://news.yahoo.com/s/politico/20090322/pl_politico/20315/print

http://www.nytimes.com/2009/03/22/opinion/22rich.html

Chapter 28

"Billllions and Billllions of Stars": ....Dr. Carl Sagan

Posted by **SENTRYMAN** on **March 29, 2009** at 5:00pm

http://www.youtube.com/watch?v=5Ex__M-OwSA

I was thinking this morning as a "global warming" cold front swept over the nation, and a local downpour knocked out my Sunday morning satellite viewing of the secular, nonreligious, and socialist CBS "Sunday Morning", without Charles Kuralt,
of which,
and very soon, the "powers at be" will also usher in a new era of the government's absolute authority over another American Freedom: the public television airwaves....So much for free choice, sounds like Venezuela!

As if the government didn't already ration-out those freedoms as slim as they are,
thus relegating my emergency back-up portable TV, along with (milllions and milllions) of other's portables and vintage sets all over America to the trash heap from now on, totally restricted & obsolete,

and "who's" bright idea was this again?

Instead of THEM concentrating on,
oh let's say: "protecting Our Daughters and Sisters from being kidnapped and smuggled across the southern border to become Sex Slaves", and eventually die an early death of disease, drugs, and violence, for instance!
That just might be something for any government to focus on, instead of
diverting $600 Million Tax Dollars for "freebie coupons" and "Bribery incentives" to guarantee elections, for instance!

As a boy in the 50s one of my prize possessions was my (one of the 1st) fire engine red metal, little plug-in portable, 6" screen, black & white television set that I could carry with me anywhere, like; to school, when the teacher would let us watch a little of the (pre-steroids) World Series, or maybe it was the Play-Offs....Long time ago, I guess!

Anyway, that was when we valued the simpler things during simpler times.
And if I didn't have my TV with me, I had my tiny turquoise 7 transistor radio to listen to the game, which I carried that in an old (hollowed-out) book with the ear-piece wire up my sleeve....Remember "Knot-Hole" Day?
Today, they would carry Drugs and a Gun, or a Bomb in that fashion!

Do We Even Consider or Worry About That?....Not enough!

"Controlling Communication, the RADIO-WAVES", that will be next,

but that's for another rant.

Pg. 147

But now, as the "weak-minded" eagerly genuflect to their Masters in Washington, and they turn-off their Saturday Night Lights with revered homage to the "Green Gods,"
but (their Epiphany) is actually very expensive and counter-productive to the National & International Power Grinds, (unintended consequences as usual)
that must now really crank-up the Juice to over compensate during this foolish symbolic anomaly, we have all gone absolutely nutz, bonkers,
and I don't want to live here anymore.

This country sucks and I want to move to another planet because this used to be the best place to live on this planet,
 and now I've got to move to one of those billllions & billllions out there that Dr. Carl Sagan used to speak about so eloquently,
("A Billion Seconds ago", count'm,) on Johnny Carson's.

But, I won't be able to leave this earthy mortal-coil, because Barack is now cutting funding for OUR future Space Travel to those Billllions of stars,
opting instead to fund;
the Thousand's of Stars in Hollywood, and the Millions of Muslims poised to kill-us from around the globe, (harsh?...that's what they said they're going to do to the infidel! HELLO)

He will also the financing;
AmeriCorps, Census volunteers and ACORN sycophants,
that will scourer the countryside, traveling the bye-ways and back-roads like Jehovah's, searching for Noviciates, and turning them to the "Green-side!"
...Isn't that right Obi-Wan, or LEFT?

And just in time too, since Our new Global Currency won't be worth the Yellow Journalistic paper it will be printed on, and most likely won't really buy anything in the future anyway "that we're not allowed to buy", tricky!
Nor will this new funny money preserve any of Our Freedoms or Our Sovereignty, while the U. N. feeds its insatiable appetite on our carcass, and plots, armed with Barack's "Collectivism" to cut up this country like a Butcher Beef-Cutting Chart,

The last of the America's taxpayer's "Greenbacks," (no Pun intended) will be replaced by their GLOBO-Dollar, "G-D" Dollar, (Pun Intended),
and will be fueling their incredible egos to empower the Laying-On-Of-Hands upon "Mother Nature", all for their own designs........ HALLELUJAH,

I am feel'n-tha Spirit to;
*conquer the Sun and quiet the volcanoes,
*hold back the tides and perfect the storms,
*shackle the winds and be still the hurricanes,
*harness the tornados and ah, ah, ah,
*change the course of the Mississippi, and Red Rivers,

all derived from a pretentious presumption that only "THEY" possess the intellect and wisdom, endowed by the Divine Right of Kings as they place the Crown upon their own heads,
with enough "good intention", yah, that's it, all they've got: "good intention", perhaps, but it'll be enough to enslave a nation and for their own prosperity!
.....And that's what we're told, paddled, and sent to bed without supper since they've cleaned out the cupboard beforehand, but who's watching?

Certainly not our Watch-dog Media. Huh!

For People That Despise and Challenge Church & STATE, they're awfully Reverent and Apostolical in their Deliverance, (Pun Intended),

so just check your common sense and intelligence at the door,
like most of the Journalism professionals from around the Globe today. Step-up
and submit to the Jim Jones on Pennsylvania Avenue; the junior Senator from Illinois,
that has never accomplished anything tangible!

Oh, sorry, other than;
*getting someone else to pay for his extremely expensive education,
*arranged to clear the election-field, and scuttle any opponents he's ever run against,
*Ghostwritten his own 2 books, and (He ain't the Ghost),
*funneled money to his Slumlord buddy and neighbor, that subsidized his mortgage and
gave him ½ of his manse side yard gratis, and (not to play sand-lot ball)
*created a BS job that overpaid his wife for another quid-pro-quo,
*and profligated devotee's to donate to: "His Cause",
"So I've Heard!"?,,,,,,,,

The "smartest guy in the Federal government",
Who's Been Instructed On Exactly How, and When, and What to Say on His TelePrompTer,
.......But by Whom?

At least, "From What I Understand"........
and it's, "Only My Opinion".........
as, I hide in my basement from real enemies, foreign and domestic!

Maybe it begins with an "S",
and coincidentally is one of only a very few fortunate people to amazingly "make a lot of
money" this past year, and without THE Bailout?.....Hmmmm

Yep, I don't want to be here anymore, just like in the movies;
"Fahrenheit 451, The Postman, The Omega Man, Planet of the Apes, The Last Man On
Earth, I Am Legend."
the deck "stacked" and surrounded by ghouls, half-wits, slackards, thieves and demons,
and all other kind of Liberal.

Well, you get the point, and I bet you could come up with some examples and illustrations
of your own, but,
like those Sci-fi movies of the '50s
there are probably even bigger A-Holes waiting for us all Out-There on some of those
Billllions & Billllions of planets anyway,
and they would undoubtedly "Tax Us" too, (an arm and a leg at a time), literally, probably
for our Oxygen!....maybe even Green House Gases, now wouldn't that be fortuitous!

Hey, there's an idea for the future, Barack.
Squirrel that one away in that cash-register mind of yours, for another day.

So, here we sit in the dark, no electric, no TV, no heat, huddled together, shivering
frightened little bunnies,
making the extremists and environmentalists in our government extremely happy,
just sitting around (making gaseous, environmentally unfriendly rabbits),
 since abstinence,
(so we've been told many, many times by our captors, and educators)
that just doesn't work to curb AIDS, or STDs, or Unwanted Pregnancies,
and those forest floor leaves just don't function as well for contraception.

All we'll have left in our new nature-balanced natural world we all must share and live-in, are those old "Chinese-made" condoms. Unfortunately, the Lead in most Chinese products does give a certain necessary firmness! (Pun Intended)

So let's see now,
we are afraid of the food, over-seen by our government peanut-brained inspectors, (bureaucrats assured will solve everything).
We are afraid of the air, thanks to our government dictating 16 unnecessary blends of gasoline that (bureaucrats assured would solve everything),
because, if you remember, we were assured EVERY ENVIRONMENTAL PROBLEM would to be totally eliminated by the sainted "catalytic convertor", (bureaucrats emphatically assured would solve everything.)

Next on the horizon was overly-expensive Green-fuels (bureaucrats again assured, will no-doubt solve everything), but depleted our food supplies and raised our food prices again, and also, not to forget, all those wonderful tree saving plastic containers, (bureaucrats really assured will solve everything), that convey $12.00 per gallon free-water,
and those (bureaucrats assured would solve everything) smokestack-caps,
and those (bureaucrats assured would solve everything) phantom Carbon-Credits.

All those faaabbulous solutions that (bureaucrats once assured would finally solve every) "imperative issue" of our times by their vast wisdom and oversight), thank God, no, we should squarely-thank the ones most responsible, giving credit to Caesar!

But fatefully, we're still afraid of too much coffee, not enough coffee, aspirin, not enough aspirin, mega-vitamins, unregulated vitamins.
Plus we're afraid of pesticides in foods, but not enough pesticides in foods shipped from South America, or the Far-East apparently,
or antibiotics in the food, and in our livestock,
and then into our water supply and into our children,
and all of our (PROTECTED by our government's miraculous intuitive SUPER-VISION) that (will solve everything)!.....thank you Caesar!

But, but, wait, I forgot we weren't afraid of peanut butter (protected by our government's oversight), but "now" we are afraid of peanut butter (ONLY inside the USA?),
 but not from outside the USA,
and we are afraid of frozen hamburgers that are (protected with our government's oversight), oh my God I'm getting dizzy!

Geez, I forget to be afraid of 2nd & 3rd hand smoke,
(that would include someone who either grew-up around, or knew someone that smoked at one time, or who's children once viewed someone smoking in an old magazine ad and incredibly comes down with a cancer....Attorneys love that one),
but those fatally-poisoning Toxins contained in "Botox" botulism-shots injected directly into the human body, in the head, close to the brain,
that's No Probleme'!

We're afraid of; EMFs, carpal-tunnel, Texting, bovine craziness, vegan-impotence, rock-n-roll, rap music, and even afraid of our Conservative neighbors "next door", Oooooo!
But, with "your Vote for Democrats", our government's miraculous "oversight-protection" (will solve everything)!

SO, THEN WHY ARE WE ALL SO AFRAID?
BUT, NOT AFRAID OF "THE GOVERNMENT", THAT HAS "NEVER CAPABLE" ENOUGH

TO EVER PROTECT US FROM ANYTHING?

Well, I'M ASK'N YOU LEFTISTS.............Well, Do Ya Punk?

But Ooooo,
we sure love, and we do trust, and we blindly obey the Wizards in Washington,
but of course, just as long as the Democrats are in power and are RUNNING EVERYTHING,
yah, as smoothly as in 2007 and 2008.

Yah, Those Democrats, who never make mistakes, or would ever go against the will of the
people, and always do "ev-er-y-thing" according to the rules,
 and "The Constitution" of the United States of America….. DON'T THEY??????????????

They do, don't they?

We Are All So Fortunate and So, So Lucky To Be So Absolutely Protected By A Wonderful,
and Infinitely Infallible Government,
 Who's "_Neutering_" Oversight (Will Solve Everything)!....Oh, sorry. I meant nurturing?

And why,
because most elected officials are Attorneys, (that might be a Red Flag),
who all swore-an-oath, and placed their hands on "The Bible",
that apparently few either respect, or believe-in since most don't defend "It", or defend our
history, or defend our heritage, our ceremony, our tradition, our goodness,
or, for that matter, any common sense, or sanity, or a profound grasp of Reality…..

Nor do our Representatives "defend the Will" of 85+% of America that would definitely
appreciate our Government Legislators, (government lawyers), the 3 atheists, and that guy
that doesn't like Christmas, to just finally Shut-Up and drop-it!
Please stop meddling in our lives, leave us alone, and let us live our lives in peace, and
stop asking us for money, and when we say: "NO"
don't go into our wallets and purses and steal our credit cards!.....How freak'n hard is that
to understand?

Yah, You guys: LAWyers,
OUR KEEPERS, OUR JAILERS, UBER-GRABBERS.

Our current government is kind of like a sick-minded adolescent, hopped-up on drugs,
drunk on perceived power, stealing the keys to the car and driving 120 mph down the
highway in the wrong direction,
tool'n-down the Coast Highway, Texting Twitter, eating an Un-Vegan greasy-burger,

headed for the big curve, with rocks & mid-air to either side, we all know this ain't going to
be pretty or end well,
and what's playing in their heads: "Bush is an idiot - Bush is an idiot,

So, what are we to do with these peevish petulant petty civil-servants?

Choose: "Communism over Islam", "Collectivism or Totalitarianism"
Some choices, 2 sides of the same coin, and neither represent the People,
or capitalism, free enterprise, liberty, freedom or America!

Did any of You Drama or Liberal Arts students every take any History or Econ. Classes, aside from Sociology, Women's Studies, Ethnic Empowerment and the Beatles-101 ?

Oops, I forgot who'd be teaching those class, anyway....forget I asked that question. Dissent, open debate, contrary opinion shall not be considered or voiced aloud, and is banned at Columbia!............"Workers Unite, power to the people" blah, blah!

Patience, and progressive Incrementalism got them here without a shot fired, and yes, along with willing coconspirators: Supreme Court, and your Guns are the next thing "They'll be coming for".

Funny, for people that do not honor "The Constitution", they surely utilize "the Law" when and where necessary to steal, undermine, and usurp our once representative-government, and this nation.
I believe that was the underlying premise of "The Judgment at Nuremberg," but some would say today that the "wrong guys" were Sitting-on-the-Bench (back them), and they live in the 57 States today!

Bad Boys, Bad Boys, what'cha gonna do, what'cha gonna do when they come for you, and you haven't any ammunition left, because they've outlawed it, since they couldn't get Your Guns......YET?....bad boys, bad boys, what'cha gonna do?

Yes, Virginia;
Elections Do Have Incremental -Consequences! ...."Eminent Domain," what's next???

I rest my case, Your Honors!

VOTE CONSERVATIVE,,,,,,,,,,NEXT TIME!

I won't tell.

SENTRYMAN

---

3 COMMENTS

Comment by Nancy on March 29, 2009 at 5:30pm
That is a great article.

Comment by SENTRYMAN on March 29, 2009 at 5:37pm

Thanks, I added the part about;
"So I Hear",,,,,,,,"From What I Understand"........"Only My Opinion".........
so I wouldn't have someone arrest me, be the only non-Muslim at Guantanamo, and they take my children away because the 1st Amendment is DEAD in America!

You have a nice day.
SENTRYMAN
--- ----

"Aide toy, Dieu te aidera". = "Help yourself and God will help you" –

the medieval French equivalent of:
" God helps those who help themselves"

Patrick Henry - May 1765, _____ (paraphrased w/artistic license in March 2009)

"Caesar had his Brutus -

Charles the First, his Cromwell -

George W., the 4th Estate

and Barack Hussein Obama - ('Treason,' cried the Speaker)
... may profit by their example.

If this be treason, make the most of it."

Patrick Henry - March 23, 1775
"I know not what course others may take; but as for me, give me liberty, or give me death!"

"Me donner la Liberté Ou Me Donne Mort."
Patrick Henry, le 23 mars, 1775

Maximilien Robespierre 1758 - 1794
April 24, 1793 - Declaration des droits de l'homme

"Any law which violates the inalienable rights of man is essentially unjust and tyrannical; it is not a law"

"Any institution which does not suppose the people good, and the magistrate corruptible, is evil."

SENTRYMAN

God and everything else
http://www.youtube.com/watch?v=HKQQAv5svkk

Carl Sagan, Stephen Hawking and Arthur C. Clarke - God
https://www.youtube.com/watch?v=HKQQAv5svkk

One of Carl Sagan's most pertinent messages for humanity
http://www.youtube.com/watch?v=hLkC7ralR30&feature=related

COSMOS
https://www.youtube.com/results?search_query=cosmos

 **Chapter 29**

Glenn Beck, Bill O'Reilly;
"Stop using Bush and Obama in the same sentence"!

Posted by SENTRYMAN on April 15, 2009 at 11:30am

Hey, Glenn Beck and Bill O'Reilly,
stop using George W. Bush and Barack Hussein Obama in the same sentence,
just to be "Fair & Balanced", Even Handed, Nonpartisan, etc., etc., when
criticizing "both" of them for spending Trillions of our tax dollars.

Bush "had" to spent $350 Billion, I might add "on His way out the door",
in another selfless act to protect OUR country, to prop-up the US economy from collapse
and the United States government from a total implosion,
(and it worked)!!!

But, Obama, in just 2 months has spent "TRILLIONS", with an "S",
 to prop-up the DEMOCRAT's All-Time "WISH LIST", and for their willing accomplices in
government, industry, finance, business and foreign governments, and while in the act of
World benefactor,
Barack's tried to expand his government's control of US "Private Enterprise", all under the
guise of: "We know what's best for You, dear"!

(Plus, Barack's refusing to allow any "Bail-out" recipients, or states' government, who
finally "Get-It" after re-considering the long term consequences,
 and thinking better on the mass-thievery, to reject their endowment, or return their ill-
gotten gains).

YET, OBAMA STILL CONTINUES TO SPEND BILLION$, & TRILLION$ MORE OF OUR
CHILDREN's FUTURES,
IN COMPARISON TO PRESIDENT BUSH'S "ONE LAST STAND" ACT IN DESPIRATION TO
HOLD THE UNION TOGETHER!.............FOOLS.
Got it.....got it?   Good Boys!

And, by the way as you're GENERALIZING;
A. Bush's White House = (Bush & Staff)
B. Bush's Administration = (Leftist enemies at Justice, State, Pentagon, and career
employees in the remainder of all government agencies,) and
C. Bush's Party = (Republicans, RINOs inc.,)

These 3 "BLAME BUSH" are all separate entities like "A TRINITY", and even different from:

D. "The Government," (Legislative & Judicial),
which has its own problems during any one President's administration, but George Bush
personally, (unequally and unjustly) takes "all the fire" for each of them; working counter,
independent and autonomously against Him, He took the hit for all (4), by the ill-informed,
inattentive, manipulated public, when just given all the $#!% about each, and none of any
credit deserved from a consummate "Media" elite!
So lay blame at the Right-Feet boys! Pg. 154

The simple reality and the TRUTH to remember is,
the latter (3) sections of the US Government: Served Him Not!

Barack on the other hand, has the sheer luxury to not accept, take, or assume any
responsibility for any actions, any events, any situations, or any consequences at all
for His government while on His watch fortunately, tee-hee, ha-ha, ho-ho,
and a big Razzzberry: it's also Bush's fault!.... And will continue to be for the next 8 years!

One fatal mistake made by Bush though instead of "cleaning house" on his Day #1,
much like the advanced "Clinton Policy": "Hillary takes No prisoners" Clean Sweep as
THEY unpacked their bags, No Pun Intended,
the Bush Administration was filled with old Clintonistas', Democrat hold-overs, career
Liberals, and plenty of PO-LI-TI-CI-AN-S, (all of whom had their own agendas),
and Bush got pilloried and hung-out-to-dry because he merely wished to ferret-out a few
Mole-Attorneys, and only toward the end of his administration tenure,
which was His right, but Who-Cares what's right, certainly Not the Courts or The Law!

"Such was the discretion of the Presidency when Clinton fired over 90 Attorneys currently
working at that time at his inauguration, and not an indignant-peep from any of the Media
Cluckers!"....that's "CI"!

George W. Bush served the American people!
George W. Bush's "Administration" Served Themselves, including; e.g.
FAA screeners that didn't pick-out any of the High-Jackers on the Watch LISTs on 9/11,
the FBI, with their hands-tied behind Jamie Gurlic's Wall, with their thumbs up their____,
the CIA, when reporting pending Armageddon with Saddam's WMDs, gave little choice,
All Of Whom Had Served Their Previous Master: Bill Clinton, went back to SLEEPER mode
but 9/11 happened and on Bush's Watch, and with George's stalled Cabinet appointments
Not-Yet totally up to speed, (Thank You Democrat Obstructionists In The Congress),
it's was now "Bush's fault", and He takes the Hit!

We had enjoyed 25 years of prosperity created by lowering Taxes and "Peace through
Strength" under the Republican, President Reagan, for which Clinton handsomely
benefited and liberally took undeserved and squandered credit constantly.

But, did anyone pat Bush on the back for all those wonderful and supremely-trained
"volunteer" service men & women, valiantly serving around the globe, and in two war
theaters created while under his administration, with required funding that Bush had to go
begging, hat-in-hand to Congress continually,
or kudos for that crackerjack SEAL-Team trained while Bush-at-the-helm, that performed
so remarkably when rescuing a Boat Captain in the Indian Ocean?????.......Nope!....

That of course, was a Master Stroke of the new rookie-President, former rookie-Senator
Barrack Hussein Obama, that "would" have cut our military anytime in the past,
and now "will" Cut The Military!.....Many Kudos bestowed upon him, our warrior President!

We waged other wars half-heartedly to mixed revues,
but then an imperative: war in Iraq "on the cheap", and we were incredibly victorious in
only 3 weeks with fewer than 100 brave men lost.
A Mission accomplished????.................damn straight!!!!!

A feat, never before achieved in history in the defense of Freedom and perhaps never
duplicated.
A Mission very "accomplished", but invariably, inexorably most definitely denied
by our own stalwart MEDIA, as they mocked and cajoled the Cowboy President.

The Cleanup, ahhh yes, unaided and all but alone, save our Anglo-American/English speaking brethren, three long years later still mopping-up, always "on the cheap", a major obstacle of opposition: leader Harry Reed, "calls the game - Kaput", and throws–in–the-towel on account of a lack of Enthusiasm from the Home Team; a failure, lost, a disaster without resolve, and "just as the patient is finally being resuscitated" and brought back from the dead. Piffle!...I have better adjectives for traitor.

That's just how things work out in Life!
Like an unfortunate few rotten-apple Abu Grebe assigned soldiers, slinking around in anyone's Army, becomes the DEM's chosen poster-children for a ineffective, inefficient and a poorly managed Republican-Military!

But, had it happened during Clinton's watch, oh, well then; "it's Not the President's Policy" and "it's Not the President's fault that a few bad apples pop-up in thousands of human beings anywhere", but again,
"human nature" so easily becomes Liberal-fodder to crucify their opposition by the un-objective? MEDIA, (with their heads so far up one parties backside, with their vision so obscured, any opposition now looks like Nazis, extremists and Terrorists, yet remember, these are our children, our citizens, our neighbors, our fellow Americans.

<u>Question:</u>
Did anyone ever check when "those soldiers" who committed the Abu Grebe high-jinks enlisted into the service?.....Small-Point....Wondered if they might have joined during Clinton's watch, not that it would be germane to this discussion, but all the same Bush always takes the Hit no-matter, but it would be interesting!

So, Bush's White House went home!

But, but, but friends, Beck, O'Reilly,
Bush's administration and all the "same players" are still right there in Washington, ensconced in The Justice Dept., in The State Dept., in The Treasury Dept., in The Pentagon and in The Congress, and were they or weren't they serving their president, Bush, or are they, were they serving Barack and Clinton?........But, but It's allllllllll Bush's Fault! RIGHT?

Miraculously though;
Now The Government is apparently "Clean and Righteous", and "Pure and Cool", and ALL "on the same Team" again……..

But hey, "they're all the same guys"!......HELLO?

<u>You think long and hard about that</u>…..Do I need to repeat it, again??...I think not.

If You didn't like Bush, if You didn't vote for Bush, if you hated, and still hate Bush, and I'm whispering here: don't tell anyone in the Media or Hollywood, but
 "<u>Those Same Crooks Are Still Running The Show</u>"!!!

<u>SENTRYMAN</u>

3 COMMENTS

Comment by Mary on April 15, 2009 at 2:07pm

Go Sentryman!

Comment by Deb on April 15, 2009 at 12:16pm

George Bush is a good man and was a good president in my opinion. With all the crisis he handled while in the White House, he still kept his dignity and faith. I believe an honest historian will find that his record in office is something we should be proud of. He kept us safe and if Congress had followed his lead when it came to reining in Fannie Mae and Freddy Mac, we wouldn't have the economic situation we have today.
God bless the Bush family!!!!

 **Comment by SENTRYMAN on April 16, 2009 at 3:02pm**

That's Right Deb;

More importantly,
if Congress followed Bush's lead when it came to reining in Islamic Terrorism "we would have won the Iraq War years ago", along with Afghanistan, and 1000s of our dead-brave soldiers "would be alive today", at home with their wives, children and families, and enjoying the fruits of their labors of our America's Freedoms they all fought and ultimately sacrificed their lives for!

"Their Blood is on the hands" of every human, American and foreign, that did not support Our Country, Our Soldiers and their President.

Look around, where are They today?
All hiding at the Treasury Dept. opening our checks on April 15th, during America's Tea Party, while there's (little gatherings) in 700+ cities across the nation that the White House "isn't" aware of,
but Obama's Security-Forces have labeled: "Extremists and domestic TERRORISTS."

"Long Live The King", that's Martin Luther,
Not the fraud in the White House!

SENTRYMAN

 **Chapter 30**

25 VIDEOs that may change the way You See The World!

Posted by **SENTRYMAN** on <u>May 1, 2009</u> at 11:30am

What do voters expect of their president?
http://www.youtube.com/watch?v=P36x8rTb3jl

Are voters well enough informed to make an intelligent, qualified Vote for the Leader of the Free World?
http://www.youtube.com/watch?v=mm1KOBMg1Y8

What happened to the Economy when the DEMs took over House & Senate at the end of '06.....
Were the DEMs protecting the citizens from Fannie/Freddie collapse?
http://www.youtube.com/watch?v=Unj-kcGOe5l

Bush gets blame! Barney Frank denies any responsibility.
What did He think & is he lying??
http://www.youtube.com/watch?v=iW5qKYfqALE

What do some world leaders think about Barack Obama?
http://www.youtube.com/watch?v=qOu-3dDQuac

Is Obama patriotic?
http://www.youtube.com/watch?v=hU9iCANi02o

How many states are in the USA......5th graders, or a Freudian slip?
There are 57 Islamic states!
http://www.youtube.com/watch?v=LuZ_5OhWhQ0

Is Obama Christian or Moslem?
http://www.youtube.com/watch?v=tCAffMSWSzY&feature=related

(guess not)
http://www.youtube.com/watch?v=0GFKqOf8EHQ

Pg. 158

VP Biden on: "Why is Obama more qualified".
http://www.youtube.com/watch?v=RDVUPqoowf8

The Greatest Orator in America Today;
http://www.youtube.com/watch?v=MyW9e5QdWxk

https://www.youtube.com/watch?v=IR5sSSqbo_s

https://www.youtube.com/watch?v=rQaJmDUN4BE

https://www.youtube.com/watch?v=eDJSVPAx8xc&feature=related

Thomas Paine: We The People: Stimulus Package
http://www.youtube.com/watch?v=jeYscnFpEyA&NR=1

THOMAS PAINE: The Second American Revolution
http://www.youtube.com/watch?v=pKFKGrmsBDk

Stimulus Package Help On The Way: "WHITES" NEED NOT APPLY
http://www.youtube.com/watch?v=nT1TkLgfinE&feature=related

Signs of Hope?
A Grass Roots: "Boston Tea Party" styled Tax Revolts for every 20 yr. old paying back the $114,000 "Interest Only" just on the new Debt during their lifetime, and Nothing on the Principle yet....Let will be their children's, children's problem!
http://www.youtube.com/watch?v=mo-Y7SStoF4&NR=1

"We are NOT a Christian nation!"
http://www.youtube.com/watch?v=AYL7gboYogo

"Barack Obama - Still Holds Muslim Beliefs"
https://www.youtube.com/watch?v=bdtirp4XdGs

Major Religious Traditions in the U.S.

Among all adults	%
Christians	**78.4**
Protestant	51.3
Evangelical churches	26.3
Mainline churches	18.1
Hist. black churches	6.9
Catholic	23.9
Mormon	1.7
Jehovah's Witness	0.7
Orthodox	0.6
Greek	<0.3
Russian	<0.3
Other	<0.3
Other Christian	0.3
Other Religions	**4.7**
Jewish	**1.7**
Reform	0.7
Conservative	0.5
Orthodox	<0.3
Other	0.3
Buddhist	0.7
Zen Buddhist	<0.3
Theravada Buddhist	<0.3
Tibetan Buddhist	<0.3
Other	0.3
Muslim*	**0.6**
Sunni	0.3
Shia	<0.3
Other	<0.3
Hindu	0.4
Other world rel.	<0.3
Other faiths	1.2
Unitarians and other liberal faiths	0.7
New Age	0.4
Native American rel.	<0.3
Unaffiliated	**16.1**
Atheist	1.6
Agnostic	2.4
Nothing in particular	12.1
Secular unaffiliated	6.3
Religious unaffiliated	5.8
Don't Know/Refused	**0.8**
	100%

Due to rounding, figures may not add to 100 and nested figures may not add to the subtotal indicated. * From "Muslim Americans: Middle Class & mostly mainstream."
Pew research center 2007   **Pg. 160**

http://www.youtube.com/watch?v=bdtirp4XdGs

"We will never be at WAR with Islam!"
http://www.youtube.com/watch?v=Z0QihHG8pus&feature=related

----

the Final 8 *are an examination of what America is up against in a fragile world, by Muslim Scholars that see the Quran (Koran) as being co-opted and perverted by sinister forces for nefarious purposes.*

"Some violent and Adult Content below"
**YouTube Videos will continue to be blocked, for whatever politically-correct excuse, but I will endeavor to find copies and reestablish them at:
http://www.sentryman.org/id8.html

#1- "100% Islam needs killing to enter Heaven", Part I
(expect a brief religious Ad during video)
http://www.youtube.com/watch?v=dJop2JkDTvw&list=PL2A849A87AADAAD69

Walid Shoebat Prophecy 101, Islam and Satan 01
http://www.youtube.com/watch?v=BD_N9t2j9jg

http://www.youtube.com/watch?v=PunDPRLnx08

#2- "Sexual Relations with Young Girls While Fasting in Islam"
http://www.youtube.com/watch?v=2t3vfDhPTIk&feature=related

#3- "100% Islam To Rule The World", Part II
http://www.youtube.com/watch?v=PunDPRLnx08

4- Who is ALLAH?
https://www.youtube.com/watch?v=eFMfViDLoEc

#5- Women have new responsibilities in Islam (1 of 2)
http://www.youtube.com/watch?v=c2AAu09xOGw&feature=related
Interview with Ex-Islamic Terrorist Walid Shoebat (1 of 2)   Pg. 161

#6- Ex-Islamic Terrorist Walid Shoebat: "Just Stop Buying Oil" (2 of 2)
http://www.youtube.com/watch?v=KC8VNZzp9Ps&NR=1

#7- *** What is the Truth?*** (Myth or Takia?)
http://www.youtube.com/watch?v=DFX9HHBqb2k

#8- The Angels Of Death….
Geez, they never taught that in my school!
http://www.youtube.com/watch?v=7atc7_Wg1lc

NEWLY ADDED FOR THIS BOOK -------3-25-2010 ------------------

C - Thomas Paine – "Open Letter to President Obama"
http://www.youtube.com/watch?v=xxDwBYjL3Fc

D - Thomas Paine – "The Broken Common Bond"
http://www.youtube.com/watch?v=Ri1b8j8gG5A

----

http://www.youtube.com/watch?v=3Wx3wkgZuf0
Pay very special attention today and every day that we don't go back to sleep again, like the world did in the 1940s, or this can happen again, even to You!
http://www.youtube.com/results?search_query=Night+and+Fog+Rare+Holocaust+Footage+&oq=Night+and+Fog+Rare+Holocaust+Footage+&gs_l=youtube.12...856662.856662.0.858351.1.1.0.0.0.0.64.64.1.1.0...0.0...1ac..11.youtube.h1XEcCw5UnQ

SNOW COMES EARLY THIS YEAR!
http://www.youtube.com/watch?v=hrxA2OcKYJc&feature=related

http://www.youtube.com/watch?v=g89rz7Za4qs&feature=related

http://www.youtube.com/watch?v=3pD4V7v6ZVc&feature=fvwrel

An Alfred Hitchcock documentary on the Nazi Holocaust
http://www.youtube.com/watch?v=PaR3qud2-e8

http://www.youtube.com/results?search_query=unseen%20alfred%20hitchcock%20holocaust%20documentary%20&sm=1

http://www.youtube.com/watch?v=482PsMEM_DI

 **Chapter 31**

NEWT & SARAH in 2012 ....beauty & brains = VICTORY!

Posted by SENTRYMAN on May 8, 2009 at 8:04pm

Email To: The O'Reilly Factor;

"TOO BAD FOR AMERICA IT COULDN'T BE IN 2010...
2012 may be too late!!

Ps, Bill, you just don't understand that "Romney scream'n, run'n Bear"
Video!

Bill, it was just Sarah saving another hapless Republican!"

SENTRYMAN
May 6, 2009

===
additional comments by SENTRYMAN to a skeptical blogger a day later:

Truth and opinion are not mutually exclusive, each valid but separate, one does not void
the other, yet TRUTH is still the truth,
and though we are all sinners in someone's eyes, non-believers alike, opinion does not
hold weight over the other...............a Yin and Yang, hanging in the balance, each needs
the other to validate itself.

The Real Question facing the GOP is:
"What do we need to do to save the Union, and to protect our children, and to win the
Prize, but with Honor?

Create another facade, another shill, another Robert Redford in "The Candidate" to fool'em
another time? ...Is that what we need, what the American people needs, Our own Obama,
or must We find a Saint since they already found The Savior?

Well, "Judge Not" and "Cast the first stone, etc.!"

None exists people, nor has for 2000 years,
and if one did, they certainly couldn't win today against the Media's "Wall of Jericho"
anyway,
and we don't need to fool'm, never did!!......We have enough trouble just trying to wake-
people-up to pay attention without any Smoke & Mirrors, Pomp & Circumstance, to just be
Circumspect!! **Pg. 163**

Most of all I am extremely tired of these unwholesome, contaminated yellow-journalists "destroying the Messengers" to Diminish the Messages, instead of standing up for TRUTH, thus compromising their own professional integrity "for-cheap", to just patronizing idealistic, know-nothing Starlets in their "15 minutes" reality society.

Even when descending upon a simple beauty queen and a young mother who's preaching faith and abstinence to somehow affect change; diminish or alter her message, and sabotage, nullify, eradicate and exterminate the Prize: Personal Freedom, Freedom of Speech, Freedom of Religion, Freedom to Assemble. The ultimate Prize: FREEDOM!

An "inalienable right" of voicing what you believe without fear of arrest, reprisal, personal destruction, or having the SNL set-you-up, and David Letterman paint a bulls-eye on your forehead, and finally Bill Maher stabs-you squarely in your back = The Liberal Trinity.

Focus People, burning Joan didn't change the message!
You can't silence the Truth forever, it always manages to find a way to seek-out sunlight.

Let US all just stop playing to the idiots in the gallery!

If we played to the "smarter ones" among us, instead of "bringing all down", just to be fair and inclusive, while honoring the mediocrity and the mundane, much more of us would desire to raise themselves above, and strive for excellence instead!.............Hey Liberals, look upon learning and not repeating the ills of historical tyranny. True freedom and free enterprise, like dance, You learn to not make the same mistakes, repeat only the best and start from there to new heights.
You must put in the work yourself with a first step, fall on your own, pick yourself-up and earn your craft, perfect your skill, be the best you can be to reap the rewards.

If you cook or clean, create or teach, build or maintain, protect and serve, we earn our own way, we do it for ourselves, we do it on our own, and only in the "only country" that allows us to do anything we wish, because of "those who came before us, and died to preserve that right" for all who would follow!

And while you're pursuing what you "freely wish" to achieve, appreciate and thank the ones (outside in the cold and dark, protecting your opportunity), and pay due homage and never forget, because without them someday you too might find yourself showering in a gas chamber, or thrown into a mass grave, still alive.
But I digress.

In 2010 "dumbed-down" Americans, who are no longer taught to learn, think or know, will blindly and obediently follow false prophets, and ACORN, and the 49.9% other Lemming government subsidized voters, just as they did in the once powerful, now collapsed Soviet U-N-I-O-N, where "everyone" was either: "On the Take" or "On The Dole", or Both,
gave up their freedoms by giving away their souls,
but that is always "The Plan."

If the inane citizen doesn't have the acumen to "see", or to understand, in order to appreciate what a simple man like George Bush was trying to do,
or open one's eyes to what has been happening to this nation just since the DEMs took control in 2006,
or what a TRILLLLION DOLLAR YEARLY DEFICIT will actually do to themselves, to their children, to their country and to our future way of life,
well, they and we are lost anyway!

Deeds and accomplishments mean nothing today without the actual work and lofty goals, with significant benchmarks and provable Standards.

It's been a foible of society for a long time now, the: "What have You done for me lately", narcissistic point of view.
It's pervasive tentacles have even entwined honored relationships between spouses, and between child and parent.
Instead of: "what can I do to make you feel loved, sweetheart"?

What has the world succumbed to: Symbolism Over Substance, every single day, created a virtue by Clinton. When did INTENTION become the substitute for DEED?

The People, the Throng, respond only to THEATRE today.
Children of the Idiot-Box, and is now the Idiot-Net,
they see what they want and want what they see, all too easy.
Whatever sensory feels good, change the channel, with the attention span of a gnat.
A cornucopia of riches, protected constituents, illegal bonuses, preferred grants, healthcare, rewarded complacency, but no real choices in schools, government, courts, unions. We're wedded and kept, cared-for and captive, all controlled the President, but someone else provides and always pays, Mom and Dad!

Watch this over here, while I pick your pocket over there, and now, a TelePrompTer for a president, an ultimate video game, but who are the puppet masters?...........NOT YOU!

Maybe an unfortunate consequence of once having had a professional-communicator for a President, this is what we've come to expect.
Fortunately, for us it was a good man In '81. Some others were not as lucky in 1933.

But what about 2009?.........Who will pay, HIM?........Not Us, we're broke.......Must be China!

"See how well He Articulates,
how well He Sounds,
how well He wears his suit & tie,
His gestures, nuanced to project resolve and determination."

Theater, matters not what He really feels in His heart, or thinks in His mind.
He has spoken freely, unabashed on the wings of His conviction, ah yes,
and now His perceived vision and intent are now too, mine,
and all that's necessary, important and significant,
the orchestrated word has won for day!...Yet, I am hungry now. Will they be feeding us?

How easy!......... All played, like Nero's fiddle,
smiles upon our faces as we march single file into the Showers, and the Quartet plays on!

What slim feeble crap....Today we sell ourselves-out so readily, and so fast, dimwitted, for anything shiny or 30 pieces of silver, no less.

You think we had these self-centered, selfish shallow-minded thoughts when a plain spoken little man approached the podium, no teleprompter of course, and president Harry Truman announced the extermination of a civilization had just transpired? Once subjected and ruled by one single idea, evil, all sacrificed at the risk of self-annihilation, our self-preservation was on his mind! These are the real responsibilities of leadership.

But today, only feeble crap we are all transfixed upon; is my 30 pieces coming in the mail today, or on April 15th? Our MEDIA manipulates the masses, skews our "reason today and yesterday", when another less articulate, less understood, plain spoken little man tried to save us once again after 9/11.

NEWS ALERT: *Robby- blinking lights, flailing arms, announcing:*
"Danger – Danger",
(if Bush screws-up, it's Bush's Fault),

(if government screws-up, it's Bush's Fault),

and when (Obama screws-up, it's Bush's Fault !)

You just can't change what someone believes,
but you can change what someone thinks if they are open to reason and logic.

One man, less telegenic, less pure, with less symbolism, but all substance,
a simple man, Newt Gingrich
has the capacity to transcend the rampant disconnect between (reason and ideology), and they are mutually exclusive.

He could be and can be OUR "Harry Truman" of tomorrow.
A more perfect Union of a Father and a Mother symbol to lead this Nation out of a darkness, that will soon befall us all.

Sarah can't make it on her own with 99% of all MEDIA against her,
were she the Virgin Mary, the Catholics would still sell her short and stone her in the square. Humans are just that, well, humanly ignorant. Sorry!

Perhaps someday, but not yet. She could be the Earth Mother to Newt, the Scholar, because that's what we need today are Ideas and TRUTH to pull back the curtain and shine the light into the darkness to make the blind see once again;
 <u>*Who Is The All And Powerful OZ??*</u>

No more show, no more symbolism over substance, no more American Idol,
Not Again!.........The next time it's going to be Real People fixing real problems.

If you think Romney, or Jindal, or some rising star from the East is coming to save our bacon, it ain't gonna happen, and We already have "One from the East", but few realize it.

What we need is a simple teacher, and a simple Mom; Idea driven, motivated, result oriented, proven business people, utilizing business principles, solving business problems with business ethics!.......
......It's Not Personal, It's Only Business!

Ideas, Reason, TRUTH!..............Not more money, We Have None!!

Keep Your Powder Dry

SENTRYMAN

posted May 6, 2009

==

2 COMMENTS

Comment by phyllis w 3 days ago

Newt is the smartest guy in the Republican party;
however, I don't think he could beat Obama.

Obama might beat himself by that time. I'll support Newt of course, but I am hoping for
somebody fresh, young, smart to be on the top of our ticket.
We have young bright Republican politicians today.

Newt could be the top advisor...when we win, how about 'chief of staff'

Comment by Canuck Gal 3 days ago

Newt is part of the old guard and would not win against Obama.
I bet you like this ticket but it would not have a chance.

I think Sarah and (senior moment here) that young fellow who took the lead in opposing
the budget would do well. Young and new .....

==

PART #2
of Comments by SENTRYMAN 2 days ago

In much older and more intellectual cultures like the Chinese and Japanese,
they honor, value and revere age, experience and wisdom.

They even have a special class of citizenry, called "Living Treasures", that are Master
Artisans of pottery, makers of samurai swords and other skills handed down over 100's,
if not 1000's of years.

We haven't the depth of character or the patience in these young United States to
appreciate human qualities and ancestral skills like that!
We would blow-off a Ben Franklin as a rummy and some kook today, I'm certain.

We like watching the shiny new penny sparkling in the sun, while a patient hand slowly
places a noose around our collective necks.

It took Dec. 7th, and again a 9/11 to finally wake-us all up!

Let me ask you something: If it was your money coming out of your pocket, (if we had any), and you were hiring some guy to build you a bridge, or skyscraper, or better yet "Operate on your Wife's heart,"
would you choose the "Flavor of the Month" cool-guy Doctor,
OR .....Michael E. DeBakey, the one with more than a few successes under his scalpel?

"People get the government they deserve!".........Ever hear that before, all you Collegians?

Presently, we obviously aren't intelligent, or lucky enough to deserve a Newt, or a Sarah!
.........but, with time and faith?

Keep Your Powder Dry
SENTRYMAN

posted May 7, 2009

===

Comment by Steve 20 hours ago

Nothing, I mean nothing is more valuable than experience.
Newt Gingrich has been there and has the drive to use his knowledge.
He shackled Clinton in '94, created the "Contract with America," and is the top guy in the area of energy policy.

Sarah Palin would make a fantastic vice president to Newt Gingrich.
Like Miller said, "he is the smartest guy in the room."
And he is, hands down.

Comment by joachim 23 hours ago

Maybe voters will have had their fill of rock star, reckless, self centered politics and be ready for a grown up in the White House again ...... just like after the Clintons left and GW came in.

Newt is sound and strong ..... just a thought...

I liked Miller's Newty and the Beauty ...
Both are patriots, wise and strong.

Let the press sling all the mud they can muster. The FNO's (Failing News Outlets) have ruined their own credibility.
They are nothing but a joke. Hardly anyone even reads them anymore.
Most have taken to alternative Credible News Sources.

Comment by Betty E 1 day ago

No to Gingrich!
Certainly there are some young Republican (Conservative) leaders out there.
Let's get rid of the "good ole boys", they haven't done much for us.

Comment by G.H. 1 day ago

Gingrich, Miller has to be kidding.
Gingrich will be 69 in 2012, just a few years younger than McCain was.

He's a smart guy, and Miller is right,
he'd do great in a debate with 0bama, but he is too much 1990's, has been married 3 times,
and has admitted to affairs, and don't think that would be left alone.

I can't see him drawing huge enthusiastic crowds, or being very inspiring.
I don't even think he'd make a good VP candidate.

Comment by K in Michigan 1 day ago

Sarah MUST be at the top of the ticket! .....She is the inspiring one.
Newt knows his facts no doubt and I could accept him as VP but Sarah must be at the top
next time and I will trust her choice for VP!

We will have to unite strong for Sarah as there will be those that try to scare us
and say "...did I mention she's a women" as sexism lurks in many!

We will have to stand against the corrupt MSM.
We'll have to convince people to base their decision on the content of character not
gender! Convince the naysayers that yes a woman can lead the USA!
===

PART #3....true today......true tomorrow?
Comment by SENTRYMAN today

Well, well, I must have hit a nerve. We seem to have somewhat of a consensus.

2 to 1 against Newt,
but of those the majority wants Newt in the mix........Promising!

I hate to be the spoiler but my pragmatic nature forces me
and I also hate being redundant but I am, and I'll repeat one question;

"If you were hiring a guy to build you a bridge that your family will cross every day,
or a skyscraper, you'd require resistant to fire and planes,

or better yet,
pick a surgeon to "operate on your little girl's heart,"
would you choose a young fresh face, or the Flavor of the Month,
OR .....Michael E. DeBakey, still operating today, way in his "senior" years?

Enough with the age stuff.
How old was Reagan the 1st time around, and he was our best man in the modern era?
And those of you that want Sarah "ONLY in the top spot",
it's an easier jump from VP once you're working at the White House.
Look at You Know Who!

I'll put it another way;
if you're going into battle,
do you want a Major, a Colonel or a General,
and if you were wise enough to think: "General",
do You want one with 1, 2, 3, or 4 stars?.............Come on now!

Experience, knowledge and wisdom are all that really matters now, isn't it!

This isn't a popularity contest.
Bye the way, Obama's only a Captain, and barely, in name only!
He may not have even rated that high in the MAFIA. Well, maybe Chicago mafia?

OK, one more analogy, and really simple:
If You were going to a Dog Fight,
you'd want the biggest, bad-ass hound you could find (disguised in a suit and tie), to
mix-it-up with their worst, flea-bitten, mangey-ass cur.

Forget about beating Obama.
He's in there ONLY as a Shill anyway, on "The FIX."
He's not the guy to beat and doesn't have the true ethic, capability, or capacity to earn his
own bones as CEO of a GE, or a Walmart,
much less be "Master of the Universe"....(well, maybe GE)!

Why do you think he's lauded and touted as the smartest guy in the government, but has
never accomplished anything "recorded" we could verify, except won a few "fixed races";

[The Las Vegas SUN......
Criminal charges filed against ACORN, two employees.....
By Mary Manning, May 8, 2009]

http://www.lasvegassun.com/news/2009/may/04/criminal-charges-filed-against-acorn-two-employees/

You have to search pretty hard for find this one. It won't be featured on NBC.
They had to make room for Sarah Palin's Ex-future son-in-law's 18th interview instead.

That's "ACORN",
the Obama community organization that He is now putting in change of OUR National 2010
census, instead of the "Commerce Department" of the US Government's responsibility as
usual.
It's been handed over to "PAID" Volunteers, (indentured friends of Obama).

ACORN will be granted Billion$ of Tax Payer's Money in the new $3.6 Trillion dollar 2010
Budget, that we will be borrowing from the Chinese, of course, if they'll still let us.....

Well, there's always the Saudi's.......Anyone up for "Drill Here, Drill Now"?....Naaahh?
Sure makes sense now, more than ever, doesn't it?

"PAID volunteers": Is that an Oxymoron, a travesty, a bad dream, or just a Moron?

Why do you think they locked up all of OBAMA's birth, health, and college records from 3
different liberal universities?

Wouldn't you think they'd be so very-proud as hell to brag about the smartest man in the
country, (on "their" team), and really desire to demonstrate, and show all His Gold Stars
that he had earned in school, like in some "traveling museum show", around the country
and finally resting in its own wing at the Smithsonian?....Wouldn't you think?....No?.........
The real "Wizard of Smart" is still behind the curtain people.

Back to my point,
we need a seasoned "War Horse" with a track record, that of (harnessing-the-Devil), and
(stomp'n-the-Snakes), like '94's Contract with America's Capo tutti di capo,
and I wouldn't wish this fight upon Sarah, but she wants in on the action, so be it.

Do you remember when Saddam's Royal Guard set those 700+ Kuwaiti oil-well fires, as
they turned-tail and ran from Bush Sr., back in 1991?
Who was the Go-to-Guy, that old Dude they all went to find in Texas, to save the
environment? ....tick, tock, jeopardy theme.....No, collegians, It wasn't Al Gore. He was
preoccupied burning ants with a magnifying glass, dreaming about man-made warming!

sidebar:
I find it hilarious that OLE AL was only worth approx. $2 Mil. after running for president,
and then after 8 years of "The Bush Economy", he's now worth approx. $100,000,000.00,
that's millllion dollllar$, and I thought the MEDIA said things were so terrible!
...Well, after the DEMs came back, but that didn't seem to hurt OLE AL either, go
figure!.........Hmmmmm!

That means that Al Gore would have had a personal net-loss of $98,000,000.00 dollars,
PLU$, would have had to be "telling the truth" for those past 8 years if he'd actually earned
the Presidency............Hmmmmm!.....He should kiss Bush's feet and send him a referral
check for a $Mil. in sheer gratitude alone!!

Mr. Obama became a millionaire during those same Bush years, also!
So did Holder, Franklin Raines, Jamie Gurlic, and the whole Clinton crew...Wa$hington?

*STRANGE how DEMOCRAT INSIDERS never suffer with any downturn in the Economy!
===

Lest we forget the "Oval office Don Juan".... that exiting "pauper" Bill Clinton, & wah-lah,
8 years later = $800,000,000.00 in his bank account.........and much of it from the Arabs,
our closest supplier of that terrible fossil fuels.

Any Democrat for: "Drill Here, Drill Now"?.........................I didn't think so!!

In case you ladies hadn't noticed,
the Tea Parties were a magnificent, proud, fine day for Grass-Roots patriotism, activism,
and freedom on exhibit,
and was totally marginalized by OUR, and THEIR President Of The United States, and
also by other discriminating US Government officials at the very top of the food chain.
The powerful significance of those events were completely shielded from the general
public, and our low-information voters by a corrupt and complicit MEDIA, insuring surdity.

You think these people give a wit about You, or for You?

I'm just incredulous why Americans of African ancestry continue to vote for these Leftists.

50 years at "War on Poverty", 11 Trillion tax dollar$ later, We still have "the same Poor",
no-kidd'n Dick Tracy, and a growing percentage of once Middle-America are going in that
exact direction too, and rapidly increasing ever since the DEMs took-over in 2007.

You would think that over the last 45 years
of basically a Democrat controlled US Government bureaucracy during the past 60 years,
we'd be living in (at-least-some-kind) of a Utopian Garden of Eden!......Well, wouldn't you?

"Oh hell, my, my, let's give the DEMs one more chance to totally finish-us-off!"....REALLY?

I'd personally like to figure out how to get them "ALL-OUT" and start over again,
so that's where I'm coming from, but having said that,
there's still 1000s of sites and millions of bloggers, each with a stone to grind, and a bone
to pick,
but the sooner we all make something happen, the sooner the problem will be solved,
and the answers certainly won't come from Washington.

"When the people fear their government, there is tyranny;
when the government fears the people, there is liberty."
Thomas Jefferson

Many of our fellow Tea Party Revolutionaries may feel energized, some may feel
disheartened, we are separated only by miles and States, gender and faith,
yet, Now Marginalized, Tabulated, Pigeon holed, Categorized and Coupled with neo-Nazis,
Terrorists, and abortion Bombers,
but, We, the people are all AMERICANS!

That yearning alone has always moved mountains in the pursuit and the protection of:
Liberty,

so, what we need tomorrow is Newt's brains, and Sarah's brawn,
her grace and strength of character, and her aim ain't too bad either!

**PEOPLE, "Rush said it much better" years ago: "The Is A WAR",**
"a war in the arena of Ideas, and a struggle for the hearts and minds of our YUTH",
(that's our children),

and the enemy holds most of the cards,
and we are playing fairly and morally with our rules, but in their backyard and on their
back-streets, and their back-alleyways,
with the absolute dregs of the New Society all playing by their own rules.
(Kind of like fighting an "Al-Qaeda"!)

Yes, it's a brave new world, yada, yada, where they want to control Freedom Of Speech, so
They can double-speak "anything", the more disgusting the better, but "you" dare not
raise your voice in opposition or criticize, or even debate anything POLITICALLY
INCORRECT, for fear of the New Hate-Speech Felonies, Old-Racism Charges and
Homophobic Accusations,
or they'll publicly excoriate YOU, take your kids, Eminent Domain your abode, and IRS
your ass!................Got'cha!!

A New World where Pedophiles will have new "protected status",
nor can you protect your kids from predator teachers,
where the Unions own the Workers, and the Government owns Everybody and Everything.

A New World where, and I said to my wife, (who is also a woman) a few days ago:
"Watch, Obama will try to fill the Supreme Court slot with: a Female, a Latina, who also
happens to be openly Lesbian, (qualified or Not), if he can find one"!.........
Watch the news today?.... one doesn't select people like things, checked-off on boxes!

But, you know what, if she's the best gal for the job, OK by me,
just don't bring your personal grist to work with you.
JUST DO YOUR DUTY and follow the Constitution like you're supposed to!

No my friends, Obama's not who we are fighting in 2009, it's;
ACORN, (now in charge of the US Census), and future voter enlistment.

MSNBC, CNBC, NBC, CBS, ABC, CNN, 2/3rds of FOX, BBC, CBC, PBS,
NPR,

the AP, UPI, The NY Times, Globe, Post, most newspapers, most magazines,

History revisionists, Book Critics, Education Book Publishers,

Hollywood, NEA, AFL-CIO, AFTRA, ACLU, SAG, UAW, TV magazine shows,
OPRAH, ELLEN, BRAVO, BET, Comedy Channel, Mahar, the Stewart's (John &
Martha), Colbert, Trump, Buffett, Soros, Huffington, KOS, LENO, Letterman,

the Music Industry,

ACADEMIA: K thru Doctoral thesis on Women's Studies, Global Warming and the
endangered white conservative male, (that class has been cancelled),

phew, take-a-breath,

our new friends in HAMAS,
every tin-pot Dictator in the Caribbean, socialists in Central & South America, and Communists across the globe,

leftist Attorneys, Sharia Law, the EU, the World Court, Geneva Convention,

Majority of the Appeals Court Judges and the Supreme Court,

leftist government workers, The White House, 95% of Press Corp.,

the RINOs, and the majority of the House & Senate of the United States Government,

and the senators from Maine, and the leftist-people's government of New Hampshire, and the City of San Francisco,

phew, take-a-breath,

some of the Pentagon, most of the State and Justice Depts.,

Bank Execs, Insurance Execs, Wall Street,

GM and their Unions,

the entire state of Michigan on the Left,

1/2 of the Catholics that turn their heads to Abortion and pedophile priests,

1.5 billion Muslims that love our President, but hate America and want to kill you and live in your house,

all of the illegals crossing our borders for the freebees, that would vote for Obama as many times as he asks,

phew, catch my breath,

and our newest Citizens moving here from Guantanamo,
that will also vote democrat, and want to kill you and your family, and don't want to live in your house, just kill you and your family,
etc.,
etc.
(If I unfairly included you in my caustic generalization, excuse yourself. I was illustrating an extreme characterization to make a reverse-point, there're no greys, "Right or Left", pick, No Independents, and if and when the bullets fly, no atheists either!)

No my friends, Obama's not who we are fighting, it's ourselves!

http://www.adherents.com/Religions_By_Adherents.html

THIS IS THE ENEMY MY FRIENDS
and Sarah can't do it alone, not without a Stick, a Brick, a Gun and a prayer!

Keep Your Powder Dry

SENTRYMAN
posted May 8, 2009

---

6 COMMENTS

Comment by Cal K on May 7, 2009 at 3:21pm
Sarah = president--------vice president = ?

Comment by Olive on May 7, 2009 at 3:17pm
Very Good summation.
I agree that Sarah will need a good right hand man...she cannot do it on her own.
While Sarah has the full-on attention of the base, she does not have the confidence of the middle-ground voters.
They are the ones who decide elections.

Comment by B on May 7, 2009 at 3:05pm
Palin / Bachmann 2012
It's going to take two strong conservative mothers to clean up the mess left by the liberal loons.

Comment by B P on May 6, 2009 at 11:50pm
Sarah, Please!!
Newt and his 3 marriages promoting family values......?   I don't think so!

Comment by Susan W on May 6, 2009 at 10:46pm
WE NEED SARAH!!!

Comment by michael m on May 6, 2009 at 9:39pm
Sarah will be atop of the ticket

 <u>**Chapter 32**</u>

"Every American has the Right to Kill the Unborn"
.....<u>So states the Supreme Court & Barack!</u>

Posted by SENTRYMAN on <u>May 17, 2009</u> at 1:30pm

<u>Remember the old joke that ends with;</u>
"Oh, we've already established: "WHAT YOU ARE",
NOW WE'RE JUST HAGGLING ON PRICE"!.............?

<u>Well, what the Hell do you mean?,</u>
"that anyone in America "doesn't already have the right"
to kill the unborn!",

now we're just trying to establish "who's Paying" to remove "IT", that;
Fetus, that blob, that piece of matter, a growth, a meaty "tumor",
fatty tissue, a "nothing" to be discarded, tossed in the trash,
crack "Its" skull---smash "Its" little head so it stops moving,
then suck "it" out, "swept away" from "Its' " Host?

That "Parasite"!

I think that "Stork" idea for delivering those "Real Babies" really works out
much better don't you, especially for the vile B/S'ers that consistently try to
(fool the Fools) and themselves!

<u>So then, what if this Tumor has "a pulse",</u>
a "heartbeat, beat, beat, beating",

a "living presents" that You can see moving on that monitor, and feel
"moving joyfully" around inside Your body, and "breathing" under-water,

that You actually observe moving right through your skin as those little
arms and tiny feet turn to "knock" on your bellybutton to say: "Hello, see
me everybody", and can as quickly give you a good swift kick in your solar
plexuses if you smoke or drink; this "entity" with its "identity",   Pg. 176

this genetic homo-sapiens-code thing,
with a very long genetic history and an ancient family tree,
with monumentally specific sponsors; a male & a female, man & woman,
a mother and a father, a Mom and a Dad,
(hopefully for the good of society husband and wife),
who each Could, who Should, who Would; teach "It" to Speak and to Walk
and to Run and to Play and Laugh, lots of laughter: tickles and giggles,

and to Ride "Its" bike, Play ball with You in the back yard, at the park,
to bring You home crayon-colored pictures of "Its" family;
that's YOU Mom & Dad, including Snuffy, or Buffy, or Muffy, or Fluffy, and
Hangs-it right-up on the frig door, that "It" and YOU both be so proud of,

and "it" Thinks, "it" remembers learning while waiting around 9 months to
say "hi" to You....WOW, now imagines how wondrous the world is all
around "It", as "It" Grows-Up big and strong, bigger than You,
picks you right-up off the ground as you think back:
"haven't felt that in a long time",
and "it" Loves and Laughs, and Writes and Ponders "Its" own existence, of
something far greater than "Its own self", way, way, far out there in that
black vast voluminous vacuous vortex,

and then "it" Cries "Itself" one day with so much joy that You permitted
"IT" to someday Witness the Birth of "Its" own "Genetic Issue"
bursting forth from "Its" own cocooned sleepy nine month journey,
much as a Butterfly explodes from "Its" own long slumber, alive the whole
time, having appeared but a blob, a Pupa, a piece of matter, a growth, a
tumor,
yet = "LIFE"...........NEW......AMAZING.......REAL......KNOWING.....,
Waiting To Love You Back, Forever Rich,...............................and so it goes!

It's so tough to get a tumor to do all that stuff these days
just so you can kill it just before all the fireworks happen!

Isn't that so Supreme Court Justices?.............Supreme what??

All that promise, all those pent-up living atoms; listening, smiling, a timed
explosion in natural science: Nature!.....Remember GREEEEN, the planet?

BUT then short-circuited, the chrysalis dishonored and aborted, destroyed,
squished under heel upon the hot pavement!.......
So then now what is "IT", but,....DEATH?.....Yes, then what was "IT"? LIFE!

Was it only truly REAL when it emerged from the darkness into the light, while in flight;
a puppy is only a dog after whelping, a baby Rhinoceros only after it's dropped on the Savanna floor?
Don't know if Mama Rhino is going to agree with that "one" after carry that "NOTHING" around for her long 16 months!

Or, will "It" be allowed, be permitted, be sanctioned, be Un-aborted,
be Un-Roe'd, be officially honored,
and nurtured, cradled warm and safe, inspiration-compelled to be free,
complete, fulfilled,.........To LIVE?

Uncompromised, Uninterrupted, the natural course of things,
that's Nature buckaroos.........It may be your body, but LIFE - "ITS" a Gift!
Try it on your own, there's NO going back!

If It Were Only Real At The Moment Of Birth, Even More "The Miracle!"
Thank You Lord For These Gifts Which We Are About To Receive,
Through Thy Bounty......Don't You Dare Touch It, Or Don't Help Make It!

***QUESTION Girls:
What's The Whole "Baby Shower" Thing For Then With Expectant Mothers,
compared to when "the 16 year old WOMAN" who wants that "THING"
wrenched-out of her body and that "Tumor-nothingness-Thing" destroyed?

Contrast these for a moment;
One happy Lady goes home thrilled, happy with promise and presents! ...
Another girl goes home with pain and guilt, loss, confusion and "the bill",
and each was concerning the same subject; what, a "NOTHING"?

Unless LIBs in America and Congress make us "all pay through the nose",
but NOT through the heart for her next bad C-H-O-I-C-E so it's even easier,
masking the true essence of this unfortunate hasty-decision by this poor
child will scar-her for an entire lifetime remembering this little M-U-R-D-E-R
F-O-R-E-V-E-R!

And, Thank You For My Life, thank you great-grandmother!

My grandfather, an abandoned Orphan at the Turnstile,
but a "living" orphan, nonetheless,
lest, go I, but for the grace of God!

SENTRYMAN

 Warning - Caution – Beware - "Do not go gentle into that good night"
https://www.youtube.com/results?search_query=real+abortions

Chapter 33

<u>Why Does The World Need A United Nations?</u>...................

Or, Should I Say: *"The LEAGUE OF NATIONS"!!!!*

Posted by SENTRYMAN on <u>May 24, 2009</u> at 1:30pm

<u>WATCH THE MOVIE: "Taken" (2008)</u>

Fact, Fiction, or Daily Occurrences?

Let it sink-in for a moment and then really consider what this movie represents in today's culture,
in today's reality for so many parents and frightened young girls from around the world, and ask yourself;

<u>"Why Does The World Need A United Nations</u>", such as it is today?
www.youtube.com/watch?v=KrzVxO9CHgo&feature=related

<u>*Does The United Nation Have A Purpose Beyond Their Own Interests?</u>

<u>*Why Do We Have The United Nations, Dead Beat Tenants On Our Shores?</u>

<u>*Why Do We Pay The Lion's Share Of Their Budget With No Advantage?</u>

<u>*Is it: "keep your friends close but your enemies closer"???</u>

<u>**Well there's too many enemies and they're all too damn close!</u>

***IF THE UNITED NATIONS COULDN'T ELIMINATE HUMAN SLAVERY IN THE 20TH CENTURY,
what makes You think they will do any better in the 21st century, especially when that isn't even a priority??..................

<u>So Then, What Good Are They?</u>
www.military.com/NewContent/0,13190,SOF_0904_Slavery1,00.html

The UN Cannot Even Stop Hunger Without a Rock Concert.

Ever Hear Of "Meals On Wheels", Just Little Woman Serving Humanity, What Could Be Simpler?....
It's Even Easier Than Stealing Donated Artwork From The UN Building, "That" They Can Accomplish, But Not Delivering Food To A Hungry World?   Pg. 179

But, Oh My, Men With Guns Steal All The Food!....blah, blah, blah
<u>"Then What Good Are You"</u>??

<u>THE UNITED NATIONS IS ABSOLUTELY "IMPOTENT" IN STOPPING</u>;
*Genocide,
*Slavery,
*Child Labor,
*Sex Trade,
*Arms Trade,
*Nuclear Proliferation,
*Nuclear Waste Black Market,
*International Drug Trade,
*Poppy Production,
*High Seas Piracy,
*Ivory Poaching,
*Whaling,
*AIDS,
*Malaria,
*GRAFT,
*"Oil for Food" Scam,
*WAR,
<u>*Or Eliminating HUNGER Outside Of The United Nation's Cafeteria,</u>

*nor stopping World Tyrants and Dictators from coming to America on a little vacation, welcoming their propaganda while addressing the General Assembly and shielding them from Arrest by the US authorities,

or *stopping any World Dictators, without simultaneously being in-bed with them, and always sand-bagging America to carry the heaviest-load, and to sustain the greatest casualties, but,
<u>*never supporting their greatest benefactors,</u>
 "Policeman to the World": the United States of American,
and always making the US the Fall-Guy, the Patsy, and the "supposed aggressor"!

<u>"So Then, What Good Are You"??</u>

But, but, but, but, but, but, but, but, but, but,

But, They Sure Can RAPE The Women While They're Protecting In Africa,

and They Sure Can STEAL A Big Slice Of The "Oil For Food" Program,

and They Undoubtedly Get A CUT Of The Poppy Field Yield In Afghanistan,

and They Can Try & Stop The USA From Freeing 25 Million Enslaved Iraqis,

and They Sure Can't Stand Up Against Saddam's Proliferation of WMDs!
...................what DMDs?????...............Ahhh,....Yuh,...Sure!

TRILLION DOLLAR QUESTION:

So Why, Oh Why, Do We Waste Our Time Being A Member Of An Incredibly Inept,
Absolutely Corrupt, Borderline Criminal World Organization,
Who, Besides Fleecing Our GREENBACKS,
 Is Going Into A New "GREEN Business" With Their New Bogus Facade!

Yes, Those Diplomatic Impersonators That Bottom-Feed Off America's Good Faith & Good
Name, Our Good Hearts, Our Good Intentions, Our Good Efforts, Our World Charity,
and Our Great Constitution THAT MAKES IT ALL HAPPEN FOR EVERYONE, providing this
world bountiful harvests that they all refuse to do adopt for themselves like a petulant Bad
Child, because we provide it all for them. Enablers that we are, Tough Love & Cold Turkey
is much smarter, and prudent parent would Kick Their Asses Right Out Of This Country
Into The Cold To Fend For Themselves, So They Would Finally Become Self-Sufficient!

"Liberals ALL", You Scratch my Back, I'll Pick Your Pocket!
They take full measure of OUR Kindness and OUR Benevolence, and when all that We ask
in return is a genuine "Thank You", some Respect, and a little HELP in the Good Fight,
Doing The GOOD WORKs for their own benefit, bites the hand and sides with EVIL!

But most importantly, the World needs to remember that no matter who is the President of
the United States at any particular moment in time,
it is still the American's OWN Money, and it is OUR CHARITY We freely provide them,
That THEY, In Essence Are Then Stealing, Without That Recognition & Acknowledgement!

The UNITED NATIONS: 191 TEMP Assistant-Managers!
Do We Really Want These Guys In-Charge Of "OUR" United States of America?....

www.cbsnews.com/video/watch/?id=4356720n&tag=related;photovideo

Do We Want The U.N. In-Charge Of The World, Plus, In-Charge Of The
United States of AMERICA With The Complete Cooperation, Permission,
Submission and Total Complicity Of Our "Current" Commander-in-Chief?
Is That What We Really Want For Our Children's Future? Well, Do Ya Punk?

"Teach A Man To Fish, He Eats Forever"...........
Give A Man A Fish, He'll Eat Your Hand Off.
When He's Done With Your Fish,
He'll Rape Your Wife, Burn Down Your House,
Steal Your Daughter, and Shoot Your Dog!

You will only have yourself to blame!!

SENTRYMAN

5 Comments

*Comment by Susan W on May 23, 2009 at 11:23pm
My husband watched it this weekend and LOVED IT!!!

*Comment by Patriot Kate on May 24, 2009 at 2:02pm
We need to support the legislation introduced by Dr. Ron Paul in February which calls for U.S. withdrawal from the U.N. The U.N. is nothing more than the means the World Banksters plan to run the military of the World. We need to get out of it.

*Comment by SENTRYMAN on May 24, 2009 at 2:25pm
(We need to support the legislation?).........Sure, but who's "WE"?

WE'VE BEEN DEALT "OUT OF THE GAME".
Barack will do anything he wants, and He likes these guys!

*THIS IS IMPORTANT......MAKE SURE TO READ THIS BELOW!

Comment by Darby on May 24, 2009 at 10:40pm
Did you know that Over 68 percent of the land in US National Parks, preserves and monuments have been designated as UN World Heritage Sites or Biosphere Reserves?

The US has 48 Biosphere Reserves and 22 World Heritage Sites. Some of these sites include Yellowstone, Yosemite, the Grand Canyon, Independence Hall, the Statue of Liberty and many others.

The UN Takeover
The UN Fund for Population Activities was started in 1969 and promotes the idea that increased welfare entitlement programs along with socialized health care reduces fertility. The UNFPA has partnered with China's one-child policy, which includes forced abortion and sterilization to reduce infant mortality rates. During a 2004 UNFPA meeting on population control, the Executive Director pledged to fight religious resistance to abortion and to guarantee young people the right to 'reproductive health services' (abortion). The US was the largest financial contributor to UNFPA during the 1970's and 80's.

In a little known Senate vote during the first session of the 91st Congress in 1970, the Privileges and Immunities of the United Nations, Executive J, was passed without one dissenting vote. Executive J gives the UN full diplomatic immunity as a sovereign government within the US. Ever since Executive J was passed in 1970, the UN has been mounting an all out takeover of National Parks and private property as this legislation came to a spearhead through multiple conventions and programs. The 1972 Convention Concerning the Protection of the World Cultural and Natural Heritage (Article 8) established the World Heritage and Biosphere Reserve Program (MAB) and legislated UNESCO as the governing body over all World Heritage sites. The World Conservation Union (IUCN) is the legislative and economic governing body of UNESCO and the World Heritage Program.

Environmental protection operates on progressive levels; 1) State Park, 2) National Park, 3) National Monument, 4) World Heritage Site and 5) Program on Man and Biosphere Reserve (MAB). The first three are maintained and operated by the state or federal government of the US. World Heritage Sites and Biosphere Reserves (MAB) are two separate designations that fall under the jurisdiction of the UNESCO. World Heritage sites are sections of land set aside as outstanding universal value for natural or cultural importance that contribute to the heritage of the world. The Program on Man and Biosphere (MAB) reserves must represent a combination of natural, biological and cultural ecosystems that are set aside as transnational boundaries for limited or no human use. The US has 48 Biosphere Reserves and 22 World Heritage Sites. Some of these sites include Yellowstone, Yosemite, the Grand Canyon, Independence Hall, the Statue of Liberty and many others.

The 1992 Framework Convention on Climate Change had nothing to do with climate and everything to do with the US handing over control of World Heritage sites to the UN. Four years later in 1996, Clinton signed Executive Order #12986 which grants the IUCN full amnesty and sovereignty as a foreign nation. This, in effect, gave the UN full control of all 70 World Heritage and Biosphere sites, which comprise over 70 million acres or 110,000 square miles of land (about the size of Nevada). Although the US still considers the land sovereign and they are still maintained by US agencies, the UN considers these sites as sovereign UN soil and integrates UN policy into current USDI and USFS legislation. Over 68 percent of the land in US National Parks, preserves and monuments have been designated as UN World Heritage Sites or Biosphere Reserves.

UNESCO is an organization of about 191 Nation Member States and over 30,000 Associate Members; Governments, Private Institutions, Corporations or Non-Governmental-Organizations are the types of entities that may become members. A 1995 UN report on global governance estimated that there are nearly 29,000 international NGOs. NGO's compose of over 70% of the total funding for UNESCO. President Bush decided to rejoin the group in September 2002. President Reagan abandoned the UN organization in 1984, calling it grievously corrupt. The US government contributes about $80 million annually to UNESCO. As of 2005, there were 812 World Heritage Biosphere properties around the world under UNESCO control, and 628 of these sites have been set aside for cultural designations.

The World Heritage Program is a massive land grab, it transfers federal and private property to control under the IUCN. Under Executive Orders, the IUCN/UNESCO is granted full immunity from US law. This means that when you stand on a World Heritage Site in the US, you're technically not on US federal property, nor are you on private property; you are actually standing on UN Land. Despite the legal framework that has clearly been established by the UN, the US Congress still maintains its sovereignty. One of the greatest testaments to US national cultural heritage and sovereignty is Independence Hall, where the Declaration of Independence and Constitution were signed.

IUCN control of this site represents a direct assault on US cultural heritage and national sovereignty.

For more information research the net and find out yourself. To start Go To Pages:
http://sovereignty.net/p/land/mapmabwh.htm

and
http://whc.unesco.org/en/list

Well, shut my mouth and shoot me in the head.

So, are you with me, or agin' me, pilgrim?

Let's see, people used to worry when Japan was buying up New York City properties,
but then some enlightened New Yorker said: OK, let them try and take the buildings home!

So, let them try to take Nevada back to DUBAI!

Seriously, that was wonderful.
Try saying that on O'Reilly and stir up a hornet's nest.

I believe you made my point with a sledgehammer though.

We need these Carpetbaggers gone,
and that goes with any politician that sides with them.

Even the Mafia got behind the War effort in the '40s, so let's get this going Paul Revere,
but if I'm the only one that's not aware of your Thesis paper, I apologize for my ignorance,
but if my enlightenment is in the minority, reprint this DARBY a thousand times from pillar
to post.

It is at the bowels of the problem, and everyone in this sleepy country needs a Good
Cathartic!

And as for THEM coming here and moving the trees,
there's enough forests burning-down because we can't tend our forests properly anymore,
and what's standing will have enough Good OLE Hillbillies, with Long Rifles protecting
them for many a year, so don't You fret none!

Up The Rebel,
and Keep Your Powder Dry.

Ps, hell, everyone's coming here anyway to be Americans,
so let them pay the fee and enjoy the woods.

SENTRYMAN

Chapter 34

"Is This A THUG Government?"

Posted by **SENTRYMAN** on **May 26, 2009** at 1:30am

http://www.youtube.com/watch?v=neGbKHyGuHU

Is there a Thug Government running Our nation today,
because things seem to be out of control and getting worse? They either can't stop it and don't care, or they know it, and it's part of a larger plan.

Either way, we're deep in it, and no one's watch'n out for us anymore.
The real shame of it is that, it just doesn't have to be that way, and shouldn't with a National Press performing their sworn duty.

The old saying: *"people get the Government they deserve",* may really apply today, but that doesn't explain one/half the country doing its best to Deep-6 the last government administration, acting like spoiled losers, and hurting OUR country and OUR military, who risk their lives protecting us all around the globe.

The loyal opposition, that other half of the nation, certainly didn't act that way biting their tongues for 8 years with Clinton ignoring many of his international responsibilities, endangering the entire country for years, while playing oval office high jinx and He was given a pass.

That, as compared to Nixon who had the personal integrity and class to resign for something he didn't create, while trying to protect his all-too jealous staffers for their high-jinx, but that's water over the bayou spillway. Tsk, tsk!

The much greater issue today endangering our national freedoms and personal liberties is that we've gotten all too complacent, sitting at our computers playing virtual-reality sports on the Holodeck, ignoring our own responsibilities and handing the decision making process to some mythical force for the American Good.
That apparently somehow assures us all snug and protected, secure in the thought that nothing can really happen to us and all will be OK, even though an economy can be destroyed overnight by corrupt politicians spending Trillion$ on a dinner we've not eaten yet, from a menu unread!

This can easily happen in a single morning while passing bills and removing Constitutional Rights of Free Speech, Free Assembly, Eminent Domain run-amuck, that No One challenges, certainly not by the 4th Estate,
but in a few fleeting minutes, late for work, clocks stop and the world ENDs, 3000 co-workers crash to their deaths, you're stuck in morning traffic....What does it all mean?

It can all end in a millisecond, a wisp of radio-active material, a breath of toxin, a spray of microbes, as we sit on our duffs trying to generate enough energy to stand-up, flex and bend-a bit-from Wii-syndrome, and other assorted foreign-born amusements,   Pg. 185

since we no longer manufacture hardly anything like We used to, and if we do, it's absent the old quality or personal pride we once insisted upon.

A list too long, embarrassing and probably surprising what we don't make, and worse, that we still do but now replete with flaws, because we no longer pay any attention to such mundane things. A throw-away society, the retention span of a small flying insect, Korean Cars, no less, are even kicking our butts, and Washington is carving up the spoils...Do we care?...Do we understand the ramifications?...We only hope gasoline is still under $3.00 today, and who got kicked off Dancing-With-The Stars last night?....That's it!

And that brilliant President Obama, well, he can do anything He likes just as long as it's not that stupid Bush, and all is well with the world!.........That's about how simplistic, how attuned, and how plugged-in we all are; instructed at respond with politically correctness, told how to think, what to think, when to think, and that's only if maybe we still can think!

We've totally fooled ourselves into claiming "victim status for everybody" and anything, dumbed-down & down-sized, conformed and capitalized, capitulated into blaming the other guy and someone else for all that's wrong, swearing, fingers pointed and raised, "not my jub-mon", holsters-emptied on the freeways hell-bent to tomorrow.

Hey, idiot, wake-up! Close your eyes and think of your grandparents. Imagine them acting anything like that, way, way back in time when they were your age?........
What's different now, what has changed, why have things changed so much, for better?

**Nowww you've got a Quest for a unholy grail of your own. If you can actually come up with the correct answer to that simple question: "why have behaviors changed so much in America since my grandparents were my age, is it for the better?", well then, you'll really be on the road to Wellsville and securing your own destiny, once again.

Ignore it, and you are doomed to repeat every stupid thing you've ever seen and heard anyone ever do, and not because we feel so powerless drifting in our despair, No, we've intentionally put ourselves to sleep, bemused, numbed, drugged into delusions, placed our own feet in cement starring at a speeding steamroller heading straight for us in slow-motion, running us down like in a Austin Powers movie...How dumb, we know better!

Everything written and rewritten, plot-lined scripted, scored and trumped-up, just to win back the White House....Oh, we are so shocked and surprised, really?
Fantasy, all fabricated, we read the lines and played our parts, knew the storyline, the plot and the outcome, self-assured we could hold-back the dawn and turn the tides in the last act. The instigators, authors and the smarter among us all knew that when the 1st Domino started to fall...deliverance?.....Noooo, reprisals and bedlam!!!

Don't get me wrong, they are all to blame;
the Dems for lying, the Media for printing and legitimizing it, looking the other way, and the GOP for acting guilty, or actually being scared and impotent up to their knees with elbows in the cookie jar, stunned, eyes glazed over as innocent deer in headlights, they asphyxiated themselves on their own self-worth,
and there We all sat, whining and watching like the Reality Show Junkies We've Become, but Forgetting We Were The Ones Being PUNKED.

Then, when We begrudgingly put an un-tempered, ill-tempered, un-proven man into the White House to appease the historians, the masses, the fates, and the winds of time for the Eastern Gods of War, like some "Rocky", or "Rudy" based exclusively on mere emotion, some repressed guilt for past sins, a little Hope and a lot more blind-faith than deserved, well, that's how the Show's supposed to End with the happy ending before the credits........isn't it?

That's just how it's all supposed to work out for the best?.....But, this wasn't any tempered steel-soldier, like: General Powell, or some war tempered-iron lady like: Secretary Rice, and without the least of any fundamental, or a minimum of a requisite examination or modicum of skepticism in choosing and determining; oh, let's say, a plastic surgeon's skill and (1) sample "nose", or
even a good house-painter's technique and a "finished abode",
or
a genius politician, yah right, but without (his grades, no health records, no birth certificate, no proof of any former achievements and No Security Clearance: zip, zero, nadda)........... not even (1) house painted and some old used brushes?
G-o-l-l-l-y?....So Then, Where Do I Sign-Up To Vote, Batman? I mean:" ACORN?

Who'd we think this guy was: Jack Bauer, Denzel Washington, another Colin Powell with 45s strapped to each leg?.....Naahh, we already had one of them.....Now, we're gon'na do it the "smart way".........a Hail Mary!
And forgive the religious connotation no longer permitted anymore in the New America, a kinder and gentler Nation!

And who is this guy we've put all our hopes-in and our money-on; this Wager, a bet, a Gamble, a Ghost, a Legend, yet another Actor?
....Whatever He Is, He Ain't No Colin Powell, and whether Colin is a RINO or not, we are going to wish We had Colin Powell when it finally hits the fan!

We've all become a nation of micro-managers today.
Uneducated, inexperienced and totaling unwilling to put-in the time, to pay our dues and learn the task. We sit at home in judgment watching the coliseum, 300 million experts: Thumbs-Up or Down, picking the American Idol winner, a surrogate to run our lives for us.

(Personally, I thought the Downey Jr. look-a-like had the best voice, but what do I know? Simon lives in a $24 million dollar hou$e that We Paid For....... dummies, and no one can see (((The Big Picture))) anymore. Not even on our $3500 Flat Screens @ 28% on VISA during these worst Depression years.

Point of fact:
Government mouthpiece spokesmen repeat (two things continually) as though they weren't connected;

#1 - Economists today predict lower Christmas sales in November, and for December!

*This un-surprisingly always manifests itself into: "now, consumer confidence has fallen again, purchases lag, and unemployment rises.".........Duuuuuhhhhh!

AND

#2 - Economists were "surprised" today with the increase in the GDP, and fewer filed for unemployment benefits.

*********Gee Whiz, Surprise, Surprise, Surprise.
Somebody's either smart enough to ignore it or fortunate enough not to have heard their manipulating government's 1st prediction....Phew!

What if those same "Wizards of Smart", (a Rush idiom), were to exclaim:

["The United States is the greatest nation in the history of man, and You Americans have, and can continue to, succeed in anything You attempt,
and we've had a little dip in consumer confidence and the economy lately,
and it would be a most prudent thing to ignore (anything and everything negative) that emanates from the "MEDIA" in the immediate and for the foreseeable future,
and additionally,
also from any foreign Government, or foreign Press, all wanting to hurt our nation's economy!...So go out there TODAY and produce the finest quality "American-made" products that only We can produce on this earth,
and also start spending again because hoarding is counter-productive, plus
live your lives without FEAR, which is what has always made this country GREAT!"

"And, oh yes, get your fat ass off the sofa and go buy your kid a baseball mitt, bat & ball, and go outside, introduce yourself and hit a few to them and shed some pounds.
The country will appreciate it, be healthier for it, and so will you both!..Have a nice day!"]

AND JUST WHAT DO YOU THINK WOULD HAPPEN THEN??

I'LL BET YOUR SWEET BOTTOM
THE DEMOCRAT GOVERNMENT WOULDN'T BE CONSUMING AND ABSORBING
EVERYTHING THEY COULD GET THEIR HOOKS INTO RIGHT NOW,
THAT'S FOR DAMN SURE,

BECAUSE THEN, THE AMERICAN PEOPLE, RE-INVIGORATED, INFUSED and ENTHUSED
JUST WOULDN'T TOLERATE THIS BEHAVIOR ANYMORE, ...NO, NO and NO,
AND THEY'D THROW THE CROOKS-OUT WHERE THEY BELONG!!!!!!

Now go out there and shag some balls Fatso!

SENTRYMAN

//
5 Comments

Comment by Susan W on May 26, 2009 at 7:26am

> This was quite a post! Yes, the country has changed quite a bit over the last few years...teenagers don't mow the lawn anymore. Instead of sitting out in lawn chairs visiting with neighbors on a beautiful summer evening, people spend nights glued to the TV, sealed up in their air-conditioned houses. Families now are so busy with their schedules that they often miss out on the simple, fun things like going out for ice cream, or catching fire flies at night....
>
> It's mostly the little things that are now missing out of our lives. Things that now seem so trivial, but did, in fact, add so much to the richness of life. Indeed, if anything good comes out of this economic crisis it will be that people will have to "slow down" and "shut down" all the 21st Century distractions that have allowed us to become so detached from each other.

Comment by Bruce O. on May 26, 2009 at 7:23am

This administration spun off from the Chicago political machine. They follow the Alinsky playbook. They threaten and bully private citizens into submission (Chrysler Bondholders), or destroy them if needs be (GM CEO). Thugs, indeed. As for the American people, while 54% voted for Obama the Infant Slayer, 48% did not. They are hard working , Tea Partying, Patriots. Many of whom are standing up and working to change things come 2010. Don't give up on Americans, the best are on our team.

 **Comment by SENTRYMAN on May 26, 2009 at 10:18am**

Excellent insight on a spring Memorial Day weekend, sentiment-waxing, bye-gone-days from a simpler, saner time in America.

But now on this Tuesday after,
the stark reality of business "as usual" in the 21st Century,
as We prepare to nominate a (*Janeane Garofalo*) to the Supreme Court,
and stare-down the barrel of a Tin Pot Dictator with a post-Harry Truman mindset,
it becomes all too clear "A Bad Moon Is Rising".

Welcome to a Brave New World where Fire-Flies will have an entirely new meaning!

God Save The United States of America.

Comment by Cowgirl Losi on May 26, 2009 at 12:03pm

A Thugocracy on steroids, which is what we have. It will take time and effort but we can bring sanity back if we simply stick together, allow differences of opinions and not play the game the Left wants us to play, and be divisive among ourselves!!
I don't think any of us realized what kind of an administration would come out of the Chicago Daly Machine. NOW We KNOW!!!

Comment by Amala on May 27, 2009 at 1:23am

It is a FASCIST REGIME !!

I don't know historically when one party controlled both the legislature and executive branch if they before this point in U.S. history became a regime that did not respect the minority?!

Maybe FDR. People are easy to scare when they are going through hard economic times. In this case the government is STEALING from us by telling us the sky will fall if we don't let them keep STEALING from us.

 **Chapter 35**

TILLER, TEACHERS, TYRANTS and TESTIMONIALS…..
"So, what's with the LEFT?"

Posted by **SENTRYMAN** on <u>June 2, 2009</u> at 1:00pm

<u>**Men that wore the Death's Head insignia "met" in the desert!**</u>
http://www.youtube.com/watch?v=Cy3aDlatrY0

German Chancellor Adolf Hitler and Grand Mufti Haj Amin al-Husseini: Zionism and the Arab Cause (November 28, 1941)
http://www.youtube.com/watch?v=BSLgbT-7U7A&list=PLB4D03A14708F4C7F

Muslim soldiers with hat showing Nazi insignia- WW II.
http://www.youtube.com/watch?v=dxCzwz7zTco

http://www.youtube.com/watch?v=HfLvP2jTVg8&feature=related

http://www.youtube.com/watch?v=PhHYS0GVbeM&feature=related

http://www.youtube.com/watch?v=EAxrg7nMcs4&feature=fvw

**all photos on this Blog Post shown at: http://www.sentryman.org/index.html

==
United States   June 1, 2009

As THE MEDIA decries the malicious death of a Great Man,
Dr. George Tiller, Kansas notorious abortionist: *"Tiller the Killer".*

Tiller, Tiller, the "Reluctant Mother Fulfiller", as All
Sides take up Arms and lines are drawn,
the obvious, as usual, will be obscured in Leftist Ideology
to vilify the "Right" and "LIFE" proponents, and I wonder:
<u>"What's with the Left"?</u>

Dr. Josef Mengele would have been proud
and a special place at the table in The Third Reich would
have been held for a man of this stature, this Great Man of
such Humanity that the "LEFT" so embraces and has exalted.

Pg. 190

Simple contrasts, why the debate the disparity in reason and reality?

This observer personally marvels at "ironic idioms" and the irony of Liberal Labels that camouflage, or rationalize deceit, all in the name of their particular brand of enlightenment and Democrat misnomers that hide the truth for their greater good.....Let's All Just Drink-Up And Be Happy! Kind of a Bait & Switch Cults, like Scientology, a New Age Jim Jones kind of thing!....No Peeking Behind The Curtain!

To their ends justifying their means, anything becomes possible, even murder? Well, well, that depends on one's point of view here, it all becomes Just Opinion!!! The US Constitution abridged, the Rule of Law ignored, common sense exploited, and blind justice denied.

The world "was" in fact: "FLAT"! Swear on a stack of Bibles, and a really tall stack too, so there!
Go to your room, young Galileo Galilei and stay there for a century, or we'll kill you!

TRY THESE "Liberal Labels" and "Democrat Misnomers" on for size;

Pro Choice = That means choose Death over Life, Right?

"Kill the Baby so I can get back into the sack, but just don't club any baby seals",ers!

Pro Life = "Don't kill people," ers!

Oh, I understand it now.....It's an anagram cipher!

A rouse, a deception to obscure and disguise the actual intent.

Just like;
Eminent Domain = The government steals your stuff!

Universal Health Care = the government steals your life, and then decides if you are viable and productive enough for the State, and whether to spend the money to keep you alive.

<u>Equal Rights</u> = the government gives you everything for
free,
just as long as you always vote Democrat,
as long as you are not a male Caucasian or a conservative
female, or a conservative minority, or a conservative.

<u>Fairness Doctrine</u> = The government repeals the 1st
amendment to the Constitution in order to protect freedom
of speech.

<u>Affirmative Action</u> = the government assumes that you do
not possess the capacity nor the intelligence to think, or
care for yourself, and then keeps your soul.

<u>ACORN</u> = takes from the rich and gives to themselves, and
if You pay them enough money they'll get you elected to
public office. Perhaps even, to the presidency, so You can
pay them off with even more Tax dollars in a quid-pro-quo.

<u>Roe VS Wade</u> = Roe isn't versus anymore! Oops, UR mistake!

<u>RACIST</u> = a 20th century pejorative,
that when used in the 21st century is a code word for:
I can extort your money and influence your new detractors,
and now have power over you by making You feel guilty for
your achievements, accomplishments, and for your own hard
work.
Otherwise, you will pay a heavy price and be publicly
castigated, ridiculed, mocked & disliked by an organized
majority (of the minority), of malcontents, who are very
faithfully determined to wreck your business and destroy
your life, your reputation, and any credibility you've
ever earned.

<u>Vegan</u> = don't eat anything with a face.

<u>Abortion</u> = kill anything with a face.

<u>Moral Equivalency</u> = "Oh yeah?," and "I'll show you!"

i.e. (If I think you've mocked me, or that you've demeaned
what I think, or what I believe in,
then it's perfectly justifiably to "Blow You Up",
or "Chop off your head",
or "burn your bullet-ridden body and hang your blackened
stinking corpse from a bridge"),

and, as a Liberal's Bonus behind curtain #3,
the "MEDIA" will not question my motives, or make any
judgments, or condemn your struggling as a crime.

In fact, they will hail my courageous fight, and give me a
total PASS and blame the corpse!

Oh, I get it now, this is fun...........................It's about Being
LIBERAL and anti-Capitalist!

Stimulus Package = Fulfilling the Democrat's Wish List:
"License To Steal".

I'm sure you can think of a few of these also, like:

TARP = The government spends money we don't have,
on things we don't need,
for reasons we're not sure about yesterday,
because we're now afraid of tomorrow,
so we'll Shoot ourselves in the Head today,
instead of "in the Foot", as usual!

"TARP!" Isn't that a dead, stinking, swollen beached
fish corpse?
No, no, that was the Omnibus Bill!

Separation of Church and State = a Dichotomy!
In education, it's juxtaposed to Islam co-opting the
American "taxpayer funded" Public Educational School System
in 2009.

(Our Federally and State monitored and protected education
system that now Outlaws: cupcakes and Christmas Trees,
yet enthusiastically condones and inexplicitly sanctions
Islamic Muslim curriculum and Mohammed's teachings, and
Islam's daily-regimented, religious ceremonies openly
taught to a captive audience of American citizen's children
in America's US government controlled public schools
without any interference by said government!)...
Can't quite understand that one, unless someone pretty
high-up in the federal government must have ties to Islam!

Moral equivalency = has become an invective. The standard
liberal response or epithet, utilized for any situational
rebuttal, actuate or not, the Double-Standard of today.

Owned by a complicit MEDIA, and proudly taught by

Progressives, where "Standards" are reviled and "Hypocrisy" is the watchword where they hold their "death grip" on the minds and a few souls of "Public Opinion".
Willing agents in the Democrat Party who govern and share increased powers with the Executive Branch of government, will now Rule as Czars by Edicts, co-mingling/co-sponsoring all of whom unanimously "abhorrer", with total distain their loyal opposition for their freedoms of speech, continuous espousing of religious freedoms and rightwing Judgementalism.

Though now, this Unholy Trinity, this Triumvirate are the most unforgiving, hypocritical, judgmental, picayune, horrific tight-asses that the planet Earth has ever witnessed since The First Grand Inquisitor - Torquemada in 1483.

So, What's with the Left?

*side-note, as an illustration of how upside-down society conducts itself presently:
The Spanish Government has petitioned the International Courts for the "rightful" return of located & legally salvaged-treasure-gold found in International waters in the Atlantic Ocean by a private concern.

This observer is again amazed and taken aback by the obvious, obscured absurdity of this issue, but applaud their intentions:
"absolutely return the gold to the "rightful owners", those that it was stolen from originally" by the Spanish Conquistadors who conquered, pillaged, murdered and I'd speculate undoubtedly also raped, decimated and destroyed 3 major civilizations,
and an entire continent and part of another,
in the name of King, Queen, Country and God, and as a bonus for being such good sports they stuck around as the New Landlords and slave masters of any remaining indigenous peoples, those that hadn't been finally finished-off by their immune European conqueror's disease.

The gall of Spanish government's hutzpah is incredible, as though the Nazis could sue, via International Courts to get-back the treasured ARTWORK the 3rd Reich confiscated, murdered-for, and stole from: Judaism en masse before they "gassed them", private collections, and sovereign Nations and galleries across Europe, and parts of Asia and Africa.

In fact, very much like the current Austrian government's claims, and International museums alike, presently holding W.W.II ART, now rightfully belongs to the former owner's Representative Country of Israel,
with the (recipients of said-stolen ARTISTIC properties) all now demanding official bills of laden, photos, proof of purchase and the receipts (that were obviously burned-up in a World War, before relinquishing their grimy-holds upon this ostensibly amoral ill-gotten contraband!

I for one, if in absolute authority to pressure the smarmy scoundrels and world governments, (including the Vatican), would demand the exact same requirements upon them, OR GIVE THE DAMN STOLEN ARTWORK BACK TO THE PROPER REPRESENTATIVES!

Much as the Egyptian's heritage and artifacts, for that matter, far flung and strewn across the World.

Interesting question: who rightfully owns anything without an authorized receipt, unless freely sold by a rightful owner, or freely bartered and purchased, not at the point of a spear, sword, gun or cannon!

But, perhaps in a case where a preponderance of rightful ownership, supported by a mountain of circumstantial evidence, where the ownership documentation, as well as the owner both went up in smoke, an allowance would be exercised and a more rational judgment would prevail. Especially when the onus should fall upon the government, or museum to produce a Bill of Laden, which would be a business administrative norm.
But, what do I know about Laws made up by men, devoid of common sense, reasoned logic, or ethics in common law?

Right is Right,
but then there's that ever-evolving and fluid: Liberal's Law!...Screw The Constitution....What day is it?.... and That's The Law We'll Use Today!............But I digress.

Again, if these elitist Leftist, tenured socialist, union pensioned academics,
along with their unsuspecting (diversity-quota'd) captive charges, all had to make it "on their own, in the real world", without their government's assistance and entitlement safety-nets, they'd learn very quickly just how the "*Law of the Jungle*" reality only accommodates "*the survival of the fittest*" and "*natural selection*"!

All of which thins out the Herd's Gene-Pool every now and then for purposes known only to wisdom of NATURE, GOD and the FATES, (that's Dumb Luck), global-warming excluded!

But, the belief in a "higher being" to keep your courage-up, and yourself grounded, well now, that takes a certain amount of "FAITH"!....Don't look under the bed, another pedophile's been freed by a Vermont Judge: BOO!.....We need some faith when dealing with a liberal's interpretation of a "fluid Constitution", but I don't think most (thinking Americans) have the intestinal fortitude and constitution for these boogiemen roaming the world today in all different disguises and purposes! I recommend no patience!

Where's a good 'ole Islamic "Hand-Chopping" when you need one?..Or chopping off something else for that matter, to end (1) problem "For Good"!!...Ahh, an Idiom with a double meaning, don't tell the Liberals, they'll Ban the Word from the Text Books!

The malevolent Dr. Tiller, on the other hand, wasn't put here on this Earth to play GOD, or be a GOD.
I'm sorry he got shot. Bad things happen don't they, no matter how hard we try to prevent them. He of all people should ultimately appreciate the significance of the "ending of human life", but,
had he unluckily succumbed to an auto fatality, for example, would he still have been deified by his sycophantic devotees?
That always opportunistically skews moral issues for one's advantage? Tiller killed in car crash = KARMA. Shot = awe!

That's an interesting question though. I would suspect not, being relegated to, but a footnote to history, forgotten!

Everyone loves a martyr. They used to be worth $25,000 ahead in IRAQ under Saddam's regime.
I just don't remember The MEDIA decrying Saddam's Payola Scheme Deal while they unanimously savaged Bush and His soldier boy's supposed savagery for 6 long years......Quite the democratic businessman, Saddam. Didn't matter how many civilians, women and children inevitably got blown-up in collateral damage along with HIS Target, Saddam awarded that same $25,000 prize to any Suicide Bomber's family just the same, with "no penalties or deductions".

Our brave soldiers, on the other hand, were severely criticized and demonized for any unfortunate collateral damage occurring, of which our fighting men went far above & beyond, way out of their way to the extreme, jeopardizing the mission and their own personal safety in many cases, as not to incur any civilian death. A tact, and a practiced American "rule of engagement" unseen in armed-conflict anywhere else on this earth in the present or the past to the United State citizen-soldier's personal detriment.

We don't hear about any Barack's soldier's suspected atrocities every single day any longer, or monthly or even yearly for that matter. Hmmmm!
Perhaps there are "our" soldiers once again instead of just President Bush's?? Same Men, same War, same weapons, same bullets, same humans, same enemy, different President! Hmmmmm!

You know, of course, what they say about "False Gods"?
(that would be called "Karma" for those in CA, CO and NY)

"It's not nice to fool with Mother Nature,"
....and it's Not just about Butter, it includes Ethanol, Dikes (that's about water), Cloning, or the dropping-off of your (much too large for your apartment) Pet Shoppe foreign born exotic snake into the local woods, being abandoned in southern Florida, (those that lays 50 to 80 Eggs), that then explode into new foreign-specie populations up to 100,000+ fat 25' foot Python Snakes that Eat=Anything in nature, including your dog, your teenager, and even you given the chance............Want to really save the environment, our planet, or your place at the party?

Don't picket, or worry about drilling for cheap oil and gas in our backyard to eliminate the deficit, and the imbalance of payments to save the US economy and your country, but at least be consistent and raise some REAL HELL about the New Anacondas eating Old Yeller and Sammie-Sue, You idiots!

Didn't hear the Sierra Club or PITA staging any Nude commercials about that, instead of worrying about the SUV, or people wearing pelts and chicken's rights.

It's the Seals and the Whales, Chickens, Goose liver and veal! Forget about loss of freedom, murderous terrorists moving next door and chopping babies like ponderosa pines.

..Oh my God, don't cut the trees, please!

Do you think Herr Doktor Tiller really made all those Million$ on just smashing baby brains, just murdering 60,000+ babies, or maybe other stellar sundry pursuits like selling some body-parts for Stem-cell and Cloning experiments as a sideline?....hmmmm

His proud family said they'll reopen the Clinic in his honor, yah, right,
and to keep The Bank Accounts Open to make further deposits and cash future checks...
I'm sure a testament to Nazi efficiency!

So, now then Liberals, is that really the traditional "All-American, Flag waving, National Anthem and Mom's Apple Pie" we are all fighting to protect today?

Well, is it Punk?

NEWS FLASH
United States
(June 2, 2009)

Hot off the Radio today, since "Press Is Dead".

Men that wore the Death's Head insignia "meet" in the desert again!

One if by Land, Two if by Sea!....What if by AIR, and where is Our Fearless Leader Today?

Obama's Government does another "Britney Spears: "did it again" for those paying attention.

Monday: all America's nuclear sites and stockpile depository locations, including their AAA Trip-Tik direction maps, were included in a governmental administrative staff newsletter about: "government secrecy", strangely enough today and was "mistakenly", (yeah, sure),
put on the World Wide Web (oops, "did it again") for a short time before being discovered and removed.

[and they used to fear Bush's access to that briefcase with the "RED BUTTON"]

"And these are the guys that are going to be in charge of protection all of us,
in addition to running Universal Health Care," so stated Rush today. Check his newsletter tonight for clarification.

OK, now since Obama is presently in a Muslim country, as I type this, and he gleefully is espousing his Muslim ancestry, maybe he feels safer over there, if We Americans over here get attacked "Right Now",
since everyone on the planet "now" knows exactly where all of our strategic soft spots are, and no longer hidden?

You can make a lot of Dirty Bombs with any of that stuff!

And, as our World President meeting with friends in the desert, once again switching hats today for a Kufi Cap,
I am reminded of other men that wore the Skull cap with a Death's Head insignia and Lightning flashes on their collars,
who weren't that happy with Judaism either, not so long ago, when first plotting their mutual dilemma of an age old hatred in the modern age of enlightenment, equipped with original WMDs; airplanes and automatic weapons,
 and *Zyklon-B*.

And ironically who did the majority of American Jews and American Catholics all vote for in the last presidential election, again?

As time and tide changes all things, and the great pendulum of human events swings back and forth, to-and-fro, on and on
FOOLISH MEN REPEAT HISTORY AGAIN AND AGAIN THROUGH THE MILLENNIA,
and STILL THEY LEARN NOTHING.

==

**as an addendum to a Blog comment that I gave in reference to: "Socialism and Fascism on College Campi",
I wish to make one last point before I'm shouted down by "Miss Anderson's" 5th grade class!

"Sure you can go to any campus TODAY and say anything you want, this is America?
1st amendment, and all that jazz..Right Dude!....NOT!"

<u>QUESTION:</u> Why do we really care what college kids think anyway?...Look who they voted for! Ever watch Jay-Walking? They don't know where they are!...Just bring the Beer Dude!

Why does the MEDIA tabulate, calculated, embellish, over-emphasize and publicized these children's opinions? They're not even weaned yet, and they are totally subsidized, so who cares? Does your kid help you make-out your budget, or pay any of your bills?...Sure, they Make-Out alright but that's where it ends!

Would a Master Carpenter give credence to an apprentice's assertions?

These students, these loaves of unleavened bread, they're like an unfinished soufflé. It's all scrambled eggs and all over the plate,
and even when it's finished and out of the oven, these graduate youths will fold in a tremor, or stiff breeze.

It's their parents that we need to hold responsible for capitulating to their babies whims and paying through the nose to proudly have their children "Half-baked".

Talk about a lack of equal value for $60.00 to $600.00 @ Credit Hour at any college or universities today. For every dollar invested, exactly what value does one receive in return?

...What are You paying for parents, and what are your children getting in return for that investment?...
If You Get What You Pay For In Life, Then When It Comes To Education, The Higher Up The Food Chain Your Valued Return Diminishes Exponentially.

What is that, reverse psychology or reverse economics?
Sounds more like a ZERO-SUM GAIN rip-off to me!
I've Learned That The Hard Way: Writing the Checks!!
...Trade Schools are excluded for this debate!

We all know that many professors, and academics are liberal leaning, ha ha ha, and some crazy-radicals, corrupt, smok'n som'thn, or all 4.

QUESTION:
Did any Engineering schools, or Nobel Laureates ever do a
class project, thesis or "case study", anyone's aware of,
on the: "Effects Of A Plane Flying Into A Skyscraper?",
(either at night, in a storm, or high-jacked by maniac-
clowns from Hell),

and, precisely: "How Many Minutes It Would Stand Before
Collapsing?",
In Order To Determine How Much Time It Would Take The
Heroic Fire-Fighters To Arrive There, And Remove All Those
"Incapable or Less Self-Initiated" Out Of That Structure.
Or, Remove People From The Neighboring Building Also, That
Had Been Told That "It Was OK" To Go Back To Your Desks And
Continue Working, As Either,
That Skyscraper Or The One Next To You Burns Down,
And,
Unfortunately Everyone That Doesn't Escape, Dies,
Including The Brave Firemen And Policeman Unnecessarily
Risking Their Lives For A Foolish "Lack Of Foreseen Proper
Procedures and Protocols?".....

I didn't hear any of that discussed over the last 8 years,
other than: that dumbbell Bush had engineered "the greatest
clandestine disaster conspiracy" in modern history, and
with No Leaks! How clever a dumbbell, who would've thought!

But of course, for the sake of this academic "case study",
It Could Be Just An "Innocent Mistake" By A Plane In A Fog,
Or A Snow-Storm Blizzard, A Radio Or Radar Malfunction,
Or Even Terrorists, God Forbid, That The FAA Should Have
Been Screening For, Whatever!......I Thought That Is What
Engineering Schools Were For, And Did:
(What if it pancakes and falls down?)

Doesn't seem like such a stretch to me to analysis and
anticipate the unknown: to determine actualities,
preventions, procedures and protocols to exit inhabitants
in any emergencies, the fastest way to get all out ALIVE!

Oh, But Not To Forget Taxable Building Codes, And Taxable
Inspectors, Taxable Emergency Fire Escapes, Taxable Mini-
Parachutes, Burn Safety Tests And Taxable Fire Retardant
Coatings For GIRDERS, Etc. Hey, Seems as though a revenue
generating opportunity was lost here, bureaucrats, or was
it? But the way to "Get People Out Fast" Missed The Grade.

Any Genius At MIT or Stanford Ever Check-out That Scenario?
Wasn't The Empire State Building Hit One Time By A Plane??

Maybe some Professors would just rather sleep with our
daughters, and (some of our sons), then earn their pay
thinking outside the box and "teaching", or perhaps grade
papers strictly on merit, without personal bias!

Our most trusted, extended family members that spend more
time with our children then We, while we work to earn the
money to pay them, The Teachers, those "all feeling and all
knowing" surrogate parents, they should be held to the
highest-standards, and recognized for their genuine
accomplishments, but also made officially responsible and
given due credit for filling the prisons with trillions of
unfulfilled Liberal promises under their tutelage, for
decades now.

When all those future-felons were their naive captive
audience on a daily basis for some, 13 to 16 long years,
kinder, grade and high schools, who personally held their
little brains in their big firm, molding hands,
  ten-times longer each day than even those student's own
parents; Moms and Dads that rushed home, made dinner,
barely time to speak, watching homework performed and maybe
read a bedtime story,
always trusting and feeling, rest assured that their
children (were-in-good-safe-hands)!....
So, <u>what's with the Left?</u>

<u>What do we need to do to get our children back?</u>

<u>What do we need to do to get our children back?</u>

Well, we could start actually making some "judgments", ooo;
creating some standards,
pointing some fingers,
holding people responsible,
not repeating the same mistakes,
getting ticked-off,
getting bad teachers "OUT", and
stop worrying about maybe hurting some feelings, or making
waves, or being embarrassed. It's our children's hearts and
minds we are trying to save here. The Hell with convention,
Teacher's conferences be damned, we want our kids back!

Consider it "An Intervention"
and if it's your friend, or a relative, or your child's or
grand kid's teacher we're talking about here who is a
little sick in the head, and they desperately need your
Tough Love to make them see the light,...INTERVENE..,
and change them for the better.

What have You got to Lose? ..Your Children!

Or, Just look in the mirror, and then take your children
away from the maniacs, and the sycophants, and the
socialists, the pedophiles and especially your politicians!

Really now, is this alternate universe we are all living in
worthy of an actual debate?
...No Testing? No Standards? No Vouchers? <u>REALLY?</u>

How many times in the '50s or '60s, or even the '70s and
'80s for that matter, did we have 9th graders "Texting"
pornographic self-images through cyberspace,
or
had "5th graders" fornicating in the classroom
with an audience of their peers cheering them on, or WOW,
knew what was going-on,
or
your daughters, or granddaughters giving BJ's on the school
bus ride home,
or
middle school teachers descending upon their students like
sex-starved harridans,
or maybe,
I just went to better schools on another planet?

50 Years of Liberal Education had set that stage
for what Obama was able to pull-off in just 90 days
that it had taken Castro, President Hugo Chavez, Manuel
Noriega, as quick examples, literally years to accomplish.
Yet, Obama did it in only 3 months and without a shot fired!

"All tyranny needs to gain a foothold is for people
of good conscience to remain silent."
<u>Thomas Jefferson</u>

"A democracy is nothing more than mob rule,
where fifty-one percent of the people may take away the
rights of the other forty-nine."
Thomas Jefferson

And You're telling Me, that we should really care what a
college kid thinks about "who should run the largest
business on the planet",
and the greatest country in earth in the history of man??

So, college kids may have helped Jane Fonda dethrone an
American President and end a war,
(that unfortunately lead to the Genocide of millions of
human beings, gone in the "Killing Fields"),
but who's counting,

and influenced the US to abandon future cheap nuclear power
to our detriment and deficits after Jane's movie, "China
Syndrome", unlike France, smart enough to consider the
advantages that has successfully, safely and cost-
effectively, to the advantage of all Frenchmen, have
enjoyed and prospered ever since Jane's outstanding
propaganda campaign,
but who's counting,

and has kept the USA forever "oil dependent" upon Arab
Sheiks, with our "No Drilling Here" policy,
or building any new refineries, which has almost destroyed
our economy and brought down another American President,
but who's counting,

and since the omnipotent oppressive Cathe' Standards, our
nation will enter a new era at risk, as usual, of its own
sovereignty and survival, as
our freedoms are absconded by a slick and cool demagogue,
but who's counting?
 .... certainly not Jane, or her ex-husband!

At least we don't have to listen to or watch Jane Fonda
anymore,
or her weak-kneed billionaire ex-husband,
that hadn't even realized that his very own ex-wife was
directly & indirectly culpable in the murder of millions of
Cambodians and Vietnamese, after we generous Americans were
forced to "high-tail-it" back home in defeat.

It was new news to Teddy-boy in a recent interview I
personally watched, he, like a baby deer in headlights, you
could see a light bulbs explode in his brain!..I think it
was on O'Reilly, check YouTube!.........

So, what's with the Left?

The "Unintended Consequences" of: "the end justifies
the means"

Just like: "Republicans starving children, in the lunchroom
program" under Bush,
went uncontested and undefended by Republican weasels,
always leaving President Bush out to dry.
Which was actually a continuation of the largest increase
in Federal school funds ever in history for a second year
in a row,
(greater than the entire US Government budget under the
Reagan Administration for the United States' government.
That's probably enough money for a lot of peanut butter and
jelly sandwiches, even at today's prices Liberals!

And again, far more monies allotted for the US Education
Dept., than was ever appropriated under Clinton's
administration, come-on!

But those mean-ole Republicans dared to make a slight
"reduction to just the automatic increases", which were
tacked on top of the massive school program from the year
before for a little fiscal responsibility, strategically
labeled by the DEMs, ("not toward over-paid,
underperforming teachers"), oh No,
(The Children's milk and cookies). BRILLIANT DEMs!

But another chink in the Republican's armor giving the
DEMs another opening to go for the jugular, and was there
any Republican outrage or defense to correct the record?
And once again this "Lunch Myth", this "Sandwich Fable" was
transmuted and translated by the Liberal-Press to their
waiting un-appreciative, un-interested, ill-informed and
un-involved, totally-managed "voting bloc" that still think
"their government gives them things for free".
..How dare that heartless Bush?

Seriously, I'm probably preaching to the choir here, and
You all know this, but for the few that might not, and any
of my past rants that have rocked your world just a little,

or started to open your eyes a bit, maybe the light is too bright with snob blindness, well then, let's all just start being those ("big, bad, evil, not really very nice, boo-hoo "mean spirited", and judgmental bass-turds"), that we've been blamed "for being" all these years, and grow a spine & start standing-up for one's convictions for a change, and taking some prisoners. Also losing some fair-weather friends, or a comatose relative for the betterment of the nation and your own sanity can we healthy as losing pounds.

This isn't a popularity contest, it's real Life and Death now, and Our Republican Leaders just won't do it, and since Journalism, now dead, once in defense of Freedom and Truth, Justice and the American Way; so, where is our Superman?

He's not coming, surprise, and it is all up to us, sorry! They are not your friends anyway when the $&#@ hits the fan, the balloon goes up, & we're finally in-it up to ours. Or do you want your great-granddaughters to be continually used as toilet paper, or
your grandsons preyed-upon by the NEA's protected members? Move your kids out of New Hampshire, or anywhere, or any schools like that while they're still innocent and alive.

Think - Think very long and hard, deep in your bones, does anyone really believe "The Left", "Those Liberals", "These Socialists" and "Them Communists" give a galloping wit about real "Civil Rights", any "Human Freedoms", true "Equality", saving Children and Women from Rape, the Life of an un-successful abortion procedure, breathing & gasping for its eternal life, left on a table, struggling alone, un-aided and watched as she takes her last breath? Senator Obama weighed-in on that when in Illinois………Check it Out!

Opposed legislation protecting born-alive failed abortions

Obama has consistently refused to support legislation that would define an infant who survives a late-term induced-labor abortion as a human being with the right to live. He insists that no restriction must ever be placed on the right of a mother to decide to abort her child.

On March 30, 2001, Obama was the only Illinois senator who rose to speak against a bill that would have protected babies who survived late term labor-induced abortion. Obama rose to object that if the bill passed, and a nine-month-old fetus survived a late-term labor-induced abortion was deemed to be a person who had a right to live, then the law would "forbid abortions to take place."

Obama further explained the equal protection clause of the Fourteenth Amendment does not allow somebody to kill a child, so if the law deemed a child who survived a late-term labor-induced abortion had a right to live, "then this would be an anti-abortion statute."

Source: <u>Obama Nation, by Jerome Corsi, p.238</u>
Aug 1, 2008
http://www.ontheissues.org/Social/Barack Obama Abortion.htm

Start Fighting Back, Notre Dame won't!
This BRAIN FREEZE Is Best Typified By This Stockholm Syndrome; After 60, that's 6-0 long years of the DEMs for all intents and purposes being in primarily control of our government and of this nation,
so, exactly "why haven't things changed"?,
since it's been a monumental progressive DISASTER of epic proportions with sycophantic rhetoric, double-speak, half-truths, BOLD FACED LIES, and enough false promises to fill the Grand Canyon with nothing to show for it but backwards looking finger-pointing, with inertia set in permanent reverse for the AMERICAN's of African ancestry by liberal PR that hasn't risen to their touted projections and hype; AND STILL The Constituency Votes-Straight-Democrat
 With A LEFTIST "Vulcan Mind-Meld"!

I-N-C-R-E-D-I-B-L-E!....U-N-B-L-I-E-A-B-L-E ....WHY?...HOW?

Ps, Obama said in Cairo:
"America is one of the largest Muslim countries"
with over 6,000,000 Muslims.
Oh, Really? What a Guy...What a Kidder?...
..NO, THIS GUY'S SERIOUS PEOPLE!
http://www.politifact.com/truth-o-meter/statements/2009/jun/04/barack-obama/obama-claims-america-one-largest-muslim-countries/

(Oooo, out of 300+ million citizens, or are those in his addition 5th columnists, only He knows about?)
http://www.theguardian.com/news/datablog/2009/oct/08/muslim-population-islam-religion

So, if He likes his own name once again so much, "Hussein", now that he's finally and securely President, then let's give him what He wants and address him accordingly:
"Mr. President of the World: Hussein Obama."
==
Photo on http://www.sentryman.org/index.html
Haj Amin al-Husseini, the most influential leader of Palestinian Arabs

==

The Nazi Connection To Islamic Balkan Terrorism
http://www.youtube.com/watch?v=dbP2EyF8d34

German Chancellor Adolf Hitler and Grand Mufti Haj Amin al-Husseini: Zionism and the Arab Cause (November 28, 1941)
Photo on SENTRYMAN.org

http://www.tellthechildrenthetruth.com/gallery/
Minutes of the meeting with Hitler and Husseini.

==

Amin Al Husseini, Head of SS Muslim Hanzar Division
 - Mein Kampf by Adolf Hitler.
Distributed by Palestinian Authority- 2003
Photo on www.SENTRYMAN.org

http://www.tellthechildrenthetruth.com/mbhood_en.html
Muslim Brotherhood

KNOWING AND UNDERSTANDING THE HISTORY OF THE MUSLIM BROTHERHOOD IS THE KEY TO UNDERSTANDING TODAY'S ISLAMIC WAR AGAINST THE WEST

With Saudi King Abdullah on June 3, 2009:
Photo on www.SENTRYMAN.org

All For ONE, and the ONE is OBAMA….._Allah be Praised_

SENTRYMAN

Ps. Remember:
It's Not About The "Black Guy",…………..It's About "That Guy"!

My choice would have been "Condi or Colin" to go up against Hillary!......

Heck, Morgan Freeman would make a far better President for these United States, than this guy who's only playing one!

Chapter 36

"How Do You Take Credit For An Abstract"? Mr. President

Posted by SENTRYMAN on June 9, 2009 at 11:08pm

Had a thought today while listening to Rush.
I had my ears-on, as I'm an independent self-employed; white collar/blue collar, iron collar
(work'in-for-the-company-store), "Pee-On";
like a lot of us today, because I can No longer afford to ever retire!

I didn't want to be totally out-of-the-loop, so I bought a head-set,
and, (follow me now),
as for our illustrious "Freeless" Leader,
<u>"How can You take credit for an abstract"?</u>

That's when the president grabs, no steals credit for something that doesn't happen, didn't
happen, might, but hasn't happened yet!

* i.e. ("didn't rain today, no one got shot, my dog didn't get hit by a car,
and bye the way, I saved (1) million jobs and some money on my car insurance!.......
So, I'll give myself a well-deserved pat on-my-own-back"),

but especially when You lack the class to "give credit where credit is due",
and for something that "didn't happen again", but could've,
to the very Man who is totally responsible for preventing it?...

(Get that?)

We didn't have a 2nd 9/11,,,,,,,FACT!
Thank you President Bush!

(Are You with me up to this point?)

*e.g. Like a school Superintendent that made a difference in America today, and stepped-
up and fought-off a Gunman down-to-the-ground, and took away the Gun in his school;
who probably,
must have,
most likely did,
you can bet your kid's life on it,
"prevented the death of at least (1), if not many little boys and little girls,
who all got to go home to their Mommies and Daddies this afternoon,
only because this "(1) guy made a difference!"

*(An "action" that <u>prevented</u> a "reaction")!

Can't prove it, no way to tell, didn't happen, but <u>He is a genuine HERO</u> all the same,

<u>and so was George Bush, all the same,</u>   Pg. 209

but, we sat on our hands, and we tolerated one/half, ½, 50% of fellow Americans to perpetrate that lack of respect, lack of recognition-atrocity against our standing President at that specific moment in time without raising a voice….Shame on us!
So now, "Thank You, Republican members of the House and Senate
for all that You never did for your Leader"!

Oh, but had a 2nd - 9/11 happened, oh, well then,
who would be the 1st person to award that distinction to President Bush for that major Cluster-F#@%;
Ms. Fonda, Tom Hanks, Steven Spielberg, (Barbar) Streisand, Susan Sarandon, Sean Penn, Michael Moore, The View, Dan Rather, Katie Couric?

Yup, and Who's The Last Person On Earth To Get Any Credit For:
 Preventing Anything From Happening, or The Total Collapse Of This Nation, After 9/11? Hmmm?

Well, now let's all remember to remind each of them
 Who's going to be responsible for any major Cluster-F#@%s from now on,
and to get "His just due", and all the credit when it happens again
with the close of the Guantanamo Water Sports & Summer Camp!

So, why won't our "Media-elite" proudly exclaim, and explain to our uninformed youth, as well as, remind the 90% misguided LEFT in America,
since our children will never learn it in our schools, just how noble "America has been" just in the 20th century,
risking life and limb defending its citizens, and FREEDOM for all,
around the world during W.W.I, W.W.II, Korea, and especially Viet Nam, when We had little to gain.

Also in Granada, Haiti, Africa, in Europe again and especially too, in the middle East,
precisely how our "American soldiers fought and died" for Kuwaiti (Muslims) that were attacked by Saddam Hussein,
and those "American soldiers that died" helping to feed (Muslims) in Somalia,
and those "American soldiers that fought" for the oppressed (Muslims) in Kosovo,
and for the (Muslims) in Bosnia,
and those "American soldiers that die" today helping (Muslims) in Afghanistan,
and "died trying to free (Muslims) enslaved in Iraq", and today and all the tomorrows,

some of our soldiers will "leave their families forever", and give away their futures and give-up their own lives, <u>because they think it's important directly protecting their country, and You and Me here at home,</u>

and indirectly defending innocent (Muslim) women and children,
<u>because it might happen, could happen, would happen again, if they weren't over there,</u>
so maybe some disillusioned Home-grown terrorist wouldn't think it's a noble, justifiably good idea to assassinate an American soldier somewhere, someday.

Any random soldier's death would do for Terrorist-Ideologies, even one of his own countrymen for his "Eye For An Eye" rational, that this mental giant "Bledsoe", didn't get the memo and kills one of our sons and is even be proud of it!

A brave young "new" recruit: Pvt. William Andrew Long, fresh out of Boot Camp that joined the Military to do his part and travel across the globe to defend The Constitution, and protect strangers, You and Me, and to also "protect the guy who killed him", another young "new" recruit to "Radical Islam": Abdulhakim Mujahid Muhammad, AKA Carlos Bledsoe, who "was told" in fact that our soldiers Kill Innocent Muslim Women and Kids!

By whom? You know,
our own stellar yellar "Yellow Journalists" in the US of A, that's who!

Thank You, NY TIMES: all the news that will fit at the bottom of a parrot cage.

And this brilliant Muslim firebrand, armed with his new radical ideological Media-driven
traitorous-propaganda that helped mold and create this moron, all deserve at least 99% of
the credit for killing our boy!
Which is fundamentally why our journalistic society, "The Media, didn't cover the story".
Instead they busy themselves in their own ideological cults like deifying Herr Doktor Tiller!
Our hats off to you Men and Women of decisive clear purpose, influencing the youth of
America for your own purposes........To bad You're on the wrong side of decency & logic!!

READ MY LIPS:
OUR MEDIA KILLS OUR SONS AND DAUGHTERS WITH THEIR WORDS
AS EQUALLY AND PRECISELY AS JIHADI STINGERS, AND ROAD-SIDE
BOMBS.......THESE AMERICANS ARE THE DOMESTIC TERRORISTS OF
THE 21st CENTURY!....YES, THE PEN IS MIGHTIER THAN THE SWORD!

Credit where credit is do!

PERFORMANCE, President Obama.........NOT ABSTRACTs,
then You'll earn some Kudos, not a Nobel just for showing up!

SENTRYMAN

//

 Comment by SENTRYMAN on June 10, 2009 at 11:57pm

Abdulhakim Mujahid Muhammad, AKA Carlos Bledsoe explained today,
and was repeated on O'Reilly:
"Murder is justified" when You have a good reason!

Who's teaching Americans that in certain circumstances:

MURDER = Good Idea,
or "WHO is Not teaching" our citizens that "Murder isn't OK" on the Planet Earth?

In certain circumstances;
Liberal Teachers? - Hollywood? - Sharia Law? - Racists? - Secularists? - his Parents?

Of course, knowing that one "can beat the rap" with many Judges today, isn't a deterrent,
unless you're stealing Football cards, right Juice?

Chapter 37

"It's like living with a Wife-Beater, a Drunk or a Democrat".

Posted by SENTRYMAN on <u>June 11, 2009</u> at 1:21am

Mr. Letterman at 11:50 PM, on his show Wednesday evening,
in an act of hollow-contrition toward the "Governor, & Mother" in question,
mocked now Mr. Palin ("Tooodd"), twice,

and He then repeated every joke (to rapturous applause) once again;
(asking the question: why then aren't Spitzer and A-rod complaining
"also"?),

while referencing the original tasteless jest, he gave his tailor-measured
"maya copa", but only apologizing about, and this is choice: specifically:
getting the ages of the joke's main-targets wrong, and for that he was truly
repentant and sorry!
For indeed, it was a mistake since "knocking–up" the "18 year old"
daughter is always "Fair Game" and Legitimized Humor, instead of the
aforementioned "14 year old" daughter, thus making HIS Joke only
<u>borderline</u> indecent, and less funny,
 ....(phew, follow that?)

Appreciate witty clever writing like that?....."Johnny" is spinning in his
eternal slumber.
If of course you have more class than watching those kind of sophomorics,
<u>"Vote with Your TV Clicker"</u>, someone is always counting and you can take
a stand and make a difference?

What's more worrisome and of greater concern might be:
What vegetable truck did this Peanut-Gallery fall off?
They didn't express even an "Ooooh" or a groan. This country is chock-full
of Enablers, which is half the problem!....No Shame anymore!

It's like living with a Wife-Beater, a Drunk, or a Democrat and watching
"Bad Boys" and "Girls Behaving Badly" all day.
One Needs A Bit Of Self-Respect Before You Can Help Others!

<u>SENTRYMAN</u>

Pg. 212

Comment by SENTRYMAN 1 day ago

CBS Won't Care! ....But, if You give a wit, write the sponsors. Vote with your feet, and vote your purchasing power.

In the same way, I have always felt that proper credit should be levied where credit is due. An obviously desperate comedian who hasn't been funny in years now, on the downside of a career must resort to baser instincts, sensationalize to be outrageous, and though "I once loved the guy", he, or I have changed, maybe both.

One should rightfully reap what one has sewn!

Liberal teachers have filled the prisons with the "less fortunate", who's momentary incarcerations will only be furloughed by weak Liberal Judging, to then wreak havoc once again upon our undeserving unfortunate society by even more talented and fortunate crooks, those who attended college, but missed the "Ethics" class, and eventually made it to Wall Street, and into the highest Corp-rat Board Rooms, and the sainted Halls of Congress.

All those less serious among us struggling to find their identities, graced with an "Excess of Vanity as a consolation prize" to mug and entertain from Burbank, were bestowed The Blue Prints to mimic (Depravity, Greed, Lust, Deception, Incest and Murder She Wrote) in their pursuit of the higher Imaginary-Truth for their Art, eager portrayals that glorify the "darker sides of man", for their own self-aggrandizement and enrichment, lest they take Vengeance upon thee, their Cross to bear, Guilt, being less serious!

To Caesar: credit is due!

Thank you MEDIA for helping kill our soldiers for cash.
Thank you Hollywood for rewarding sloth for cash.
Thank you Network TV for compromising values for cash.
Thank you Music Industry for corrupting our youth for cash.
Thank you UAW for destroying the Auto Industry for cash.
Thank you Democrat Party betraying America for cash.
Thank you President Obama impersonating Icarus for cash.
Thank you Bill Gates for Pandora's Box with No Lock, for _____?

The Enemy isn't coming from Guantanamo, the Enemy is already here!

SENTRYMAN

Postscript,

and Thank You "Speaker Pelosi" for still fighting to release those
Guantanamo interrogation photos,
no matter how many of our sons and daughters "lives will be jeopardized
and sacrificed" in the never-ending pursuit of "your" TRUTH.

In case you weren't aware of the Jihadist rules of engagement,
Madam Speaker,
when You are responsible for the death of an American infidel, "you" are
required to kill Yourself in order to reap your reward!

Halleluiah, I think You just won the LOTTO Lady!

SENTRYMAN

---

2 COMMENTS

Comment by naner on June 11, 2009 at 10:56am

They are not held accountable for anything and do as they please.
We must show them by protesting - Washington DC on July 4th.
We must not let this continue.

Comment by SENTRYMAN on June 11, 2009 at 1:39am

'All that is necessary for the triumph of evil is that good men do nothing'
Edmund Burke

"The people get the government they deserve".
Joseph de Maistre, Alexis de Tocqueville

 **Chapter 38**

A MAN FOR ALL SEASONS.........WE NEED HIM NOW!

Posted by SENTRYMAN on June 14, 2009 at 1:03am

When the people fear their government, there is tyranny; when the government fears the people, there is liberty.
Thomas Jefferson

The democracy will cease to exist when you take away from those who are willing to work and give to those who would not.
Thomas Jefferson

The spirit of resistance to government is so valuable on certain occasions that I wish it to be always kept alive.
Thomas Jefferson

Our country is now taking so steady a course as to show by what road it will pass to destruction, to wit: by consolidation of power first, and then corruption, its necessary consequence.
Thomas Jefferson

My reading of history convinces me that most bad government results from too much government.
Thomas Jefferson

Never spend your money before you have earned it.
Thomas Jefferson

Timid men prefer the calm of despotism to the tempestuous sea of liberty.
Thomas Jefferson

No man will ever carry out of the Presidency the reputation which carried him into it.
Thomas Jefferson

Money, not morality, is the principle commerce of civilized nations.
Thomas Jefferson

All tyranny needs to gain a foothold is for people of good conscience to remain silent.
Thomas Jefferson

A wise and frugal government, which shall leave men free to regulate their own pursuits of industry and improvement, and shall not take from the mouth of labor the bread it has earned - this is the sum of good government.
Thomas Jefferson

Peace and abstinence from European interferences are our objects, and so will continue while the present order of things in America remain uninterrupted.
Thomas Jefferson

Do you want to know who you are? Don't ask. Act! Action will delineate and define you.
Thomas Jefferson

A democracy is nothing more than mob rule, where fifty-one percent of the people may take away the rights of the other forty-nine.
Thomas Jefferson

Educate and inform the whole mass of the people... They are the only sure reliance for the preservation of our liberty.
Thomas Jefferson

Every citizen should be a soldier. This was the case with the Greeks and Romans, and must be that of every free state.
Thomas Jefferson

Every government degenerates when trusted to the rulers of the people alone. The people themselves are its only safe depositories.
Thomas Jefferson

Experience hath shewn, that even under the best forms of government those entrusted with power have, in time, and by slow operations, perverted it into tyranny.
Thomas Jefferson

For a people who are free, and who mean to remain so, a well-organized and armed militia is their best security.
Thomas Jefferson

I own that I am not a friend to a very energetic government. It is always oppressive.
Thomas Jefferson

I predict future happiness for Americans if they can prevent the government from wasting the labors of the people under the pretense of taking care of them.
Thomas Jefferson

I would rather be exposed to the inconveniences attending too much liberty than those attending too small a degree of it.
Thomas Jefferson

I'm a great believer in luck and I find the harder I work, the more I have of it.
Thomas Jefferson

If the present Congress errs in too much talking, how can it be otherwise in a body to which the people send one hundred and fifty lawyers, whose trade it is to question everything, yield nothing, and talk by the hour?
Thomas Jefferson

In matters of style, swim with the current; in matters of principle, stand like a rock.
Thomas Jefferson

It does me no injury for my neighbor to say there are twenty gods or no God.
Thomas Jefferson

It is always better to have no ideas than false ones; to believe nothing, than to believe what is wrong.
Thomas Jefferson

It is in our lives and not our words that our religion must be read.
Thomas Jefferson

It is neither wealth nor splendor; but tranquility and occupation which give you happiness.
Thomas Jefferson

It is our duty still to endeavor to avoid war; but if it shall actually take place, no matter by whom brought on, we must defend ourselves. If our house be on fire, without inquiring whether it was fired from within or without, we must try to extinguish it.
Thomas Jefferson

It takes time to persuade men to do even what is for their own good.
Thomas Jefferson

One man with courage is a majority.
Thomas Jefferson

The advertisement is the most truthful part of a newspaper.
Thomas Jefferson

That government is best which governs the least, because its people discipline themselves.
Thomas Jefferson

The care of human life and happiness, and not their destruction, is the first and only object of good government.
Thomas Jefferson

The man who reads nothing at all is better educated than the man who reads nothing but newspapers.
Thomas Jefferson

The moment a person forms a theory, his imagination sees in every object only the traits which favor that theory.
Thomas Jefferson

The most successful war seldom pays for its losses.
Thomas Jefferson

The natural progress of things is for liberty to yield and government to gain ground.
Thomas Jefferson

The strongest reason for the people to retain the right to keep and bear arms is, as a last resort, to protect themselves against tyranny in government.
Thomas Jefferson

The tree of liberty must be refreshed from time to time with the blood of patriots and tyrants.
Thomas Jefferson

The whole commerce between master and slave is a perpetual exercise of the most boisterous passions, the most unremitting despotism on the one part, and degrading submissions on the other. Our children see this, and learn to imitate it.
Thomas Jefferson

Truth is certainly a branch of morality and a very important one to society.
Thomas Jefferson

Walking is the best possible exercise. Habituate yourself to walk very fast.
Thomas Jefferson

We did not raise armies for glory or for conquest.
Thomas Jefferson

We hold these truths to be self-evident: that all men are created equal; that they are endowed by their Creator with certain unalienable rights; that among these are life, liberty, and the pursuit of happiness.
Thomas Jefferson

Were it left to me to decide whether we should have a government without newspapers, or newspapers without a government, I should not hesitate a moment to prefer the latter.
Thomas Jefferson

When a man assumes a public trust he should consider himself a public property.
Thomas Jefferson

When angry count to ten before you speak. If very angry, count to one hundred.
Thomas Jefferson

That's Barack's 1st 100 days, then really get angry! ...(*referring to the quote above*)
SENTRYMAN

When we get piled upon one another in large cities, as in Europe, we shall become as corrupt as Europe.
Thomas Jefferson

That would be in Chicago, in Detroit, in New York and in LA. (*referring to the quote above*)
SENTRYMAN

Whenever a man has cast a longing eye on offices, a rottenness begins in his conduct.
Thomas Jefferson

Whenever the people are well-informed, they can be trusted with their own government.
Thomas Jefferson

Where the press is free and every man able to read, all is safe.
Thomas Jefferson

God Help The United States Of America

Where are the MEN like this today when we need them most?

(Awaiting their diplomas, coming in the mail from Phoenix Internet University or Harvard?)

SENTRYMAN

"Government is not a solution to our problem, government is the problem." by Ronald Reagan.

Chapter 39

Obama is a "Can-Do" President?......Is He Funny or Just Prophetic?

Posted by SENTRYMAN on June 19, 2009 at 10:00pm

Ali Noorani, the Executive Director of the Board of the National Immigration Forum, advises Laura Ingram filling-in for O'Reilly,
that Barack Obama is a "can-do" President, ..."who's all about solving problems",
like fixing the "Economy", developing "Universal Health Care",
and now, our free-less leader will tackle and solve the Illegal-Alien issue with "Amnesty".

Wow, I hadn't realized our new, young inexperienced rookie president had accomplished so much, and in so little time!

Well, you can do "some things" with 4 Trillion Dollar$ worth of Monopoly Money,
and then the threat to use another 3 Trillion Dollar$ on Health Care.

Of course, I heard that Michelle O., with her Quid Pro Quo job she attained through her Senator husband, (is that nepotism or graft?),
devised exactly how to "farm-out" the old, poor and indigent (shallow-pockets) patients in her Chicago Hospital, in order to raise the Hospital's bottom line....
(Do you learn that in Law School or in Advanced Accounting class?)

Guess she hadn't heard of the millions of illegal's swamping the border State's Emergency Rooms with all their FREE services, on-demand,
thus causing those hospitals to close their doors permanently,
or maybe She had?

And I thought Barack was still trying to "find new homes" for ardent Killers in Guantanamo before his Dec. 31, 2009 Deadline, accessing William Shatner's Price Line on his Blackberry, I'm certain,
since the 1st few days of his fledgling presidency and was still coming up empty.
Maybe somewhere in the Bahamas, or the South Sea's Islands might work???

Travel-Obamacity Theme Song:

"Just sit right back And you'll hear a tale, A tale of a fateful trip,
That started from this tropic port, Aboard this tiny ship.
With 240 prisoners left at Guan-tan-a-mo Bay,
worst of the worst" & mastermind: Khalid Sheik Muhammed, ya don't say,
cause if they don't really figure-out, where to dump these guys today,
they'll be com'in here to your house, cause Holder wants them to stay,
With endangered MINNOW, silver fish, kicking out the migrants someday,
We'll have plenty need for cheap labor then, Khalid & Friends won't stray!"

by SENTRYMAN 2009

Pg. 220

And as far as fixing the "Economy" by our most learned scholar / businessman /
community organ / President is concerned;
much like ignoring an abusive alcoholic uncle that likes to baby-sit your kids,
who don't smile anymore upon hearing of his arrival,
(Obama and his posse) in the 2nd branch of government
created and caused the entire damn catastrophe.
But, Uncle Bart's not such a bad guy.
Ooops, just be quiet, he's coming in the room!

Really now, Is half of America asleep or just stupid?
(and Thank You Barney Frank and the NEA)

Jeepers folks, "This was a put-up Job", and everyone knows it!
Why is everyone to a man, afraid to say it?

Bush was dealt a bad hand too, and turned the country around very rapidly. Remember
Bush, the dummy,
the only President with a Master's Degree, and from the "Business school", no less?

Like him or not, he started-out his presidency with an impending Recession, (in a bomb
crater),
and in a very short time, and along with some "Tax Cuts",
we had the "lowest interest rates" and "lowest unemployment in 40 freak'n years",
and with "more people working than ever before",
including the approx. (12 million to 45 million) "illegal workforce", having infiltrated
America over the last 20 years, "as a handicap" for any president besides,
 and "his economy still soared" till the DEMs took over.

Everyone knows that, come-on!.......
Had He Been A Democrat, He'd Be A GOD today!

Plus, ...the Dow was over 14,000, and....
Bush crippled Al Qaeda,
Bush turned Iraq around,
everyone was working, and *everything was looking rosy,*
 and the Private Sector still owned its own assets, and itself, (pre-Czar's "Obama Motors"),

Uuuunnnntttttiiiiiiiilllllll,
the DEMs scared the be-Jesus out of 70% of those "Chicken Little" Voters in 2006,
and they believed all the DEM's tripe, and "THEY" won-back the Congress,
 and then the DEMs did such a Good Job of terrifying everyone "that the sky was falling",
(they should work that hard "solving" real problems, instead of manufacturing false ones),
that when the Dominos started to fall, (along with the SKY),
No One could put the Eels back into the "Live Well" Of Souls....Maybe was "the Plan"?

And as for "Health Care", this genius in Washington
is developing a "15 member panel" to write "the protocols"
to Rule and Govern the Doctors and Hospitals, and the Drug Companies,
(without a single Doctor) on Barack's Board of Experts.....ARE YOU SERIOUS?
.......IS ANYONE PAYING ATTENTION HERE?......

WHERE IS OUR 4th ESTATE TO EXPOSE THIS 5th ESTATE?

Brilliant!.......Just Brillant! ....30. Kh1 Qg1+ 31. Rxg1 Nf2# = CHECKMATE!

Maybe these same 15 EXPERTS could stop up to "Obama Motors" in Detroit and change some oil and a tire or 2, paint a few cars, and then call themselves "veteran mechanics", before firing anymore CEOs?

Oh, I forgot, "The "Energy Policy"..................There isn't one!

"Drill" yourself into the ground, "Here".
Just shoot yourself in the foot, no, the Head! We're already bleeding Red Ink, who'll notice.

You're just a little wicket, and Obama wheels a mean Croquet Mallet like no-other tyrant....
"Walk Loudly and Carry A Little Stick"

"Date Night" in Bangkok for Thai, Sweetie?.....He doesn't pay for the gas!

**Catch Obama's Speech on YouTube at the "Radio & TV Correspondents Dinner"
and tell me if He's Funny, Or Just Prophetic?..........I said: Pro-fe-tic!

http://www.youtube.com/watch?v=KxNJg7d7D_s

Don't forget the Tree-Huggers:
"Stave America to save an Endangered little Fishy in the San Joaquin Valley!"
(Perhaps Cesar Chavez's followers would like a Presidential recount? a' amigos)

Was that "create" or "save" 5,000,000 jobs, or 5,000,000 Minnows??

What can WE Do when 1/2 of our neighbors are On The Dole??????????????????

Move to Mexico or Canada?....Heck, everyone's here!......Actually, that might work!

SENTRYMAN

---

5 COMMENTS, and a little debate

Comment by Rocco 1 day later:

> *"While I totally agree with you about Obama, there is some serious revisionist history going on about Bush. Bush was so bad he made Obama possible."*

A rebuttal by SENTRYMAN:

Rocco said: "some serious revisionist history going on about Bush."

Don't generalize Pal, I hate that!
Geo. Washington, Jefferson, Lincoln and FDR weren't perfect either,
and hindsight is always 20/20.

Personalities aside, facts are still facts,
even with expert Revisionists like the DEMs spinning them! "FAULT ME!".....No,

really, FAULT ME!
Read any of my Blogs........Plain speaking and plain spoken.

You want HINDSIGHT?

#1- If Carter had done his job, and Clinton had arrested Bin Laden even once,
No One would have died in a 9/11. = **A FACT**

#2- If Bush hadn't taken the fight to THEM, (and there was exactly a Home Country to pick
a fight with the biggest Bully in that sandbox over there),
 Los Angeles would have fallen next = **A FACT**
and then probably Chicago, or Washington again after that.

That "little wrinkle" would have certainly destroyed the US economy for a decade,
and that's without co-opting GM!.... **A FACT!**

Would You have been happier with them stats Pal?

But, We Did Have 14,000 on the Dow.... **A FACT!**

and the DEMs did take over in "07 and the S#&t Hit The Fan.... **A FACT!**

and Harry Reid DID SAY; along with other heroic Democrat Statesmen;
"That (our murderous soldiers) had lost the War," ... **A FACT!**

And after the NY TIMES had told the Enemy exactly how We were electronically surveilling
them, an "extremely valuable asset dried-up",...TRAITOROUS... **A FACT!**

But, BUSH refused to arrest those American Traitors in the 5th Estate...**A FACT!**
*There Bush made a mistake, too nice a guy...Roosevelt would have tossed them all in an
Internment Camp!

(Valerie Plane = Red Herring c@%p)
The NY Times: more CIA leaks commits murder!.... **A FACT!**

More of our sons and daughters died, due to any War "being extended" by Leakers,
sycophants, dooms-sayers and pacifists; that 90% of the weak-kneed national MEDIA,
and a complicit NY TIMES by continually were aiding and abetting the Enemy (traitors),
along with the Leakers, sycophants, dooms-sayers and pacifists outside the media who
all "to hurt Bush", Our brave volunteer Soldiers Be Damned. .... **A FACT!**

Do you know why W.W.II , an actual WORLD WAR, was shorter,
(with the 60's Nam-whiners always complaining and reminding us),
it was because We All SUPPORTED our children fighting for their country,
way back there in 1942, '43, '44 and 1945,
unlike TODAY!......... **A FACT!**

My Dad was in that one,
and my Grandfather was in the Great War, having newly arrived from the Old Country,
and I joined for Nam before being drafted, Paesan! .... **A FACT!**

Rocco said: "Bush was so bad he made Obama possible."

SENTRYMAN rebuttal:
 NO MY FRIEND, "THE MEDIA" WAS "THAT GOOD", DARN'IT !

"THE MEDIA" HAD WRITTEN, DIRECTED AND PRODUCED A "BARACK HUSSEIN OBAMA" POSSIBLE. .... A FACT!

That's the trouble about a Representative Democracy with Leaders that don't listen to the people, and without TERM LIMITS,
it doesn't really matter who lives at 1600 Pennsylvania Ave;
The Same Players Still Hold The Purse Strings On Capitol Hill, ... A FACT!

and a "Barack", or a "George" can only do what the "MONEY CHANGERS" will allow!
Oh, like raiding Fannie and Freddie, like another Capitol Hill "Post Office's" ATM.
I suppose that's revisionist too, right Pal? .... A FACT!

Of course, The MEDIA wasn't sleeping with George W. Bush in the Oval Office, back then.
Noooo, they reminded us "every single day" of the "Body Count in IRAQ". .... A FACT!

Funny, don't hear any "Numbers everyday" with Obama's Afghanistan!.... A FACT!

"You hear want You want to hear", You remember nothing! .... A FACT!

SENTRYMAN....
Keep Your Powder Dry!
----

4 COMMENTS

Comment by Lora H on June 19, 2009 at 10:20pm
I nearly choked on that guy with Laura Ingram, too. Yeah... I guess he's "doing",
alright.........Doing a lot of damage, that is.

Comment by Tess on June 20, 2009 at 2:09am
America better not be asleep.

Comment by SENTRYMAN on June 20, 2009 at 3:12am
The patient's been comatose for so long, it's on total Life Support and Brain Dead,
and the only reason it's not euthanized is that it generates government funding,
from China, for just filling the bed.

There might still be help for those Brain Dead over 55 with Obama's Universal Health Care,
and they can be kept alive indefinitely like vampires in perpetual twilight.
But, No Jell-O!

Comment by T.C. on June 20, 2009 at 8:34am
Watched a segment of "the dinner" last night.............Obama is more of a comedian than Letterman.
Now as I see it, he has the possibility of either a preaching or doing Late Night comedy when He loses to Sarah in 2012,
so B.O. start working on your speeches, and or your routines.

Chapter 40

"Ever hear of Margaret Thatcher or Golda Meir?"......Sarah has of Melinda

Posted by **SENTRYMAN** on **July 4, 2009** at 1:30am

Inside Politics Daily
Melinda Henneberger, Editor in Chief

"Sarah Palin to Step Down as Governor of Alaska"
Posted: 07/3/09

An excerpt from Melinda:
"Roll the stone away, let the guilty pay; it's Independence Day." –

"In a rambling, borderline bughouse decoupage of sports metaphors and intimations that the forces of darkness"
were running her out of public life,"

"Listening to her talk in furious circles, it was hard to say whether a) some new scandal was about to break, b) she'd had enough of politics, thanks"
Melinda Henneberger

///

SENTRYMAN weighs-in;...Now, now! ......**rrrrraaaeerrrrr...scratch!**

Hey Melinda, sweetheart; why the angst?
Are you concerned about the "WHYS", or the "TIMING"?

Or, are You talk'n about Hillary constantly whining about that mythical:
Republican's "right-wing Conspiracy"?
(that Hillary's own minions had invented, fabricated and perpetuated)!
Or, about Yourself; complaining about a successful, clean articulate,
(oh, had a Biden moment there), an All-American conservative woman
who "actually worked" her way up the ladder to the top,
without being the wife of a President, or bribing and paying-off "voting
blocs", leapfrogging life's (work-your-way-up) system by-passing hundreds
of legitimate, more experienced, and qualified local, career public servants,
to covet, (not earn as a real New Yorker), that high political position. Pg.225

Or, for instance;
managing to garner more votes in one's winning tally, than there are citizens "living" in a specifically "democrat districts", but I digress.

Or, are You really complaining about a self-assured lady with a happy life and a happy family,
who doesn't want to ever kill her late term baby,
who has a satisfied happy husband that's not insecure being married to a strong, moral, working wife, and He loves her,
who's also an accomplished business woman that doesn't like the "good OLE' boy", "politics-as-usual" funny-business in her midst?

A woman that just might not enjoy hundreds, if not thousands, of sycophantic plotting zealots,
so frightened of her influence and her future in the American politic, that they will do and say, and act anyway necessary to destroy, her, her family, her career, her public office, and even her state,
to suit their purposes to derail her future ambitions,

and, not withstanding, hurting fellow Americans, and wasting Alaskan taxpayer's time and money with an unending barrage of, no less than 11, premeditated, frivolous lawsuits to date, and with more to come I'm sure, and with no, fair impartial-government entity, coming to her aid, short of the exhaustive and "personally expensive" defense litigations for each......"The Plan"!

But she, in an act of self-sacrifice and self-preservation at this moment in time,
dares to disrupt "The LEFT's" deification of a pedophile, singer/entertainer, probably succumbed or murdered by his own excesses;

Is that what your journalistic-tripe is supposed to convey with your innuendo, and aplomb?

Nonetheless, a man has died, a life snuffed-out, young and before his time, always a tragedy to be sure,

unlike, of course, the purposeful, premeditated poisoning, suffocating, and then smashing the skull of a fully formed living unborn baby,
in order to make room to drag it's squirming, gasping, clinging to life, dying carcass out of the customer's incubation-chamber,
who is a diabolical professional henchmen,
(contrary to one's former professional, ethical Hippocratic Oath),
routinely exterminate, minus the Hollywood glitz, fanfare or ceremonial eulogy,
just as a comparison!

Yes. Sarah Palin how dare she, of all times to be self-effacing, selfless and all too generous to her fellow Alaskans, than to pull this prank on the eve of the "anniversary of another Birth",
that many other henchmen also tried very hard for hundreds of years to abort, yet, It survived,
to one day become the greatest nation and the last hope for personal liberty on this earth known to MAN!

Ohhh, and for women too. Yeah, even lady editors.
HALLALEUYA SISTER!!

Gee, wouldn't it be terrible if Sarah actually wanted to the Executive Officer of the entire country, and essentially becoming a real Commander-In-Chief one day, protecting you too Melinda?

So, better sharpen that pencil and ax to grind Honey,
she just might earn it the ole' fashioned way,
since the current positions occupant knows little of LIBERTY, JUSTICE and the American Way!!

You think a sleeping giant awoke when Japan paid a surprise visit, and then Hitler, then Russia, Korea, China, Iran, Iraq, al Qaeda,
Korea and Iran once again, who all dared to make the earth tremble?

Well, You just watch what happens when America finally wakes-up from its materialistic, drug-of-choice self-anesthetized, government-induced entitlement-comma, and realizes there's a Socialist
 in the White House?

Do you remember, or have you ever hear of Margaret Thatcher, or Golda Meir, Melinda?...

They may not have educated you about those strong-willed conservative women in your "Women's Course" at whatever Lib College you may have attained for your journalism credentials donated from,
but remember this name too: "Sarah Louise Palin."

SENTRYMAN

 # Chapter 41

Selective Indignation and Moral Relativism of President Obama.

Posted by SENTRYMAN on July 11, 2009 at 4:00pm

"The Truth, The Whole Truth and Nothing But The Truth, Your Honor."

As the President tours a former Ghanaian coastal emplacement site where slaves, once captured & delivered by their own countrymen, then temporarily corralled before their perilous inhuman voyage to the "New World", and elsewhere to satisfy the world-wide demand in daily commerce,

Obama takes advantage of an excellent teaching moment for his daughters:
"that life can be evil, and cruel and unjust."

REALLY?!!!....That's it?

But, with the singular perspective of "moral relativism",
one can perhaps miss the total picture and a greater issue;
"THAT SLAVERY STILL EXISTS TODAY",

and

"WHAT ARE WORLD GOVERNMENTS DOING ABOUT IT,
OR EVER WILL?

Should Be Simple Enough, Right?

Lord knows those governments will soon monitor "what we eat"
And the "kind of light bulbs" we'll be allowed to use in our own private homes,
behind closed doors, and purchased with our own earned money!!

But, I sure hope Our President doesn't neglect to mention to his girls during his undoubted dissertation on the Evils of the "White Man", leaving out: The Evils Of "MAN", and "The Evil That Men Do",

because Men of that Day, as well as today, all existed, no, survived on the backs of their countrymen and fellow residents of this same planet, en masse in most instances.
.......That is how the Pyramids were built remember?

It wasn't personal, Only Business!... Where have I heard that before?

Pg. 228

But especially, with this "Barack Teaching moment",
#1: <u>Chronology Of The History Of Slavery: 1619-1789.</u>

400 year ago African's raided, murdered and caught their brethren in order to "market them for sale",
to transfer them from this "transport facility" to the anxious White European merchants,
as well as other Vendors of varied complexions elsewhere on the planet, all awaiting their cargo,
of which Barack is so aptly showing his daughters today.

(By the way girls, the Americas weren't the only customers, or destination for the "daily catch". Don't know if you got that message too.)

Much like the Jews in the '40s being rounded-up from all over Europe, and FED/EX'd East;
their wealth, expansive and extended worlds totally forfeited and confiscated by the State,
(Eminent Domain any one), to eventually also include their very lives and existence.
…..Governmental "Incrementalism" at its best!!........Gee, that's sounding familiar!........

Then, there's the Spanish Kingdom, a little before the European and African slavery cartel, of the 1600s to 1900s,
during the 12th Century "Inquisition" when actually tearing-apart the human bodies of White & Brown & Black Jews,
and Brown & Black Moslems, and White Christians, with their women included, by a whole array of evil invention and contraption that was the standard "sport of the day".

A truly "equal opportunity" and unrestricted, non-denominational Torturer,
state-of-the-art, a head of its time, oh, but not to diminish the rampaging exploits of how "The MOORS" slaughtered their way across African and up into Europe,

or how "Genghis Khan" slaughtered his way across Asia and eastern Europe,

or the ultra-professional expertise of the Conquistadors who decimated Central and South Americas, and obliterated 3 ancient Empires for some shiny golden metal,

or the way the Tutsis and Hutus hacked each other apart 50 years after the NAZIs had improved on the original Grand Inquisitor's vision, thus making people actually disappear into thin-air, a puff of smoke, just like a Vegas magician. POOF! Applause, "Danke Schoen"

Then there's wholesale death in Nigeria and Somalia, and on, and on, etc., etc.

<u>See girls, some things can always be worse!</u>

There isn't a moral equivalent for the insane savagery of man, preying upon men,
because all other species on this planet perform this insatiable process for their own nourishment and survival, but,
with Man, it is an unparalleled ritual incompared in the Animal Kingdom.

I think ALL but the perpetrators would agree, NOT!

With further examination, to compare one atrocity over another, it would be an academic folly, since throughout the so-called civilization the history of man's inhumanity to man is, of course, earth shattering and things haven't changed all that much.
….Death, has just become more efficient now than ever before!

But, for the sake of argument since there are men, still today, making their livings keeping

these old wounds open, and (peoples apart), festering old scores and old sores, just picking away so the Healing Never Ends to round-out their education, I certainly hope the President also took his daughters with him for his Photo-op at the Death Camp in Poland, or was it Germany? There were so many,
and pointed out the ash'ed remains of those "white slaves", who were starved to Death or worked to Death, or merely put to Death,
since it was more "cost effective" to gas their exhausted huddled-hulks of standing bones, instead of wasting valuable ammunition to shoot them in the head,
before Cooking-up their Remains in the bright ovens.

See girls, some things can always be worse!!

Then, he should take his daughters to the Coliseum in Rome, not the only ancient location for this exercise during that Empire either,
to enlighten his daughters just where those "lucky" slaves got to shovel-up the Lion's and Tiger's manure, where <u>the remains of the "less-lucky" White Christians ended up,</u>
as a result of the National Sport, and were reposited!

See girls, some things can always be worse!!!

And I could continue Through Time, In Memoriam but hopefully made the one point
 all too often ignored,
<u>Selective Indignation Never Sees the Forest through the YEARS, or is it Tears?</u>

At least, and with all due respect for human dignity and life, in the case of the African Slaves they were considered valuable chattel, that were,
to some or greater degree, cared for enough so we are still having this debate 400 years later with their descendants, plus,
we've got Alex Haley and Michael Jordan, and 40 million other light-skinned and dark-skinned African-descended AMERICANs today.

Juxtaposed to "all the other slaves throughout world history" that didn't get that Economy-fare One-way Ticket, and just got Their ticket punched!
......We're all just damn lucky to be here at all, alive today so;
Enough of it already!

Besides, Clinton "Officially" apologized on behalf, and for the United States Government, way before Obama got elected,
and thousands and thousands of "white" men and their families suffered, and died to FREE those ancestors under that Republican LINCOLN,
and those "white men's" families received "no remuneration" or "reparation", or accommodation, or appreciation, then, or even today either.

The White Man "Paid His Debt" In More Than A Pound Of Flesh!

We're here today, we're all together, and we're all ALIVE, ala 9/11,
And We're ALL AMERICANs and we've got bigger fish to fry without hashing over the past
again, and again, and again, aaaaaannnnddddd AGAIN!

In the Importance of Full Disclosure:
I'm Roman Catholic on one side and Ashkenazi on the other,
and my ancestors started out from Africa, just like all of YOURS,
So shut-up already!!!!!

<u>SENTRYMAN</u>

PS, The "United States" of America only had Slavery some 89 years, not for 400 years, AI, and they got rid of it as soon as more honorable "white" men could stop the Democrats back then!

If you have an "ax to grind" take it up with the (English, the French, the Dutch and those Spaniards), oh,
and those humanitarians: those "African" Trappers and "African" Merchant-middlemen!

I'm still waiting for my reparations-check from Caesar and Hitler!

PPS, Remember, the slaves were owned by Democrats,
just like many of their descendants today!

PPPS, if one has (1) "white" ancestor in their genealogy, You are also a white European-American too!
Glad to meet you, Fellow "AMERICAN"!

===

3 Comments

Comment by Henry's Mom on July 11, 2009 at 4:37pm

Most slaves captured in Africa were sold in slavery by their BLACK or ARAB captors.
Most slaves ships sailed to Brazil, not North America.

None of Obama's ancestors were enslaved. Obama never talks about the "white" half of his family, except in one of his books, where he exclaims that if he "could remove every drop of white blood from my body, I would".

NOW who is racist?

Comment by farmgirl on July 11, 2009 at 5:01pm

It was the Portuguese and the ENGLISH and the Spanish who participated in the slave trade....the English just didn't allow the slaves to be brought into England. After the Revolutionary War, they were here and so was the institution of slavery.

However.....Africa still can't seem to get over the slave trade business. It's STILL going on!!

In my opinion, instead of crying out for Reparations here, black people should be thankful they are here and not there. Who's to say they wouldn't be sold into modern day slavery today?

Not every black in the US was a slave, either. Not every black person here is a descendent from slaves.

I remember when our English boys were here visiting and made a comment about the US and it's foundation of slavery and I said, 'Yep....and it was the English that made all the money from the slave trade.

What are you going to do about that?' He got real quiet and shook his head. These poor Oxford students.........

Correct, correct FarmGirl.........Every hour on FOX they're reporting that OBAMA spoke to "ALL OF AFRICA",
because "Only He" could have the "credibility to be believed" by "the countrymen of his ancestral roots", than any other President that in the past have been too afraid to use such stern-talk...........
What? .,,,,,,,Unlike Clinton, the unofficial 1st black President?
http://www.brookings.edu/

"The U.S. refusal to intervene, to halt the "Rwanda genocide of 1994" remains a blot on the foreign policy legacy of:
the Clinton Administration."

"Responsibility for the failed international action in Somalia, led by U.S. troops, is widely shared. By pulling American forces out of Somalia in March 1994 after a score of American soldiers were brutally killed in October 1993, the United States signaled the limit to the sacrifices it was prepared to shoulder to contain African humanitarian catastrophes.".......Well then, unlike Bush,
that did more for Africa than any other President in History?

Unlike FDR, who kicked the Nazis out of Africa?....Well, that was a detour on the way to Germany, but still.

Unlike [US "donations" to Africa outstrip Europe donations by (15 to 1), Scotsman.com ^ | Frasier Nelson, Posted on Sunday, July 03, 2005]

Obama apparently told "Africa" to straighten-up and fly-right,
do things the way he suggests, or they'll get no goodies........hmmmm

Which on the whole isn't bad, but if He wants to shape Africa like he's doing to America, (in his own image), I feel sorry for the Africans.
Do Africans "in the bush" have to use those lousy "coil, environmentally-friendly light bulbs", that if one's broken, do they have an Asmat-Team on-the-ready to swoop-in & scoop-up the dreaded mercury before We All Die?

Or do they "burn" wood, and cook food with fire, and fill the air with unchecked emissions?............Me/thinks they better re-think that behavior for the good of the planet, to be equitable and fair. ....Don't thee?

Of course,.........India — Population: 1,147,995,904,
and..................China — Population: 1,330,044,544,
both told Obama where he could Park his GREEN Light Bulbs, and to Take A Hike!

Maybe Obama will have more luck with Africans, and bring all their Youths back to America for free college education's, like the Arabs, working from the middle/up toward total World-Domination, Mini-Me? *Nothing like TRAINING your competition*!

I don't know!.......He is very tricky and calculating, and He's 1/2 White you know, and "You just can't trust Whitey"!

SENTRYMAN

Chapter 42

WOE IS ME!.... What can we do??
…..................ATTACK!…………..
Forgo the Head….Chop up the Snake!

Posted by SENTRYMAN on <u>July 16, 2009</u> at 1:47am

("The 'Cap and Tax' Dead End"

By Sarah Palin
Tuesday, July 14th, 2009

"There is no shortage of threats to our economy"

Read full text of Washington Post Op-Ed)

http://www.washingtonpost.com/wp-dyn/content/article/2009/07/13/AR2009071302852.html

===

SENTRYMAN weighs-in;

"president's cap-and-trade energy tax would adversely affect every aspect of the U.S. economy" By Sarah Palin

THAT'S THE WHOLE POINT,
AND IT EXTENDS BEYOND OUR BORDERS TILL THERE ARE NO BORDERS!

A SINGLE GRASSROOTS NATIONAL REFERENDUM EFFORT, DRIVEN BY PATRIOTs;
RIGHT & LEFT & CENTER, TEA PARTIERs AND ALIKE, AMERICANs ALL!

Pg. 233

STATE BY STATE,
PETITIONED AND PLACED ON THEIR OWN STATE's BALLOTs,
JUST AS CALIFORNIA FIGHTS THEIR ESTABLISHMENT, BUT THIS TIME FOR THE WHOLE ENCHILADA…..

FOR THE GAME, THE CLOCK, THE FIELD AND THE STADIUM STOLEN BY EMINENT DOMAIN, WHICH USED TO BE YOUR NEIGHBORHOOD,

TO MAKE AN "END-RUN" AROUND A PURPOSELY BLOCKED-PROCESS, A CLOGGED SYSTEM: OUR OWN GOVERNMENT "HOLDING US RANSOM",
(ALL IN A DEATHGRIP, BY THE THROAT)

IN ORDER TO FORCE OUR "EMPLOYEE" JAILERs TO RELEASE THEIR STRANGLE-HOLD ON THE LIFE's BLOOD OF FREE UNFETTERED COMMERCE,

CONTAMINATING OUR CONSTITUTION,

TAINTING OUR CHILDREN'S EDUCATION,

THIS HEATHCARE "RED HERRING",

IGNORING TORT REFORM,

FOR WRITING THEIR OWN; PAYCHECKs, ANNUITY RETIREMENTs, CUSTOMIZED HEALTHCARE, PERKS UPON PERK, ETC. and ETCETERA,

TAXATION WITHOUT REPRESENTATION,

AND BRIBING EACHOTHER, AND THE POPULUS INTO SUBMISSION!

<u>AND THAT'S JUST FOR A START!</u>

HOW?………….2 WORDS = TERM LIMITS!……………………

<u>By: "2-TERM LIMITS FOR ALL ELECTED OFFICIALS."</u>

NOTHING ELSE WILL WORK, OR WILL WORK AS FAST
TO SAVE THE UNION, OUR NATION AND OURSELVES!

SOME LONE KNIGHT, OR ANOTHER SINGLARLY OMNIPOTENT SAVIOR, WOMAN OR MAN CANNOT SUCCEED ALONE TODAY, ESPECIALLY WITH 535 QUISLINGS RUNNING INTERFERANCE.
THIS VICHY GOVERNMENT WILL CONTINUE TO HOLD-BACK THE TIDE, AND THE DAWN ON OUR LIBERTIES FOR ANY TRUE FREEDOM FOR ALL OF CIVILIZATION.

**So, we're just going to have to do it ourselves for our children's, children's, children's future!

1.

**THE "2 TERM LIMIT" IS THE ONLY CHANCE WE WILL EVER HAVE
AND RIGHT NOW IS THE EXACT PRECISE MOMENTOUS TIME
TO MAKE IT HAPPEN,**

**(<u>Synchronicity</u>: Coincidence of events that seem to be meaningfully
related, conceived in Jungian theory as an explanatory principle on
the same order as causality.)**

**UNLESS YOU'RE PERFECTLY HAPPY TO BE "FOREVER-ENSLAVED" BY
YOUR OWN GOVERNMENT,
(SOON TO BECOME A "WORLD GOVERNMENT")!**

**TAKE YOUR POWER BACK FROM A GOVERNMENT THAT NO LONGER
HEARS YOU,
AND PUT THAT POWER "BACK INTO THE HANDS OF THE PEOPLE"!**

**FOR AN OPEN AND FREE GOVERNMENT,
NOT USURPED BY SELF-INTEREST GROUPs, FOREIGN GOVERNMENTs,
GREENs, REDs, PINKs, LEFTISTS, PROGRESSIVEs, LOBBYISTs,
ILLINOIS / MINNESOTA STYLE ELECTIONs,
RINOs,
THE NEW ACORNs, AND THE 5TH COLUMNISTs,
STEALTH TRADERS and TRAITORS,
<u>NOW THAT THE FORTH ESTATE IS DEAD!</u>**

"One if by Land / Two if by Sea!"................

"The British Are Coming"… "The Russians Are Coming" …"The Terrorists Are Coming!"

**And they all came, except this time,
THEY ARE ALREADY HERE............. >2 TERM LIMIT!!!**

*PROPOSITION #86, (to eighty-six the government and FREE The People)
<u>www.SENTRYMAN.org</u>
===
<u>ref·er·en·dum</u> (rĕf'ə-rĕn'dəm)

n. pl. ref·er·en·dums
**The submission of a proposed public measure or actual statute to a
direct popular vote.**

<u>SENTRYMAN</u>

Chapter 43

THE AMERICAN THINKER and An American Thinker.

Posted by SENTRYMAN on July 17, 2009 at 3:30am

Excerpts from our own lives and experiences. (re-print)
AMERICAN THINKER
July 15, 2009
Sarah Palin vs. the Marquis de Sade.....By Robin of Berkeley

I grew up with a mean older brother who was ten when I came on the scene
Tom's main passion in life was tormenting me.

After I grew up and became a psychotherapist, I learned that there was a name for Tom's behavior, sadism. Sadists get a thrill out of being cruel and watching others suffer.

Let's call them by their true name. When an actress calls for gang raping Palin, she's a sadist. When people torch Palin's church with children inside, they are sadists. When bloggers call her a c__t and scorn her disabled son, they are being sadists.

the growing power of the Left. Adults who have the impulse control of two year olds marching around, unhinged and uncontrolled, like Lord of the Flies. Teens beating up each other and teachers and uploading the video on YouTube.

Evil, unacknowledged and unrecognized, takes root and becomes a virus so virulent, it threatens everyone whom it touches. Because evil changes people; it wipes out what makes them uniquely human; it turns them into something completely different, unrecognizable, alien.

And goodness is not just some old fashioned concept, some relic of days gone by. It's a privilege bestowed on us from the universe and we must cradle it and protect it as we would a newborn babe. We must never take it for granted, mock it or abandon it because it's the only thing that stands in the way of us and total anarchy.

Philosopher Jacob Needleman tells a story of walking on a bustling San Francisco street with a religious scholar from Tibet. Needleman asks his friend, "If it is so rare to be born a human being, how come there are so many people in the world?" His friend ponders the question silently for several seconds. Then he looks at Needleman and responds quietly, "How many human beings do you see?"

I look around each day and ask myself the same question, "Where are the human beings?" I see fewer and fewer each day. But there's a shining example in Alaska of a woman who maintained her integrity in the midst of cruelty that would have crushed many of us; who never descended to the level of the thugs; and who exits the scene with something that the sadists will never have, not even in their dreams -- her humanity.

A frequent AT contributor, Robin is a recovering liberal and psychotherapist in Berkeley. **Pg. 236**

http://www.americanthinker.com/2009/07/sarah_palin_vs_the_marquis_de.html

(someone doesn't want you to read this, so you'll have to hunt for this one at the LINKs below, using: Palin vs Marquis) ...also TRY:
https://www.google.com/#q=Palin+vs+marquis+de+sade+American+Thinker

http://www.freerepublic.com/focus/f-gop/2293842/posts

http://www.americanthinker.com/
+++

SENTRYMAN weighs-in with an Obama 2 cents, NOW only worth (1) penny!

This brief remembrance is but an echo repeated a billion times since man sprang from the ooze; "An uncle that returned unexpectedly so often to help baby-sit the babysitter!"

Heroes and anti-heroes

<u>Non-fiction:</u> Bush, Reagan, King, Kennedy, Gandhi, Truman, Teddy, Earp, Custer, Lincoln, George, Elizabeth, Joan, Jesus, Lionitus, David and Moses......

<u>Fiction:</u> (Willis, Eastwood, John Wayne, Roy, Moore, Glenn Ford, Harry Carey and Kirk Douglas' "characters"),
and Zatôichi, Grimm, Charles Darnay, Robin Hood, Arthur, Ripley and Our Superman.

How many times must We hear of another Woman Being Raped in the street below and no one lifts a finger to physically help, or even screams-out: "STOP, WE SEE YOU! THE POLICE ARE ON THE WAY"!

Then "Synchronicity" occurs, as if divine intervention and by divine providence, and the fates provide the "one" individual at that moment in time to deal with major A$$ H@!&$,
....and the lone "pale rider" comes out of the shadows when all hope is lost,
....but unfortunately, not often enough!

It's never going to change, there's always going to be idiots, morons, half-wits, imbeciles and "evil-doers".
That's why God invented the Four Horseman to cleanse the Gene Pool.

It's when you start screwing with Mother Nature, you start getting into real trouble Al!
Even if you're making $100,000,000.00 dollars, it doesn't give you the right to Fool with Mother Nature....Al!

"What does change" is the length of time that it takes for people "not to take-it anymore", because the more civilized we seem to get
the greater the risk is for the many, since we've become numb to it all in this electronic communication age, and "conditioned", as that's all that is on TV and in movies anymore!

So, perhaps employ some old, old standards to see if anything improves?

<u>Islamic Law:</u> ....Steal = lose the hand = No More Stealing.....VS.....

<u>US Jurisprudence:</u> Murder your wife = (Ever do any acting or run with a ball? Well)

<u>Harsh?....How about some legislated "organized" Karma for some real change?</u>

Blind Justice: whack Your 3 wives; in barrels, dry bath tubs and a Martian abduction = Your final destination should be in a barrel over the falls! (hope a Martian beams you up)

Blind Justice: You kidnap a mother and child, and drown them = You get water-boarded permanently, = "no more kidnapping"!

Blind Justice: You kill a living fetus anywhere, anytime, in Anyone = You lose your license, You go to jail, Your inmates make You real welcome, = no more babies murdered!....Real simple in Kansas!

Blind Justice: You rape a little girl = We remove your penis, = (little girls are safer)!...Real simple in New Hampshire!

Blind Justice: You rape a little girl & put her in a garbage bag "alive" = You get buried in a garbage bag Alive, = (little girls grow into ladies and live happy lives)!..Real simple Florida!

I seem to recall that the Ancients called that "an eye for an eye", in the Old Testament, so I guess that's why Justice has both eyes covered!....huh?

Want to be safer in an insane world?....Stop acting like a 10-year-old Liberal and Grow-up!

Just remember, you strap a bomb on your back and take someone's life, (hate to break it to you Pal), because frightened Liberals won't tell you, since they too, live in a fantasy world also, there are No Virgins waiting for YOU!....wherever you travel there's no place like home!

But if, by some strange quirk of fate, You survive the blast = We're Going To Blow You Up, Again!.....JUSTICE, like Karma, should be a bitch!...

How many times must WE be taught this same lesson, "eon upon eon", and told these same stories again, and again, throughout time, while sitting silently opening unpaid bills at the dinner table watching Obama on-mute, worry and wondering why our daughters aren't home yet, and having to send our children to die on foreign shores to constantly defend ourselves against the same mental defectives, "eon upon eon"?

It's almost as if We're in an alternate-universe Loop, all players in the same clichéd rerun where Reality is clicking the channels from; Fox News to Sponge Bob, to Lucy to HBO, to The View to American Idol, to Flavor Flav, and back to Fox: "Al Franken winning in Minnesota" to Turner Classics; "The Tale of Two Cities" and "On The Beach", and on, and on, and>>>on!

All dutifully just playing our part in some old SNL skit.....phew, just a bad dream....

Who won in Minnesota again?

PEACE,
SENTRYMAN

Chapter 44

One if by Land, Two if by Sea...... "Too Late"!

Posted by SENTRYMAN on July 19, 2009 at 3:00pm

"The Fall of Capitalism and the Rise of Islam."

An alert was aired this morning on Fox News, if you missed it,
warning that, at this very minute in Chicago an elite Muslim extremist organization,
and I don't believe is included on the current
"Terrorism Watch List" (AKA, friends of Obama) yet,
are planning the "2nd" of a "3 phased assault" upon the United States.

Phase One, an intentionally invisible, clandestine, "blending-into" the population program,
much as 5th columnist's German-Americans did prior to WWII.

Today the 2nd Phase becomes the overt stage, a "coming-out of the closet", as it were,
declaring to the world: allahu akbar....Here We Are! (AKA, out from Spider Holes),
Ha, ha, in your face, what are you going to do about it, as We are protected by your
Constitution too!

They are now drawing public attention to themselves physically as a recruiting tool, and
most vocally as the fund raisers, fully utilizing the US Constitution "as cover" under the
1st amendment previsions,
and at the same time coordinating their actions in a massive demonstration tomorrow,
also in Chicago,
supported by new US legislation sitting "on the Hill" as I write this, that will provide these
particular Muslim Activists "free rein and freer Reign" under: "Free Speech",
and "Freedom of Religion",

and can now openly profligate and preach sedition to their impatient minions of the
clamoring throng, of the benefits of Sharia Law,
with the specific intent to over-throw the government of these United
States, (contrary to their host country's generosity and Constitution),

and call for the total overthrow and fall of Democracy in America, and anywhere else
freedom exists in the world,

for the total Dominance of Islam Across the Globe,

but, at the same time our benevolent, (malevolent), leaders in their great wisdom have
seen fit to create and pass other new legislation; (that it will become a felony for anyone,
(Americans), when even voicing an opinion, or openly expressing an opposing view
contrary to those held by these;
(AKA:_____, You fill in the blank, I don't wish to be arrested.)

Pg. 239

Muslim Activists, soon to be protected under the new Hate Speech Laws, that our brilliant "paid" Representatives are about to enact in Washington.

Check it out for yourself....... I hope I'm wrong, dreaming, or asleep in my bed........Nope, pitched myself, we're in major trouble!

"The Fall of Capitalism and the Rise of Islam."

http://www.youtube.com/watch?v=W8Wg3j6MTJg

Hizb ut-Tahrir (Arabic: حِزْبُ التَحْرِير; English: Party of Liberation) is an international pan-Islamist, Sunni, vanguard political party whose goal is to combine all **Muslim countries in a unitary Islamic state,** or caliphate, ruled by Islamic law and with a Caliph head of state elected by Muslims.

http://atlasshrugs2000.typepad.com/atlas_shrugs/2009/06/islam-in-america-fall-of-capitalism-and-rise-of-islam.html

http://hizb-america.org/

http://righttruth.typepad.com/right_truth/2009/07/the-fall-of-capitalism-and-the-rise-of-islam.html

http://nocompromisemedia.com/tag/the-fall-of-capitalism-and-the-rise-of-islam/

The Khilafah Conference 2009 is scheduled to be held July 19, 2009 at the Hilton Oak Lawn hotel.
Protesters gathered outside a Chicago area hotel Sunday as an Islamic extremist group reportedly linked to Al Qaeda held its first official conference on U.S. soil in an attempt to step up Western recruitment efforts. https://www.youtube.com/watch?v=W8Wg3j6MTJg

Members of Hizb ut-Tahrir — a global Sunni network with reported ties to confessed 9/11 mastermind Khalid Sheikh Mohammed and Al Qaeda in Iraq's onetime leader Abu Musab al-Zarqawi — met Sunday inside a Hilton hotel to host a conference, "The Fall of Capitalism and the Rise of Islam."

Hizb ut-Tahrir insists that it does not engage in terrorism, and it is not recognized by the State Department as a known Terror Group..... Well, that's reassuring, I feel much better now!

http://www.youtube.com/securefreedom

http://www.foxnews.com/story/0,2933,533880,00.html?test=latestnews

http://www.youtube.com/securefreedom#play/uploads/1/KlOZqdHXZDE

http://www.centerforsecuritypolicy.org/

Man, if this ever comes to fruition, when these Islamic Extremists go after their sponsors and benefactors on Capitol Hill,
I hope we'll have enough of a heads-up to launch a counterattack and annihilate them before they succeed in reaching our towns and families, unless they've been so cleverly insidious and patient
that we find ourselves surrounded and over-run by our own "home-grown" idiot followers.

Sounds like Red Dawn, Conspiracy Theory, or a Bruce Willis movie right? Well, where do You think these primitive Neanderthal cretins get their ideas from, but Hollywood!

One if by Land, Two if by Sea......Too Late.....They're Here!

Keep your powder dry.
SENTRYMAN

2 TERM LIMIT FOR CONGRESS   and   1 TERM LIMIT FOR PRESIDENTS

4 Comments

Comment by Nancy on July 19, 2009 at 3:32pm
　　　No wonder B Hussein is changing the Terrorist Alert (remember the color coding)

Comment by Tess on July 19, 2009 at 3:16pm
　　　I miss Dubya.

Comment by Dean on July 19, 2009 at 3:14pm
　　　God help us as we move toward this threat!

The New "Alert Color Code" Is Black & White!

Say, do you really think that "people of color", (the preferred label for today) who make such a big deal out of Michael Jackson as the 3rd coming,
since Barack is the 2nd coming, aren't also major RACISTS,
or than perhaps I don't understand double-speak, double-standards and HYPOCRISY.

YOU KNOW,
WE'RE ALL RACISTS, AND BIGOTS, AND HOMOPHOBES, AND HUMAN,
and a new batch is born every day, and us big kids, make lousy examples for them.

*Question:
If ARABS aren't hating Jews and Americans,
the Individual Tribes "can't stand each other"....So what is that called? ....
Racist? ...Bigoted? ... Homophobic? ...Or Human? Maybe B. Hussein calls them ?

**Questions about labels:
Do Wahhabi Muslims support interracial marriage with Black Muslims?

Seems they can fight and die for Allah all day long,
but,
will they become a new 2nd class in the New World Order for those at the top of the food chain that don't wish to get their hands dirty any longer? Are they closet Segregationist?

I know Black Muslims are brothers, but I never see any ARABS in the posse, standing in front of voting precincts for the Nation of Islam, or on TV, or while keep'in Michael Jackson hostage. ....Racist?

Now, having speculated that, let's all try to be a bit more tolerate of that neighbor across the street with the bright yellow house, and those plastic lawn flamingos..........Hypocrite!

Enough already........We've all read Black Like Me, and seen To Kill A Mockingbird, and Inherit The Wind........ So ENOUGH! ....OK?

Or, if you really want to get mean, START CALLING BARACK WHAT HE IS = "WHITEY"!

Either We Are All "Americans", And WE Protect The Constitution, Or You're The Enemy!......... Constitutionalists!

That's The Only Difference That Should Ever Separate Us From Being AMERICAN!...........Patriotic!

And If You're Not American, "Go Home After Your Friendly Visit"!..........Tolerance!

SENTRYMAN

Chapter 45

The Movie: "SWING VOTE", or "SWING SHIFT", or maybe "SWING BLADE"?

Posted by SENTRYMAN on July 19, 2009 at 3:30am

You know, it dawned on me as I watched "Swing Vote" w/Cosner tonight, I was reminded of "just how much time" presidential campaigns and elections actually take. I'm sure You've thought the same thing once or a hundred times.

Barack started, what was it, 19 months previously by June of '08, and all the while on his (only "maybe if") Voyager trek, He is collecting a check from the people of Illinois, and when not in Washington his (only 145 or so days) doing the job He was already PAID to do by the constituents, his employers, he was Not tending to "his sworn duties" to the entire country as a Representative of the US Government.....Maybe, He was on sabbatical, or had a note from his Grandma?.......I'm not sure!

Not to single him out alone, but, in any case that type of behavior and dereliction of duty includes even, and all sitting Presidents; the Bush's I and II, Clinton, all of them, except for LBJ and a few others for this reason or that.

My gosh, FDR for 4 times and today with a minimum $100 Million dollar war-chest, expense account to the challenger, not to mention (all the promises, favors and quid pro quo's, black bags of cash from Chinese restaurants owners, and Internet foreign-donors alike, and all that entails), there's a lot of money in-play. What a tremendous disadvantage is placed on any New Guy trying to battle an Incumbent, who Himself in the interim, is not tending to his own duties to the nation and isn't doing his job very responsibly either!

I've been concentrating all my attention and Blog efforts to cleaning up the House and Senate by pushing for 2 Term Limits, to send them all home to where they belong after their shortened patriotic service stint, (not to get rich),

but, in order to protect their solemn oath of office, the Election process in general, everyone's personal integrity, including The Republic's, and finally, hopefully for us to actually get our monies worth as the American Taxpayers who have always paid for this Liberty thing, and are eternally footing all the bills,

Pg. 243

someone's, everyone's got to think very seriously about this process and fast, before we are all corrupted!

What genius thought this stuff up in the first place, or has it morphed into another monster, like those 18,000 Gun Laws that protect "no-one", but the criminals?......What a con!.....We poor zhlobs!

This is a Job we actually paid them to do, plus, with all those perks they give themselves, with very little or no results to show for it, year after year, after, yah, and now they've wrecked the country and they still get paid!!!??? Hoorah

So, then it occurred to me that while a President, newly in office, only one day, is immediately reminded by his handlers that there's another election "just 4 years" away, the whole process [RE-SETs] and starts all over again,
so,
exactly "how many days" do these men actually spend "working" on their (required tasks, hired-for) conducting the "affairs of state" we all pay them to do, and by AFFAIRS, I certainly don't mean "chasing a skirt around the Oval Office on company time". (I think that would fall into the PERK column....Yah, definitely), but actually "keeping us all, (all Americans) safe from our enemies, foreign and domestic, while representing ALL the PEOPLE!

Point: What if we took that burden off their shoulders, and off the one man that we've saddled with that crushing responsibility, the toughest job on the planet?

Think of it, to actually have the luxury and the required time to concentrate, uninterrupted by mundane raising of cash, or calculate bribing some guy with a Judge appointment for his brother, to grease Locals to get out the Vote in his reelection bid, for instance; Wow, just to have the time to Do One's Job Really Well......Man, wouldn't that be great? ...America, "Limit Terms" Can Save Us All!

To have enough time for mindful contemplation, forethought and consideration. To use your intellect with patient, reasoned judgment, honor and wisdom for a change, instead of manufacturing staged performances and subterfuge to fool & camouflage hidden agendas and benefactors.

Simply inspire us, and lead with diligence and dignity, deciding the weighty life and death issues facing America every day. Then give us all a break! Stop lying to your employers, get your damn government off our backs and out of our pockets, stop spending money we don't have, thinking up way to rob us, then just defend our country and the Constitution of the United States! Not thinking about reelection tomorrow, frees you up to think today.

To actually work for the entire "full four years at the toughest job on the planet", being the Leader of the Free World, just might be a pretty rewarding, cool job!

*Don't You really think any person needs that much time to do the work properly? How much time do you spend away from your kids as a responsible good parent before they turn into gangsters or burn down the house.

Well, the President of the UNITED STATES, all 300+ million of us, is the surrogate father of our country, and if We don't do a good job and set some rules, then how do we expect him to represent our wishes? Not to make our decisions for us, but to do his very best with our vital interests of first and primary importance, like; NOT buying foreign oil "ever again" and drilling in our own back yards for $1. a gal. gasoline for starters, also natural gas, coal, solar, winds, etc.!....Do ya think?

Why does that seem like such a stretch?...I mean, really? I'll bet any self-employed businessman, or even the CEO of Wal-Mart spends more hours at their jobs than any President does working, as they simultaneously think about opinion polls and reelection!......No More _Lame Ducks_, just EAGLES!

I'm afraid we've all been conditioned to accept mediocrity today, and "symbolism over substance", lowering our standards and expectations, like tolerating an idiot uncle, we cheat our children, neighbors and ourselves! Let's start facing problems again and stop fooling the world and ourselves. Wouldn't it be refreshing to get a (day's worth of work) out of elected politicians "for each day paid". Isn't that what we'd expect as employers from any of our own employees within our companies? We expect that of ourselves, we should certainly expect that of them. Who works for who?..... Keep saying this to yourself: "We Are Their Employers", people! There is No free Lunch, and THEY are eating ours!

"Why" Don't We Demand More For Our Money?
If A President Is Going To Spend $75,000 Dollars MINIMUM For A Saturday Night Out-On-The-Town-In-Manhattan Using Our Money, I at least want to know how good the steak was, and to see some pictures, and hear a few interesting stories, if only, from some fellow Peon employers in the same restaurant at the next table!

*2 Terms for all elected government officials,
but, ONLY (1 TERM) FOR ALL FUTURE PRESIDENTs.

FOUR LONG YEARS SHOULD BE AMPLE TIME TO GET ANY JOB DONE WELL, OR, SCREW IT UP ENOUGH SO YOU DON'T SNEAK BACK-IN FOR ANOTHER 4,

AND JUST MAYBE WE'LL GET OUR MONIES WORTH AND SOLVE EVERY DARN PROBLEM ON HIS PLATE, ESPECIALLY A FREE $75,000 STEAK!

WOULDN'T THAT BE NICE FOR A CHANGE, AND MAYBE WE'D ALL HAVE SOME "CHANGE" LEFT IN OUR POCKETS..........IS THAT TOO MUCH TO EXPECT?????

SENTRYMAN

---

1 COMMENT

Comment by Gina on July 19, 2009 at 10:56am
I believe Obama needs to be a One term President before he completely destroys America and defaces our Constitution! You made some really good points, thanks for sharing!

 <u>**Chapter 46**</u>

$$
President Obama says: America can never pay its debt"

Posted by **SENTRYMAN** on <u>July 26, 2009</u> at 3:00pm

Glenn Beck agrees with a Theory I've espoused on my Blog for the past 9 months, and now Obama has provided Glenn with the specifics.

President Obama says: "America can never pay its debt" to AFRICAN-AMERICANS for 400 years of Slavery,

(p.s., Barack, we've only been the United States for a little over 200 years),

and that apparently a continental Civil War, that raged from 1861 thru 1865, pitting neighbor against neighbor, brother against brother, wounding and killing over a quarter of a million "white" American "Republican" Union soldiers; by fighting and dying to (end the Democrat's institutionalized Slavery Policy, wouldn't ever be enough?

**I know! I have one ancestor that when 20 years old, He enlisted at the beginning of the Civil War from Ohio,
and then He re-enlisted into a 2nd unit for the second half of that War,

and my other ancestor at 16 years of age was drafted at the start of the Civil War, and He also made it all the way to the end of the War, alive also…He, "twice wounded", was (1, of only 3) surviving enlisted men, out of the 95 men in his Company at the Battle of Sayler's Creek. He was at Appomattox Court House when General Robert E. Lee [CS], finally surrendered to Lieutenant General Ulysses S. Grant [US] on April 9, 1865, and then
Lee's Army was paroled, and went back home!....*thanks anyway fellas*!

Yes, each of my Ancestors trying to kill each other, each on opposing sides, but, as The Fates would have it their paths forever entwined with each other's future, providing "the one his daughter, the other his son", who would someday fall-in-love and marry one another ………..
<u>**a Union truly Un-divided?**</u>   Pg. 246

So now, almost 150 years later, not just "White" Americans, but "all Americans", including even those that came to the Americas after the Civil War ended, who obviously bore "no direct or indirect culpability or involvement" in that episode, will also be forced to pay "into-the-Kitty" for a Universal Program for perpetuity, giving all "African-Americans"; PREFERENCES = AKA: MORE-FREE-STUFF!

It would seem to me that if Barack's got an ax to grind, especially since he's not even a slave-descendant, (even if He is, or isn't a legal American citizen), I'd "target" those specific family's ancestors who bought, kept, and benefitted directly from their Plantation Slaves in a Class-Action Suit, if still riding that train.

I'm sure John Edwards would love to bring that suit if his ancestors weren't involved, and while You're at it, contact all those "white" northern families directly affected, damaged and destroyed, having sustained wounded or killed family members that were soldiers of that "Republican" Union Army for their fare share of that "Restitution Kitty", for the same remunerations and freebees!.....

That' equitable: don't you think? Especially, since the aforementioned Slaves lived-on, with some of the progeny eventually producing $Millionaire descendants in sports, industry, the arts, literature, music and education in that greatest nation on earth,
but all of those old "white" patriot "Union soldiers" just remained scared, crippled or DEAD, and with their families and descendants forever altered, or destroyed!

But, it always seems to just work out like that for our soldiers though, doesn't it!

In case you didn't catch Glenn Beck's programs on related subjects, try;

A New America for racial and social justice through;
Affirmative Action, Health Care, Cap & Trade (Cap & Tax)
http://www.youtube.com/watch?v=RELWULoyIn0

part 2
http://www.youtube.com/watch?v=hqdKYbbDmH0

We're on the "Road to Socialism"
http://www.youtube.com/watch?v=pLT0IDwZNNM&feature=related

Why is there an Offices of Civil Rights & Minority Health Care
http://www.youtube.com/watch?v=89MeB4_CbOI

And so the circle is now complete Obi Wan,
Darth is now "The Teacher".

SENTRYMAN

$$

Comment by SENTRYMAN July 22, 2009 to another Blog:

* *"Protect Life, Liberty and Property In Our Health Care!"*.........*Posted by Bill C.*
* *"So WHAT does President Obama want to do with his health care plan?"*

SENTRYMAN response:

1) - Reverse History, of course.
2) - Put Caucasians in Chains, having them submit and commit to OBAMA's subservience to the State,

3) - Euthanize White People With "Final Solution" Health Care For The Elderly, once Private Insurance fails with SSI & Medicare collapsing,

4) - Welcoming-in a more enlightened secular multi-national, color-neutral, New World Order, after opening the cage doors of tyrants, dictators AND the acquitted Terrorists for total global chaos,
in order to undermine and finally destroy the "white"- "white"- "white" corporate-elite power structure underpinnings,
(as if "greedy-bankers" wasn't enough of a curse) of the "oh, so unfair" Old World European Imperialistic-Colonial Civilization,
thus welcoming-in the stability, the fairness and tranquility of a newer U.S.S.R., Maoist, Cuban, Czarist, National Socialist Global Society!

Yah, "since those all worked-out so well",
but this time a Rookie with "no track-record", "no practical experience" "no managerial business experience", who has
 "sequestered all his academic grades and personal records" that would show us and prove to the world "Just How It's Done", with HIS totally new regulated system, dominated by a rigid-minded all-controlling fascist-ordered society, modeled on Islam!

I think I've seen that "SYSTEM" sold on late night TV at 2:00 AM for $199.00, right after the Real Estate Course, and the Knives that never-need-sharpening, and Sham-WOW! ...SENTRYMAN

* *"Sooooo, What do we need to do next?"* ....Posted by Bill C

SENTRYMAN response:

Well, Pay more attention, wake-up & Vote Them: "All Out Of Government," in favor of "Only Conservative" candidates who will make sure You keep most of what You earn, and "Not steal your stuff", but don't trust them either!.........THEY may just be Wolves in RINO Conservative clothing!

Be better stewards of Liberty and vote-in: **"2 TERM LIMITS"**

for ourselves, our kids and OUR OWN SURVIVAL!!

SENTRYMAN

==

SENTRYMAN postscript:

TERM LIMITS - "IT'S THE ONLY WAY TO SAVE THE REPUBLIC!"

Pay heed to the lessons learned by our newly "American", early Pilgrim Settlers first dabbling with Socialism out of desperation during the original "New World Order" experiment!

You see, I really believe this stuff of dreams!
As "one", of the many thousands of descendants from just (1) of the families depicted here in this illustration below, of the original 102 Mayflower Pilgrims who gathered in prayer, giving thanks to their Creator, asking for strength and wisdom to find a better way,
"they were willing to gamble everything on an Idea": LIBERTY!

"FREEDOM for His family"; they took the ultimate risk to venture into the vast unknown.......not with an Army, not with modern weaponry, not with radar, not with refrigerated food stocks, not with hearth and home waiting: but in a wooden boat and Faith in the Lord!

Though He didn't live to see "The Hope" fulfilled, of the 45 to die that 1st winter in a brave new world,
He was my Ancestor and a better man than me, but, for the grace of GOD go I.

And You Too!

SENTRYMAN

The Pilgrims' Financial Crisis

http://spectator.org/articles/42565/pilgrims-financial-crisis

By Peter Ferrara on 11.26.08 @ 6:09AM

The Pilgrims who landed at Plymouth Rock in 1620 were an idealistic lot. They were part of the broader Puritan movement believing that the Anglican Church, recognized in law as the official church of England, had strayed from true Christianity. The Puritans were devoted to the Bible as the only true source of Christian doctrine and practice and objected to Anglican traditions and practices that had been added over the years from outside of the Bible.

The Puritans more generally wanted to reform and purify the Anglican church from within. But the Pilgrims were a subset of Puritans that wanted to separate themselves from the Anglican church entirely and practice their own true form of Christianity on their own. The Anglicans in turn persecuted the Puritans as heretics rebelling against the officially recognized Church of England and their obligations to it under the law.

This is what led the Pilgrims to leave England seeking full religious freedom. First they migrated to the Netherlands, which practiced religious tolerance of alternative religions. But the English Puritans wanted their children to grow up in an English culture, not as Dutchmen. That is why after a few years they sought to establish their own colony in the New World, where they could control their own government, religion and culture.

Due to unexpected delays, wandering off course, and searching for the best settlement site, the *Mayflower*, carrying 102 settlers, finally anchored at what was to become the settlement of Plymouth on December 21, 1620, the dead of winter. William Bradford, destined to become the second governor of the colony and the longest serving, wrote in his diary while still on the ship and contemplating "this poor people's present condition": "Being thus passed the vast ocean, they had now no friends to welcome them, nor inns to entertain or refresh their weather-beaten bodies; no houses or much less towns to repair to, or to seek for succor....And for the season it was winter, and they know that the winters of that country [are] sharp and violent, and subject to cruel and fierce storms, dangerous to travel to known places, much more to search an unknown coast.

Besides, what could they see but a hideous and desolate wilderness, full of wild beasts and wild men—and what multitudes there might be of them they know not....If they looked behind them, there was the mighty ocean which they had passed and was now as a main bar and gulf to separate them from all the civil parts of the world....

What could now sustain them but the spirit of God and his grace?" Pg. 250

In these precarious conditions, it was natural for them to work together and share their food and shelter. Even so, 45 of the original 102 died that first winter, including 13 of the original adult women, with one more passing away in May. During 1621, they discovered a couple of English speaking Indians, who had learned the language from fishermen hauling off fish from the New England coast, but who had not settled. This included the famed Squanto, who showed the settlers how to best hunt, fish, plant, and mine essential commodities in the New World, served as their exploration guide, and developed their relations with the surrounding Indian tribes.

****OK now students,
how do you think things would have worked out for our earliest American adventurers, seeking to throw-off the yoke of oppression for religious freedom and a new opportunity, had they all just waited around for their checks to come on the next mail-ship, and had they only relied upon ole' Squanto to hopefully feed and provide "Cradle to Grave Care", for these European misfits?......Me thinks: more would have reach the grave, before any arrivals in the cradle!................SENTRYMAN.................

By 1623, four additional ships of settlers had arrived. The colony had initially prospered just collecting wild growing food, and securing plentiful game such as turkeys and deer providing venison, supplemented by their own agriculture. Given their religious devotion, their concern for personal wealth was not a top issue for them, and even in that time idealistic notions of communal property and sharing communal resources as offering an ideal society of happiness had a strong appeal for those striking out to start a new civilization from scratch.

But as the colony grew, this initial quasi-socialist community of share and share alike was not working to produce enough for essential basic needs, let alone the prosperity that was expected in the new world. Available wild supplies of food, in particular, were no longer enough. Bradford again wrote in his dairy,

All this while no supply [of wild corn] was heard of, neither knew they when they might expect any. So they began to think how they might raise as much corn as they could, and obtain a better crop than they had done, that they might not thus languish in misery.

At length, after much debate of things, the Governor (with the advice of the chiefist amongst them)
gave way that they should set corn every man for his own particular, and in that regard trust to themselves; in all other things go on in the general way as before. And so assigned to every family a parcel of land, according to the proportion of their number, for that end....This had very good success, for it made all hands very industrious, so as much more corn was planted than otherwise would have been by any means the Governor or any other could use, and saved him a great deal of trouble, and gave far better content. The women now went willingly into the field, and took their little ones with them to set corn;

which before would allege weakness and inability, whom to have compelled would have been thought great tyranny and oppression.

As indicated, this experiment in private agriculture was hugely successful, with the colony's agricultural output soaring. But the settlers still increasingly complained that the colony's remaining communal practices and lack of complete private property were constraining and unfair. Bradford wrote further in his diary in 1623,

The experience that was had in this common course and condition, tried sundry years and that amongst godly and sober men, may well evince the vanity of that conceit of Plato's and other ancients applauded of by some of later times; that the taking away of property and bringing in community into a commonwealth would make them happy and flourishing, as if they were wiser than God. For this community…was found to breed much confusion and discontent and retard much employment that would have been to their benefit and comfort.

For the young men, that were most able and fit for labor and service, did repine that they should spend their time and strength to work for other men's wives and children without any recompense. The strong, or man of parts, had no more in division of victuals and clothes than he that was weak and not able to do a quarter the other could; this was thought injustice….And for men's wives to be commanded to do service for other men, as dressing their meat, washing their clothes, etc., they deemed it a kind of slavery….Let none object this is men's corruption, and nothing to the course [meaning communal policy] itself. I answer, seeing all men have this corruption in them, God in his wisdom saw another course fitter for them.

Thus was capitalism born in America, sentimental notions of socialism having been tried and failed, not only as a matter of economics, but also because it was seen as a regime of unjust restrictions on personal liberty. The colony adopted private property and free trade, ending its own critical financial crisis, and creating the trademark bountiful American prosperity, which drew waves of new settlers seeking the American dream that had already been born.

http://spectator.org/archives/2008/11/26/the-pilgrims-financial-crisis

----

There Is No Free Lunch, NOT even With OBAMACARE...

and no free breakfast or dinner either.
Never has Been, Never will Be, and now it's bitter cold outside and snowing, even with global warming……ha ha ha, ha ha, ha ha ha, brrrrrrrr!

SENTRYMAN

<u>1 Comment by Natalie from Australia, on July 26, 2009 at 3:44pm</u>

Glenn Beck laid it out very clearly, it is there to be seen.
Isn't that what Acorn is really all about?

Blind Freddy could have, SHOULD have seen who Obama was and what his Real Agenda and modus operandi were. Sean Hannity tried to show people, they in the main did not want to see.

Bill O, Reilly did not want to see, I kept emailing him prior to your election in the US, asking him to get his production team to research Obama and from my perspective, he sat on the fence.

I always felt if Obama had been just another white man, Bill's treatment of him would have been extremely different and I felt, he did not want to be tagged as "racist".

The thing is, it has nothing to do with the colour of his skin, he makes it that way himself, it is all to do with some deep-seated hatred, a chip on the shoulder, it was his wife Michelle who spelled-it-out clearly for anyone prepared to listen.

 # Chapter 47

"Click The Emblem" To Make A Difference on Beck! ....yadda, yadda

Posted by SENTRYMAN on August 1, 2009 at 1:30pm

Hello again Patriots.

Been away for a while at a survivalist camp in Idaho, for Americans
 Wanting To Take Back Their Country and Constitution.

Ever see the movie "The Postman" with that commie-Lib Cosner,
talk about being miscast, should have been an Eastwood, or Bruce Willis "type" instead?

["Click The Emblem" To Make A Difference On Beck"!]

VOTING-IN: "www. INTERNET POLLS & SURVEYS", TO WHAT END Glenn?

Isn't that what they do in Iraq, but with an evidenced "purple" finger? ...
Well, we've all gotten "The Finger" long enough!

Glenn had a couple of important shows last week, but it's all the same, the same, the same!

These people in Washington, they know "exactly-what-they-are-doing."
Or, need I say: "They don't care WHAT they are doing to Us",
 and nothing We say or Do will deter them from their appointed rounds:
Special Delivering Our Immediate Concerns To The Circular File@ Talk is cheap Glenn,
and so is their value as a representative-government, they do as they please!...Surprise...

We'll get the results from Bobby Jindal's Investigation of A.C.O.R.N. in 7-1/2 years or
so!....... WATCH @~@

Did you see that brilliant inquisition of Bernanke "testifying before the congressional
committee" with his "deer-in-headlights" responses?

And when Bernanke responded, paraphrased: "((Bush)) only did what he did last fall to
hold the nation together", and I think;

"as well as he'd done for the previous 7 years", boy, did that fall on deaf ears.

I didn't hear the Press, nor even one of Our Guys exclaim in utter amazement:
"OHHHHHHH, I SEE NOW.....HURRAH, HURRAH FOR "W"!"
"Hurray For The Vital Job Pres. Bush Did Saving America Once Again"!......I can't type any smaller!!

[Nope!!!].....I could hear the crickets-chirping in the weeds outside Washington.

Geez, Louise,....... "If That Wasn't A Teachable Moment People"....
Are All These People Really That Stupid, or Moles, or Deluded Commies,
or just: Deaf - Dumb & Blind?....... A Trifecta of bewilderment!   Pg. 254

These sycophants wouldn't credit Bush if He ferreted-out 1 of the most nefarious, heinous, infamous Dictators on the planet, and freed 25 million of his captive subjects from decades of his murder, rape and servitude...
.......Wait A Minute!!!

That should have made every Republican so proud, and maybe even, at least 1/2 the DEMs ....well, 1/3 the DEMs....well. OK, forget that.
(If any of them really and truly cared about their Country) someone on our side should have leaped-up and yelled in the halls of Congress: _"That's It, we're not gonna take this anymore", a'la Peter Finch,_ and lead a mob to storm the White House with torches.

You know though, Mr. Beck,
Glenn, knowing how many ways your enemy is sticking-it to you, well,
That Don't Impress Me Much!.... (Shania).

(How To Affect That "Symptomatic Cause-Celeb" For The Big "O",
Is The Only Thing We Need To Know, and The Precise Way To Alter The Effect.)
I know when someone's slapp'n me in the face, stabb'n my children in the back, and pee'n on the Constitution, and I don't need that examined to infinitum.....What I NEED,
"I need ideas, battle plans, solutions", not a grocery list of every offence....I want Results!

I don't care about How Many Ways I Can Get Screwed turning a light bulb,
I wanna know "How To Stop Getting Screwed" = light bulbs are outlawed!

(You Go "Click" <<<<<< and "Call Beck" on the Internet)<<<<<<<<<<<<<<

It's useless and about the same as making a futile response to an O'Reilly Poll:
"Do you agree with how Obama is taking the country into the Abyss? ......Yahhhh, Duhhhh!

or......"Do you think Cronkite was an honorable guy"?.....WHO CARES!!!...
and who cares about ineffectual useless polling either! Never meaty questions.

I have filled out so many of those GOP and Congressional questionnaires that have been sent to me by "Special Delivery" mail to My house over the years,
and I've even been dumb enough to write-in (above and below) each question, editing and expanding, and illuminating their inept simplistic, inane questions, while qualifying ALL my answers Infinitum with explicit footnotes and ideas,.......ALL CRAP!!....SUCKERRRRR!

It's all a sham, a futile endeavor, designed to extract that last drop of blood from me with a politician's Kiss of Death, a raspberry ruse! .....Oh ya, and another request for a donation!
Nothing ever changes, Nothing, Nothing, Nothing; Zip, Zero Nada, Zilch EVER CHANGES, and that was when the GOP had the Presidency and both HOUSEs....WHOA...
and We Were Supposedly In Power!....ha ha ha ha ha, (&$&%#@%+^$?&*)

And, just as we were about to lose "the power and the control", and the last of our checks were quickly processed and cashed, as our surveys were unfiled & shredded "UN-READ", in the circular file, and the air went out of the balloon, I got a "New" Questionnaire!.....Send us money so We can win back the House and Senate to fulfill President Bush's yada, yada.
I no longer care about responding to poll studies or listening to their pitches on the phone, or opening newsletters, or getting membership cards in the mail, or listening to opinion reports from "Talking Heads",
or being wired into one of Frank Luntz's straightjacket: Lie-Detectors,

or even making Good TV and advancing Glenn Beck's ratings, that He always brags about to O'Reilly. Who in return, brags about the same, back to Beck on more than 4 occasions lately when they're together!

*I just want to know (1) SIMPLE thing from these nattering-nabobs that none of these guys have bothered to ask each other, or anyone for that matter, or even "queried an answer":

"EXACTLY HOW DO WE BEAT THESE GUYS NOW, AND PERMANENTLY???"

And Stop The Madness Before We Are All In "The Commune or Speaking Arabic"?

What's that quote again: *"When more people are voting than are working?"*....

THEN WE'RE DEAD, D-E-A-D!....STICK US WITH A FORK, WE'RE DONE!

Well, we are almost there folks!.......Their knives and forks a'ready, and there's just a few grains left in the Hourglass!

"All that is necessary for the triumph of evil is that good men do nothing"
... Edmund Burke

We even have RINOs voting with the DEMs on Sotocracker, & One Representative Is Not Even Running Again, But Retiring. What's his deal? And these votes are not even needed, bi-partisan traitorous Hockey-pucks!

........What the HELL does that tell YOU about the caliber of individuals that We hire to represent OUR interests in WASHINGTON?
........Are We Blind or Just Fools?........No, damn fools, with blinders on!

You go tell our Saviors that We don't need them anymore, to ponder this one: A state by state referendum, a lack of confidence in this Government:
2 Term Limit for Congressionals

and

1 Term Limit for Presidents

and just watch the Manure hit the Spreader!

........It's all up to You now........ I can't get anyone to pay attention, so, I'm going back to Idaho!

SENTRYMAN

10 COMMENTS

Comment by Donna the teacher on August 1, 2009 at 2:08pm
Thank you for your comments. I appreciate you.
Keep it coming...

Comment by Natalie from Australia on August 1, 2009 at 4:26pm
Your frustration and anger is warranted,
but in this case I think you are a little unfair 'shooting the messenger'.

As an Australian the major part of my learning of your recent politics has been via Fox. Of course they work for ratings, unlike C.N.N and NBC, they would be off the air if they did not. Do You really believe Glen Beck has wasted his time writing a book "Common Sense", because he doesn't care?

These people have a job of informing the viewing audience, interviewing people you would otherwise not be exposed to. Then it is up to you to bring about the changes you want.
The New Republican site on Team Sarah advises you how to work at the grass roots level of the party, be involved in who is nominated to represent you, do your homework and find out who they actually are.
Stand yourself, you have an election next year, you Americans should all be working to the best of your ability to achieve change.
If Acorn could get people registered to vote and many of these people were only doing it for the money, surely there are so many of you with principles, who really care, you can do it, only with much greater success.

At the end of the day, it is up to you, the people, Not Beck and O, Reilly, they only have one vote each.

Comment by SENTRYMAN on August 1, 2009 at 6:12pm

Natalie, I love ya.
You are 100% correct,
but only in a perfect world.

Australians, Australian/Americans, African/Americans, Americans, rational beings, human beings, whatever,
we just watched our ("chosen-for-us") Presidential Straw-man candidate "torched" faster than a Burning Man Festival,
and if you don't think the whole thing isn't rigged, and there's almost nothing that can be done, we wouldn't be here, in less than 1 year.

But, don't fret, I'm not getting on Glenn's case as much as You are, on Mine.
I have no more patience for the "symbolism over substance",
 and I've seen through the B/S since I was 8 in my father's saloon.

"Just show us what to do to resolve this ASAP"
 if you've got any bright ideas Glenn, not how to embellish your ratings.

We're already knee-deep in a Septic Tank. We don't need you to identify anything for us specifically.
(Glenn did the same theatrics at CNN, but has now come to "The Audience",
not the Audience coming to Him.)

"Rush" reiterates periodically that his popularity is based on:
("Not that he tells people what to think, but that he voices what people already think!")

And I think, and have thought these things for a very long time, along with most conservatives going on 60 years, having had the advantage of a good mother, Church, Cub Scouts/Boy Scouts, many public schools (before taken over by Ideologues), with GYM and Intramurals, Religious Instruction after-school, playing baseball in front yards, in open fields and a sandlot or two, always outside in the fresh air, (no video games), but Board-Games with friends, 3 channels on B&W TV, The Lone Ranger, Roy & Dale (married), NO INTERNET, 3 colleges, the military, hard knocks and working for myself over 40 years, and I stood-up for myself, Natalie.

FOX is popular because it mirrors what: WE ALL THINK ALREADY, MR. OBAMA!
Not what FOX tells us to think, MR. OBAMA!
Fox just does its job, that no one else does anymore, and it's called Journalism, Mr. Rather.

It's Not "The Messenger", we've come a long way since Rome.
We've had our own "Ides of March"!
We don't need messengers, we've got too many messengers.
We need results, and we're Not going to get it from "Our current Crew" in Washington!

They Deserve to be Traded-in for a New Bench.

VOTE-IN ONLY CONSERVATIVES whenever possible.

REAL CONSERVATIVES, LIKE SARAH with a track record, not promises or rhetoric, and with a real Birth certificate, and a School Transcript to prove You're a Genius!

And as I watch the last of my 4 businesses get swallowed-up in that septic tank called Washington; as You sip a brewski in OUR backyard to protect your halo,
"It IS The Economy Stupid", and "It's YOUR REALITY", Mr. President!

But unfortunately, no one that really knows how to fix-it is listening, or wants to....YET!

SENTRYMAN

Comment by Miss Lavenia 10 minutes ago
Indeed, there is nothing new under the sun...

"A government that is big enough to give you all you want, is big enough to take it all away. Government control is the name of the game."
- Barry Goldwater

Comment by SENTRYMAN 40 minutes ago
Thank you MW.

I had forgotten to reiterate the "power of perception" and the crippling effect of Junk Science and FEAR.
We've gotten to this point because of one stupid movie: The China Syndrome, that castrated an entire country for 30 long years, from ever producing its own cheap fuel
 to eliminate a perceived fear,

and stymied construction of any more Oil refineries with their touted impact on the environment,
hampered too by its own "over capacity" maintenance shutdowns, storm susceptibilities and production issues, again, all to eliminate a perceived fear that also stopped any new drilling for our own domestic cheap oil,
forcing us to unnecessarily manufacture gasoline into (18 varieties) of evil Gas like blends of champagnes to eliminate another perceived fear,

thus forcing us to triple our dependency of "artificially priced" foreign oil,
placing our economy in a noose while performing our self-imposed duties as the World Cop protecting the engine of Democracy.....OIL!
That allows Futures-speculators to manipulate it's price, and simultaneously rapes the nation, where all involved, including our own government, could benefit on the backs of American Taxpayers who always foots-the-bill,

and ultimately brought down an administration, once again eliminate another perceived fear, the "power of perception".....BOO!

So we Tilt at Windmills for The Solutions!

SENTRYMAN

Comment by MW 2 hours ago
good message Sentryman!

Comment by SENTRYMAN 8 hours ago

Hey Patriots;
This isn't Mickey Rooney and Judy Garland,
and the only way we can save the OLE' clubhouse is to buy the land before Grandma looses the house In Foreclosure.
So we'll put on a big "Tea Party show" to save the day, and have a big closing number with everyone smiling and singing!

"The Enemy" denied the Permit for the Show,
"the Press" has been told to turn their backs,
"They" already stole the land through Eminent Domain,
"They" ground-up Grandma's clunker so she can't drive, or get away,
and "They've" shipped her off to the Soylent Green Factory in a chauffeur driven Ford Fusion Hybrid by a (PAID A.C.O.R.N. Volunteer).

It doesn't matter what you tell "Them", or plead, or threaten, or scream at "your Representatives", "They've" already crossed-over to the Dark Side,
and "the opposition" doesn't need your votes anyway.
"To Them", Progressives, Leftists, Socialists, Communists, Jihadists, "We" are irrelevant!

And if anyone thinks that an emotion-driven, vacuous, amoral "celebrity", or even some reasonably rational actors who don't believe as strongly in (the Purpose and the Vision), as if it were a Jim Jones's anti-Christ Call-to-Arms,
or that "They" don't have the smarts or the gumption to wholeheartedly follow through and enthusiastically influence the vast majority of the great uneducated,

unwashed and unenlightened,
right up to, and right past that very point of the total ruin of this nation, AMERICA,
well then, you've never seen a Macy's (bargain basement) "Wedding Dress Sale"
in action, or a Sale on Manolo Blahniks, to die for,
or watched Glenn Close, or Demi Moore make Michael Douglas' life a living hell.

This is "THEM" on display, for REAL: What "They" think, what "They" write, how "They"
act, what "They'll" do, and ....what is so very important to "Them", ONLY!
"These" people helped orchestrate that "Actor's" ascension into the White House.

We once had a politician that played an actor, a long time ago, in the White House,
and now we have an "Actor playing a politician"!

Just because we think "They're" really just fooling, or perhaps just plain crazy, or
delusional, and "They'll" see the light at the last minute to redeem "Their" souls, yuh sure!
Well, that only happens in real life, and in "Their" fantasy world, "They" aren't dying yet.
"These" people don't live in the real world earning $10,000 to $1,000,000.00 a-Week,
depending where on the food chain "their" SAG or AFTRA card is.

HEY, WHO ARE THEY ANYWAY?....."THEY ARE" ACTORS!.....JUST MAKE-BELIEVERS!

And if we think we'll finally succeed because We are Right and Just, and Fair, and Play by
the rules because we are The Good Guys, and God and/or karma will come to our rescue
in the end, well,
the ghosts in the Concentration Camps & the Internment Camps are still waiting for help!

Let me remind everyone that we only won W.W.II because we were late to the game and
"we cheated" (so to speak) with the Enigma, and we had to invent a world-shattering bomb
to save the bigger-picture and defeat Evil! But, a lot of people died waiting, before our own
brave soldiers died also, coming to their rescue. Lincoln was proactive, but still no kudos!

Granted many of us wouldn't be here today having this discussion, of course, and it'd be a
different world with all of us speaking German, or Japanese and Italian.
Oh, and Hitler even had to shoot himself before we got the chance!
.......We haven't been that lucky or have seen that in a while!

All's fair in love and war I hear, and there is no love out there for us it seems, no matter
how many times America Saves The World.
"These" people want to kill Santa Claus, for cripe sakes!

The Rules have changed again, and "They've" seen to that,
and We are now playing "Their Game", on their "Home Court", and we're down 202 to 233,
and most of our guys have sat out the 1st half,
and if we don't change the "entire bench" in the 2nd half
we'll all be praying for a Hail Mary!

But, by then, even "she" won't be able to help unless "she" comes out of Alaska.

JUST Bypass The Crooked Congress.

People's Term Limits Referendum: PROP #86 and eighty-six the congress with
(2) - Terms for Congress and (1) - Term for Presidents!

SENTRYMAN

Comment by Billie 1 day ago
This is on the AOL homepage right NOW!!.......... They are such liars!!

"Another Sarah Palin Switch?
She was billed as a featured speaker for an event at the Reagan presidential library next week, in what would have been her first public appearance as an ex-governor.
But now Palin has decided not to go."

I really can believe the audacity of them!! She and her lawyers have made the statement last week or so that she wasn't invited and didn't care to attend or speak at the event!!
And people will actually believe the lies too!!
===

Comment by SENTRYMAN 23 hours ago

Hey Billie;

Ever wonder why Jimmy Carter never learns or mellows?

Why Huffington, or Sarandon, or Streisand never learn, or evolve.
Well maybe if al Qaeda bombs Rodeo Drive, but aside from that happening, You just can't let it get to you, or ponder WHY. Expect it, Nature of the Beast.

In the grand scheme of things they are different animals.

A tiger can't change its strips or better put,
you can't tame your pet Python not to eat your dog,
no matter how nice you are to it, or how long you have it.

Remember that old C&W song with the sympathetic woman that rescues a snake frozen in the snow, and nurses it back to health,
 and when she hugs her new little friend she's bitten in the breast?

Or, did I just imagine that. ha ha
They're never going to give You a break, and that's one on one.

Now what are You going to get from a pack of Jackals in the Press Corps, <u>BLOOD</u>!

If Mary Matalin can't change her husband James Carville's mind,
or Bob Beckel sitting there while Shawn Hannity lists off 100 documented things
Obama did wrong this year, Bob will smile and say: "Well, Yuh, But!"

And then there's Dr. Lamont on O'Reilly's factor, now there's a "lost cause" and He'll be teaching children at Columbia in the fall.
And thank yous; to that "phony Indian" professor in Colorado, and the "Bomber" professor in Chicago, and the NEA!

The "only things" that can change anything on this planet is "The Sword" & "The Vote."
Take your pick!
After that we're all treading water, just watch out for the sharks.
Have a great day just being in "the Right". The other side is always angry and sad.

<u>SENTRYMAN</u>

9 Videos for Social Justice, Health Care, Slavery Reparations, GREENs and Computers
http://www.foxnews.com/topics/politics/glenn-beck.htm?&start=10

http://www.foxnews.com/search-results/search?&q=glenn+beck+archive&mediatype=Video&start=10

Glenn Beck Clips now on FOX NEWS site, not "YouTube" any longer.
07- 28- 09 -- Seg. 3- America You Need To Know Community Organizers!
Chart.
http://www.youtube.com/results?search_query=glenn+beck+7-28-09&oq=glenn+beck+7-28-09&aq=f&aqi=&aql=&gs_sm=s&gs_upl=104156l110297l0l123172l7l7l0l6l6l0l282l282l2-1l1l0

http://www.youtube.com/results?search_query=Glenn+Beck&oq=Glenn+Beck&aq=f&aqi=g10&aql=&gs_sm=s&gs_upl=2640l6437l0l10578l10l10l0l3l3l0l313l1327l1.3.2.1l7l0

New Health Care Bill has shades of the movie Soylent Green
http://www.youtube.com/watch?v=ho-0SHFEgGo&eurl=http%3A%2F%2Fwww%2Eteamsarah%2Eorg%2Fgroup%2Fglennbeckfansforsarahpalin%3FgroupUrl%3Dglennbeckfansforsarahpalin%26id%3D2330231%253AGroup%253A151638%26page%3D1&feature=player_embedded

"Cars for clunkers" Seg. 4- @ Cars.gov allows government to take over your computer
http://www.youtube.com/watch?v=KZxaWDqUmho

Glenn Beck Clips are now on the FOX News site 07-28-09 Seg. 5- Ben Stein: Obama Is No Friend of Israel!....Google It
http://www.youtube.com/watch?v=33ZfEdKQKTk

Glenn Beck Clips now on FOX site 07-28-09 Seg. 1- At The 6 Month Mark, Obama Says 'It Is GOOD' and Goes on Vacation..Google It_____ http://

Glenn Beck Clips now on FOX site 07-28-09 Seg. 2- Michelle Malkin Guest 'Culture of Corruption' Author..Google It
http://www.youtube.com/watch?v=4HsZw58Lr0A

Glenn Beck Clips now on FOX site 07-27-09 Seg 4- Rep. John Conyers Says: 'What Good Is It To Read The Health Care BILLS?'..Google It
http://www.youtube.com/watch?v=mzAEoKs0kWM

Obama on Healthcare and Social Justice through Reparations and US can never pay its Debt for Slavery.
http://www.youtube.com/watch?v=RELWULoyIn0&feature=related

SENTRYMAN

Chapter 48

Free Money & High Gas & Environmental Global What?
Politicians = "All Clunkers"

Posted by SENTRYMAN on August 5, 2009 at 12:18am

CASH FOR CLUNKERS????

How about just $1.00 @ gal. Gasoline again??

"Drill Here, Drill Now" ...."E-V-E-R-Y-B-O-D-Y"   BENEFITS!!!

Everybody Works Again and Not "On The Dole", and Not "On The Take".

WE ALL WANT TO SAVE THE ENVIRONMENT ?

"A Socialist Ploy To Enslave A Nation and Abscond With Their GNP!"

So stated German Scientists, and Meteorologists who petitioned their
Government to officially label "Man-Made Global Warming" a Sham,
and a Pseudo-Religion!

http://www.freerepublic.com/focus/news/2308036/posts

http://wattsupwiththat.com/2009/07/30/american-chemical-society-
members-revolting-against-their-editor-for-pro-agw-views/

http://www.iceagenow.com/Climatologists_Who_Disagree.htm

http://www.climatedepot.com/a/2597/Exposed-Climate-Fear-Promoters-
Greatest-Fear--A-Public-Trial-of-the-Evidence-of-Global-Warming-Fears-
Inconvenient-Developments-Continue-To-Mount

Pg. 263

http://www.breadandbutterscience.com/OSGWD.htm

http://www.climatedepot.com/a/2165/Climate-Fear-Promoters-Try-to-Spin-Record-Cold-and-Snow-Global-warming-made-it-less-cool
http://politicalape.com/2009/07/10/gore-is-a-liar-no-global-warming-nasa-planet-cooling-since-2003/

SHAWN HANNITY STATES: "POLITICIANS USE THE LAW TO PROTECT THEIR POWER TO RAM SELF-SERVING LEGISLATION DOWN CITIZENS THROATS?"

SENTRYMAN STATES: "TERM LIMITS"

....

IT'S THAT SIMPLE!........EASY AS 1 - 2 - 3

AND WE JUST SAVED THE AMERICAN TAXPAYER A TRILLION DOLLARS
and No "Bills" Were Needed, That Invariably Are Intentionally Never READ!

See,.....Running the Government isn't so hard when One wants to accomplish something significant, lasting and meaningful!

Now, What Do You Want To Do Tomorrow To Save Our Countries "Insignificant Citizens" A Lot More Money?...Oh, I don't know?
Why not buy 535 pairs of "reading" glasses for the House and Senate?

That could save another QUADRILLION Dollars over 15 Years,
and just maybe "FIX something", and give some Americans a job?

***An IDEA -

If We can Reward a Wall-Street "Commodity Trader": one lone individual, with a Gold Star & a whopping $100,000,000.00 sun-blocking "sales bonus", by using the US Taxpayer's IOUs to write His Bonus Check,

No, NOT a "great" ($1 Million Dollar Bonus and a new Corvette) sales reward for example, oh no,)
that would be a "One "Hundred" M-i-l-l-i-o-n D-o-l-l-a-r Bonus check", folks, for ostensibly "manipulating and Artificially Tripling" the Price Of Oil by his own devices, but NOT on behalf of his "struggling fellow Americans", or the world's poor, NOPE!
.................................FOR HIMSELF AND HIS BUDDIES...........…..............

Thus Raping His Own Nation In A Traitorous Act Of Un-patriotic Unimaginable GREED! Are any of YOU Americans awake and watching Fox or listening to Rush?

Why Not Use Our Borrowed Money To Better Use: $100,000,000.00 BOUNTY on Bin Laden and Al-Zawahiri Each, To End This? = a BARGAIN!!

For that matter, for a soft bed and 3 Squares in the tropics, including ObamaCare, they might even turn themselves in for the cash, skip the ObamaCare......<u>Show Me The Money!</u>

Man-made Global Warming?

http://www.youtube.com/watch?v=XFmOi6G2x6s

http://www.youtube.com/watch?v=GLGKTZHzsZk

http://www.youtube.com/watch?v=_u81qXOYfKg

Ice Age Precursors 2 - Global Warming
http://www.youtube.com/watch?v=MDtQa5SuwlE

Ice Age Precursors 1 - Ice Age Climate Normal Climate
http://www.youtube.com/watch?v=8XFy75dlc4Q

Hell, "Double-it".... it's Only Obamapoly Money Anyway!
It's A Madison Avenue PR Bargain Dream-Date!

In fact, it's probably "chump-change" compared to the Quid-Pro-Quo's it took for Bill Clinton to spring those "Environmentalist Babes" from Mr. Karaoke, not excluding those Nuclear Spare Parts ole' Bill brought his old Buddy, that he'd given that Nuclear Power Plant present to (back-in-the-day), that Korea-Kim promised Slick Willie would never be used to make bombs, which ultimately brought us to this very point "right now"! ...Thanks Billie.

....I know this song, and I think we've danced to this tune before!.......Déjävu anyone?

Hey, do you think Bill "partied" on the plane-ride-back with the Environmentalist Babes?.......Naaah.....Sure!

Well, There's A Lot Of Monkeying Around And Some Monkey Business, and We All Sit On Our Hands, like the "The 3 Monkeys" Listening To The Same Piper, Over and Over Again!...

<u>Al Gore sued</u>
http://www.youtube.com/watch?v=FfHW7KR33lQ&feature=related

and, *"that's the way, uh-huh uh-huh, I like it, uh-huh, uh-huh"*

<u>SENTRYMAN</u>

Chapter 49

2nd Shoe Dropped: Atty. Gen. Going After Bush Policies, Or Bush?...

We Can Wait Our Turn: "Obama For Treason!"

Posted by SENTRYMAN on August 24, 2009 at 9:06pm

Attorney General Eric Holder, an Obama front-man, has finally gotten a Green Light
 to go after the CIA for "coerced interrogation",
(one thing that Obama claimed "He never wanted"), but, will now
Let Loose the Dogs of War!

Eenie, meenie, minie, got'cha George!

(That's a Stab-In-The-Back political War there, figuratively and practically speaking,
if I've ever seen one),
especially since "today's" DEMs are basically cowards in any shooting war; with Obama
always being against Iraq when in Illinois,
and then against "the surge", and "proud of it" when in the Senate),

and Holder was applauded by Conyers and Nadler today
for the appointment of a Special Prosecutor, "Ta-Daah"!,
that both stellar Patriots want a much broader mandate for greater powers to
go-right-after Pres. Bush and VP Cheney, and also of course, with a wink-wink-nod-nod,
for keeping us ALL safe, by their politically-incorrect methods.

Fantastic!............Full disclosure!...........Yup, feel safer all ready, check, we're out'ta here!

Heck, let it all hang-out, and let's not stop there for a NEW, improved "Transparent
Government"! ....Indonesia? …..Hawaii? …….Islam? …..College transcript?
….Ghostwriters? ….Ayers? ….Wright? …..Rezko? …..and, ACORN? …..anyone?.....

OK, Let's keep digging in <u>Washington Landfills</u> to include <u>Clinton</u>: dropping bombs on
anyone, including civilians from 50,000 ft. in Kosovo,
and also never aggressively going after Islamic-Terrorist striking US military personnel
and US interests,
and for supposedly accepting foreign donations for his election campaigns
from Communist governments, heck, forget sex scandals, unless on Company Time,
Oooops!

Yah, and for <u>Kennedy</u> and <u>Johnson</u>, posthumously,
for those "Democrat Wars" we always forget were "Democrat Wars" when slamming the
Bush's, and always ignore the sex scandals, unless on Company Time. Oooops!

Pg. 266

And, with <u>Carter</u> for "gross stupidity" by destabilizing the entire Middle-East
section of the globe and **"<u>for starting the entire Terrorist thing</u>,"**
and all the radical-Islamic WARs to follow that have besieged us for 30 years,

oh yah, and for "thinking about" having sex once, without his wife, in Playboy Mag....
No, for being "dumb enough" to say it!

Then there's <u>Truman</u>, oh boy, posthumously of course,
but, all the same, for shortening WWII with The Bomb,
and saving too many American servicemen's lives, Environmentalists hate that one!

And, <u>Roosevelt</u>, again posthumously!
What's with us?.... We're so slow to crucify these old DEMs. I guess the Republicans are
just easy pick'ns!

Let's get <u>FDR</u> for his Jap Internment Camps, and for rousting-out those poor
German/American Bund members, and for "killing" Nazis spies......Whoa,
actually KILLING non-combatant, how novel!!!
Then there's the New Deal, Old Deal, Same Deal and the Social Security Lie,
and for sex scandals, well, we'll give him a pass on that, but Get'm on all Them DEALS!

And finally President <u>Wilson</u>, posthumously again.....Man!......For the Great War- W.W.I.
He must have killed someone there, because enough people have Bit-The-Dust after His
"Revenue Act of 1913", and the "Federal Reserve Act", and for sex scandals?....I think.
Must be, he's a Democrat!

<u>Democrats All!</u>   *(Sorry to include you Harry in that bunch)*

Then, after we've nailed the **Bush's**, and dug–up all the bodies,
indicted them in the Name-Of-Transparency-In-Government, and re-buried them all,
We'll ALL wait for President Obama, "Not", to be Reelected in just 3-1/2 years, and then
Arrest Him for Treason....Sounds like a plan to Me!...
What goes around eventually Comes Around!......Think that's called KARMA!!

And, we'll get'm for "supposedly" accepting foreign donations for his election
campaign.....1/2 a Trillion dollars, in nice little $10.00 untraceable Internet-Donations.
Sounds like another plan....heck, even "if it's bogus", we've got to have that ole'
 (Obama team's "pound-of-flesh" out of your opposition) tact, don't We,
Pay-Back, and rub-in-the-salts, just like all His cronies,
 put on the scent to go hunting for the Bush's, Right?

Obama will probably have a closet-full of Skeletons at the end of his 1st term, so We won't
have to search too far!

We can all fine-comb his first 4-year old administration, if that's how he wants to change
the "once civilized" congressional-statesmanship's Rules and Codes,
and just for Laughs,
for never unsealing his school records and exposing himself: not the "genius" as
advertised,
we can give him an "F" on the next AOL Presidential Poll!

Be extremely careful for what you wish for Attorney General Holder,
You just may get it, and how did You earn that $90 million dollars during those terrible
Bush years again?.........

We remember you and Mark Rich defending Terrorist Bombers.
we can patiently wait for You too, Attorney General!

Folks, see how stupid this all sounds, it's certainly counter-productive and unpatriotic, but, do We hear anything from the MEDIA? They are lick'n their chops for Bush bones.

During the blood-letting and dragging our troops through the gutters,
We Should Go After "The Media" For Aid And Comfort To The Enemy, And Having Given Away All Kinds Of National Secrets During War. .....So Keep it up NY TIMES,
You're Next, if We get the Government Back.............Traitors!

If "revenge is a dish best served cold"
and You DEMs want to play like that,
then You better hope global warming is real,
because an ICE-MAN, or maybe an ICE-WOMAN Cometh
and hell's about to really freeze over!

SENTRYMAN

===

8 COMMENTS

Comment by Catherine on August 24, 2009 at 9:35pm
 You forgot the Black Panthers!

Comment by SENTRYMAN on August 24, 2009 at 10:17pm
I know there's a grocery list on this guy, but this wasn't the time for that rant, he's not calling the shots.
His day will come if that's how he wants to deal out Justice in America.

If they don't believe in the mercy of God, maybe KARMA might save them,
but I doubt it.

Comment by Barbara on August 24, 2009 at 10:24pm
 I don't know why we aren't trying him for treason now.

Because they're all corrupt.
Both sides!

But to be fair, "all of their side",
and "most of ours", and the few brave ones we've got are still on a leash, to be controlled and quell the waters.

Why don't you think we nailed Clinton when we finally had him (dead to rights) and Republicans were in power?
Not only for his admitted peccadilloes, but after countless quid pro quos, trading missile technologies to the Chinese military for campaign donations, giving Korea the Bomb, etc., etc., and letting Twin Towers happen twice,
and now He's sold his sole to the ARABS for $800 million.

Bush gets nailed for Katrina for using inept FEMA "career" government employees and old policies, in-place for decades under many Presidents,
and Clinton bears no blame for building "The Wall", (dismantling the entire Intelligence Network), and opening the Front Door after 8 years of attacks that could have prevented "the 9/11",

but now, Bush gets nailed for protecting this Nation too well,
and with all his new "immoral and unlawful" surveillance procedures and techniques, that now Our,
oh so ethical new fearless-President has decided to keep in-place, and even broaden,.....(1st good idea),
and now we've got this Dog 'n Pony Show and Obama hasn't closed Guantanamo yet.

Is anyone paying attention, or keeping score out there,
besides the other-side "lying through their teeth" every-single-day,
and they get a total pass, PLUS Our Guys Say Nothing As Usual?

One thing we must give the President's followers credit for though,
just like standing behind The Emperor of Japan, IL Duca and Der Führer,
Ayatollah and bin Laden, not to forget that crazy little guy in North Korea,
they are loyal to the death....go figure...

We could learn some of that.
Well, not all of us out here in the Hinterlands, or our soldiers,
but our Leaders in general certainly could and earn our respect.

While "W" was too busy defending "all of us", and never stopped long enough to defend himself,
Our Leaders never fought for their President, like "They do for theirs today"!

But we could certainly Eat-Our-Own and nailed Nixon for trivial crap,
(almost like a "Scooter Libby" mishmash), let him sleep with the Red Herring.
The guy's honorable enough to take the hit for his A-team,
and he didn't even know that Dean and The Plumbers were doing an errand for Dean and his wife, but it didn't matter. Ask Liddy!

That poor sap who no one seemed to like, really loved his country so much he'd let Kennedy steal an election without a fuss, so as not to let his country suffer.
(Al Gore could learn about some class there!)

He also opened-up China, started the EPA and OSHA, stopped Nam, and brought the guys home, and they all hated him and still do today.
He personally did more for the LIBS, Dems, Greens, the economy and foreign trade deficit than any Democrat President ever,
and The Left is so blinded with conceit by their own supremely narcissistic, self-admiration of self-worth, they're totally incapable to recognize their own insignificance on the planet as they challenge the 4 winds, mother earth, and God.

We, on the other hand, only have the balls to go after old men;
hiding in restroom stalls, and building roads in Alaska,
(while ignoring highways and airports in W. VA and PA, respectively),
and can give-up on an old shell-shocked ex-POW hero,
shot out of the sky and had the vinegar tortured out of him,
till after 35 years later He can't see the enemy sitting right next to him.

Final Solution: Trade them-all-in for a new team,
and start a national referendum to end-run around Congress,
and vote in TERM LIMITS: Twice for Legislators, and Once for Presidents,
to take our country back,
Or Stick Us With A Fork, Were Done!

SENTRYMAN

Comment by AJ on August 25, 2009 at 4:07am

What the current administration is doing (so-called justice dept) is TREASONOUS...Our intelligence personnel risk their lives for us...This is beyond belief...that they are trying to prosecute people who did nothing wrong...

I just can NOT believe they are doing this... Obama the traitor is BLOWING the hard fought fight in Iraq by pulling out too fast. If he lets Iran go into chaos, then all will have died in vain...IT MAKES ME SICK...I will not tell you what I think of Obama because it will not be readable...

Obama is only keeping the war going in Afghanistan for political reasons, so he doesn't lose complete credibility of the American people, while he passes through his FASCIST agenda...And yes Sentryman, I believe the Repukicans are almost as bad....it is the selection of the lesser of the evil...I find the Repukicans enough to VOMIT over...but what we have right now is just PURE EVIL...

Sarah is NOT part of anyone of these corrupt parties...They are BOTH trying to destroy her for obvious reasons...

I totally agree with you about Bush too! He is a real patriot who PROTECTED us...And his policy in Iraq was really forward thinking and BRILLIANT...History will show that unless Obama is able to unravel all the GOOD that was done in Iraq...

HA HA good job there !! maybe we should FAX this to him daily, like a daily VITAMIN PILL, whad'da'ya say ?

I can't stand this horrible little dictator. He is both a coward and a bully (usually goes together). I would NOT want HIM in my foxhole at any time, this man is an enemy of AMERICA and should be prosecuted for treason.
Can you imagine they are after PANETTA now, he wasn't liberal enough, with his daughter and their family affair with Chavez, that wasn't good enough, I hope he RESIGNS and makes a big stink. When a weasel like Panetta gets upset you know things are really in the toilet

---

I think it would be great if you all bombarded the media, Senators, congressmen and of course the White House,
advising you wanted the President impeached for Treason. Eric Holder is his man, Obama playing good guy, letting Holder be BAD guy. Either he is the leader or he is a puppet having his strings pulled by others.
Every person deserves a holiday BUT, the hypocrisy is just wonderful, swanning down there with all the wealthy 'elites', I wonder if Georgie Soros is funding this particular 'junket'.

I would have thought a community organizer would have invited many of the homeless down to enjoy the spoils of all their hard work'in getting him elected?

and Guess "Who Isn't Coming To Dinner",
when He asked permission to stop-bye the Kennedy Compound
while in the neighborhood?

Oh well girls, there's always Graceland and Neverland Ranch
while the Obama's are on summer vacation!

Chapter 50

Premise: "CAN TRUTH BE MANIPULATED"?

Posted by SENTRYMAN on <u>August 27, 2009</u> at 3:56pm

The Premise, a query: "Can Truth be manipulated"?

In today's post modern- Flower Child, free love, goodtime rock 'n roll, no tomorrow generation, where there is no judgments, no Right and Wrong, Rules can be bent in a supposedly "Living document" like the Constitution, with only Perception and Relativism, Opinion with Perspective in America!

No Judgment = No Foul?.... Jibber Jabber!...

The Haves and The Have-Not's, as old as TIME, and The Haves Always Rule!

HOPE?..... Can't We Just All Get Along?...... Piffle!
Sure!....Just As Long As "They" Are Calling All The Shots For The Rest Of Us!

"Can Truth Be Manipulated,
and replaced by a greater TRUTH for the greater GOOD. Truth no longer stands! ...A guise, an attitude, a pose, a phenomenon, a specter, an epitome, a SAVIOR"?

Riddle Me This!

Yin & Yang Idioms;…….
"Symbolism over Substance" and "Perception Is Reality"!

In our current culture's lexicon that would precisely mean;
No Right or Wrong, Just Light and Shade!................... All Things Grey and Grave?
<u>TRUTH IS NO LONGER RELEVANT IN OUR SOCIETY!</u>

I've heard it stated somewhere: "Barack Obama is a really smart guy", again and again and again and again and again and again, and once more again!

I've also heard it stated that: "George W. Bush is a really stupid man", more than a 1,000 times, a million times?....Well, maybe a few less, right Will?

*Perception = Fact or Belief?

*Belief = Truth or Opinion?

*Opinion = Right or Wrong? Conundrum, or does it depend on Ones Perspective?
Pg. 272

***QUESTION:

<u>How is it that George W. Bush;</u>
whose grandfather was a US Senator,
and his Father was the 41st President of the greatest country in history, to date,
who attended a Prep school as a boy and an Academy high school,
and who was a Yale graduate,
and was in the Air National Guard and logged-in more than 500 hours in many aircraft, including multi-million dollar military fighter jets,
who is perceived as a stupid, numbskull, idiot dolt?

And whom is still called names, and perceptions persist from supposedly the smartest and most educated amongst us! At least that's what they claim about themselves and their own pedigrees from the academic and entertainment élites, Rappers and Will Ferrell!....Hmmmm!

"When interviewed by the Associated Press, in February 2004, flight instructor Maj. Udell recalled that Lt. Bush was one of his best students, saying that: "I'd rank him in the top five percent.""

He earned scores that included 100% for flying without navigational instruments, 89% in flight planning, and 98% in aviation physiology.
Bush also completed two weeks of survival training during this period."

(Hell, everyone can do that in Alpha Phi Alpha Kappa Alpha Psi Omega Psi Phi Phi Beta Sigma Iota Phi Theta house! ....<u>No big deal?</u>)

In addition, P-r-e-s-i-d-e-n-t of the United States, George W. Bush, the only US President to have earned a Master's Degree, and in Business no less,
and from Harvard, no less again,
(who's life is an open book, and all of his grades and personal records aren't locked-up in one of Al Gore's Lock Boxes, like some Presidents require).

Plus Bush "worked" in the real world in the family oil "business" as a young man, married an intelligent, pretty woman,
was a successful businessman,
was a Governor of one of the largest states in the Union,
was President of the United States, "twice",
and managed to bring the greatest country in the world - back from Sneak Attack and Wars,
a recession,
and the US back, kicking and bitching from the brink of more than a few disasters, short of (1) city, amongst 5 states; (that refused to get off the tracks of a speeding train 5 days in advance),
a man, who would need to see through lead, and bend steel in his bare hands to prove his worth to his detractors, but, is apparently, with no thanks for keeping "them all safe" for 7 years, still perceived by most, if Not every Democrat, most in the MEDIA, most Journalists, most of Hollywood, most Broadcasting companies, most TV pundits, most TV Talk Show Hosts, most Stand-up comics, most Network TV News Magazines, Michael Moore, Susan Sarandon and SNL,
as a big stupid, bumbling jerk, and dumb as a bag of rocks,

but "THEY" in turn,
have influenced most of the "uneducated" by their liberal teachers, most of the un-informed minorities, most illegals, and almost ½ of the US voting population, of which the majority accepts and depends for their subsistence from the U.S. Taxpayer's paid Federal Government,
who have been instructed "never to watch FOX News" to learn anything from opposing points-of-view, contrary facts, or any information for themselves, but ordered to exclusively and only listen the THEM, alone, period, ever!

As compared to, oh, let's say,
someone that all of Bush's Detractors adored; like Barack Obama, for instance,

WHO, with no practical business experience, is now accentually running the largest corporation on the planet for the past 8 months with only US Taxpayer's IOUs
WHO's own academic records have been personally sealed from the public, shielded from exposure, and any public scrutiny to legitimize any of his claims. HE is perceived to be a "self-proclaimed Genius" by all of "THEM", and thus is believed to be THAT by slightly more than ½ of the current US voting population!

I.e. And these "smartest guys in the room", running and protecting the US Financial Systems, the very foundations of this free Democracy,
who can't even spot Barney, or Bernie Making-Off with our Piggy banks,
but Bush is an Idiot and Barack is a Genius, so states these smartest guys.

INTERESTING QUERY:.......Yin and Yang, or Dumb and Dumber?

Me thinks, there's a bit of a sound judgment disparity out there, or it's jealousy?
Of course, whoever said judgment was taught in schools,
or for that matter, even in the home anymore today?

Not casting any aspersions, of course, since we're all Grading-on-the-CURVE now and we all have the right to be as dumb or as enlightened as we want to be in America, as long as it's utilizing our public School Systems. All FREE, to take full advantage and without any vouchers, or teacher testing, or Choice, who needs it?

FREEDOM to be what You want to be, except a conservative, or with the military!

***QUESTION:

Does then "Truth" need to be (empirically correct) to be "TRUTH",
or just Reasonably Correct, or Sort of Correct,
or is it just a Point of View, from One's Perspective, kind'a correct?

How many ways do You want to cut this pie up, to be correct?.....Geee, hmmmm?

I know what I'd answer as a Conservative, and I know how I'd answer if a Progressive……..These are simple concepts people,

Both Can't Be RIGHT!.......Stop sitting on the sidelines, or at a goal line, and make a damn decision to take a stand.

Your ability to do so is almost gone. That's You, You INDEPENDENTS!!

***QUESTION: Can beliefs be manufactured?
 .....Can we trust ourselves to know the difference?

THAT's "FAITH"!........I know, I believe, for I am SENTRYMAN?.....Faith!

This Is All Blind Faith, Hope, and a whole lot of Charity!

This is the smartest guy on the planet?...Well, They told us so, so it's so?

Maybe the smartest Guy in the room, in some auditorium, talking to undergrads at Columbia, ...BUT , NOT AT "WEST POINT"!

THE "UH" Count on Late Night
http://www.youtube.com/watch?v=ThEAO0lt4Dw

I Give "uh Good um" Speech
http://www.youtube.com/watch?v=eHgH5i8ug6E

Obama's Prompter fail
http://www.youtube.com/watch?v=5TMrxqdX64Q

Obama without his teleprompter, winging it!
http://www.youtube.com/watch?v=4_Ju6kWfXEk

AND THE BEST FOR LAST.........
THIS GUY ACTUALLY BEAT HILLARY?

A WORD FROM THE SMARTEST GUY IN THE USA:
EVERYBODY KNOWS THAT IT MAKES NO SENSE
http://www.youtube.com/watch?v=cxxxGUeZtno

With Faith, Hope and a Charity.....Their Faith, his Hope, our Charity!

SENTRYMAN

Chapter 51

Glenn Beck, Great Week's Work,
but Friday's "Solution" *anti-climactic*!

...."I HAVE A SOLUTION!"

Posted by SENTRYMAN on August 29, 2009 at 2:00am

GLENN WANTS US ALL TO WRITE TO WASHINGTON AND "LIST",
AND DEMAND,
AND ASK,
AND WHINE,
AND PLEAD,
AND PRAY,

AND MEANWHILE THERE'S AN 18 WHEELER BARREL'n DOWN THE HIGHWAY AT 86 MILES PER HOUR, HEADED STRAIGHT FOR YOUR FACE GLENN, and WHAT,

AND YOU'RE GOING TO MAKE THE MEANEST SCOWL THAT ANYONE CAN IMAGINE, TO WHAT, INTIMIDATE, TO STOP THESE MANIACS BEFORE YOU'RE VAPORIZED? ....THAT'S YOUR PLAN?..........THAT'S IT?..........THAT'S ALL YOU GOT?..............

.................WOW!...............THREATS!..............VERY INNOVATIVE!...............

I CAN'T TELL ENOUGH PEOPLE, ENOUGH TIMES, TILL I'M BLUE IN THE FACE, ABOUT THE DIRE SITUATION WE'RE REALLY IN, OR ADEQUATELY EXPRESS THE INCREDIBLE URGENCY WE MUST ALL REALIZE, TO EMPLOY EVERYTHING WITHIN OUR MEANS TO AVOID THIS JUGGERNAUT THAT'S HEADED RIGHT TOWARD US AT THIS CRITICAL TIME IN AMERICA's HISTORY, JEOPARDIZING ALL THAT WE HOLD SACRED AND DEAR, THAT IS ABOUT TO BEFALL WE AMERICANs. ("We few, we happy few, we band of brothers")

EMINENT DOMAIN, IMMINENT DEATH HEALTH-CARE AND DISMEMBERMENT OF PRIVATE INSURANCE, THE FINANCIAL INDUSTRY, NATIONALIZING MANUFACTURING, INTER-NATIONALIZING FEDERAL PARKS, LANDS AND NATURAL RESOURCES, CONTROLING COMMUNICATIONS, EDUCATION, OVER-REGULATING SMALL BUSINESS, REAL ESTATE, TRADING-OFF OUR SOVEREIGNTY BY FINANCING SHAM WORLD GREEN INITIATIVES WHILE BORROWING ($.50 cents) OF EVERY DOLLAR ALLOCATED, and CONFISCATED BY OUR RENEGADE GOVERNMENT,
WITH THE INTEREST and LONG TERM CONSEQUENCES, BE DAMNED,

BY THIS MAFIOSO-CABAL OF VITO OBAMALONE's STEALTH CZARIST QUASI-DICTATORSHIP, STRANGLING THE VERITABLE "LIFE'S SPRING" OF THE INDEPENDENT AMERICAN SPIRIT.

WITH THE "ONLY POSSIBLE WAY LEFT, TO LEGALLY" BREAK THIS SATANIC DEATHGRIP AROUND OUR NECKS, BEFORE THE CRAZIES TAKE A HAND, AND BLOOD STARTS TO FLOW IN THE STREETS, AS IN EUROPE,

IS TO "VOTE EVERY LAST G-D LEGISLATOR OUT" OF OFFICE, ASAP

WHILE WE STILL HAVE A CHANCE.........AND ONLY THEN, AND PERHAPS ONLY IF
THERE'S ENOUGH TIME TO BREATH SOME FRESH OXYGEN,
THAT WE DERIVE FROM PLANTS THAT FEED ON DREADED CARBON IN THIS
SYMBIOTIC RELATIONSHIP WE ALL SHARE AND BENEFIT FROM, (MMG/W reference)
INTO THIS BLOATED-CORPSE OF A CONSTITUTION, OF WHICH GOVERNMENT HAS
BECOME A PARASITE ON BOTH,
AND "TRUTH" MAY RE-EMERGE!...

REPLACING THEM ALL WITH A LEGITIMATELY AUTHENTIC "CONSERVATIVE"
GOVERNMENT PARTY, IN TURN, WOULD BE A FRESH START, LIKE "Minnesota Michele"
AND Sarah, of course, ALONG WITH A FEW "JOHNNY-COME-LATELY" TOKEN
REPUBLICANS, PRESENTLY PUTTING-UP A HALF-HEARTED FIGHT.
  BUT ABSO-DAMN-LUTELY "NO RHINOS"!..........
THEY CAN RETURN TO THE DEMOCRAT PARTY, IF IT WAS ONLY POSSIBLE,

ELSE WE ARE ALL BUT DOOMED, SLAVES FROM A ONCE FABLED LAND,
 AND WE WILL HAVE NO ONE BUT OURSELVES TO BLAME, ONCE AGAIN!

.................BRAVE SOULS TAKE HEART.... "TAKE A-C-T-I-O-N"...................

RIDE TO THE SOUND OF THE GUNS, TAUNTS, SIGNS, BANNERS & JEERS

"WE THE PEOPLE", MUST DRAFT LOCAL PETITIONS IN EVERY STATE,
 STATE-BY-STATE WITH CITIZEN PROPOSITIONS, CREATING THE 1st
SYMBOLIC "COLLECTIVE" NATIONAL REFERENDUM TO SAVE THE USA

BY VOTING OURSELVES, FOR OURSELVES and OUR CHILDREN:
"TERM LIMITS"......."TERM LIMITS"......."TERM LIMITS"

FOR OUR OUT- OF- CONTROL GOVERNMENT EMPLOYEES!

Note; AS THE CITIZENRY SO APTLY DOES IN CALIFORNIA WITH REGULARITY,
VOTE OURSELVES A STATE INITIATIVE FOR AN "END RUN" AROUND CONGRESS',
(by STATE and then NATIONAL REPS.),....THAT IS OUR ONLY HOPE FOR RECOURSE,
REPUDIATION, RETALIATION, VINDICATION, PRESERVATION AND SALVATION.

DO YOU REALLY THINK ANY LAWYER - LEGISLATOR WOULD "EVER", "EVER" VOTE
AGAINST THEIR OWN INTERESTS, OR THAT ANY REPRESENTATIVE WOULD EVER VOTE
TO DIMMISH THEIR OWN POWER AND AUTHORITY OVER THE PEONs, US? NOR WOULD
THE CURRENT RECIPIENTS OF ALL THEIR GENEROSITY WITH OUR MONEY!....NO WAY!

THEY WILL NEVER DO IT, NOT ON THEIR OWN?...TORT REFORM?... FORGET IT!

WE'VE GIVEN THEM OUR CHECK-BOOKs, AND THE KEYS TO THE ARSENAL, AND ANY
POWER WE ONCE POSSESSED, GONE BY A CONTROLED & CONTRIVED COMPROMIZED
VOTE. WITH NO RECOURSE, WE MUST NOW CUT OFF THE SPIGOT and THE SKINNY
LEGS OF EVERY CAPITOL HILL "SWELL", RIGHT OFF AT THE KNEES TO REDRESS OUR
GRIEVANCES, ONCE AND FOR ALL.......

"PROPOSITION #86"

TO "EIGHTY-SIX" THE CONGRESS WITH: **"TERM LIMITS"**;

2 TERMS FOR LEGISLATORS,
(4 yr. for Senators and 2 yr. for Congress Persons)

and **1 TERM FOR PRESIDENTS,**

and **"20 YEAR" TERMS FOR SUPREME COURT,** (while we're at it!)

***They are "Keepers of the Truth", since Keepers of the Faith is no longer allowed!

….They are only human, and as such, twenty years may even be too long.

TRUTH – Understanding "Right from Wrong" is NOT a 4 to 5 Split Decision. It's perhaps 7 to 2, hopefully 8 to 1, because 9 to 0 isn't humanly possible! Since there's always 1 in every group, and can never be Objective…tsk, tsk

****THIS IS THE FASTEST, EASIEST AND QUITE FRANKLY,
THE ONLY POSSIBLE WAY WE CAN EVER GET OUR COUNTRY BACK….

FOR **THE 20 DEMANDMENTS TO THE CONSTITUTION**
AS A GAME PLAN, AN ARMADA FOR A BETTER AMERICA FOR TOMORROW…
OUR OWN TROJAN-HORSE AS THE VEHICLE WITH PROPOSITION #86
AS THE ANSWER. THIS IS WHERE THE LAST STAND FIGHT SHOULD BE,
UNLESS YOU THINK THERE WILL BE ANYTHING LEFT TO VOTE FOR IN 2012!

ACT NOW BEFORE IT'S TOO LATE…. **"IT'S OUR COUNTRY!"**

THE HOURGLASS IS ALMOST EMPTY AND WE'LL ALL BE MELTING…..
BECAUSE THERE IS NO "KANSAS" ANYMORE DOROTHY. THEY'VE DESTROYED IT, WITH ALL THE UNBORNS, AND ANY "WILL" TO FIGHT FOR THE "RIGHT" IN AMERICA!

IT'S US vs THEM!

IT'S MORE THAN ½ THE CONGRESS,
MORE THAN ½ THE COURTS,
MORE THAN ½ THE CIVIL SERVANTS,
MORE THAN ¾ THE JUSTICE DEPT.,

THE SECRET SERVICE IS BOUND TO DUTY AND NEUTERED,
THE NSA BELONGS TO THEM NOW,
THE FBI IS THEIRS TOO, AND THERE'S NO J. EDGAR, (dress or not),

......WHO IS LOOKING OUT FOR ALL OF US, ANYMORE?....

and THEN THERE'S AmeriCorps AND ACORN!....."Enemy Camps"!!!

THE CIA DAREs NOT ...(Imminent castration)!

THEM - VS - US,
WE PRECIOUS FEW, BAND OF BROTHERS & SISTERS, FREE Americans.

WE, the People...
ALL THAT's STANDING BETWEEN THEM AND OUR CHILDREN!

HALE!.......HALE TO CAESAR......HALE OBAMA, "Heil, mein Führer!"

SENTRYMAN
===
Add a Comment
Comment by Lance hours 9 ago

Start here with a ten-minute video introduction:
http://www.youtube.com/watch?v=TzEEgtOFFIM

http://sustainabledevelopment.un.org/index.php?page=view&nr=23&type=400

And we see the plan attended and started by George HW Bush 41,
was made an Executive Order by WJ Clinton 42,
furthered by Dubai 43,
and crash-plan implementation (so far) by BHO 44 ,
and the 545 Congress and Supreme Courts-persons.

We don't need Black Helicopters or Area 51.

Make sense of the seeming incomprehensibility of Congress the last 19 years,
regardless of who's in power. Be afraid, be very afraid....

We need more outcries!
Makes sense of Death Panels (oops, The CENTER for Comparative Effectiveness
Research),
Sanger-Eugenics mandated abortions,
seizing Control of Internet,
multi-national corporations,
CAP & TAX, (trade what, our souls?)
Famines, (No matter what Rock Concerts try to help eliminate),
AIDS,
government manufactured food scares, recalls - beef, tomatoes, lettuce - that
bankrupt thousands of Small Business farms,
health scares by The Media (including FOX) Pandemics, Epidemics, and Outbreaks
heightening panic not awareness,
racial divisiveness,
religious wars,
terrorist attacks making one seem helpless without government intervention giving
up liberty for 'security' (Patriot Act); formation with arrogance of Civilian National

Security Force as powerful as our military, UN Forces holding maneuvers on US Soil...
'Cash for Clunkers',

Spiraling Debt and Unemployment being 'Global'.
The manufactured Enviro-Wackos getting away with international with enviro-terror, intentional 'dumbing down'
revisionist history and science in Textbooks (with Texas leading the charge).
Changing the meaning of words themselves and on and on and on and on....
an Entertainment Industry that is geared to the vilest of human behavior,
destroying the true God, and making a pseudo-religion of environmentalism...

===

SENTRYMAN response:

WOW, nicely put....... I don't think you left anyone out.
It gets really scary when the bad guys get organized and government sanctioned the likes of ACORN, AmeriCorps, (soon to be equipped with an internal private security force), that start wearing uniforms like the Brown Shirts, who eventually morphed into the SS when they got full government financing.

I'm going to begin to wonder where are all the sane voices from the 99% patriotic (PC correct, "of color") Americans that are strangely silent.
Just like the 99% normal intelligent, civilized Muslims "we never hear from", condemning what their "Radical Brethren" have been doing for the past 30 years, of which OUR Media has been spinning about for the last 7 years, which We rarely hear from until just before they're shot in the head by their own brothers for speaking out. Sound vaguely familiar?

I think I've seen this movie (8 ways to Sunday) and it's getting pretty tired.
So when is the Rambo, or Eastwood, or Willis, or The Rock character going to ride in on a Pale Horse to save us all? It sure isn't going to be (Arnold anymore) since he's been turned to The Dark Side by Mrs. Meow, puurrrr! .....Yah, yah Huney!

This is now like an all too clichéd game of Tit-4-Tat, 1 Ups-manship, and Hangman, "Now It's Our Turn" on a tape Loop! How dumb do these people think we are all across this vast free nation? Maybe "The Media" wants to ask us: "what magazines we read?"...guffaw

They may have successfully dumbed-down the Youth-of-America, but there are still a lot of us out here that weren't taught by those-type-teachers 40-50-60-70 years ago, and that kind'a crap doesn't impress us at all.
Perhaps That's Why They're Getting The "Death Panels" Ready, and Dusted Off "The Death Book" For Our Retired Warriors!
There's always idiot on both sides and in every quarter, and always will be, which is probably why The Four Horsemen are inevitable in nature to screen the Gene Pool.

The real problem in this Saga is keeping all the players straight in the credits at the end of this ensemble cast, B movie,
and which ones are playing, and which ones think this is for real.
I feel like some Jiffy-Pop...............See you at the movies. Bring your own gun, THEY might start shooting. Only Kidding?

SENTRYMAN

Agenda 21 For Dummies
http://www.youtube.com/watch?v=TzEEgtOFFIM

Obama on Track For Agenda 21
http://www.slate.com/articles/health_and_science/onearth/2013/03/agenda_21_no_the_gov
ernment_isn_t_going_to_confiscate_your_property.html

http://politicalvelcraft.org/2012/01/11/obama-signs-his-86th-executive-order-13575-ron-
paul-executive-orders-being-taken-too-far/

*United Nations Dept. of Economic and Social Affairs
Division for Sustainable Development

Core Publications Agenda 21

Section IV, Means of Implementation, Chapter 35
Science for Sustainable Development
http://www.un.org/en/development/desa/index.html

 Comment by SENTRYMAN on August 31, 2009

Elections Do Have Consequences, Mostly Bad
 since we rarely get what's advertised....Such Is Life!...

Let's just assume our Officials can be turned to the "dark side" when they leave home for Washington, like our college Freshmen, off to a first All-Night Kegger.

Next our daughters who never had boyfriends yet, are up dancing-on-the-table, unclad, and our sons are sneaking off to Argentina on Father's Day. S#!+ happens and listen, We Must Put Leashes On These People "Permanently".

We have to be protected from human nature. Our Forefathers never envisioned that, far off in the future, "Everyone" would be on the Take and "on the Dole", or could somehow be compromised and turn into RINOs.....Do you think they had "On the Dole" back in 1776? ......I suppose a form of it, and called them British!

I don't know why Our Side acted as they did during the first 6-Bush years in Washington, or why they have laid down as "door mats" in this last 3 years. Maybe it's all those FBI "personal profiles" that the Clintons were able to strangely obtain, (an automatic Felony) on everyone in Congress during their Reign….Nixon got NAILED for just having (1) file in his possession, go figure!

*Just goes to show you, when You own the Attorneys what you can get away with, and Barack's Sure Got Everybody's Number!
(We'll probably learn about "The grassy knoll in Dealey Plaza" before We can ever get see the Boy Genius' school grades), but We Are Stuck Here Now, they brought us to the dance and Our Guys Let It Happen, and They're Doing Nothing To Stop The Onslaught.

We Can Blame Pres. Bush For """"Everything"""", But He Was Only As Good As His Congress, who 373 out of 535 agreed with their President to use "affirmative action"…Capish?.....(WASHINGTON (CNN) -- Friday, October 11, 2002
the Senate early Friday voted 77-23 to authorize President Bush to attack Iraq if Saddam Hussein refuses to give up weapons of mass destruction as required by U.N. resolutions.
Hours earlier, the House approved an identical resolution, 296-133)

If 49% "YEA, or 49% NAH, 50/50, or the 40/60 for/against TODAY.
It's The Same Gang Of Petulant Thug Players Every Term,
(those Children Away From Mom & Dad, Too Busy To Monitor The Little Buggers), but This Ain't High School, And It Certainly Isn't College, It's Real Life, Life And Death (And The Same People Have Been There For Too Many Years), and "They All Got Us Here To The Point In History", and They're All Just AS Culpable, People!

Good or Bad,….. The Next Batch, No Matter Which Team Is Top Dog Then, and Even If We've Got A "Sinner" Or A "Saint" In The White House,
 We Must….MUST ….Geld These Stallions and Fix These Fillies With TERM LIMITs.

"TERM LIMITS" IS THE ONLY STOP-GAP THAT CAN PROTECT OUR LIBERTY, BECAUSE IT'LL STILL GIVES THEM MORE THAN ENOUGH TIME TO SCREW-UP!

BUT, AT LEAST WE CAN "JUGGLE THE PLAYERS" WITH A LITTLE MORE SPEED, AND QUICKER HANDS-ON TO "CUT THOSE TENTACLES" THAT ARE ALWAYS TRYING TO TURN THEM DELUSIONAL.
IT WOULD HAVE A DEVASTATING EFFECT ON THE LOBBYEST INDUSTRY ALSO!

WE NEED TERM LIMITS and WE NEED THEM – RIGHT NOW!

DO YOU REALLY THINK WE ARE EVER GOING TO GET "TORT REFORM" FROM L-A-W-Y-E-R-S-?
……………WAKE-UP……….
THEIR GAME = THEIR RULES !!!!

SENTRYMAN

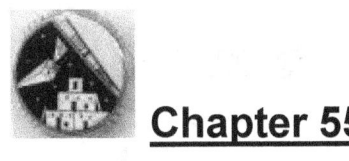

Chapter 55

Does The President Consider Himself An American, Or?

Posted by **SENTRYMAN** on <u>September 10, 2009</u> at 12:53am

JOHN WAYNE Video: The Hyphen #2

http://www.youtube.com/watch?v=PbOlg1Wy9Zo&feature=player_embedded

http://www.youtube.com/watch?v=xaPA8fGeRUc&feature=related

The President of the United States obviously allows, approves, condones, and "lets remain" this current description of himself existing on Wikipedia, <u>http://en.wikipedia.org/wiki/Barack_Obama</u> the free encyclopedia as of 9-9-09.

"Barack Hussein Obama II, born August 4, 1961
is the 44th and current President of the United States,
the first "<u>African American</u>" to hold the office. He served as the junior United States Senator from Illinois from January 2005 until he resigned after his election to the presidency in November 2008.

In November, Obama won the US presidency with 52.9% of the popular vote to McCain's 45.7%, and (365 electoral votes to 173) to become the first <u>African American</u> to be elected President. Obama delivered his victory speech before hundreds of thousands of supporters in Chicago's Grant Park.

<u>Obama's granting of his first television interview as President was to an "Arabic cable network", Al Arabiya,</u>

Obama explained how, through working with "black"-churches as a community organizer while in his twenties, "he came to understand" the "power of the <u>African-American</u> religious tradition" to spur social change.

"Categories: Barack Obama | African American academics | African American history | African American lawyers | African American memoirists | African American politicians | African American United States presidential candidates | African American United States Senators" |

Pg. 283

Red Skelton's Pledge of Allegiance
http://www.youtube.com/watch?v=TZBTyTWOZCM

---

3 Comments

Comment-1 by BILL [AR] AKA Freedomwarrior on September 10, 2009 at 3:55am

> Excellent video. You're an American, or YOUR NOT.
> Which is it Obama???????

Comment-2 by SENTRYMAN on September 10, 2009 at 4:31pm

> Well, I guess he's an <u>African-hyphen-American</u>,
> like all those other African-Canadians and African-Mexicans we
> always hear about,
> like that "Horse of a Different Color" in the Wizard of Oz!
>
> A rose by any other name, should smell as sweet,
> why does He bother to alienate one-half of his nation's citizens then?
> Unless, He really doesn't give a Wit <u>for / about</u> "That Other Half"!
>
> I guess the "American Half" (of His ancestors) would be saddened
> with his rejection of their/his American heritage, being an American
> President,
> and His (other half), the "African Half" (of His ancestors) would be
> gladdened by that choice!
>
> <u>I think I smell a betrayal in there, African-Quisling President?</u>

Comment-3 by SENTRYMAN on September 11, 2009 at 12:44am

> Living in the shadow of a; Hippie, Yippee, Yuppie, MTV weaned,
> Pong, Atari, SEGA, Nintendo, "overweight" Wii generation,

where now Friday nights are spent at DVD-Blockbusters for your $3000.00 Flat Screen (recession?) "substitute",

when a perfectly good, well-functioning $300. rabbit-eared 36" color Sylvania TV, w/ BETA or VHS,
that unfortunately also "replaced our great Friday evening" High school basketball game, and once was followed by Sock Hops, then after a short-stop for a "burger & fries", served on roller-skates at your Drive-In Burger Joint on the way home in a '58 Chevy.

But we all expected it to work-itself-out for that "Happy Days ending" in just an "hour & a half", and we would have never suspected that our own leader could be, would be, to be a "Quisling" Pawn involved in some world-wide conspiracy of El Shaitan, with Lieutenant Wayne hot on his trail! ('40s & '30s serials ref.)

Pull back the curtain and this Big Brother, this great and powerful OZ is "a Hologram, with a script",
ill-equipped to think-his-way-out of a tight spot
without a bevy of sycophants, more than eager to fall on his sword, quite reminiscent of the SS, or Hara-kiri seppuku!

The real danger in America today is that <u>3 generations</u> of "War Protesters", that couldn't muster the courage
 of any descent 18-year old female Israeli teenager out on night patrol, for their "required" Patriotic Duty, which in fact automatically builds self-worth and character when Evil comes'a knockin the next time around, and around, and around is never too far off.

Our Youths on the other hand, may just be more than willing to happily capitulate and "go along, to get along", and gratefully "place the collar around their own throats" in order to receive their automatic government subsidies deposited into their debit-accounts, as the Post Office will finally be bankrupt, and but a butt-memory.

*Press 1 for Spanish,
*press 2 for Arabic,
*press 3 for FARSI,
*press 4 for Chinese,
*press 5 for ACORN.

*<u>Texting is accepted in "French"..."English" is no longer recognized!</u>

<u>SENTRYMAN</u>

Chapter 61

Hey, It's Not About "The Black Guy",
……………….It's About "That Guy".

Posted by SENTRYMAN on <u>September 20, 2009</u> at 3:00pm

All we're hearing about today is *Race, Race, Race*!.... What is this,
Daytona?.........

Racism, Race Baiting, Racial Unrest!.............. Bologna and Hockey Puck!.........
......Where did all this come from as of late?.......Who's spreading this and why?

......Maybe we should ask Mr. Cosby about that of Mr. Carter, a modern southern
plantation owner!

<u>Someone "doth protest too much"</u>!!!

Ever watch the "Talking Heads" on TV and you're listening to their tripe, and they
say something entirely "off the wall", or as usual a bold-faced "Lie",
and You scream at the set, saying: "wait a minute, what about this fact, or that
fact"?, or "You forgot to remember to say this, you idiot!", and
 "That's just total crap! Why doesn't he challenge that, and call him on that one".
Instead of "Letting Every One Of Those False Statements" Just Stand Out There?
...I.e. "<u>Bush Lied</u>" for the millionth time!.......................<u>crickets</u>...............<u>Waiting</u>!

For me, it's usually Bob Beckel or Ellis Henican, or Anthony Weiner or Marc
Lamont Hill, who are Slinging IT so thick they'd need a permit for a Landfill,

& it's Hannity & O'Reilly I'm usually yelling at. <u>They know better</u>!

Laura Ingraham, and Michelle Malkin, and Megan Kelly, or Ann Coulter
<u>Take-No-Crap, and Take No Prisoners! They are some courageous broads!</u>

The <u>Left</u> has been hiding behind their sanctimonious-facades ever since, it seems
they could no-longer own any Slaves. Then their "3 legged" Voting for a time
worked to their advantage, when Equal-Voting was finally forced-out of the DEM's
vice-like grip. Then, the marches In the South, aided-by? RIGHT, "white" northern
Libs against southern DEMs remember! Students restricted from attending
southern colleges were barred by Democrats, police and Sheriffs, who had long
held separate/equal? "Everything", ever since those good ole days, banjo playing
Dixie, since 1866. Even DEM Presidents, were blocked by their Party, & needed the
Republican's limited muscle to push-through every piece of civil-rights   Pg. 286

legislation necessary to fulfill the new American ethic facade, of a FREE America for every citizen, once held back by old DEM's Racism....yuh, sure, sounds-good.

Which again, if you were taught that children, all started with, "No Thanks Today" by a Republican President and his Northern Republicans Patriot soldiers, just 144 years ago! Who had fought, who were wounded, and who died, forever altering their families lives in order to change the status-quo, (banjo playing John Brown's Body), to FREE a People, their fellow Americans.....remember, but,
the Left just won't let-up, just won't let-go. Who keeps saying: Uncle Tom?

Which group continues to "keep the term a pejorative invective" to wound?

The "Left" Is Still In Control, and I Just Don't Get It!

How did the Slavers get to be the Saviors? Can only be "Stockholm Syndrome!"

*"WHO DOESN'T PROPERLY EDUCATE" BLACK CHILDREN EVERYDAY IN DETROIT, CHICAGO, LA, on and on, TO EDUCATE AND ESCAPE THE GHETTOS?

*"WHO'S IN-CHARGE OF ALL THE EDUCATIONAL INSTITUTIONS IN AMERICA?"

*"WHO SPECIFICALLY LEGISLATES TO PANDERS, TO ISOLATE A "SEGMENT" OF OUR PEOPLE?"

WELL?...SAY IT!...SAY IT OUT LOUD, SO "YOU" CAN HEAR-IT YOURSELF!

*Riddle me this , Batman: ANY OTHER GROUP OR CONSTITUENCY FROM ANY STATE, OR ANY FOREIGN ÉMIGRÉ, FROM THE FARTHEST CORNERS OF THE PLANET, AND ESPECIALLY AFTER THE DEFEAT OF IMPERIAL JAPAN, NAZI GERMANY, FASCIST ITALY AND COLD WAR RUSSIA, MAO'S CHINA,
and even the dreaded Viet Nam,
HASN'T FOUND-IT TO BE A-HINDERANCE, OR A-HANDICAP TO ACHIEVE THEIR SUCCESS IN AMERICA! ....THAT INCLUDES DARK-SKINNED "EAST INDIANS", SAMOANS, AUSTRALIANS, OR THE ACTUAL AFRICANS, WHO DON'T NEED, OR RELY, UPON ANY SPECIAL LEGISLATION TO ACHIEVE WHAT THEY ASPIRE TO!

*TODAY, AMERICA WELCOMES AND EMBRACES NEW FRIENDS AND OLD FOES ALIKE, EVEN MILLIONS OF "SANTA ANNA FORCE'S - DESCENDANTs" POURING OVER OUR BORDERS......SO WHAT THE HELL'S EVERYONE BITCHING ABOUT ?

WE PROBABLY EVEN HAVE ex-AL QAEDA DRIVING-CABS IN NYC, AND MAYBE A FEW CURRENT MEMBERS TOO!

So, what is it?....When You hear Carter, or Jesse, or Al, or Rangel, or now Old Bill say these things, you just wanna scream: Awe, come-on now, that's B/S, and throw anything in-hand at your TV!....SHUT-UP, GIVE IT A REST...GROW-UP.

Maybe it's a perception, maybe a perspective, maybe a inveigled frame of mind, certainly a fallacy, or we wouldn't be to over-flowing in AMERICA, from every corner and every color on the planet...Heck, maybe it's the "same syndrome" that keeps the Republicans from standing-up for themselves, and their President after being down-in-the-mouth and the catacombs for so many years, and waking-up to the light, finally stepping-up-to-the plate, acting like they're Winners for a change.

Maybe just a little confidence and "to hell with everybody else", is just what the Doctor orders for anyone with this confidence problem, regardless of skin tone who has a skewed view and vision of: "Just How Wonderful This Idea" Really Is.

This is after all AMERICA, and everyone seems to be breaking-in here from somewhere else for something very special; CHOICE, FREEDOM, OPPORTUNITY?

"America, Land of Opportunity"
 "O'er the land of the free and the home of the brave"!

(Why do they keep coming here?......Can't be to spend those required $1000s a season, on a ticket to watch Michael or LeBron bounce a ball, I can't! Or Adrian catch one, or Donovan throw one, or Tiger whack one, or Barack having one...or, maybe it is?)

It's certainly not to hear Michael Steele talk about one, since all the DEMs say repeatedly: "things are so damn bad here", or is it just what they want us to think?

WHAT DO YOU THINK, DOCTOR COSBY?
http://www.youtube.com/watch?v=1FLN4uVoOes

Think about that for a while Bill....We Still Love You,
But You're Asking The Wrong Questions Doctor!....
Maybe ask that of the NAACP, or the DNC, or the NBCC, or the NUL, or the Nation of Islam, or the new kinder-gentler Black Panthers?
I'm wondering about any organizations based solely on the color of a man's skin, "A COLOR"!....REALLY?

Seems counter-productive doesn't it, and contrary to the point "at hand"?

I'm so glad Bill noticed the two skin tones on each side of "his hand too."

***It would seem to any rationally thinking human being having lived upon this earth over the last 25,000 to 1-1/2 million or so years ago,

that the "only TWO differences" = (2), between one man and another man on this planet were primarily based on;

(#1) the "position of the Sun",
with respect to their approximant locations standing on this spinning ball in space, in relation to the other without enough sunscreen,..............glib,
and the only real one,
(#2) their "attitude", toward each other!.......................

http://www.physorg.com/news154880690.html

Everything else is pure chance, irrelevant, immaterial and clearly political!
As with Chinese to Chileans, Monrovians to Moravians, Aleutians to Australians,
Russians to Rwandans, Vikings to Visigoths, Inca to Inuit, Japanese to
Jordanians, Moroccans to Zulu, Spanish Conquistadors and Aztecs
(oops, too close a reference, a bit of friction there),
and San Franciscans to NY Greenwich Villagers (sorry, they're the same),
but You get my point ....It's Location, location, location!) ....
Happenstance and chance, as to when and where you're born on this big blue and
green ball spinning in infinite space.

***People are just people, and humans are all the same, no better, no worse,
all flawed with genetic attitude to some degree, probably to keep one alive!
.......And then there's "The Dutch", but that's another story! ....Only Kidding,
blame that one on Austin Power's father!

Like the lines in "The Merchant of Venice";

Shylock: I will buy with you, sell with you, talk with you, walk with you, and so
following; but I will not eat with you, drink with you, nor pray with you............

I am a Jew. Hath not a Jew eyes? hath not a Jew hands, organs, dimensions,
senses, affections, passions? fed with the same food, hurt with the same
weapons, subject to the same diseases, healed by the same means, warmed and
cooled by the same winter and summer, as a Christian is?
If you prick us, do we not bleed?.......
......If you tickle us, do we not laugh?......... If you poison us, do we not die?........

http://www.youtube.com/watch?v=_Gh3_e3mDQ8

You want to see people pull together? You need a common disaster which always
brings out the best in humans, or a common enemy that can bring out the worst.
Until We have interstellar-extraterrestrials landing their ships in DC, we mere
mortals will be squabbling between each other like **Cain** & Abel for a scratch of
earth till the Environmentalists outlaw everything on the planet but Dish Gardens.

"Then" We'll All Have A Common Enemy To Join Forces Against!!!.......Till then,
everyone just try and behave yourselves. That's the best anyone can hope for!

I'll tell you what We might try though, along with little ribbons for just the Movie
Stars to wear, to absolve themselves of any responsibility or guilt to the human
race for their exceptionally excessive and massive inordinate wealth but I digress.

As a (standard retort), this simple "come-back" in the form of a "national slogan
campaign" to defuse and extinguish inane ignorant bigotry in any form, especially
the LEFT's go-to fallback position when defending Barack Obama from anyone
disagreeing with any of his politics or positions, their RED HERRING: "RACISM".
Their daily reframe to shift everyone's attention away from what they are really

trying to do to America's Free Enterprise System, Democracy, Capitalism, Liberty & our Freedoms. So, when responding to any mental-deficients, or those old "like-minded" white southern Governor/Farmers type constantly lamenting the old days of Free Labor with Chained Hearts; you know: <u>Liberals,.....................</u> <u>all You just need to say is</u>;

(A) "Hey, It's Not about The Black Guy, it's about That Guy"!

(B) "It's always been about Left & Right, Not Black Vs White!...
.......Grow-up......Get over it ....Get a Life ..... Get a Job !".......

As for the conservatives: "Condoleezza or General Powell were fantastic choices, especially over "McCain" who was specifically <u>anointed and hand-chosen for the Republicans to lose with.</u>"

Even Morgan Freeman, a fine Actor, could make a better President, and probably a better showing against our enemies. Certainly, he wouldn't have our country in this peril that we all find ourselves in right now, even as a civilian, versus a professional politician.
This peril, NO, this calculated cacophony of Obama blessings, strategically and totally based on "rumor, speculation, crystal ball, innuendo, false supposition, demagoguery, erroneous: (facts, figures and stats), along with a clogged "kitchen sink", "the sky is falling", B/S and Malarkey-Fark!"

***Want to be self-righteous Jimmy C.?
Put down your hammer and try worrying about real Slavery in the modern age, like kidnapped children, young girls and young women grabbed off the streets, hidden in basements, backyard lean-tos, and sent overseas and across our borders; used as "Sex Slaves", and other sundry depravities around the world and "at this very moment" as you're reading this, FOOL, (not Savannah 1860)! ....Thanks to your "turn-a-blind-eye & do-nothing" buddies at that useless "United Nations" with their worthless agendas.

One would assume you at least have the power and influence to clean-up some minor-league Sleaze-Balls around the planet. Well, don't You punk? We all know you're hapless and helpless with Radical Muslim Students, but the U.N. can't even cope with goofy, teenage Somali pirates either when everyone knows right where they're hiding, and it's not Tortuga......Arrrgg!

Look, just forget the question....We'll just have to wait for another Lone Rider: Republican or Conservative, to actually have the conviction and strength of moral character to ride into the White House on a pale horse, and kick-some-ass again to solve some real problems in the World, instead of creating them!..........SENTRYMAN

*HERE WAS A PHOTO OF SARAH PALIN HOLDING THE NECESSARY DEFENSIVE WEAPON OF THE UNTIED STATES ARMED FORCES, IN ORDER TO MAINTAIN AND SECURE AMERICA'S FREEDOMS!

Google-IT!.........Or go to: *http://sentryman.org/id8.html*

Comment by Mary 5 hours ago

The only group of people being racist is the media. They do not hold Barry to the same standard as anyone in history that has ran for president or has been president.

Comment by Irene 6 hours ago

It is hard for me to believe that our Gov. Republicans or Democrats did not know or else they are pretty stupid not to know we were on the fast track for communism. They did not know Soros was trying to bring down the U.S.A. when even the newspapers in Canada!!! I think we should throw all of them out... We seriously need something about the CA farmers .. That is our bread line. One thing we can do is pray for rain. God has turned back time because of prayers. Do you think the God of this Universe Jehovah cannot bring rain.... God bless the U.S.A.

Comment by Gina 4 hours ago

SENTRYMAN...I don't mean to date myself but I grew up working in the cotton fields of Alabama with my family and back then there was NO racism, race baiting or racists among people black and white picking cotton, working and sweating together to earn a days' wage.

There was indeed a mutual respect for one another and a common thread between cotton sharecroppers. I know we are in different times but to simply compare the two times is such a contrast.

HERE WERE 2 PHOTOS OF AMERICAN FAMILIES DURING THE
SO-CALLED "GREAT" DEPRESSION,
EXCEPT FOR TAXPAYERS, THAT DIDN'T MAKE THE CUT.

I'LL POST ON www.sentryman.org/id8.html

Sorry Gina

Comment by Gina) 4 hours ago

oops! Typo...we had a mutual respect and also I used the
two different times as a comparison.
I forgot to say Thank You for an enlightening post!

Comment by SENTRYMAN 20 minutes ago

No, I read you right.....It's all good.

It is a different time....WHY?.....50 years of LIBERALISM.
and "The Divide" Is Getting Wider.......WHY?.......50 years of LIBERALISM.
and it's all being ginned-up & manufactured...WHY?..... 50 years of
LIBERALISM

The DEMs brag they Own the subject...The Saviors of the Downtrodden and
Disenfranchised.....and they do, by choice, They Own The Franchise....
<u>and shouldn't be proud of it!</u>...

The DEMs have been totally responsible for keeping an entire race, and 3
generations subjugated to second-class-citizen status, in a country where
even former enemies from Santa Anna to Germany, to Viet Nam to China,
and Russia can all come to America and thrive and prosper,
but yet, at the same time trapping its own citizens that have been in the
Americas perhaps longer than many other immigrants, and then relegating
those Americans to entertainment fields, and playing with balls as the
primary avenues to make it really big.
....WHY?.......50 years of Liberalism.

And Lord, You even have to be half-Caucasian, but not a 1st generation
African to become President......and WHY?.........YOU KNOW!

I've wondered for 45 years, if everyone is supposed to be equal, and have
equal access to every opportunity in America, and the Federal government
is supposedly guaranteeing fairness and equality in Education; why is
there such a disparity between inner-city schools and the suburbs, from
the facilities, to the educators, the standards and the opportunities?
........50 years of Liberalism?

The DEMs have been in 100% control from the beginning of the Liberal-era,
<u>50 Years Ago, to theoretically "correct" all the injustices in this savage land</u>
A-M-E-R-I-C-A!
.... What happened? …....Screaming: Show ~ Me ~ The ~ Money!

Oh please, George W. Bush provided more money for education than
Ronald Reagan had to run the entire United States government in the 80s.

"Show me the Money"! ….They've Had It!...What did they use it for, over the
past 50 years of LIBERALISM? ..The kids didn't get it with their propaganda
lessons. It must have gone to the 700 N.Y.C. teachers sent home on those
<u>variety of charges</u> on full salary, & contemporaries in the other 49 states?

So, if you've got any problems with any facet of anything in the education industry,
LOOK TO YOUR LEFT!!!!

Why then are standards and testing "fought against" so vehemently by teachers and the NEA?..... LOOK TO YOUR LEFT!

Why do these unions possess the ultimate power to object to anything the Federal government mandates or tries to enforce?...LOOK TO YOUR LEFT!

Why has studying "The 1st Thanksgiving and the Founding Fathers" been reduced to (1) Chapter, but masturbation instruction for transgender, gay penguin has been expanded to "thesis status" for elementary school.
LOOK TO YOUR LEFT!

We can't have Christmas trees, or Cupcakes, or Dodge ball, or any Prayer before the Big Game in schools anymore,
and hamburgers and sodas are next,
but a black kid isn't guaranteed a descent education in the United States to develop his secure future?...Why the hell NOT??..... LOOK TO YOUR LEFT!

The 64 Thou$and dollar question would be, and today that would be $64 Billion dollar question): Why do American citizens continue to buy into the DEMs false promises?......50 years of unfulfilled PROMISES! ......
Is that like battered spouse syndrome, always thinking it's going to get better tomorrow? ..... LOOK TO YOUR LEFT!

That was 50 years of empty Tomorrows for failed children,.................that is Faith all right?.......Sounds more like False Hope and Stockholm Syndrome!

SENTRYMAN

Comment by Gina) 4 hours ago

Thank you Sentryman.....I love your posts! They really make me think!

Gina

Chapter 78

Whistling In The Dark and Spitting Into The Wind ...
"TERM LIMITS"

Posted by SENTRYMAN on October 2, 2009 at 4:50pm

I'm reposting this SENTRYMAN "TERM LIMITS" Blog
from September 14, 2009, to all those planning; Rebellion Parties, Marches,
Petitions, or contemplating just burning down the White House with
torches, so He'll listen.
It's a handy guide, and I can keep this effort in the loop.

Plus, I don't have to rearticulate it 1000 times for those with onset of A.D.D.
==

***Hope whatever campaign efforts there are result in something tangible,
but I'm afraid that all the Petitions, Tea Parties, TOWNHALL parties, 9/12
Parties, slumber parties, and even future Inaugural Parties aren't going to
change anything, and we will all just go back to sleep as usual very soon.

We cannot "root-out" the insidious players ensconced in the <u>Civil Service sectors</u>
of our ever-expanding government bureaucracy at HUD, Food & Drug, EPA, FEMA
and at the State Department and the UnJustice Department, or the moles in the
Pentagon, the VA, not to forget the Energy Dept., and the Edjukacian Department.

Bush could not even (excuse, relief, fire) a few of his renegade-lawyers toward the
end of his Presidency, which He supposedly possesses the complete authority
and legal right to do, at any time He sees fit, but, but, but, motorboat ,,,,,,,NOT!

But, Clinton "Axed-All Of Bush Sr.'s Attorneys" Going In The Front Door,
and Bill additionally, as a consolation prize to his Party, "stopped every"
investigation of crooked DEMs throughout government that afternoon,
and No-One peeped!...........

So, where was the impartial FBI?

Is Anyone Ever Protecting The American People, and consistently......Or
Do You Have To Be A Black Panther To Get A Presidential Pass?
(hey, not to pick on any subversive, radical Para-military racist organizations
that aren't White, of course!)

If Palin ever got in the White House she'd need a Food Taster!   Pg. 295

Want to put some real teeth into your Petition Drives?
Start with every state petitioning for a referendum, for; TERM LIMITS!.......

TERM LIMITS!.......If it has to be at the state's level first to work, so be it,
but the end result will be the same, and quite emphatic, and watch the rats scatter!

Figuring out exactly how the American People can shove "TERM LIMITS"
right-down ALL their collective throats, should be the #1 Grassroots Campaign
prior to the next fraudulent, fixed election, (i.e. Minnesota),
(within a national 50 State block, creating ostensively a national referendum,
 just as, so many of California's state's initiatives have been courageous!)

(PROP. #86 = to "eighty-six" the Congress with "2 Term Limits")

2-Terms for Congress ...(cut sloth Senators from 6 yr down to 4 yr)

1-Term for Presidents ....(so they might actually work during their
"entire term", instead of starting their "reelection campaign"
 the day after Inauguration Day, January 20th)

This Is Probably The Only Thing That Can Ever Return The Reins Of Government,
That Will Neuter These Stallions For Virtue, Along With Their Feminine – Partners-
In-Crime Accomplices!...............................NOW, That's A Party Worth Attending!

Not to forget:
"TORT REFORM" and REVERSING "CAP 'n TRADE",

and any HEALTHCARE BILL, (AKA, taking over every facet of your lives
with impunity, under the guise of: "We Really Care" B/S, etc.)

And finally:
"LIMITING LIFE APPOINTMENTS TO THE IMPERIAL COURT TO 20 YEARS",
while we're slapping-down all the children, just for good measure!

Anything less, is just "spitt'n in the wind" for another 4
years, or 8, or 16, or maybe forever!

Good luck........and God bless, to us all.

SENTRYMAN

==

3 Comments and 3 videos

Comment by SENTRYMAN on October 8, 2009 at 6:50pm

THEY NOT ONLY STEAL FROM US,

BUT WE PAY THEM TO STEAL FROM US,

AND WE PAY THEM TO INVESTIGATE EACH OTHER, STEALING FROM US,

AND IF WE DARE TO INQUIRE ABOUT JUST HOW MUCH THEY STEAL FROM US

<u>WE GET AN ANSWER LIKE THIS:</u>

Rep. Charlie Rangel swears at Jason Mattera over scandal
http://www.youtube.com/watch?v=rdtFWCrCh0s&feature=player_embedded

AND THIS CLASSIC EXCHANGE:

Bill O'Reilly flips out on Barney Frank - BANKING CRISIS mad screaming match
http://www.youtube.com/watch?v=alm5Mp-mmRU&feature=player_embedded

And "The OLD Administration" Setting The Record Straight:

From The "Architects" Mouth, Mr. Rove On Obama's Olympic Failure, Fannie and Freddie
http://www.youtube.com/watch?v=tm9im091qdw

==

Comment by SENTRYMAN on October 7, 2009 at 8:07pm

THIS POLITICO Article from 10-7-09 "MAKES MY POINT".......................

((((((-- I TOLD YOU SO --)))))),
And how do You think We can possibly ever stop this?

POLITICO................ EXCERPTS;
House: Working hard or hardly working?
By JAKE SHERMAN | 10/7/09

Like most Americans, members of the House are expected to report promptly — no excuses — when summoned by their bosses for the start of another workweek.

One difference: For lawmakers, starting time doesn't come until about 6:30 Tuesday evening.

After taking control of the House in 2006 — and again when President Barack Obama was elected president in 2008 — Majority Leader Steny Hoyer (D-Md.) boasted that lawmakers would work four or five days a week to bring change to America.

The House got off to a fast start this year, approving a stimulus plan, an omnibus spending bill and climate change legislation, as well as getting health care reform bills through three committees.

But now lawmakers and staff are enjoying an Indian summer of sorts; Mondays are dead, and Fridays have the Hill set clad in jeans and oxfords, awaiting the next vote four long days away.

Two-and-a-half-day workweeks are not exactly what Hoyer had planned.

Midway through President Barack Obama's first year in office, Steny Hoyer's House has settled into a rather leisurely routine. Photo: John Shinkle

But while some GOP lawmakers grumbled in 2006 when Hoyer first talked of a five-day-a-week schedule, at least one was willing to look at the bright side Tuesday.
*an average of three hours and 36 minutes of legislative debate and voting each day, according to a POLITICO analysis of House voting records.

"Two and a half days a week is plenty of time to consider the ideas coming out of this Democrat-led House," said Rep. Roy Blunt (R-Mo.).

"Imagine the damage they could do with five-day workweeks."

PROP. #86,......................(to eighty-six the Congress with 2 Term Limits)

2 Terms for Congress (cut Senators from 6 yr to 4 yr)

1 Term for Presidents (so they might actually work during the entire term, instead of starting their reelection campaign the next day on January 21st)

SENTRYMAN

==

**Chapter 14 *(repeated: in case you've missed the point of this book!)*

The 20 Demandments of the United States of AMERICA.

Posted by SENTRYMAN on January 8, 2009

"A Peaceful Citizen's REVOLUTION"

"Our" government has its Own self-satisfying, self-indulgent, *self-aggrandizing* Death-grip wrapped around Our collective necks,
and their Own greed will never serve or protect US, their employers!

Demand of OUR Government with a Citizen's National Referendum
by a (PEACEFUL) Non-Violent Ultimatum For:

"The 20 Demandments"

No GOVT. Committees,
No blue ribbon Sub-Committees,
and without any idle Legislative Debate,

We must demand of "OUR" elected, non-representative, government employees.
(since they'll never comply or permit any reduction of their power or authority,
that We their employers, The America Taxpayer have granted and entrusted to them,
nor would they ever Vote-It "Out Of Committee" to make these viable as any of OUR LAWs,
with the following provisions;

#1- (2 Term) Limits for all elected officials, & Presidents only (1),
This Civic Duty Is Not a Career, nor an Annuity, and certainly not a Life appointment.
It's a Calling, a Service, a Sacrifice and then Go Home as OUR Forefather's envisioned.
"THE MOST IMPORTANT and IMPERATIVE of the 20"

#2- Tort Reform,

#3- Outlaw all "Lobbyists",
we didn't elect, hire or pay these representatives to travel to Washington
to be professionally bribed, or made millionaires.

#4- Give the President the "Line Item Veto"
or, "No Bundling Bills."
All Bills Voted On Separately, equaling = No Ear Marks = No Pork, unless
voted upon its own merits, with a majority approval for the general good!

#5- No Pay Raises for Government Officials
unless and until "we, the people" vote them one, when it's deserved,

#6- Freeze All New Spending,
and tell Government to go home until they are actually needed to solve a
problem, dilemma or pressing issue.
No Idle Hands!....They're not serving us anyway.....
i.e. "TRILLIONS In-Debt, with Bailouts to friends and past associates",

#7- 12 months Freeze: NO INCOME TAX.
No More Bailouts,
Keep Our Own Trillions Of Dollars In Our Pockets and That Will Solve The
Problems Immediately,
(that's "RIGHT NOW", for you Washingtonians),

#8- FLAT TAX, or Consumption TAX,

or a combination there of, and <u>Dismantle the IRS from going after citizens</u>
or businesses for political retribution, then the Congress will stay home till
needed.

…..<u>On second thought, Dismantle the IRS</u>,

#9- "Don't Buy Any Foreign Oil,

Drill Here, Drill NOW, and use Natural Gas!"
Continue to research, experiment, invent and design all the Wind Mills,
Solar Panels, Geothermal, etc., etc., that private Industry wishes to create,
but in the meantime, break the yoke of our oppressive pseudo-green
government and,

#10- No More Eminent Domain,

or Reconciliation for Corporations or Private Business,

#11- Election Funds Limit,

i.e. a FLAT $100 Million (for all contenders) to divide!
(NOT McCain's $140 million Vs Obama $700 million),

#12- "3 Strike" GUN LAW

The confused police shoot'm or lock'm-up, and the Courts let'm out.
Do You really think the 18,000 guns laws on the books are working?

And who runs the Government? .....LAWYERS!
And who teaches the Lawyers? ......LIBERALS!
And who wants to charge the Taxpayers $400. @ hr.
for anything and everything? ....LIBERAL LAWYERS!

Hey, Geniuses, this is how to "make a Law in 1 minute":
A - Carry a Firearm in the commission of a felony = 10 Years

B - Fire a Firearm in the commission of a felony = 25 Years

C - Kill someone in the commission of a felony = Life!

Do you know how many trees I just saved, or how many court dockets I just
cleared???.......(that's real "Green" Government)

and how many lame-brained villains and felons just decided not to "Carry"
Firearms in the commission of their chosen professions = ?
but hey, a lot more than 1 minute ago!

**So why must this be a lifelong debate while lives are ruined and people die??

***Now we can start working on their compunction and propensity for committing Felonies in the 1st place!

And while we're discussing the psychological, philosophical and sociological ramifications,
who runs and ruined their Education in the first place???.......GUESS!

#13- ENGLISH, the official language of The United States of America!

#14- Military on the Border and Finish The Fence,
Train new recruits with duty-guarding our country's 4 sides with our already paid Military. It's FREE!

#15- Legalize all Non-Criminal Illegal Aliens with a <u>5-year Green Card,</u>
& immediate citizenship by joining the US Military.

#16- Every Citizen has a national Voter Registration,
(Thumb Print - Photo ID) card or "YOU Can't Vote".

No more calamities like:
I.e. (More people voting for Obama than even lived in the town!)

#17- No one leaves Prison without a GED and a professional skill,
which means; teaching inmates what they never learned in our Liberal Public Schools that We Paid For, That As Children They Didn't Receive,

#18- Returning Military will be employed by Our government of 1 year stateside, to insure a safe-integration back into civilian-society, this for all our valiant former warriors and volunteer protectors.

#19- Give the Military and active Troops whatever they need to properly Defend OUR Country, with Full Health Benefits for our returning Military.

#20- "<u>Marriage</u>" is between a Man and a Woman!
(If you can't make babies, you don't need this ancient ceremonial rite!
A religious precept & custom based on rightful-heritage for the "<u>offspring</u>")

The Constitution of the United States of America

~~~~~~ <u>Here was a picture of the constitution!</u> ~~~~~~

<u>Preamble Note</u>

We the People of the United States, in Order to form a more perfect Union, establish Justice, insure domestic Tranquility, provide for the common defence, promote the general Welfare, and secure the Blessings of Liberty to ourselves and our Posterity, do ordain and establish this Constitution for the United States of America.

==

****MAKE MINE FREEDOM...video**

<u>http://www.youtube.com/watch?v=mVh75ylAUXY&feature=player_embedded</u>

All tyranny needs to gain a foothold is for people of good conscience to remain silent.
<u>Thomas Jefferson</u>

Timid men prefer the calm of despotism to the tempestuous sea of liberty.
<u>Thomas Jefferson</u>

Every government degenerates when trusted to the rulers of the people alone. The people themselves are its only safe depositories.
<u>Thomas Jefferson</u>

I predict future happiness for Americans if they can prevent the government from wasting the labors of the people under the pretense of taking care of them.
<u>Thomas Jefferson</u>

When the people fear their government, there is tyranny; when the government fears the people, there is liberty.
<u>Thomas Jefferson</u>

The spirit of resistance to government is so valuable on certain occasions that I wish it to be always kept alive.
<u>Thomas Jefferson</u>

Our country is now taking so steady a course as to show by what road it will pass to destruction, to wit: by consolidation of power first, and then corruption, its necessary consequence.
<u>Thomas Jefferson</u>

My reading of history convinces me that most bad government results from too much government.
<u>Thomas Jefferson</u>

Never spend your money before you have earned it.
<u>Thomas Jefferson</u>

Do you want to know who you are? Don't ask. Act! Action will delineate and define you.
<u>Thomas Jefferson</u>

Every citizen should be a soldier. This was the case with the Greeks and Romans, and must be that of every free state.
<u>Thomas Jefferson</u>

A democracy is nothing more than mob rule, where fifty-one percent of the people may take away the rights of the other forty-nine.
<u>Thomas Jefferson</u>

Educate and inform the whole mass of the people... They are the only sure reliance for the preservation of our liberty.
<u>Thomas Jefferson</u>

<u>***For More Pearls from Thomas Jefferson visit my blog listed:</u>

"A MAN FOR ALL SEASONS.........WE NEED HIM NOW!"

(Posted by SENTRYMAN on June 14, 2009)

GOD SPEED,

<u>SENTRYMAN</u>
KEEP YOUR POWDER DRY

 **Chapter 100**

JOHN STOSSEL TAKES ON THE WORLD....WITH Charlton Heston
"World Class Global Warming B/S'ers"

Posted by SENTRYMAN on <u>December 11, 2009</u> at 1:30pm

<u>Charlton Heston on Global Climate Change</u>
http://www.youtube.com/watch?v=ozO4YB98mCY

<u>John Stossel Rips Apart Global Warming on ABC</u>
https://www.youtube.com/results?search_query=John+Stossel+rips+global+warming

https://www.youtube.com/watch?v=r78-bZfy8oU
<u>John Stossel tackles global climate change (part 1)..12-10-09</u>
http://www.youtube.com/watch?v=RiYX09H4Q6k

<u>John Stossel tackles global climate change (part 2)..12-10-09</u>
http://www.youtube.com/watch?v=eRiapFd5Uyo&feature=related

<u>John Stossel Moving to Fox Business, Says Goodbye to ABC</u>
http://www.youtube.com/watch?v=kilzbXmyRpY

<u>John Stossel's Debut On "O'Reilly Factor"</u>
http://www.youtube.com/watch?v=cQER0w_vORc

<u>John Stossel Government Mistakes!</u>
http://www.youtube.com/watch?v=LmoS4cZ1p7Y&playnext=1&list=PL1671559C672F6F24&index=31

https://www.youtube.com/watch?v=IAYRm0ggMjg
<u>John Stossel : Free People Create Jobs!</u>
https://www.youtube.com/watch?v=7QOSX5vvO_I

<u>12/1/09 (1/2) John Stossel on Eminent Domain</u>
https://www.youtube.com/watch?v=Zym47P5Cc2k

<u>John Stossel GLOBAL WARMING SCANDAL O'REILLY FACTOR FOX News 12-1-09</u>
http://www.youtube.com/watch?v=qJdEtPbMXgU

<u>John Stossel on Glenn Beck</u>
http://www.youtube.com/watch?v=-8_ne_CV8Fc

John Stossel on Glenn Beck on Fox News Channel 01/22/09
http://www.youtube.com/watch?v=aUtlZbUgDhA

https://www.youtube.com/watch?v=bctRYvUJKe4&list=PL122E50E7D33B0F76
John Stossel Fox Business 01-21-10 'Green Jobs' 1 of 5, watch all of them!
http://www.youtube.com/watch?v=lYSFZLOGmWA

U.N. Agenda 21- "There Will Be No Private Housing" Peter Schiff, John Stossel, Judge Napolitano.
https://www.youtube.com/watch?v=3Ee6S9_H1Vk

http://www.youtube.com/watch?v=O2I37RT3TCo&feature=autoplay&list=PL981A8
1183E7352C4&playnext=2

Hey, World News, Reporters and Journalists,
this is what professionals in your industry used to do for a living
when they had integrity, honor, values and souls.

Here <u>was</u> a photo of John Stossel's book
"Give Me A Break"

<u>**But anyway, watch every one of these and think long and hard on them:</u>

<u>ARE WE GODS, OR ARE WE ANTS, DRONES, PAWNS and SERFS???</u>

<u>Thank You; John and Charlton, Bill and Glenn, Peter and the Judge!</u>

<u>**SENTRYMAN**</u>

Chapter 137

JUST PASS'n IT ALONG..... "BORN IN THE USA?"

Posted by SENTRYMAN on APRIL 12, 2010 at 12:30pm

(*SOME LINKS IN THIS CHAPTER ARE SLOW, NEED DOUBLE OR TRIPLE CLICK, WHY?)

BORN IN THE USA?

Kenyan official: Obama born here

In debate over constitution, minister urges African nation to emulate U.S. inclusion

---

Posted: April 11, 2010
6:22 pm Eastern

By Drew Zahn
© 2010 WorldNetDaily

http://www.wnd.com/index.php?fa=PAGE.view&pageId=13
9481

WAS PHOTO of
Kenyan MP James Orengo

A Kenyan lawmaker told the nation's parliament last month that Barack Obama was born in Africa and is therefore "not even a native American."

During debate over the draft of a new Kenyan constitution, James Orengo, the country's minister of lands and a member of parliament for the Ugenya constituency, cited America's election of a Kenyan-born president as an example of what can be accomplished when diverse peoples unite:

James Orengo photo at Link above

"If America was living in a situation where they feared ethnicity and did not see itself as a multiparty state or nation," Orengo posited, "how could a young man born here in Kenya, who is not even a native American, become the president of America?" http://www.wnd.com/files/kenyanparliament.pdf

Orengo held up the U.S. as a country no longer "living in the past," since Americans elected a Kenyan-born president without regard to "ethnic consideration and objectives."

A new strategy has been unveiled to demand answers to Obama's eligibility questions. See how you can help.

http://www.wnd.com/validationofbarackobama

Debate is then recorded in the Kenyan government's official March 25, 2010, hansard – a traditional name for printed transcripts of a parliamentary debate – as continuing with no other MPs mentioning or attempting to correct Orengo's comments about Obama.

As WND has reported, several other sources – including National Public Radio – have claimed Obama's birthplace as Kenya prior to his election as president.

WND also reported when a video appeared in which Michelle Obama said her husband's "home country" was Kenya, though her comments didn't specifically suggest his birth there.

The video, posted April 3 on YouTube and forwarded by a score of Internet e-mails, shows Michelle Obama saying, "When we took our trip to Africa and visited his home country in Kenya, we took a public HIV test."

"Michelle Obama says Obama is Kenyan"
http://www.youtube.com/watch?v=YqrTsz1wQIM

http://www.youtube.com/watch?v=R6fiSfBh9-4

The reference drew attention because of the claim made in numerous lawsuits and other challenges to Obama's occupancy of the Oval Office that he is not eligible to be president under the requirement of Article 2, Section 1 of the Constitution that the president be a "natural born citizen."

But the NPR reference and Michelle Obama's comment are far from the only ones of their kind.

At one point, there were reports that even Obama's grandmother claimed being in attendance at his birth in Africa.

http://www.wnd.com/index.php?fa=PAGE.view&pageId=107524

According to a compilation of images at a military forum, another reference was made in 2008 in the Nigerian Observer.

http://forums.military.com/eve/forums/a/tpc/f/4960045241001/m/9440076532001

Under a byline from Solomon Asowata and a Washington dateline, the report says, "Americans will today go to the polls to elect their next president with Democratic Party candidate,

Senator Barack Obama largely favoured to win.

The Kenyan-born Senator will, however, face a stiff competition from his Republican counterpart..."

NIGERIAN OBSERVER PAPER

A commentary at The Post & Email website said, "It is no wonder that many doubt Obama's claim of a Hawaiian birth."

http://www.thepostemail.com/2010/04/07/evidence-against-obamas-hawaiian-birth-story-mounts

It cited another report from African Travel Magazine that said, "As Kenyan born U.S. Senator Barack Obama jets into Kenya today as part of his African tour, concerns have once again been raised on the security preparations for other visitors and residents. ...."

The Post & Email commentary also cited a report from "Indonesia Matters" that includes similar references.

http://www.indonesiamatters.com/2952/barry-soetoro/

WND documented earlier several other statements linking Obama and Kenya.

http://www.wnd.com/index.php?fa=PAGE.view&pageId=113004

These included the apparently archived article from the Sunday Standard in Kenya.

http://web.archive.org/web/20040627142700/eastandard.net/headlines/news 26060403.htm

The report begins, "Kenyan-born US Senate hopeful, Barrack (sic) Obama, appeared set to take over the Illinois Senate seat after his main rival, Jack Ryan, dropped out of the race on Friday night amid a furor over lurid sex club allegations."

SUNDAY STANDARD PAPER

The article is credited to the wire service Associated Press at the bottom of the page. However, the article could not be found either in the AP archives available to the public online or the archive on the newspaper's website. WND telephone calls and e-mails to the newspaper did not generate a response.

Last year, an African news site and an MSNBC broadcaster referred to President Obama's birthplace as being outside of the United States.

http://www.wnd.com/index.php?fa=PAGE.view&pageId=103638

Network correspondent Mara Schiavocampo was reporting on the celebratory atmosphere in Accra, Ghana, immediately prior to Obama's visit to the west African nation.

Interviewing a person who appeared to be a shop operator, she stated, "Barack Obama is Kenyan ... but Ghanaians are still proud of him."

<u>The video of the report is at this link.</u>
http://www.msnbc.msn.com/id/3032619#31856235

Also, a report at <u>Modern Ghana</u> posted in advance of the president's visit cited his birthplace on the continent of Africa.

http://www.modernghana.com/news/226379/1/history-beckons-as-prez-obama-arrives-tomorrow.html

"For Ghana, Obama's visit will be a celebration of another milestone in African history as it hosts the first-ever African-American President on this presidential visit to the continent of his birth," the report said.

WND has reported on dozens of legal challenges to Obama's status as a "natural born citizen." The Constitution, Article 2, Section 1, states, "No Person except a natural born Citizen, or a Citizen of the United States, at the time of the Adoption of this Constitution, shall be eligible to the Office of President."

Some of the lawsuits question whether he was actually born in Hawaii, as he insists. If he was born out of the country, Obama's American mother, the suits contend, was too young at the time of his birth to confer American citizenship to her son under the law at the time.

Other challenges have focused on Obama's citizenship through his father, a Kenyan subject to the jurisdiction of the United Kingdom at the time of his birth, thus making him a dual citizen. The cases contend the framers of the Constitution excluded dual citizens from qualifying as natural born.

Complicating the situation is Obama's decision to <u>spend sums exceeding $1.7 million</u> to avoid releasing an original long-form state birth certificate that would put to rest the questions.

<u>http://www.wnd.com/index.php?fa=PAGE.view&pageId=106138</u>

<u>WND also has reported that among the documentation not yet available for Obama includes</u>; <u>http://www.wnd.com/2009/06/100613/</u>

WORLDNETDAILY EXCLUSIVE
OBAMA: WHERE HAVE ALL HIS RECORDS GONE?
Footprints of president's own history either vanish or remain covered-up
Published: 06/09/2009 at 8:34 PM

his; kindergarten records,

Punahou school records,

Occidental College records,

Columbia University records,

Columbia thesis,

Harvard Law School records,

Harvard Law Review articles,

scholarly articles from the University of Chicago,

passport,

medical records,

files from his years as an Illinois state senator,

his Illinois State Bar Association records,

any baptism records and his adoption records.

<u>http://www.wnd.com/index.php?fa=PAGE.view&pageId=100613</u>

Pg. 311

Because of the dearth of information about Obama's eligibility, WND founder Joseph Farah has launched a campaign to raise contributions to post billboards asking a simple question: "Where's the birth certificate?"

http://www.wnd.com/index.php?pageId=112208

WND also reported previously when Michelle Obama contradicted Obama's story that he lived with his mother and father for several years in Hawaii after he was born before his father left to pursue a graduate degree.

http://www.wnd.com/index.php?fa=PAGE.view&pageId=114259

Michelle Obama said her husband's mother, Ann Dunham, was "very young and very single" when she gave birth to the future U.S. president.

Her comments undermine the official story as told by Barack Obama – that Dunham was married to his father, Barack Obama Sr., at the time of birth.

The remarks were made by Michelle Obama during a July 2008 round table at the University of Missouri. Obama was responding to criticism of her husband's presidential campaign speeches about fatherhood and faith-based initiatives.

http://blog.showmeprogress.com/showDiary.do?diaryId=1297

Hmmmmmmm! ......and We all thought "Arnold" wasn't eligible, good news for 2016.

Come'n to AMERICA...............where Laws are just for keep'n the Little People In-check,

and the Constitution's has been suspended and stored in Al's freezer, in a Lock-Box!

Condoleezza / Sarah 2012

OR

Sarah / Condoleezza 2012

YOU MUST ACT NOW

YOUR LIBERTIES ARE SLIPPING AWAY AS FAST AS YOU CAN READ THIS,
AND ONLY YOU HAVE THE POWER TO MAKE A DIFFERENCE

YOUR TIME IS UP

ONLY YOU CAN EFFECT REAL CHANGE.
IT DOESN'T COME FROM THE OUTSIDE GIFT WRAPPED,
DOWN THE CHIMNEY, OR IN THE MAIL BOX,
WE ALL KNOW THAT.

IT ALL COMES FROM WITHIN,
AS HARD AS THAT MIGHT TO BE TO ADMIT TO YOURSELF,
BUT YOU KNOW THAT TOO, OR AT LEAST YOU SHOULD.

WASHINGTON WILL BE HAPPY TO DO IT FOR YOU "FOREVER"

GOVERNMENTS CAN / WILL ALWAYS RUN OUR LIVES!

JUST SIT THERE FOOL, COLLECT YOUR STIPEND AND,

BE VERY, VERY SILENT! ~ *BYE-GOOD AM3RIKA!*

Check out some of these other Blog posts at: www.SENTRYMAN.org

FIRE THEM ALL: Book Video's Blocked-Addresses Re-established

Want To Defeat HILLARY?

YOU SAY YOU WANT A REVOLUTION!

LIARs & TRAITORs - Loose Lips Sink SEAL-6, Pakistani Doc, Ambassadors & America

*HOLOCAUST: The GLOBAL SPORT

Valley Forge. 11-11-11

OBAMA, Agenda 21, Smart .... A thought for a HAPPY 4th of JULY, 2011

Peace For Our Time. Memorial Day weekend, Get Out JEWS! 5-27-11

LIBERAL TOLERANCE ....1860 to 1917 to 1935 to 2006 to 10-24-10 to 11-14-10

RACISM in AMERICA 10-16-10

BUSH's Stupid...Gee, Never hear that stated often enough! Yah RIGHT! 9-9-10

Terrorists, Now We're Coming For You! .... Aug 25th to Oct 8th, 2010

SOCIALISM: The Gateway Drug......... Jun 14 to July 2, 2010

US Oil; Spills or Tears of our Fathers .....NAZIS, Warf Rats and Pyrates. 6-1-10 to 6-12-10

SENTRYMAN

Chapter 138

The Millionare$ Club Under BARACK and a HARD PLACE!

Posted by SENTRYMAN on March 14, 2010 at 2:09pm

The Millionaires' Club Increases Its Ranks

http://www.theatlantic.com/business/archive/2010/03/the-millionaires-club-increases-its-ranks/37253/

http://www.unz.org/Pub/AtlanticWeb-2010mar-00470

All HYPE aside, exactly how this chart has been Analyzed and Interpreted according to "the DEMs", who remind us daily of the disastrous economy that Obama has inherited, and then was interpreted, nuanced, and SPUN by the smartest guys in the NEWS Room, (without benefit of a CPA, or any bright Econ-101 student to explain to the experts that what they're looking at is, in fact, "not an Eye Chart"), belies it's real significance.

If one would analyze this chart for a critical moment, they would easily determine precisely what was happening to that "supposed", much touted "wonderful Clinton Economy" just prior to Bush "inheriting his": (Top 2 Lines - 1999 to 2001, that was invariably dumped upon Bush who was equal to the challenge),

and when Bush took-over, and then supposedly created the "worse Economy in history" according to "the DEMs", exactly what happened then in the US after "9/11" on this chart,

What Bush was able to do with that "Mess", and "Turning the Economy Around", all while "Defending Us on 2 War Fronts", as well as "Stopping Any Further 9/11 Attacks" for the benefit of an ungrateful nation, and (without a "Bail-out"), until the DEMs took full control of the US Economy and were in-charge, necessitating the first Emergency Recovery Fund prior to George W. Bush leaving office, is to this day unrecognized & miraculous in scope.

"Right Up, Until The DEMs":

TOOK-OVER-TOTAL-CONTROL-OF-THE-CONGRESS-IN-JANUARY-2007;
(ALL 4 LINES from 2002 to the beginning of 2007 were BUSH),

then, and from then-on, what happened to OUR Economy "really was Historic"!

EXAMINE THIS CHART FOR YOURSELF!........WHO'S TELLING THE TRUTH?
http://www.theatlantic.com/business/archive/2010/03/the-millionaires-club-increases-its-ranks/37253/?rss=37253

But Then, Who Profited "The Most" From
YOUR MONEY BEING GIVEN AWAY BY OBAMA and THE DEMS?

Pg. 315

*SO MUCH FOR "TRUTH IN ADVERTISING", "TRUTH IN JOURNALISM", "TRUTH IN OUR GOVERNMENT", and FOR "IN TRUTH", IN GENERAL!

THEY'RE PITTING AMERICANs AGAINST AMERICAN WITH "CLASS-WARFARE" AND "CLASS-ENVY", WHILE FILLING THEIR POCKETS, UNDER THE GUISE OF "HELPING THE LITTLE GUY"!.....RIGHT, DNC?....RIGHT BARACK?....crickets...

"GOT MILK"?........HA HA HA HA

YAH, I've "got milk, got gas, got electric, but by "inordinately" expensive pricing, AND plenty of unpaid bills to boot"! My mother used to say: without a pot to....etc. Well, we're all in the same pot now, aren't we! Class-Envy still preoccupying You?

GOT MONEY? - GOT JOBS?? - GOT CONFIDENCE IN WASHINGTON??? ....BUT, IT'S ALWAYS, ALWAYS, ALWAYS "BUSH'S FAULT"?

..................HOW LONG ARE YOU GOING TO ACCEPT THAT, AND LET THEM GET AWAY WITH THEIR LACK OF RESPONSIBILITY, OR FROM THEIR CULPABILITY???...................

I JUST "DON'T REMEMBER BUSH WHINING ABOUT ANYTHING", EXCEPT THE DEM'S RELUCTANCE TO FINANCE HIS EFFORTS TO PROTECT OUR NATION, AND TO AID OUR TROOPS EXPEDITIOUSLY!   It's Tough running a War "on the Cheap" & They ALL knew it!

Oh yah, and for the DEMs "not helping Pres. Bush fix" Social Security, or Healthcare, and stopping HIM from nominating the 1st Hispanic Supreme Court Justice......Actually, I don't remember him whining about that one either. He must have been just doing his job!

Does anyone ever remember any of this stuff, since I rarely, if ever, hear from our "GOP" or the "Republican leadership" reminding anyone, except THE FEW conservative pundits!

SENTRYMAN

==

*A comment by SENTRYMAN to a Patriot, whose Blog analysis I'd posted:

The Patriot stated: ("Don't understand your question, but it looks like B/O is making his buds more and more money!")

OK... I didn't want to make it too easy, but for those I lost with my dry, abstract-quips, my point was;

#1) - there wasn't any "wonderful economy" from Bill Clinton's "surplus" that Bush was touted daily as "having had inherited" for 9 straight years by the DNC, that Bush also "supposedly squandered". It was already headed SOUTH into the Dumper!

#2) - Bush was dealt a major "bad-hand" by The Fates, and He, a Rookie President, not only stepped-up to the plate and also accomplished the impossible on 3 Fronts, (9/11, America's 9/11 shell-shocked economy, and 2 War-theaters), but, He made the "most" Lemon Ade out of a kamikazes' load of lemons, ever since 1941, and then, America began to soar "as illustrated BY THE CHART ABOVE"..........................
GOT THAT?.............Check it out yourself!

It's "quite obviously" demonstrated by the graph! ....(Remember "trickle ! down",
and Free Enterprise raises~all~boat, and We were riding~that~wave till the Demagoguing?

Right~Up until the (all-knowing, all-powerful Titans-of-Totalitarianism) The DEMs,
took-over-total-control of the United States government's "purse-strings" once again!

And once again poised to wreck-havoc on the country's economy, but "for Real Reason":
laying the foundation for their Party's re-taking (of the Presidency) in 2009,
and as always usual, continuing to damage Bush even further & His entire administration,
(i.e. Scooter and Karl, the Judges, Grebe, water~torture, and fired MOLE-Attorneys, and
a full "kitchen sink" of War Crimes, and Ooops, so sorry but, "No Money for: Military units
Armoring-the-Troops, or for better retro-fitting their Humvees"...<u>and whose fault was that?</u>

<u>WHAT?....Are We All Asleep Here?....HELLO?....Wake "the hell up", damn it!</u>

Granted, the Republican's needed and deserved a major comeuppance,
but; Bush, and the nation, with millions of Retirees, and US working men and women with
their 401k's "full of GM stock" <u>ALL LOST EVERYTHING</u>, along with those unnecessarily
unfortunate NEW 6% "unemployed-over-night" Americans, who didn't deserve their rug
pulled-out from under them either: were all (stabbed in the back)! ..Was that Bush or DNC?

Oh that stupid, guileless, dumb nincompoop, who can't talk, or tie his own shoes: Bush?

So then, what were the Genius, Wizards of Smart in the Democrat Congress doing while ol
dumb, stupid Bush single-handedly tore-down in just 1 year, Without the DEM's Necessary
AND Required Authorization, what Bush worked so hard to create for America in 5 years??
And OUR new 6% unemployed Americans are now incredibly blamed on Bush again, too!

BUT, NOT the 535 Legislators with the power of the Congress, the Laws and The PURSE,
NOOOOO! Those newly-unemployed 6% were strangely added to Bush's stellar "<u>40 year</u>
<u>unemployment record LOW</u>",
(including the unavoidable and usual static 4% career unemployed, as well).........WHAT??

#3) - <u>Obama turns around the economy, but ONLY for Millionaires' Reversal-of-Fortunes,</u>

<u>(And again, as illustrated on the chart),</u>

that Barack's own Party so ably prepared America for the DEMOCRAT's Prophet
Coronation by succeeding to "temporarily destroy" and Deep-6 the American
economy, but,
Not for the America's 10%, or 16%, or 40% and 60% respectively, of the
"unemployed" segments of the population in different demographic class and
ethnic groups across our Nation,
nor for that ONLY (flat 10% unemployed-reported), then heralded downed to 9.8%,
with most of us still in the $#!%s after Barack's Mortgaging of the Family Farms,
printing his Funny Money, and Trading his IOUs with Foreign Gangsters with his
"Trickle-Up" economy, THAT WAS JUST FOR Millionaire$ and Billionaire$ ONLY,
..."O" baby, all financed from the real "negative-positioned" trillion-errored
taxpaying "under-water benefactors", the poor schlub American Tax Payers!
Unfortunately, the DEMs did too good a job DEEP-6ing, and the patient drowned!

<u>Trust that clarifies what I was trying to be so glib about, Bud!</u>

SENTRYMAN

Chapter 139

ANOTHER BEACHHEAD TO FAR

Posted by SENTRYMAN on <u>March 14, 2010</u> at 2:45pm

Geez, how many times do we have to go over this?
"Hollywood has been portraying "The Ugly American" for how long now?"

Here was a movie poster of Marlon Brando in "The Ugly American".
Viewable at: <u>http://www.sentryman.org/id8.html</u>

['The Pacific' on HBO: Previewing the WWII Miniseries From the 'Band of Brothers' Team

• March 11, 2010 , By: Gary Susman

Historians like to say that each new war usually finds its generals trying to re-fight the previous war. So it is with Steven Spielberg and Tom Hanks, who are ready to fight World War II one more time in 'The Pacific,' a 10-hour miniseries debuting March 14 on HBO.

"Another difference from the European war: the <u>often racist nature of the propaganda directed against our enemy, something that strikes Hanks as similar to anti-Arab and anti-Muslim sentiment whipped up during the current wars in Afghanistan and Iraq.</u>

"Back in World War II, we viewed the Japanese as 'yellow, slant-eyed dogs' that believed in different gods," he recently told Time<u>. "They were out to kill us because our way of living was different. We, in turn, wanted to annihilate them because they were different. Does that sound familiar, by any chance, to what's going on today?"</u>

Pg. 318

The result is a portrayal of war that's reportedly even more intense and more gruesome than 'Band of Brothers,' with more <u>moral ambiguity in its portrayal of American servicemen and more depiction of atrocities committed by both sides</u>.

At least one WWII veteran, however, praises 'The Pacific' for coming closer to getting the big picture and small details right than any previous screen depiction of the war."]………end

----

Touted as: <u>*"The one war movie that closest comes to the truth of what really happened out there"*</u>

Well, how can there be any "real" truth, or the "one" truth,
when seen through the eyes of millions who lived it, <u>with their own truth</u>?

The reality of life, in general, is that "it's all truth" from a million points of view,
but what our new liberal Progressive, mealy-mouthed, whining, soft'n fuzzy Hollywood micro-managers shaking the bushes (forgive the pun) today,
looking for the answer in pure concentrated "TRUTH" in a bottle,
in order to inoculate themselves from having to make any real life and death decisions, is to assign blame!....

Dealing with the "real bullets" is what the unprofessional "real people" have had to do since the beginning of recorded history. Along with this a self-indulgent, counterproductive useless venture for the "regular folk", all designed to obscure reality, for profit, individual and political agendas.

This is "Real Life" Jack!..
It ain't pretty, and we're all lucky to be here today arguing this minutia, and having the luxury of wasting ones time, when many of the earth inhabitants must fight everyday for their own survival from a variety of nemeses, and even a portion of each day just locating fresh water for their family tonight .

You Guys continue to miss the big picture, again, and again,
Mr. Hanks…….Steven.

IE. *"often racist nature of the propaganda directed against our enemy, something that strikes Hanks as similar to anti-Arab and anti-Muslim sentiment whipped up during the current wars in Afghanistan and Iraq."*

"They were out to kill us because our way of living was different. We, in turn, wanted to annihilate them because they were different. Does that sound familiar, by any chance, to what's going on today?"

"moral ambiguity in its portrayal of American servicemen and more depiction of atrocities committed by both sides."

Wait, Wait Tommy, You almost stumbled on to it….ohhhh, You Missed It!

**BECAUSE:………..…"They were out to kill us"!

There's Your "Lightening in a bottle" moment, boys………….TRUTH!

http://www.amazon.com/gp/product/B000KA21X4?&tag=shopwik i-us-20&linkCode=as2&camp=1789&creative=9325

THIS GREAT MOVIE POSTER OF JOHN WAYNE IN
"THE SANDS OF IWO JIMA"
 ILLUSTRATES EXACTLY WHAT MOTION PICTURE STUDIOS LIKE:
MGM and Republic Pictures and WARNER BROS. Studios

KNEW, ALL TOO WELL IN THE 40s,

AND THEY UNDERSTOOD THAT WE NEEDED TO WIN, AT ALL COSTS,

AND BY ANY MEANS TO PREVAIL, TO LIVE, TO EXIST AS A PEOPLE,

TO REMAIN "THE UNITED STATES of AMERICA"…LAND OF THE FREE!

Here was a great poster of the DUKE charging up the "Sands of IWO" that you can see at http://www.sentryman.org/id8.html

A real (John Wayne - IWO) poster today can fetch ($600.00+) on eBay because it was a depiction of a critical event in American history that could be symbolized at a glimpse, …………………..easily depicted and illustrated by a patriotic Film Industry that understood the score a long, long time ago, in a land far, far away!........$6 bills…So much for a sagging economy?

Great '40s movies used to inspire Americans to courageous feats, and to desire only the valor of VICTORY for their country and families,
and too, unfortunately in a similar way "The Ugly American", and "The China Syndrome", and others not worth mentioning, would uninspired another generation after the 50s, to prefer cynicism and defeatism, toward their own military heroes, to hobble, cripple and castrate its Nation!

AND "THAT", YOU TWO (band of brothers, wannabes), WILL NEVER GET!

FROM ANZIO to IWO, and FROM 9/11, TO BORA BORA and BAGHDAD;

BECAUSE "THEY WANTED TO KILL US"!

Yup, from Gettysburg to China Beach, Kuwait to Somalia, to Kosovo; because "savages were holding lives hostage", and We wanted to HELP others be FREE, always to our own great peril, you two simple fools!

If We as a people, were such racists
then Japan wouldn't be holding your President's government together, boys, and You two Jokers wouldn't be driving Lexus, and NSX down Rodeo Drive,
and We, American Imperialists, wouldn't have stupidly opened our country up to legions of 5th Columnists and 9/11 Terrorists because their skin color, features, and accents would have kept them off the damn planes, idiots!

Such is the price of "FREEDOM" in a democratic open society.

So grow up, and grow a pair, look in the mirror You Ugly Americans, and grab a shovel and a rifle, stack some sand bags and start becoming "Racist Americans", because, when They come for us the next time, and THEY finally get to You TWO, Better Men Will Have Fallen Before Then,

and that guy "wired nine ways" from Sunday,
 ready to explode,
pointing that AK-47 at your head, no matter his ethic heritage,
<u>he doesn't really care who you are Jack</u>.

Rich or poor, Pinko or Greenie,
just as long as You are an American,
he's come here to take your Life, and then blow-up your stuff!

<u>That's Life!………..That's Reality!………….That's TRUTH!</u>

So, keep your powder dry Boys!...

It might get real damp out there after the Global Warming Floods
WATERWORLD.

Glub, glub, glub………Ha ha ha!............. Allahu Akbar

<u>SENTRYMAN</u>

 **Chapter 140**
"Hey America, You are one of my 20" ....

Posted by **SENTRYMAN** on <u>March 28, 2010</u> at 1:06am

<u>Subject:</u>   One if by Land, Two if by Sea, Three if by Email!....

An Email from a friend, pass'n along, not breaking the chain to the 300 Mil

An idea whose time has come!

   For too long we have been too complacent about the workings of Congress. Many citizens had no idea that members of Congress could retire with the same pay after only one term, that they didn't pay into Social Security, that they specifically exempted themselves from many of the laws they have passed (such as being exempt from any fear of prosecution for sexual harassment) while ordinary citizens must live under those laws.

   The latest is to exempt themselves from the Healthcare Reform that is being considered...in all of its forms. Somehow, that doesn't seem logical, equitable or even rational coming from our own employees. In America, We haven't had an elite class that is above the law since We kicked the British Empire out. I truly do not care what banner they fly, if they be Democrat, Republican, Independent or from New Hampshire.

These self-serving elected Public Servant-Representatives must be stopped. This is a good way to do that. It is an idea whose time has come. If each citizen contacted a minimum of Twenty people on their Address list, and in turn Ask Each Of Those To Do Likewise....in just three days, most people in The United States of America will have gotten the message. This is one proposal that everyone should be in favor of and passed along.
<u>Proposed 28th Amendment to the United States Constitution:</u>

"Congress shall make no law that applies to all citizens of the United States of America, that does not apply equally in value, intent and consequence to any and all Senators and/or Representatives, including the Executive, of these United States of America;
and, Congress shall make no law that applies solely to the Senate and/or The House of Representatives and the Executive, that does not apply equally to the citizens of the United States of America". So Help Them God!

DONE- B!.....Thanks, SM

Pg. 323

 # CHAPTER – 141

ONLY "1" WAY LEFT TO SAVE AMERICA BEFORE 2012
Without Getting Arrested, Shot, or Imprisoned For a Lifetime
Of Slavish Capitulation and Serfdom Servitude in a Fiefdom!

~~~ AND IT'S NOT VIOLENT OR COMPLICATED, NOR ILLEGAL! ~~~
Tea Party Patriots. and 9/12'ers, Citizens and Patriots All:

How can You channel Your passions into some kind of meaningful result that can actually be great enough not to be dishonored by Your President, or ignored by His/Your fellow citizens in the MEDIA, ignored by the loyal Opposition from either persuasion, nor abandoned by Your neighbors and friends, or disrespected by even Your own relatives and Your frozen-brain children; all who either don't know, don't want to know, don't care, couldn't care, don't believe it and just want-it to all go away? Including the passive, that just want "to get along", whining: "do we always have to fight"?............Yes, YES We Do!!.........And even dangerously worse, "Those That Really KNOW The SCORE"!

We, the People............YOU FILL IN THE BLANKS FOR YOURSELVES....!
IT IS YOUR COUNTRY!.....IT IS YOUR FUTURE!....YOUR TIME IS NOW!

YOU can "now actually change something for the 1st time", at the right time, at the right place, and for the right reasons to "Save the Republic" from this shadow-government that is finally exposed, Out Into The Light, unafraid as vampires with a SPF-99 Sun Block. We can NOW "identify them all" for the very first time!
VOTE-IN "TERM LIMITS" YOURSELVES & TAKE YOUR COUNTRY BACK!

TAKE-IT-BACK FROM THE PYRATES, SNAKES & VAMPIRES IN BOTH PARTIES;
those in the STATE DEPARTENT = working against Republican presidents,
and in the JUSTICE DEPARTMENT = working against Republican presidents,
in the Department of Energy, TREASURY, HUD, and the DEPT. of EDUCATION;
all working against Republican presidents & not in OUR Children's best interests.

Take-It-Back from the "Department of the Interior" not protecting our sovereignty from the U.N., back from the Department of Veteran Affairs working against our Vets, back from the EPA now becoming the "NEW Enforcement-Arm" within this Shadow-Government.... We are all asleep at the switch!! ...FANNIE & FREDDIE, The FED, The IRS, FDA all complicit with A.C.O.R.N. and the CENSUS BUREAU!

AFTER BLANKET AMNESTY, THE REPUBLIC WILL CEASE TO EXIST = AM3RIKA'

Researchers Find The "Liberal Genes";
http://www.sciencedaily.com/releases/2010/10/101027161452.htm
http://www.nbcsandiego.com/news/weird/Scientists-May-Have-IDd-Liberal-Gene-105917218.html
http://www.foxnews.com/scitech/2010/10/28/researchers-liberal-gene-genetics-politics/

"Give Me Liberty Or Give Me Death!" St. John's Church, Richmond, Virginia 3-23-1775
Pg.324

MR. PRESIDENT: No man thinks more highly than I do of the patriotism.....

It is in vain, sir, to extenuate the matter. Gentlemen may cry, Peace, Peace but there is no peace. The war is actually begun! The next gale that sweeps from the north will bring to our ears the clash of resounding arms! Our brethren are already in the field! Why stand we here idle? What is it that gentlemen wish? What would they have? Is life so dear, or peace so sweet, as to be purchased at the price of chains and slavery? Forbid it, Almighty God! I know not what course others may take; but as for me, give me liberty or give me death!.....*Patrick Henry*

http://history.org/Almanack/life/politics/giveme.cfm

"MAKE MINE FREEDOM" VIDEO,

http://www.youtube.com/watch?v=mVh75ylAUXY&feature=player_embedded#

Our watchdog Media wants us all to ignore, but be very afraid of these fanatical crazy radicals that are endangering our freedoms and Liberty in their desperate attempt to shift America away from its decade's old secular roots, and as one of the largest Muslim nations on earth, we are duly warned!!

Thank you NBC, NY Times and president Obama.

www.youtube.com/watch?v=78GMsv6fKQk&feature=player_embedded

and a humble request: **Please Donate to these important vital charities;**

#1- Children of Fallen Soldiers Relief Fund,
#2- Freedom Alliance,
#3- The Wounded Warrior Project

===

#1   http://www.cfsrf.org/

FREEDOM ALLIANCE By Freedom Alliance Monday, 29 March 2010

"Today, Freedom Alliance was attacked with baseless complaints. There is absolutely no merit to the scurrilous charges launched against Freedom Alliance from two of the most left-wing organizations in the country. "The smear-mongers who have launched this politically motivated witch hunt against Freedom Alliance will be proven wrong as we aggressively defend ourselves in the days and weeks ahead." - Freedom Alliance President, Tom Kilgannon

----

Freedom Alliance "Thanks Sean Hannity" By Freedom Alliance

Monday, 29 March 2010

Forty days ago on his radio show, Sean Hannity discussed his book, Conservative Victory, and announced that he would donate his net proceeds from the book to Freedom Alliance. The donation, he told us, would support Freedom Alliance's Scholarship Fund for the sons and daughters of America's military heroes.

#2   http://www.freedomalliance.org/

#3   http://www.woundedwarriorproject.org/

*Acknowledgment: A Tribute & Dedication to Rush Limbaugh

If You want to be on the "cutting edge of Societal Evolution" each day, just catch a little "Rush" just like 20+ million other fellow Americans over 20 yrs Getting-to-the-Truth "unfiltered", before watching it on their nightly News; misquoted, slanted, misconstrued and propagandized by the Government's Media Wing to fool all those less fortunate Americans that can't listen daily!

Classic Rush Limbaugh aired 2-17-2010, in case You're forced to listen to Air-America and NPR by your Union Bosses on-the-Job!

For Full daily transcripts, Live feeds, Stack of stuff, and 24/7 Library = RushLimbaugh.com

RUSH:

"The Big Lie today is the stimulus worked. They're doubling down on this and the reason why they're doubling down on this is because it's been such an abominable failure. The polling data — we had this yesterday — only 6% of the American people think the stimulus created any new jobs. Therefore, 94% of the American people know it didn't work, so what does Obama do? The only thing he knows how to do is to double down and tell them they're wrong and incorporate the Big Lie. We got some sound bites here from this morning just to illustrate this, blaming Bush, not reading the polls. The American people are not buying any of this. This is part of Obama's new communication strategy: Blame Bush and claim the stimulus saved us from depression. What's new about that? Not one thing. It is the same lie, it is the same strategery continued."

OBAMA: "—if dramatic action was not taken to break the back of the recession, the United States could spiral into another depression. That was the backdrop against which I signed the American Recovery and Reinvestment Act."

RUSH: "Yeah."

OBAMA: "And one year later, it is largely thanks to the Recovery Act –"

RUSH: "Yeah."

OBAMA: "—that a second depression is no longer a possibility."

RUSH: "Meanwhile, homelessness is at an all-time high, we have that story, amazingly, in TIME Magazine, and we also, ladies and gentlemen, have the news now that Terry Jeffrey, Human Events, has run the numbers, Obama has spent more than FDR did on the New Deal and of course there's nothing to show for it, zilch, zero, nada, this is the Big Lie. Now, I don't know whether this next is Obama continuing to display his ignorance of economics or if it's just his obstinate stubbornness."

OBAMA: "During a recession when businesses pull back and people stop spending, what government can do is provide a temporary boost that puts money in people's pockets –"

RUSH: "Didn't do that, though."

OBAMA: "—keeps workers on the job –"

RUSH: "Didn't do that."

OBAMA: "—cuts taxes for small business –"

RUSH: "Didn't do that."

OBAMA: "—generates more demand –"

RUSH: "Didn't do that."

OBAMA: "—gives confidence to entrepreneurs that maybe they don't have to cut back right now."

RUSH: "None of that happened! Zilch, zero, nada. Be cool, Rush, be calm. This is nothing new. You've heard it all before. It's the Big Lie. None of that happened. Now, Obama continuing the Big Lie tells you stupid idiots that he cut your taxes next."

RUSH: "There were no tax cuts. There was a one-time tax credit. There were no tax cuts and there aren't going to be any tax cuts as long as this guy is running the show. Nothing but tax increases are heading down the pike. Let's go back to bashing Bush and let's call it The Lost Decade, you keep in mind now the Bush decade showed almost no unemployment. It was at 4.7% starting in 2003 after the recovery from 9/11 began."

"Do you hear this? "Over the past year alone, the amount the US government owes its lenders has grown to more than half the country's entire economic output, or gross domestic product." Past year, ABC? You slipped up here. I thought Obama inherited this from George W. Bush. "Even more alarming, experts say, is that those figures will climb to an unprecedented 200 percent of GDP by 2038 without a dramatic shift in course." Can I translate that for you? We are busted, and your kids and grandkids are screwed, thanks to one man and his party: Barack Hussein Obama and the Democrats. Your kids and grandkids are busted and screwed -- and it's not because of George W. Bush, it's not because of Republicans, it's not because of "the lack of bipartisanship," and it's not because of the "dysfunctional" Washington. It's because of this plan."

RUSH: "Let me read you one more sentence here from this ABCnews.com story, Drowning in Debt, what the nation's budget woes mean for you. Listen to this one sentence: "The government's ability to cut taxes or provide a safety net would also be weakened, economists say." Now, this is strictly inside the Beltway Democrat liberal groupthink. John F. Kennedy -- I know you're tired of hearing me say this -- John F. Kennedy and Ronald Reagan showed that you must cut taxes to increase revenues to the Treasury, because cutting taxes will lead to new jobs. Folks, this administration does not want new unemployment while they tell you that they do. When Obama goes out there and says businesses are responsible for growth, which he did today, you need to ask yourself, then what the hell are you doing starving them? What the hell are you doing punishing them? Why don't you incentivize them? Why don't you get out of their way?"

"The Big Lie continues to roll off of his fluent tongue as well as anybody has ever told a Big Lie. You cut taxes to increase revenues and grow your way out of a deficit. Reagan's tax cuts doubled the revenues to Washington in eight years, $500 billion. When he took office in 1981, there were $500 billion coming into Washington. When he left office, close to a trillion, cutting taxes from 70% down to 28%, 31% for some. That's all that's needed here. Why the hell is this so hard, and why the hell do we need a commission? We don't need a commission. The purpose of the commission is to give cover to the Democrats. Erskine Bowles, when are you going to realize you're being used here, sir, and you're being made a fool of? The Clintons made a fool of "Irksome" Bowles. And Alan Simpson, come on. Both you guys ought to tell these guys to stuff it."

"Now, I want to go back and play for you something that we did last week. This is a little two minute, 15 second segment from the movie Back to School. Rodney Dangerfield is the star of the movie and he is the owner of a Tall and Fat clothing chain all over the country. His son and he are estranged, the son's going to college, Rodney Dangerfield never graduated college, decides to go back to school with his son to establish the relationship, get his degree and ends up in an economics course with an Obama type professor, an arrogant, conceited snob who has no understanding of what really happens in the business world."

Rodney Dangerfield's First Economics Class
http://www.youtube.com/watch?v=YlVDGmjz7eM

RUSH: "That's Rodney Dangerfield with Back to School. And that's the reality of what we face out there up against Obama, the arrogant, impudent snob who thinks he has all the answers. Let's go back to the audio sound bites. This is number 10 and 11. We played this for you last year, October 22nd, 2009. It's on Capitol Hill before the joint economic committee, the Council of Economic Advisors Chair Christina Romer testified about the economy and the slush fund, the stimulus, and this is what she said."

ROMER: "The fiscal stimulus will have its greatest impact on growth in the second and third quarters of 2009 and by mid-2010 fiscal stimulus will likely be contributing little to further growth."

RUSH: "That was a little distorted so let me translate for you what the woman said. "The fiscal stimulus will have its greatest impact on growth in the second and third quarters of 2009 and by mid-2010 fiscal stimulus will likely be contributing little to further growth." So they basically said the big bang for the buck was 2009, anything after that, it's over."

She's changed her tune today, Good Morning America today, the co-host George "Stephy" Stephanopoulos talked to Christina Romer. "With unemployment still about 10%, is the biggest bang from the stimulus behind us?" He didn't add this but I'm going to add, "like you said last October."

ROMER: "Absolutely not. Certainly in terms of the level of the things we care about like employment and the unemployment rate, those effects are going to grow over time."

RUSH: "The Big Lie continued. She stepped in it back in October. Somebody came in and got her mind right and so now she's part of the Big Lie as well."

RUSH: "If the stimulus is working, as Obama said today, and if jobs are being created out there, wouldn't the world believe that our deficit would be going down? Well, the world doesn't seem that. A shocked AP: "The government said Tuesday foreign demand for US Treasury securities fell by the largest amount on record in December with the [ChiComs] reducing its holdings by $34.2 billion." They're dumping our T-bills out there! Japan now the largest holder because of the ChiCom dump. This would not be happening if our stimulus was working and jobs are being created and the deficit was coming down. The Big Lie. Barack Hussein Obama."

END TRANSCRIPT

Read the Background Material...
• ABC: Drowning in Debt: What the Nation's Budget Woes Mean for You
• ABC: Economists Predict Cutbacks, Tax Increases That 'Aren't Even Imaginable'
• Gateway Pundit: FAIL Just 6% of Americans Believe Obama's $787 Billion Stimulus Created Jobs

• Politico: Bayh: Congress Has Created No Jobs
• CNS News: Obama Defeats FDR (in Spending Other People's Money)
• AP: Suburban Homeless: Rising Tide of Women, Families
• Reuters: On Anniversary, Obama Defends Economic Stimulus
• The Hill: Dems try to Avoid Overselling Jobs Bill
• Republican.Senate.gov: One Year Of Spending Taxpayer Dollars Studying Malt Liquor And Marijuana, Researching Drunk Mice, Funding Martini Bars And Steakhouses, And Examining Facebook

RUSH: "The Obama administration is one gigantic, Big Lie. The Democrat Party is one gigantic, Big Lie. From the Richmond Times-Dispatch: "Virginia Attorney General Ken Cuccinelli turned up the heat on global warming yesterday. On behalf of the state, Cuccinelli filed a petition asking the federal Environmental Protection Agency to reconsider its December finding that global warming poses a threat to people.""

RUSH: "Big Lie continues. Dr. Jones, University of East Anglia has admitted there hasn't been any warming since 1995. All of his data he "lost." It's a hoax. The e-mails from the university prove it's a hoax. Responsible people, smart people are backing away from this now. But it's government people, politicians, who will be the last to give this up because it's a political thing. They wail and they moan about everything being politicized. They're the ones that are politicizing even the weather! She says forget the evidence. Forget the evidence. Global warming is happening. A reporter, Karen Schuberg, from the Cybercast News Service. I'm wondering your opinion on what climate change expert Phil Jones, former head of the Climate Research Unit at the University of East Anglia when he told the BBC last weekend he agreed with the statement that from 1995 to the present there has been no significant statistical global warming. I'm wondering do you agree with Dr. Jones there has been no statistically significant global warming since 1995?"

RUSH: "The Big Lie. Jane Lubchenco of the National Oceanic and Atmospheric Administration, the Obama administration. Not only did Phil Jones say there hadn't been any warming between '95 and the present. He also pointed out that the hockey stick graph (of this fraud scientist from Penn State, Michael Mann) was also wrong, that there was medieval warming, much warmer than it is today. The whole thing's a hoax, folks, but they're not going to give it up. Because it's not about global warming, and it's not about "saving the planet." It's because advancing socialism, Marxism, whatever you want to call it; expanding government and taking away people's freedom and liberty and raising their taxes and making you feel guilty and responsible for all of this destruction that has taken place."

END TRANSCRIPT

Read the Background Material...

• Climate Depot: Continuously Updated 'ClimateGate' News Round Up
• UK Daily Mail: Climategate U-turn as Scientist at Centre of Row Admits:
There has Been No Global Warming Since 1995

• Wall Street Journal: The Continuing Climate Meltdown
• American Thinker: Evidence of Climate Fraud Grows, Media Coverage Doesn't
• Richmond Times Dispatch: Va. Challenges EPA's Stance on Global Warming
• American Spectator: The Disappearing Science of Global Warming

Classic Rush Limbaugh in case You missed it on 2-18-2010

"The comedy continues. I'm watching this morning, there's Obama, he's got "Plugs" Biden with the carbon no longer on his forehead today, and he's got "Irksome" Bowles up there from the University of North Carolina and Alan Simpson, and we're going to have a blue ribbon deficit commission. What is the liberals' answer to out of control government spending? You create more government to study it! There's not a person who is engaged in this in the world who doesn't know why this has happened. It's called Barack Hussein Obama Barry Soetoro. Who spent us into this state of ruin in one year? Barack Hussein Obama. And now he's calling in these two retreads with 18 other people or 16 other people to study this? Here. Listen to it and laugh. This is Obama announcing all this."

OBAMA: "Alan Simpson and Erskine Bowles are taking on the impossible. They're going to try to restore reason to the fiscal debate and come up with answers as co-chairs of the new National Commission on Fiscal Responsibility and Reform. I'm asking them to produce clear recommendations on how to cover the costs of all federal programs by 2015 and to meaningfully improve our long-term fiscal picture."

RUSH: "Why are these guys even accepting the gig? What's in it for "Irksome" Bowles and Alan Simpson to accept the gig? Because if they're going to approach this honestly they can produce their report today, and it would say: "Mr. President, either resign or put somebody else in charge of spending because you are bankrupting and destroying the country. We've studied it here for the past year, and there's nothing that can be done to fix this if you don't change, and if you don't change then you're going to have to for the good of the country resign." We don't need study it. Nobody needs to study this! What we need to do is change it. Here's Obama, who is on track, if he hasn't already, he's on track to spend more than anyone since FDR, now tells us this."

RUSH: "Which means there's going to be no end in sight to the spending no matter what "Irksome" Bowles and Alan Simpson and their 16 other worthless blue-ribbon panel people -- What in the world is the president for? What is Congress for? What are all these czars for? Why do they have to go out and get these two guys and 16 other people to absolve everybody of responsibility, everybody that is culpable in this is to be absolved of responsibility. I can't wait, I really can't wait 'cause I bet you I can predict what the outcome of this blue-ribbon panel is going to be. These people are going to fix it so that there is going to be a quiet revolution in November and virtually anybody that reminds the voters of this country of anybody in the past year and a half is gone, never to get back to Washington ever again."

END TRANSCRIPT

Read the Background Material...

- AP: Jobless Claims Rise Unexpectedly
- Reuters: U.S. Jobless, Price Data Fan Concerns on Economy
- AP: January Wholesale Prices Jump 1.4 Percent
- CNBC: Jobless Claims, Inflation Jump as Economy Wobbles
- AP: Leading Indicators Rise 0.3 pct in January
- Wall Street Journal: It's the Spending, America

http://www.rushlimbaugh.com/home/today.guest.html

EIB...Rush Limbaugh

Stack of Stuff Quick Hits Page

April 1, 2010

Story #6: Obama to Crush Economy with Massive CO2 Taxes

RUSH: This first story -- now, keep in mind, this is April 1st, but this is Canada Free Press. "Obama to Crush Economy with Massive CO2 Taxes as Early as Next Week." Why do you shake your head? "Abandoning all loyalty to the democratic processes this nation holds dear, President Obama has made the decision that getting energy tax legislation through Congress with the approval of the American people is just too much of a pain to bother with. Instead he will have the EPA declare as early as next week that CO2 is a dangerous global warming gas and will start regulating its emissions immediately." Now, the Supreme Court has given the EPA the legal right to do this.

"Obama's promise to open up vast stretches of ocean on the East Coast and Gulf of Mexico to energy exploration is simply a ruse to soften up the public for soon to be announced draconian regulations. Similar to how Obama used the $50 million dollar study on healthcare companies competing across state lines to sell Obamacare as a bipartisan bill, his recent decree allowing energy companies to explore (not drill, not produce energy from … just explore) new stretches of ocean for oil is also meant to be a trivial, yet impressive enough sounding carrot for conservatives right before he stuffs his Marxist trash down their throats." This obviously is an opinion piece. If this were an American publication, of course it would be standard news. "Every American who doesn't live in a technology adverse commune in California will now pay even more of their hard earned cash to the federal government for absolutely no good reason."

So that's one story, that basically cap and tax is going to be announced next week, and we have heard that they were considering doing this because the votes are not there in Congress for it.

RUSH LIMBAUGH_____

"CANADA FREE PRESS"
Environmental Protection Agency (EPA) is plotting a new massive job-killer that the American people can't afford
Obama to Crush Economy with Massive CO2 Taxes as Early as Next Week
 …..*By Fred Dardick* - Thursday, April 1, 2010

http://www.canadafreepress.com/index.php/article/21566

Story #7: Bailout: Look for Union Agenda, and Get Ready to Pay

RUSH: From Mark Hemingway, the Washington Examiner: "Anybody who thinks the multiple trillions of federal tax dollars spent by President Obama and the Democratic Congress on the Troubled Assets Relief Program bailouts for Wall Street and the auto industry, the economic stimulus bill, and Obamacare were excessive better get a good grip. The mother of all taxpayer bailouts is right around the corner. Union bosses want taxpayers to foot the cost for bailing out the labor organizations' many failing pension plans that millions of their members are counting on to 'be there' when they retire. Unfortunately, the average union pension plan has only enough money to cover 62 percent of its financial obligations. Such a low level of funding puts those plans on the government's critical list. Pension plans funded below 80 percent are considered 'endangered' by the government. Below 65 percent is 'critical.'" And we're talking about union plans that now only cover 62%.

"With union membership declining, that puts these funds into a tailspin from which they'll likely never pull out. The government's Pension Benefit Guaranty Corporation only guarantees pensioners $12,000 a year. ... Concern over underfunded pensions is the real reason behind nearly every legislative item for which unions are currently agitating. One of the top union priorities is 'card check' legislation that would eliminate secret ballots in workplace. ... No wonder the unionized United Parcel Service recently shelled out a whopping $6.1 billion to get out of the multiemployer pension plan in which it was formally enrolled. Prior to UPS shelling out the money, the company's pension liabilities were estimated to be in the neighborhood of $4 billion, but turned out to be much higher. That's because unions are trying to hide the severity of the problem from their own workers. The union officers know this. ... And after $400 million in campaign donations in 2008, if unions want a bailout -- it's going to be hard for Democrats to say no." And particularly hard for Obama to say no.

If you are willing to throw away a trillion dollars and lie about its purpose, if you're willing to make up a bunch of horrific reasons, most of which were not true to justify TARP and then change the rules and the purpose after the money's been allocated, if you are willing to bail out General Motors and Chrysler and then take ownership of them and transfer majority ownership in one case to the unions, is it really hard to believe that Obama, who cares nothing about spending money or printing it, or taxing it, is it hard to believe that he would bail out these underfunded union pensions? It's not hard to believe it at all. So there's just two stories, cap and tax by executive order next week, and sweeping bailout for union pensions essentially right around the corner.

Now, if you still don't believe me about this bailing out of the union pension plans, what do you think the bailout of General Motors and Chrysler were all about from TARP money? It was about bailing out the unions. It was about saving union jobs in case those companies had to declare bankruptcy.

So pension plans, underfunded pension plans, the UAW via the Chrysler and General Motors bailout, had their pension plans totally bailed out and their retirement benefits totally bailed out. You know who got screwed? Let's not forget, the bondholders, the people who Obama said were being unreasonable. They wanted their full investment back, and they were told to go pound sand. So, $108 billion for UAW health benefits is in the Senate version of the final health care bill. It is in there, page 48. You will see it.

And they just keep coming at us. **THE WASHINGTON EXAMINER**
"Mark Hemingway: Look for the union agenda, and get ready to pay"

By: Mark Hemingway Commentary Staff Writer - April 1, 2010
http://www.highbeam.com/doc/1P2-21475198.html

http://3gn.ar15.com/archive/topic.html?b=1&f=5&t=1022441

http://www.rushlimbaugh.com/home/today.guest.html

Thank You Rush!....Thank You For Being There At The Right Time In History, and Thank You For Voicing;
 "What We Already Think", What We All Know, and What We've All Felt, because We Have No Other Way To Express To Our Relatives, Who Won't Listen and To Our Friends, Who Won't Hear!

A Man For His Times.......A Man For All Seasons.......A Man, Just In The Nick!

QUOTES and DICTIONARY

"I tell ye true, liberty is the best of all things; never live beneath the noose of a servile halter." .<u>William Wallace, Address to the Scots, circa 1300</u>

"In the beginning of a change, the patriot is a scarce man brave, hated, and scorned. When his cause succeeds, however, the timid join him, for then it costs nothing to be a patriot." ......<u>Mark Twain</u>

"WE WHINE AND WORRY - THE DEVIL IN THE DETAILS - HIP DEEP IN OBAMACARE MINUTIA ...A RUSE, LITTLE TO DO WITH HEALTH CARE, WATCH THE OTHER HAND: THE CARROT!.............................A SNARE!" ....<u>SENTRYMAN</u>

<u>Main Entry:</u>	"ruse"
Part of Speech:	*noun*
<u>Definition:</u>	trick, deception
Synonyms:	<u>angle</u>, <u>artifice</u>, <u>blind</u>, booby trap, curveball, <u>deceit</u>, <u>device</u>, <u>dodge</u>, <u>feint</u>, <u>gambit</u>, <u>game</u>, game plan, gimmick, <u>hoax</u>, imposture, jig, <u>maneuver</u>, <u>ploy</u>, <u>scenario</u>, <u>sham</u>, <u>shenanigans</u>*, <u>shift</u>, <u>stratagem</u>, stunt, <u>subterfuge</u>, <u>switch</u>*, <u>twist</u>*, wile

----

<u>Main Entry:</u>	"snare"
Part of Speech:	*noun*
<u>Definition:</u>	trap
Synonyms:	allurement, <u>bait</u>, booby trap, <u>catch</u>, come-on, <u>deception</u>, decoy, enticement, entrapment, inveiglement, <u>lure</u>, <u>net</u>, noose, pitfall, quicksand, seducement, <u>temptation</u>, <u>trick</u>, wire
Antonyms:	<u>freedom</u>, <u>liberation</u>

<u>Remember this QUOTE?</u>

It's why teachers "ONLY" teach "their" American History to their students!
"the KKK was essentially the "terrorist arm" of the Democrat Party"
<u>Rush Limbaugh 4-5-2010</u>

HEADS-UP: Tea Party, Who they are really.

April 5, 2010

(portions of transcript text from EIB, dealing with the "previous" quote;)

"RUSH: Does anybody know what the tea party actually stands for? What does t-e-a stand for?

Nevertheless, as you well know, the State-Controlled Media and the Obama regime and the Democrat Party are doing everything they can to discredit and to marginalize members of the tea party. They are casting them as racists, old, angry white guys, a bunch of sexists, largely Southerners, they shout the N-word, they shout homosexual epithets at Barney Frank and so forth, when none of this happens, nobody can document that it happened. And all of these Congressional Black Caucus members, as we now know, were deliberately trying to provoke an incident on Obamacare Sunday by walking through the crowd, which was totally unnecessary.

These are sexists, by the way, who happen to love Sarah Palin, for example. These are racists, by the way, who happen to love and respect Shelby Steele and Clarence Thomas and Thomas Sowell.

Regimes don't put up with being protested. And regimes target average citizens. Presidents do not. Regimes do. Regimes lead the targeting of average citizens. So I have three polls here today on just who the tea party people are.

Hotline National Journal: "The Winston Group conducted 3 national surveys over the winter -- one in each Dec., Jan. and Feb. -- to find out who Tea Party members are and what drives them. Over the course of the surveys, they found that more than half (58%) identified themselves as GOPers, with 28% claiming to be Indies and 13% DEMs.
But 65% identified themselves as conservatives, while 26% said they were moderates.

Tea Partiers also skewed older and male. Of those associated with the Tea Party, 56% were male, compared to 48% of the electorate as a whole. Just 14% were between the ages of 18-34, while 20% of all voters are under 35."
Tea Partiers are quite representative of the public at large." That is from Gallup.

We go to another poll reported at TheHill.com. "Four in ten tea party members are Democrats, or independents."

but the Representative Steve Cohen, a Democrat from Tennessee, was the guest. And here was the question: "The pervasive feeling in Washington right now, all this vitriol, all this hate, what's being done in America about all this now? What about the tea party?"

COHEN: "Tea party people are kind of like without robes and hoods"

All the KKK, the vast majority of them were southern Democrats. It's amazing how history has done a complete 180 on all of this. These tea party people are nothing like the KKK. They are not racists or bigoted, they're not homophobes, they're none of these things.

Most of the KKK were radical Democrats, such as Robert "Sheets" Byrd, such as Bull Connor, all of the old segregationists were Democrats.

The original targets of the KKK were Republicans or blacks who might vote for them (the republicans). The KKK was in solidarity with Democrats because the Democrats were the segregationists. J. William Fulbright, Senator from Arkansas, Bill Clinton's mentor, he says, segregationist. The history revision on this is pretty amazing.   Pg. 335

These Tea Party people understand full well that what this regime wants is a permanent underclass that has no upward mobility, and the best way to get that is to pass a monstrous health care bill with massive taxes on everybody and high unemployment. If you don't have a job your mobility is nowhere, other than downward. The Democrats need a permanent underclass, dependent on them for their power and their election, and that's what health care is all about. That's what most of the regime's agenda is all about.

Remember, the KKK was made up of Democrats. It was founded to be the domestic terrorist arm of the Democrat Party. Their original targets were Republicans or blacks who might vote for them, and of course blacks in general. Never forget that.
You think I invented that? I didn't. PBS. Let me read to you from PBS. They grudgingly acknowledged it on a show they did called: "The Rise and Fall of Jim Crow.
Dressed in robes and sheets, intended to prevent identification by the occupying federal troops and supposedly designed to frighten blacks, the Klan quickly became a terrorist organization in service of the Democrat Party and white supremacy.
Between 1869 and 1871, its goal was to destroy congressional reconstruction by murdering blacks and some whites who were either active in Republican politics or educating black children." PBS.
KKK became a terrorist organization in service of the Democrat Party.
Oh, and how about this? Obama announces that we're going to unilaterally get rid of one-third of our nukes? And the next thing we know there's Vladimir Putin down in Caracas meeting with Chavez to help him get nuclear power and selling him combat weapons."
Rush Limbaugh
www.rushlimbaugh.com/home/daily/site_040510/content/01125112.guest.html

(for complete transcript go to www.rushlimbaugh.com , 24/7)
-- ---
A WARNING: This is critically important information people, so take it very seriously, and listen to RUSH everyday to get the news deciphered before the government Media skews and censors it, to spoon-feed YOU every night......
First Carter lets a fanatic Student Leader make him the Goat!...Then Clinton lets the first Somalia Pyrates make him the Goat also, then Clinton gives the CHINESE military "missile technology" so they can fly straight to LA. Then Clinton gives Korea "nuclear technology" (who crossed their hearts & gave the finger: "It'll only be used for peace", Only For Peace) Then Clinton Blocks the FBI and CIA sharing any information!........But, Saddam Hussein crosses a border and Bush whacks-him!....yeah!......Then Saddam Hussein just whispers "Dirty Bombs at Bargain Prices" & Bush whacks-him! ...yeah!....So, what's your problem?

But, GUESS WHO'S NOT BEING STOPPED FROM DEVELOPING THE NEXT "HOLOCAUST HARDWARE" IN IRAN, WHO WE WERE ALL PROMISED A YEAR AGO WOULD NEVER GET TO THIS POINT?? ......DO THE WORDS: "16 SANCTIONs" SOUND AT ALL FAMILIAR??

AND WHO'S GOING TO BE THE "GOAT" ONCE AGAIN, AND BY THIS SAME GUYS?......
HELLO!....DOES ANYONE SEE A "YELLOW STAIN" GROWING LIKE A CANCER HERE??
At least FDR, Truman, JFK and LBJ all fought-back for their country, and their people; but since then, "Socialism has raised its ugly head" once again, and now openly reigns!

Good thing "Dear Jane" wasn't skulking around FDR in the '40s or We'd all be speaking German or Japanese, instead of Spanish and Farsi!

IS ANYONE PAYING ANY ATTENTION TO ANYTHING MORE VITAL AND MONUMENTAL THAN THE PERSONAL LIVES OF "AMERICAN" GOLFERS?....THAT'S ANOTHER REASON WHY WE'RE ALL HERE RIGHT NOW and WITH "PUTIN DOWN IN CARACAS"!

HELLO; Are We All Just Saps, Just Asleep, Just Stupid, Traitors, or all 4?......SENTRYMAN

A Look-Back at a HERO…… Wisdom Forgotten Or Ignored!!

Make some room on Mount Rushmore!

Ronald Reagan quotes Norman Thomas, 1961.
www.youtube.com/watch?v=AYrlDlrLDSQ&feature=player_embedded#

—"The American people will never knowingly adopt Socialism. But under the name of 'liberalism' they will adopt every fragment of the Socialist program, until one day America will be a Socialist nation, without knowing how it happened."

www.youtube.com/watch?v=AYrlDlrLDSQ

www.snopes.com/politics/quotes/socialism.asp

A TRIBUTE to Ronald Reagan
www.youtube.com/watch?v=h8_G-mlKxTY&feature=fvw

The liberties of our country, the freedom of our civil constitution are worth defending at all hazards; and it is our duty to defend them against all attacks. We have received them as a fair inheritance from our worthy ancestors: they purchased them for us with toil and danger and expense of treasure and blood, and transmitted them to us with care and diligence.
It will bring an everlasting mark of infamy on the present generation, enlightened as it is, if we should suffer them to be wrested from us by violence without a struggle, or be cheated out of them by the artifices of false and designing men.

~ Samuel Adams (1722 - 1803)

"Government is not a solution to our problem, government is the problem."
by Ronald Reagan.

http://www.youtube.com/watch?v=XObcP69dhCg&feature=related

mea culpa

Ever say something to your spouse, or your kids, or your mother-in-law, or your Boss, or anyone today for that matter, and before You can finish your sentence THEY respond with: "NO"!.........?

<u>"Everything expressed in this book is ONLY- My Opinion."</u>
I have not personally met any of the individuals discussed here-in, and information learned and assimilated has been chronicled "second-hand " from Barber Shoppe to Internet, from Radio, and by Book, by LIVE broadcast TV Hook, & Print Media Propagandist Crook, and by Teachers, inside and out of the classroom,

(of which, I had some fine ones long, long ago, and I didn't even know how "They" <u>personally felt</u> about the subject matter taught. Each professionally Objective, and Honest to their Calling). It's ostensibly "really all the same thing" since, isn't it.

Gathered around the fire, Communication; from the cave paintings in Lascaux, France, to the Dead Sea Scrolls, Egyptian Hieroglyph, the Dominican Friars held The Bible's Hebrew, Greek and Roman transcriptions too close to their vest, and with the histories of China and India, to the ascension of Incan, Mayan and Aztec Temple to Sun Gods, it's calculated conjecture "Hear-Say" today. All subject to politic, priority and interpretation; suspect and tainted by time and mortal vanity!

As for the current topics for discussion, Our Forbearers, Forefathers, Titans and Champions of The New World, as seen thru Liberal Progressive Socialist GREEN Eyes, <u>these brave men of resolve</u>, are minimalized, marginalized, and "rightfully" diminished in stature?? Their importance and accomplishments reinterpreted and redefined with fresh eyes, skewed for children's consumption to fit "The Agenda", so now a "Founder is but a Racist" and old Honest Abe: a depressed homosexual! SO WHAT!!.....NO REALLY, SO FREAK'N WHAT?.....WAS ANYONE THERE, DUDE?

<u>Why Does Lib's Constant Character Assassinations Always Nullify: Truth?</u>

In this The New GREEN Reality "this caliber" of committed fanaticism in "Protecting Their Agenda" hasn't been witnessed since the 1930s and '40s in Germany, Japan and Italy, when they (not only "Killed The Messenger"),
They Destroyed the "Sender", and Crushed the "Recipients"!......
Not since "one ascending Pharaoh" totally obliterated all evidence to completely erase the existence of his former Pharaoh, has this technique been so blatantly employed, and on unabashed-full-display, with approval and full compliance of the <u>once honorable 4th estate</u>!

With Family, Heritage, Tradition, and Country All In Jeopardy Now, For Every American, Any Republican Presidential Achievement's Denied, Any Patriotic Tea Party Endeavor, and All Conservative Mores Are Caricatured, Ridiculed and Humiliated........And By Whom; Endowed By Their Own Ego, The Superior, Scurrilous, Decadent Effete Elitists: <u>LIBERALS!</u>

SO WHAT??......But why does matter?..... ahhhhh Yes;

<u>To the Victors Go The History Books......Rewritten, To Protect The Agenda!</u>

Pg. 338

Ever see the old movie: "Fahrenheit 451"?

With books soon to become obsolete today, relegated to Cyberspace Archives, and our "World Government" in-controls on the (Light Switch for The Internet), TRUST ME, in just a mere TWO generations "KNOWLEDGE and TRUTH" will once again be in short supply with ONLY a CLICK: hyphen, comma, edit and DELETE! Revisited by A New "Darker Ages", becoming the legacy of any Keepers-Of-The-Flame <u>to keep Truth uncontaminated</u>.

Perhaps, in the 22nd Century, "Truth" will be more valuable than Sunscreen, or Gold, or a breath of Pure-Air, or, a safe drink of Water! <u>Truth is precious</u>!

Am I An Alarmist?......You Think Me Crazy?......Over The Top??......A Little Bonkers? Eh? How long did it take Nintendo and Grand-Theft-Auto to replace "going outside to play Baseball"?.....Now half of our kids are overweight, vain, or underweight with sore throats. How many kids even own a Ball Mitt? But, I'll bet they've got the newest Universal remote wireless video game Controller, and Designer Sneakers, they don't want to get dirty!....

It's not up to "The Food Police", there's nothing wrong with McDonald's occasionally!... These Blobs won't get off their lazy butts to go have some fun out in the sun and work up a sweat, but, Oooo: Take Your Sunscreen and Don't Get Hurt!..Ohh pleassse, shuttt-uppp! Go run, and laugh, and play, build a Tree House and skin your knees!...But I digress!

Knowledge gained from One's Own LIFE Experiences and from "Moms who are never wrong", are timeless and unalterable. <u>Of ONLY THAT, I am Truly Confident</u>!

But here again, as a byproduct of the old Public School System, though "Private Education" at 5xs-the-price for some institutions, or, at 2xs-the-price for a "Parochial Education" (a far better value with GOD thrown-in for sanity) Discipline is pretty-well dominated by the same ilk, and ideological mindset today, so getting Your money's worth can be a challenge in our brave new world, where there is <u>No longer</u> "Fact"..........<u>No</u> "Absolutes"..........<u>No</u> "Right or Wrong",

<u>No "Black or White", with "Everything" Challenged! ....IT IS "ALL OPINION"</u>!

An Entire Nation Brought To Its Knees, Choked-On One's Own Fears, All Based On Rumor, Hear-Say; A Perspective, A Feeling, An Ideology! This "Fragile Society" No Stronger Than Its "Weakest" Student. <u>Life "On A Curve"</u>!

<u>Leveraged By Gamblers On Wall Street, Their Very Own "China Syndrome"</u>

And what is most intellectually and intriguingly paradoxical, but also the most alarming and disturbing feature about it, is that when ["<u>GOD</u>"] has finally been mandatorily-stripped from everyone's lives and psyche by an Imperial Edict, much like a State's sanctioned removal of that "Unborn" appendage, and "The Deity", all but a distant memory upon this infinitesimal spinning-ball, in the back-waters of infinite black-space, with the "absence of FAITH" replaced by the great dark VOID, The Hubris Of Man,

<u>WHO'S TO KNOW ANYTHING, OR BELIEVE IN ANYONE WITHOUT THE GUN</u>

<u>TO YOUR HEAD? .....THEN, MANY GODS WILL ABOUND</u>!

This morning on FOX News of course, since no other NEWS Network will broach anything of real gravity on ABCCBSNBCCNBCMSNBCPBSROSECNNKING, aside from Tiger's swing-ing, like: "Total World Annihilation" by some little smart-ass, or blaming Bush entirely for a few board, sophomoronic idiots at Abu Grebe, who themselves needed a good spanking. But then the ACLU would switch gears and "condemn the Violence" against our own for using a hand, or mother's hair brush, as though the CEO of GE is responsible for something (so far down the chain of command), like selling "Parts to a U.S. enemy" to blow-up our soldiers, but hey! Who was keeping track of anything else besides what BUSH ate for breakfast??? I'm just say'n!

So anyway, Karl Rove is being interviewed, and asked a series of questions dealing with the Obama Administration's handling of "pending Nukes" in Iran, how to stop them, sanctions, the lack of help from China and Russia (what's new), and what's with Pres. Obama's "negotiating-away" the U.S.'s stock-piles of defensive Nuclear Weapons, and "in return For What"?........yadda – yadda

All while the Usual Suspects are "building-up their own Nuclear stockpiles" in order to be the new "Tough Guys" on the block, and Black-Mail their neighbors, but, of much greater urgency is Iran's repeated threats to:
"REMOVE ^ISRAEL ^FROM ^THE ^FACE ^OF ^THE ^EARTH", as they've repeatedly "sworn to do" for years now.
And You know when an radical-Muslim swears, You don't bet with This-House! (i.e. Korea, who wasn't supposed to have any NUKES in the first place, if ever & Thank You Bill Clinton, traitor or moron?)

The much more vital question in the 21st Century <u>is thrown to Karl</u>, an ex- gov't. employee, (instead of the Administration), who responds with the rhetorical retort: "What did "We" get out of all this?" (And by "WE", I'd assume he meant: the American People footing all the bills and paying the salaries for these idiots!)

<u>My Question To Him Would Be:</u> "Why must it be left to an Ex-Government official to "Answer that Life & Death question", on behalf of everyone in America?" …..And again, this same man has to be "the ONLY one to ask" the Most Important Question Of Our Age, Since Adolf Hitler Failed At What Iran Is NOW Emboldened To Finish, (aaaaannnndddd Thaaaaank Yooouuuu Barack Hussein), and "<u>that Question is never being asked</u>" by OUR OWN (41 and 178) respective, (PAID for ?) U.S. Representatives, or the condescending and ignoring U.S. Media! Or at least asked as few times (laugh) as we have heard: "Bush Lied", which would equal-out to "at least once every single day" for 8 straight years: <u>"What Did "We Get" out of all this "peace-in-our-time" capitulation Baracster?"</u>

<u>Mr. Rove aptly makes my point again, and again, and again: "FIRE THEM ALL"!</u>

Of course, that's only my opinion!..................... "John Adam's Project" Anyone?

Everi Mann – "SENTRYMAN"_____4-7-10

<u>www.historyofscience.com/G2I/timeline/index.php?id=2623</u>   Pg. 340

Last Minute Entries;
Hot Off The FOX-News Presses At 11:30am, April 13, 2010, in Case You Missed It!

According to ex-CIA, ex-Homeland Security Officer, "Chad Sweet" with the Chertoff Group, who informed listeners today that the Native born,
("over-seas contingency" blah, blah, blah, thank-you Barack),
"Radical Islamic" and "home-land terrorist" top Al Qaeda; Arabic: القاعدة, al-qāʿidah,
"the base", alternatively spelled Al-Qaida Leader: "Anwar Nasser Abdulla Aulaqi",
born April 22, 1971 (age 38) in Las Cruces, New Mexico,

Who Was Personally Responsible For That Ft. Hood Traitor; "Nidal Hasan",
And The Christmas Day Elf-Bomber; "Umar Farouk Abdulmutallab",
Who Had Illegally Managed To Embarked On A Plane From A Foreign Country,
Which Makes All Of Our Intrusive X-Ray Machines And Precautions "Mute Points",
(thankkkkk-youuuu, Barack's "FAA" and "Homeland Security" experts),

who was educated at Alma maters; Colorado State University; San Diego State University;
The George Washington University Graduate School of Education and Human
Development, and from CSU at least, with Your generously benevolent Tax Dollars at
work, administered by your "all-knowing, all seeing" government bureaucrats,
(thankkk-youuu "Fannie & Freddie"),

and from the University Admission's Offices doing their jobs, most inadequately, to stop
people from scamming their systems,
whom obviously don't comply with Government Regulation "Guidelines",
(apparently "Not" mandatory, thankkk-youuu "Dept. of Education")

to "properly screen" their applicant's legitimate Visas, (of which He had none),
and "Grant" recipient qualifications, (of which He had none),
opting to submerge their heads as usual squarely in the government trough, and
"going for the Gold" rather than protecting the American Taxpayer's dime, or,
in this specific case, those who would eventually Die from Aulaqi's minion:
the Ft. Hood "Nut-Job", another case of "Red-Flags Waving and Horns Blaring" ignored,
(thankkkkk-youuuuuuu Government hired & paid watchdog Doctors),

and, for those who could have died in the air, and on the ground Christmas Day
(THANK YOU GOD, and the Merriest of Christmas')!

All this, from another disillusioned, poor little Rich Kid, who is still at-large in Yemen
rabidly recruiting on that Internet!
(thankkkk-youuuu government of Yemen and Bill Gates.)

Of course, that's just my opinion in Connecting the Dots......................>C*<...................!

Granted, the Fates could have provided other avenues for these Angels of Death to do
their worst, but We, The Government of the United States
Could Do A Much Better Job, and At Least "Not Finance" These Idiots!
Another unintended consequence of a Liberal Society, with its Liberal Education System,
and an unaccountable government, filled with graduates of those institutions!

(and, as always Thank-You FOX NEWS)...SENTRYMAN

http://video.foxnews.com/v/4148412/terror-suspect-received-government-money
Pg. 341

Obama's *"Remarks"* to the Open Nuclear Security Summit
(video + transcript + analysis)

http://www.casavaria.com/cafesentido/2010/04/13/6263/obama-remarks-to-open-nuclear-security-summit-video-transcript/

"Two decades after the end of the Cold War, we face a cruel irony of history — the risk of a nuclear confrontation between nations has gone down,"
(Ironic to You, not to Us, and it ain't gonna get any easier either Pal!...And why do you think that threats gone down?....RONALD WILSON REAGAN – "Peace Through Strength"!)

"but the risk of nuclear attack has gone up".
(And why do You think that?....Barrack Hussein Obama – "Peace Through Appeasement"!)

"Nuclear materials that could be sold or stolen and fashioned into a nuclear weapon exist in dozens of nations. Just the smallest amount of plutonium — about the size of an apple — could kill and injure hundreds of thousands of innocent people"

(This guy couldn't stop a young malcontent with an explosive **apple in his shorts**, much less stopping Ahmadinejad playing Chess in the desert with ICBMs.
Remember Saddam Hussein hiding his blister-wrapped MIG-Jets under the sands of Iraq, and his "very special trucks" with those "hidden compartments" for some kind of ASMAT "decontamination" functions, and every Iraq school turned into An Armory for munitions, and an AK-47 under every Iraqi's bunk bed?
And everyone just mocked "Bush and the ARMY" searching high and low for those 1990's (Liters, Barrels, Boxes, Cases and Shells for liquid and biological WMDs, that tough U.N. Inspectors just could NOT get Saddam to prove he "had yet destroyed", "cat & mouse", which "created the entire debacle" in the first place!) Rat and cheezy mice!
 http://www.youtube.com/watch?v=N5p-qlq32m8&feature=related

"Terrorist networks such as al Qaeda have tried to acquire the material for a nuclear weapon,"
(Yes, NOW You're Talking! Right from ready suppliers in Iraq and our old buds, the Russkies, who pilfered plenty. .....Thank you, thank you "W", and rest in peace Saddam!)

"and if they ever succeeded, they would surely use it. Were they to do so, it would be a catastrophe for the world — causing extraordinary loss of life, and striking a major blow to global peace and stability". .....(Thank you, thank you "W")

"In short, it is increasingly clear that the danger of nuclear terrorism is one of the greatest threats to global security — to our collective security". .....(Thank you, thank you "W")

(Late to the party Big "O", but NOW You get-it!.......Welcome to the Club, Tough Guy!)
"And that's why, one year ago today in — one year ago in Prague, I called for a new international effort to secure all vulnerable nuclear materials around the world in
 four years."

(Ah, ha, ha, ha...4 years? What is it about (16 sanctions) You don't UNDERSTAND Dude? That was 10 + 6 = 16, till President Bush said "NO MORE"! And we've been safe since!)

http://www.thenewatlantis.com/publications/the-future-of-chemical-weapons
How do you like DEM apples, Johnny? ....Pg. 342

This is one part of a broader, comprehensive agenda that the United States is pursuing —

(Oh, here it comes. Pie in the Sky, Wish upon a Star…This Guy "couldn't" get the brothers to disarm on the Southside of Chicago!)

including reducing our nuclear arsenal and stopping the spread of nuclear weapons — an agenda that will bring us closer to our ultimate goal of a world without nuclear weapons.

(Oh man, and I thought he finally got-it!….Stop trying to re-invent the wheel.
Just continue with what has kept us all safe since 1945, Jack!)

Over the past year, we've made progress. At the United Nations Security Council last fall, we unanimously passed Resolution 1887 endorsing this comprehensive agenda, including the goal of securing all nuclear materials. Last night, in closed session, I believe we made further progress, pursuing a shared understanding of the grave threat to our people.

(What did You share?…..A Dom Perignon White Gold Jeroboam???
Hello, did I say 16 U.N. Resolutions??…..16!
Why don't you guys just pack-it-in before Putin eats all your lunches, because Ahmadinejad just nailed all the hors d'oeuvres?)

And today, we have the opportunity to take the next steps.

(And I thought Barack was ONLY interested in Global Warming!…Wait till Iran turns Israel Into The Temperature Of The Sun In Just 7 Seconds…)

(But, maybe Barack can get Ahmadinejad to change his mind if he gave Ahmad his Nobella Prize?…Unfortunately, Barack's only going to satisfy Mahmoud's Blood-Lust with a piece of America as the prize!)

(You're obviously the smartest guy in the room, or everyone would have already left, but, as for those that marvel Barack's "multi-tasking" with-so-many-things-on-his-plate; Ohhh, poor, poor Prez!)

(This guy's got so many people carrying his water and lunch bucket, He needs a Nametag pinned to his $1500.00 dollar Hart Shaffner Marx to tell the Driver which stop to let him off at: the intersection of Ahmadinejad and Kim Jong Alley!)

(Want to experience authentic Multi-Tasking;
try 9/11, an impending Recession, while not having a budget in place yet = thank you DEM Congressmen playing games dragging those confirmation hearings thru the summer, then going to War, and some of your compatriots, including the U.N., are all "ON THE TAKE", with No-Less than, the very guy you're all going to WAR to stop! DEVILs IN THE DETAILS.)

(Plus, you've gotta go "begging the DEMOCRATs" for bullets, and on top of everything else, you are responsible for 300+ million people, half of which hate you, and have no intention of ever supporting anything you'll try to help them all. Now that's a multi-task Smorgasbord!)

This isn't funny, we're going to Die with this Rookie!

SENTRYMAN

***The Brave Citizen Patriots Of Arizona Made My Point;

If You Can Vote To Keep Illegals "OUT", You Can Also Vote To Keep Out Old Wood,
---------Dried Wood, Drift Wood and Dead Wood From The Halls of Congress!----------
" Send Them All Home After 2 Terms"!
<u>Now Go Get Those Signatures For Mandatory Evacuation With "Term Limits"!</u>

Alien Border- youtube.com/watch?v=zgnqpMP3GYE&feature=related
Ariz. Illegal Immigration- http://www.youtube.com/watch?v=w4Khgvjdc78
Support for Law- youtube.com/watch?v=Jm-IJykfEKo&NR=1&feature=fvwp

PS. If the Supreme Court or any other Courts, or Legislatures, right down to your County
governments, try to circumvent the Will of the People;
well, we'll leave that for my next Book - Part 2...
For now, let's start from the bottom-up, and find honest citizens that will honor their
solemn mission for what they've been sent to Washington to do.

"The greatest [calamity] which could befall [us would be] submission to a
government of unlimited powers." --Thomas Jefferson: Declaration and Protest of
Virginia, 1825. ME 17:445

"Our government is now taking so steady a course as to show by what road it will
pass to destruction; to wit: by consolidation first and then corruption, its necessary
consequence. The engine of consolidation will be the Federal judiciary; the two
other branches the corrupting and corrupted instruments." --Thomas Jefferson to
Nathaniel Macon, 1821. ME 15:341

+BACK SLEEVE SYNOPSIS+
Most of us really know the score, even if some are afraid to admit it to themselves, and to
others if only on their deathbed confession, or a death house conversion the rest will too.
So there's still hope Ms Garofalo & Mr. Moore, and Barack! On 2nd thought, He knows too!

My idea for this "Survival Primer in a Progressive World", where Sin doesn't exist,
there is no Right & Wrong, no Black & White, and all things are but shades of Grey,
is to Crack Open just a few minds and coconuts, break some eggs and open some eyes,
to raise some eyebrows about what they probably once knew, and most assuredly once
had heard from their grandparents or great-grandparents long, long ago.

Through MY series of sensory impressions, memories and expressions, inner thoughts
and rants as I watched my 3 businesses dissolve over a 12 month period, while screaming
at the television, confusing my children, angering my liberal relatives, writing and calling
my Representatives, and asking, begging, demanding of these Washington weasels;
"How do You collect a pay check for doing nothing?"...and,
"I could get that done before lunch!....Why does it take You months to do anything?..and,
"Send our Troops the damn supplies by 5:00 PM. People are dying! Bet they're not yours"!

So, I started writing my little Blog to lower blood pressure & help keep my sanity, I took on
everything and everybody, and I spared No One, including myself......I Take No Prisoners!
SENTRYMAN............truth whence came from northern skies
11-8-08 to 4-13-10......All photos and deleted materials on Website: http://www.sentryman.org/id8.html

344 pages – (revised to 388 pages) - Nov. 11, 2010

BACK COVER

This Treatise Advocates That Any and All Actions; implied, suggested, intended and demanded: Be conducted and waged by "NON-VIOLENT" means and "with-in the Limits of the Laws" of the United States of America.

In closing: a Special "Thank You" To The Ones That Mean The Most, those brave women and men of the United States Armed Forces!

a poem:

Thank You To Those That Watch And Wait....
Thank You To Those That Stave Off The Hate....
Thank You To Those That Stand Through The Night..
Thank You To Those That Never Abandon The Fight.....
Thank You To Those That Stay And Serve A Third Tour....
.....When Leaving The 2nd Their Own Lives They'd Secure....
Thank You To Those That Protect Brothers Protecting Our Sons..
Thank You To Those That Always Remain Till The Mission Is Done....
Thank You To The Fallen, For Our Lives and Our Daily Bread,.................
Thank You To The Fallen, Homage To Your Sacrifice: Freedom Never Dead,
Better Men Than We, That Guard As Peter; Upon This Rock,
May He Watch Over You As You Shepherd Your Flock!

"Thank You" Can Never, Will Never Be Enough!

SENTRYMAN 4-6-2010

God Bless the United States of America!

==
Our watchdog Media wants us all to ignore, but still be very afraid of these fanatical crazy radicals that are endangering our freedoms and Liberty in their desperate attempt to shift America away from its decade's old secular roots,
and as one of the "largest Muslim nations" on earth, so states BHO, we are duly warned!!...

Thank you NBC, NY Times and president Obama for the heads-up!

SENTRYMAN

www.youtube.com/watch?v=78GMsv6fKQk&feature=player_embedded

Pg. 345

BONUS pages added;

October 29th, 2010 …….Vote-in each election, America, "once"!
And remember <u>who fought and died to secure you that RIGHT</u> for you!

No person shall be capable of being a delegate for more than three years in any term of six.
<u>Thomas Jefferson</u>

The security intended to the general liberty consists in the frequent election and in the rotation of the members of Congress. <u>James Madison & Alexander Hamilton 1782</u>

My reason for fixing them in office for a term of years, rather than for life, was that they might have an idea that they were at a certain period to return into the mass of the people and become the governed instead of the governors which might still keep alive that regard to the public good that otherwise they might perhaps be induced by their independence to forget. <u>Thomas Jefferson</u>

Those who have been intoxicated with power can never willingly abandon it.
<u>Edmund Burke</u>

Where annual elections end, there slavery begins … Humility, patience, and moderation, without which every man in power becomes a ravenous beast of prey. <u>John Adams</u>

Whenever a man has cast a longing eye on office, a rottenness begins in his conduct.
<u>Thomas Jefferson</u>

I am for making of terms annual, and for sending an entire new set every year.
<u>John Adams</u>

Term limits would cure both senility and seniority – both terrible legislative diseases.
<u>Harry S. Truman</u>

A (constitutional) amendment (for congressional term limits) could never achieve the blessing of Congress; it could be initiated only by the states. <u>Dwight D. Eisenhower 1965</u>

The short memories of American voters is what keeps our politicians in office. <u>Will Rogers</u>

Politicians are like diapers: they must be changed often and for the same reason.
<u>Paul Harvey</u>

The issue today is the same as it has been throughout all history, whether man shall be allowed to govern himself or be ruled by a small elite. <u>Thomas Jefferson</u>

If the voters really understood what we were up to they'd vote us out of office.
<u>Senator Robert Byrd</u>

We hang the petty thieves and appoint the great ones to public office. <u>Aesop</u>

They make the point better than me, but then who speaks of it: "Fire Them All", I.
<u>Sentryman</u>

It's time we asked ourselves if we still know the freedoms intended for us by the Founding Fathers. <u>James Madison said,</u> 'We base all our experiments on the capacity of mankind for self-government.' This idea that government was beholden to the people, that it had no other source of power, is still the newest, most unique idea in all the long history of man's relation to man. This is the issue of this election: Whether we believe in our capacity for self-government or whether we abandon the American Revolution and confess that a little intellectual elite in a far-distant capital can plan our lives for us better than we can plan them ourselves. <u>Ronald Reagan Oct. 27, 1964</u>

No man is good enough to govern another man without that other's consent.
<u>Abraham Lincoln 1854</u>

http://www.dennis.polhill.info/archives/376

FIRE THEM ALL??...............<u>SENTRYMAN</u>

Chipping Away Our Liberties (1) Barrel at a Time ....gulp!

<u>From my Blog</u>
<u>SOCIALISM: The Gateway Drug...Jun 14 to July 2, 2010</u>
http://www.sentryman.org/id11.html

Home in the Hinterlands - - I SAID IT FIRST, but who cares, Points Are Ignored Anyway!

LIB TOLERANC E 10-24-10

We're Coming For You Aug 25th to Oct 8th

"I answer specific points in Miss Cupp's article;

Who's afraid of Barack Obama?...."Nobody"
by S.E. Cupp....
in the NYDailyNews.com., of 6-9-10,

"I Beg To Differ!"

- *Posted by SENTRYMAN on <u>June 14, 2010</u> at 5:34pm*

    An open letter to Miss Cupp; a young Captain in the War against "The Tide"!   Pg. 347

-

Dear Miss Cuff:

I agree everyone outside our nation is Not afraid of our President because they're (in on it), aside from our allies, and everyone inside our government is scared to death of this man for what he can do and has done, but most importantly, WILL DO!

I watched your usual stellar performance on Hannity, Sunday evening, but they are always mired in minutia, micromanaging the tree's bark, while ignoring the greater issues in the forest blaze beyond, oh, like ;

#1- What if "The Gusher" had been an American well operation,
then who would Obama blame and sue?

#2- Has Obama declared the incident, made now a saga, a National Disaster Area yet,
even though we've declared his presidency a national tragedy?

#3- Having allowed this to expand into a national tragedy for ineptness, or for purpose and TREASON,
why hasn't there been a Contingency Plan, or Plans in place for 30+ years for these 4000+ wells?
<u>Did they all just pop-up one day?</u>

#4- Specifically, which US Legislators signed-off on "slackening the government regulations" for this FRIEND,
wink- wink, nod- nod, thus jeopardizing our back-door "grocery store", and endangering our national treasures and the national economy?

In less tolerant countries where national honor trumps personal profit,
i.e. China,
you're Hung or Shot "for far less"!

#5- Who polices the Oil Police while they aren't supervising or following regulations and codes, while accepting bribes, sex and watching porn, and who ultimately writes the "safety protocols" for this type operation, over the past 30+ years?
I thought that was all Capitol Hill did, was write red tape!
...I know no can READ RED TAPE!

#6- Since it's been dragged-out to incredible lengths of human stupidity for 50+ days,
why not hand-it over to the states to accelerate any and all possible solutions, overseen by the military, as is the US Coast Guard's specific mandate and jurisdiction to "guard the coast", and should supersede any "standing vacillating President".
Why hasn't the military developed contingency plans for this or similar incidents over 30+ years already?

#7- Had it been a unfriendly foreign government's Well, like China or Venezuela, instead us tolerating an over-jealous Obama picking on our greatest, longest, and most loyal-ally to this nation, like picking on the defenseless Christians who'll turn the other cheek, while smashing them in the face again, how would the Macho-Man handle the incident then?
.... As ably as Iran or Korea?

If you have a food inspector or meat inspector, and a school kills children with bad hamburgers, heads should roll.

If the Fire Inspector allows all the people to return to their desks <u>while the skyscraper next door is burning down</u> with an airplane stuck in it, and ultimately everyone in the 2nd tower inevitably and coincidently dies too, <u>someone's head should roll</u> and The Protocols should be re-written, examined, reviewed, updated, supervised and enforced, or then

why do we have a Government Legislature in the first place?

Just to spend us into the poor house,

while half the country cheers, waiting for their bribery–checks to come on the 3rd, and the other half politely watches millions of lives float out to sea, as the oil comes ashore.

#8- Are these "Statesmen" all either inept, distracted, corrupt, scoundrels, or bandits, yes traitors, to their country and their countrymen?.....<u>So then all should be replaced!</u>

<u>Is "only" BP responsible on the planet,</u>

<u>after "Bush" of course?</u>

Or,
#9- when is someone going to have the backbone and hutzpah to ask if this President of the United States who let this THING get so bad, He would incite the hysterical Public, allowing, no clambering for All Oil Production In The Gulf Be Shut-Down, For Purpose, thus Collapsing The Economy, the way Roman Senators would whip-up the Throng for Blood and conspiratorial skullduggery,

*or a southern Sherriff from yesteryear, get the Mob to break
into the jail to dispense justice, and forget American honor
and jurisprudence.*

*The same way President Obama has destroyed the greatest
economy in the history of man, just Call Him Out, and take him
to task?....That's not racist, that's Representative government.*

ENOUGH cowardice, what do we pay you people for?

........To represent Us, or Yourselves?

Are they afraid or complicit?

*There are just a few things that I haven't heard discussed on
TV news, young lady.*

Take care,
SENTRYMAN

+++++++++++++++++++++++++++++++++++++

<u>3:12:36 PM</u>
<u>Jun 14, 2010</u>

Ps, and We hear today the President will now use the limitless
gusher Oil Spill to force Cap 'n Tax, AKA Cap and Trade,
to Tax everything we'll ever do aside from breathing, but give
them time!...

By the way,
I thought this entire "Alternative Energy" Ploy was based-on
the "known" assumption
that there wasn't enough "oil left" to meet our future needs
because the earth was ebbing in this natural resource,
...but I gotta tell you,

*I know where you can get lots of oil, no one seems to
have any use for!...*

A Great Lie: To Toss The Baby Out With The Oily Water,
That Has Fueled The Engine Of Industry and Freedom,
Now Used To Harness People & Minds,

Not To Power Wind Turbines Of Prosperity For The Better
Good!!

…<u>SENTRYMAN</u>

<u>http://www.nydailynews.com/opinions/2010/06/09/2010-06-</u>
<u>09_whos_afraid_of_barack_obama_nobody.html</u>

<u>OBAMA's TRUTH or DARE</u>

Posted by SENTRYMAN on <u>June 16, 2010</u> at 3:30am

(These entries from my Blog <u>"SOCIALISM, A Gateway Drug"</u>
are viewable with photos and illustrations at the LINK below:)

<u>http://sentryman.org/id11.html</u>

OK, so America sits-up this evening, like a good "battered spouse
syndromed" puppet, heads reeling with 55 days of B/S,
already for the next episode of;
"today's a new day and I'll believe anything He says,
and He won't hit me anymore 'cause He said so,
and I'm too stupid to admit to myself "He is lying",
and I know it,
but too insecure and weak to stand-up for myself, to either leave,
or to develop some self-respect and kick His fool, lie'n, ass out,
instead", of all sitting agog to the image on the screen. ….Pg. 352

The redundancy is for the "acronym and metaphor" challenged!

And it went something like this:

LIE #1 – our only choice for energy independence is by drilling in
deep water which has now shown to be "unsafe", with no
alternatives, but serfdom and total dependency on the Saudis
and other good foreign dictating potentate suppliers,
short of solar generated, steam powered bicycles, and living in
tents like fellow Bedouins!

But, you better learn to cuddle with the same sex to keep warm
because "no Campfires" allowed to increase your
Carbon Footprint, thus simultaneously circumventing
procreation, which would require an abortion
that may temporarily spur the economy, but there's that
"Footprint" thing with the off-gassing corpse, men!...

That's the "dead body" kind, not the "servicemen" kind,
the President is so fond of speaking about!

("UNSAFE"....after 30+ years, 1000s of wells, 1st accident
of its type (after doing nothing to stop it's spreading)
because The Government fell short on "their" responsibility)
.........Hmmmm.....
Does this mean that Planes, Trains and Automobiles will be
banned in the future too?

<u>I think they collectively have killed maybe more than 11 people
since they started rolling in 1804!</u>
[The invention of the steam engine was critical to the invention
of the modern railroad and trains. In 1803, a man named
Samuel Homfray decided to fund the development of a
steam-powered vehicle to replace the horse-drawn carts
on the tramways.
Richard Trevithick (1771-1833) built that vehicle,
the first steam engine tramway locomotive.
On February 22, 1804, the locomotive hauled a load of 10 tons
of iron, 70 men and five extra wagons the 9 miles between
the ironworks at Pen-y-Darron in the town of Merthyr Tydfil,
Wales to the bottom of the valley called Abercynnon.
It took about two hours.]

LIE #2 – a Green Tax is inevitable, timely and again,
the only alternative to finance the Alternative Energy Sources;
the ones that are so vastly over-priced, and only cost effective
if you're independently wealthy and can wait the 37 years
to break-even, and the ones that have been erroneously touted
and highly inefficient, and the ones that are total fabrication,

and the ones that haven't been invented yet, but are certain
to be cost-effective, super efficient, most sufficient and totally
eco-friendly in maybe 1, or 2 hundred years from today,
but today's a good enough time to start cutting our losses and
 our wrists
when the country is on the verge of collapse, the summer of
"hurricane, bankruptcy and foreclosure" languish is
about to start, and thoughts of revolution
may not only be an Al Qaeda dream,

by abandoning cheap and plentiful fossil fuel exploration and
production on American soil,
now and forever made "OFF-LIMITS" to any Americans,

so says, WHO exactly?....
I THINK IT'S TIME AMERICA FOUND OUT
WHO IS MAKING THESE RULES
FOR THE 300 MILLION OWNERS OF THE COMPANY!

LIE #3 – Wind turbines, Solar Panels, small efficient
over-priced ugly little cars, and those
($1000 ea. Replacement Windows) that Obama's advisor's husband
makes, cute, will be the panacea for our salvation!
...Saith the WORD! This is where the B/S Syndrome comes-in again!

Well, Beam Me Up, Scotty, to get some Dilithium Crystals,
because Barack wants me to go to "Io",
and since NASA is in mothballs, like our drilling for independence,

 I won't have to
increase that old carbon footprint.
But, I'm OK, because I bought some credits from a little old guy
in Omaha,
that had a few left after Al Gore purchased all available credits
from the residents of Kansas, so he'd remain in compliance ....

Kansas would have had more to trade, but there was that "Abortion Guy" who put a dent in the population there.

so says WHO exactly?....

I THINK IT'S TIME AMERICA FOUND OUT
WHO IS MAKING THESE Carbon Credit B/S RULES
FOR 300+ MILLION OWNERS OF THE COMPANY!

LIE #4 – "I can't stop the GUSHER in the Gulf, but I can make BP Pay through The Nose! I will use this accident as an excuse to push my Green Agenda for "Cap & Tax" right down the American's throats, like I did with Healthcare,

so my Administration and my Party, (did someone say PARTY?) can control the new unlimited Slush Funds, to be generated by BP, and the new Taxes on My fellow Americans",

("like the greater portion of the $778 Billion "Stimulus" I haven't spent yet to create any jobs, that everyone's forgotten about, that I could say: I'm going to give to those Coastal States' companies and employees,

……..but I won't!")
(Oops, wait, correction)….That was a TRUTH…..geez….. sorry!

SENTRYMAN

==

5 Comments

Comment by Denise on June 17, 2010 at 12:36am

http://www.nwofighters.org/oil-disaster-update-and-detailed-analysis/

http://anticorruptionsociety.com/2010/06/02/the-real-reason-oil-still-flows-into-gulf/#more-1494

<u>Comment by Patrick S. on June 16, 2010 at 9:53am</u>

ROTFLMAO!
The picture (crying out laughing, pounding the floor),
the picture. lol lol lol the picture.
Oh man, I have to use this picture in one of my blogs.
I may even use it on my webpage. holy cow I can't stop
laughing. That's great!

<u>Comment by Joseph W on June 16, 2010 at 9:15am</u>

I see that Toys are Us has a LeapFrog toy.
Send it to your visionary friends.

<u>KIM A. M., M.D. on June 16, 2010 at 9:11am</u>

Bravo. The empty suit is right on.
Don't forget the lie that there are few places to
 drill for oil on land
or in shallow waters in our country.

<u>Comment by Joseph W on June 16, 2010 at 9:08am</u>
In short,
Obama simply doesn't know that in every
thousand mile journey it takes a first step.
He's in a game of leap frog.

"SPILL WHAT??.....YOU SPILLED YOUR DRINK??

THE WORLD'S COMING TO THE, WHAT??............

IT'S TOO LOUD IN HERE, TELL ME LATER.

I'M BUSY NOW SING'n WITH PAUL!"

Posted by SENTRYMAN on June 22, 2010 at 11:49pm

http://www.youtube.com/watch?v=Vvorqcgcdtw

"YOU BROKE MY HEART STANLEY,
I KNOW IT WAS YOU!".....You're Out, David's Back-In!

Posted by SENTRYMAN on June 23, 2010 at 2:04pm

You're Out...........David's Back-In!

and um, those 40,000 troops you guys asked for last summer
so We could win the war quickly to have fewer losses of our
brave American soldier's lives,

well, I'll be sending some reinforcements real soon,
upwards of 30,000 eventually, just like I said last December,
but, Stevie Wonder and Earth, Wind & Fire will be stopp'n-up
to my Big House

so I'll be a bit busy and I'll get right on it, right away!

http://www.youtube.com/watch?v=FcFlp6kl508

Now Malia, No, I haven't plugged the hole yet,
but I've plugged a hole in Afghanistan, and the Clean-up
things there should go as well now as the Gulf clean-up
here!.......tee hee!

"Plugging Holes".....Hmmmm...
about that hole in the southern border fence!

.............Hey, I gotta better idea!!........
.............RAHM, bring me a pen,

and tell our Gardeners that their President said:
 "they can unpack"!

The President Welcomes New Subjects:

Posted by SENTRYMAN on July 1, 2010 at 4:06pm

As I started listening to Our Father this morning,
this time about "the tired and huddled hungry masses",
and my gag-reflux began to kick-in, so I turned him off.
I said aloud: "Oh, please Dad-dy, read me that sto-ry a-gain"...
 My wife chuckled.

I thought to myself how strange it would be to connect with my
own Dad if he was the only one that could make my life safe and
secure, prosperous and meaningful, but he never delivered
on the Promise.

But, he still had all that power over my life, just like in a family
business, and could keep me from providing these vital things
for myself and my own family, and how long would I allow him
this power over me?

Pg. 358

How long could I take it, or ever respect and believe in him
ever again?

1) - A million or so unfulfilled Promises from 2007, and 2008
 "aside", Our Father is asked to provide 40,000 additional
troops 1 year ago, and with those reinforcements my neighbor's
son can come home alive. 6 long months later Our Father finally
commits to a 30,000 man Promise, that has yet to be honored,
but Our Father Does Fire His Lancelot. Now My neighbor's son
will never walk in the door to ever hug his Mom again,
so I take pause!

2) - The ocean has a convulsion with earth's black blood
bleeding from a wound and
Our Father Promises the waters will part, and all will be well
with the Well,

but after TWO MONTHS, and over a dozen sympathetic foreign
Governments with their expertise, equipment and experience
are rebuffed, and Flotillas, Barges and Floating Barricades,
Booms are still in storage, and Stone Jetties and Sand Berms,
Skimmers and Pumpers, and COREXIT and straw, mats
and socks,

that Spin-It and Compact-it, Eat-it-up and Break-it-down,
Skim-it-off and Suck-it-up Contraptions, and Ideas galore,
a machine to suck-up and blow the oil set-afire,
in a midnight cascade blaze, why not a 100,

a simple blaze which should have been continually Stoked
on calmer seas (two months ago) to control the Oily Tsunami
for never reaching land from Day-II,

ALL Is Mired, Beset and Scuttled In Bureaucratic Environmental Red
"Tape Insanity" and for Purpose, a breathing Slime
 much thicker than a Trillion Spills,

while Millions of creatures die, Life-long Family Businesses
perish, Livelihoods wither, as local unemployment soars,
and a nation finally begins to bow from the ankles as Our
Father gears-up to challenge the Courts, but Not the Tides,
so I take pause!

3) – Meanwhile in Arizona a 17 year-long Locust Plague
(Doubles-Down) in the wake of human carnage,
a savior, our Batman search-light is lit, and the
Call-Goes-Out to Our Father, who once again PROMISES
the clouds will part and all things will be set Right-Again.

And as Governor Brewer waits this morning with her hand
on her .45 cal., Our Father praises Emma Lazarus and
all those immigrants who craned their necks at the
Statue of Liberty in the harbor, after their long perilous boat
ride to Liberty's shore, when all they needed to do was enter
by the new Revolving Back-Door, that Our Father will install
in his imaginary fence along the Rio Grande, El Paso,
Columbus, Douglas, Nogales, Lukeville, San Luis, Yuma,
and Calexico to Imperial Beach,
<u>so I take pause!</u>

<u>Why?...No, I want You to answer this question for yourself,
American citizen, Why?</u>

Compassion?....What's Fair?....Votes?.... No Borders?
....Everybody comes here?....
Your Taxes pay for The World?....
We all eventually work for The State?

<u>....Sharia Law instead of the Constitution?...</u>

I don't see The Constitution even honored anymore
with a 5 to 4 Gun decision in Chicago....
It's a Crap-Shoot, an Opinion rendered by WHO, by WHAT?

Who are these humans We doth place in judgment over us,
over life and death, that don't honor or obey
The US Constitution, but opinionate it?

<u>A simple piece of fragile paper unlike any on earth!</u>

What if that decision fell to 4 to 5?...
Good-bye USA!....That'll be next year!
When there is no more money for taxes, we use Chits & IOUs?
<u>....We're already doing that, stupid!</u>

And as we'll soon officially celebrate The Day of the Dead,
and Ramadan, in lieu of Christmas,
it seems to me and who am I to think for myself,

I don't work for the government yet,
this is all going to end with an epic struggle between
a pure and righteous Communist Oligarchy,
and a pure and holy Islamic Theocratic Republic.

Basically the same thing,
just one wears a suit and tie and the other a robe
and turban, tagelmust, shemagh, keffiyeh, pashmina,
both cut from the same cloth as Our Father!

The United States is almost GONE,
and so I take pause and a few final breaths!

http://www.youtube.com/watch?v=-u_0pBMoDhY

http://www.youtube.com/watch?v=-oZVesUmspU

http://www.youtube.com/watch?v=C3Bqbg7P-es&feature=related

**Finally exonerated by His Attorneys General of the
United States of America,
the New "Keepers of the Flame" - The Panthers Will Now
Protect Our Right To Vote!...Whoa, thanks, we're lucky!
Who knew that was in jeopardy, thanks again BHO.
We all have His Promise on that!!**

****Not to forget the new "government subsidized ACORN"
under its 50 new state's aliases!**

http://www.youtube.com/watch?v=LFSY2dnTSZQ&feature=related

http://www.youtube.com/watch?v=2fO1Q45U6Yk

http://www.youtube.com/watch?v=56DpgM0F9io&feature=related

http://www.youtube.com/watch?v=U6dRucFth98

SENTRYMAN   Pg. 361

From a recent military dispatch, leaked to the
Media to warn the enemy, just to make things fair;

<u>2010-05-12,</u> <u>18:05:00</u> <u>Kunduz,</u> <u>Afghanistan</u>

<u>Action Report:</u>

A large mass of Taliban soldiers are moving down
a road when they hear a low voice calling-out in
English from behind a sand dune:
"One Texas soldier is better than ten'a
you Taliban."

The impatient Taliban Commander quickly sends 10
of his best soldiers over the dune....
whereupon a gun-battle breaks out and continues
for just a few minutes....
pop-pop....pop-pop-pop......then silence.

Again, the unidentified voice calls out:
"Yep, One Texan is sure better
than a'hundred Tal-i-ban soldiers."

Furious this time,
the Taliban Commander sends his next best
100 fighters over the dune.... instantly
another fierce firefight ensues.
After approx. 10 minutes of continuous exchanges,
the firing falls silent.

Once again the voice calls out in a slow Texan
drawl:
"That's right,
one Texan is just plenty for a'thousand
a'you Taliban."

Now enraged, the angry Taliban Commander musters
most of his remaining fighters and sends close
to a thousand men over the dune.
Mortar fire, rocket explosions and AK-fire ring-
out in rapid volleys as the huge battle
continues.......

Then, abrupt silence once again, an eerie calm
looms as the smoke clears.

Finally out of the haze one lone wounded Taliban
fighter slowly crawls back from over the dune,
and with his dying breath, he gasps to his
commander:

لا ترسل بعد الآن من اخواننا. انه
فخ ، وهناك اثنان منهم

"Don't send anymore of our
brothers;
It's a trap; ....
There are two of them."

(from an Aug. 25th Blog below)
<u>The kitchen sink;</u>

("<u>Yes We Can</u>: The Schott 50 State Report on Public Education and Black Males 2010. Calling it a "national crisis," the report found that only 47%, percent of black males graduated from high school in the 2007-2008 school year."…

"Black Unemployment Rate Increases 700% More than White. Sept 6, 2010")…....<u>Guess They Couldn't!</u>

(National Assessment of Educational Progress (NAEP) scores – considered the "Nation's Report Card"– Only about half of low-income and minority students in US high schools graduate, and many of those who do are unprepared for college)

(2010 Cornell Grads Find Fewer Jobs, Earn Less Than In Previous Years)…<u>Oops</u>!

You just can't beat a "Liberal Education",
taught by Liberals, in a Liberal country, with a Liberal government,
that all hate Capitalism….....or can you?…

Vote with your head in Nov.
……*You're Not in Kansas anymore, and Mayberry No longer exists*!
www.youtube.com/watch?v=5bDtHSAzYXI

www.youtube.com/watch?v=6WHdWgES-Uw

www.youtube.com/watch?v=vOIbgd5qcrg

www.youtube.com/watch?v=hH6Ht-nK8vk&feature=player embedded

*Muslim Mickey Mouse Clone Teaches Arab children Hatred & Islamic Global Supremacy
http://www.youtube.com/watch?v=IZEGsnWZKh8

http://www.youtube.com/watch?v=9-KsVjuJxF4

http://www.youtube.com/watch?v=yw2EisVqKZ4

www.youtube.com/watch?v=agOU2R6MTbg

Pg. 364

While polite and civil American taxpayers, (no doubt from the "Right"), who very soon will be supporting the World, if the ("Left") can squeeze it out of them,

idly stand bye, subdued by civility, honor, class, tradition and fear of political correctness, patiently watch as the 2nd Half of the TARP II – Stimulus $782B, sum?, is squandered on "political payoffs" and maneuvering by a corrupt administration for their own political Party to be distributed for reelections in 2010 & 2012.

And, just as the 1st half was frittered away for State's and Union deficits, and to only create & expand new government jobs for eager participants, I'm reminded of the children's story of how the smartest and proudest among us,

the people, the throng, the subjects, hadn't the common sense "to see the obvious" before them. An inherent inability from pride and the indoctrination of unnecessary Red Tape, to recognize problems for what they are and simply rectify them with the easiest of solutions.

To "demand" that the ($400 billion-2nd Half of the TARP II – Stimulus) be spent on private-sector-job stimulus, for which it was originally borrowed, but stolen for, in the first place.

I.e. Re-employ America's Americans,

not to be determined by greedy banks, or selfish legislators taking their CUTs,

but a transparent "Citizen's Commission for Public Works" for starters! Headed by patriotic "unpaid, volunteer Industry CEOs", trained experts to start projects in every state "Right-Now". In part, by fixing every bridge in our nation "tomorrow". Thus stimulating all the outgrowth businesses on the periphery necessary to support such projects. That "was so vital" at one time for the DEMs continually beating over Bush's head, that now seemingly is totally irrelevant and forgotten for obvious reasons.

Nothing New, Just Fix What We've Got…."Washington = Not Necessary"!….

It could also be combined with a opt-in pathway to "legal-citizenship" for every illegal alien worker willing to come out of the shadows, solving another problem and at no additional expense to the American Taxpayers.

Who's country is it anyway?……..

Here's a suggestion,

"No", a demand while Washington's throwing our money around on bailing out banks in Europe,
jobs for cronies here at home, keeping bankrupt Democrat run states operating, and bogus research projects for Academics,
<u>how about giving our Stationed Troops anything and everything they need</u> to do their jobs professionally and correctly protecting Us and Themselves, <u>and give Our returning wounded Heroes anything they need to heal their bodies and minds,</u> to start their lives over again here at home!

And let's get back into OUTER-SPACE, the last frontier with its proven spin-offs to indirectly re-employ the world......... And the "coup de gras"; skew the result by changing the rules by out-lawing free enterprise, by "drilling our own oil on the edge of the tundra", thwarted, under the guise of protecting the planet, as though (300 million Ants in lockstep, all trading Carbon-Credits out on your lawn) could change what you'll do with your day, on Saturday, when you start-up your mower,
much less effect the solar system, or the temperature of the sun, or a billion "new drivers" in India and China,
but the DEMs and GREENIEs cleverly frame the Debate to be:
"why be a slave to Foreign Oil, buy a $1000. storm window from my Advisor's husband, or buy a Solar Roof Unit, that properly serviced and maintained "may at least pay for itself" in 20 years or so"! .....Brilliant!

How about drill for our own resources; bring back our $1.00 a gal. Gas, sell Wheat for $100 a bushel and pay all our bills in 1 year,
and grow-up and smell the freedom?

Do you think $1.00 a gallon gas, or even a stable $2.00 might stimulate a job or two? ....damn straight, Dudes and Dudettes!
Plus, the money goes back to Us and stays at home besides! That's power.
Ask a trucker, you darn greedy fools in Washington, & State's Legislatures!

Oh, the children's story: The Emperor Hasn't A Clue!....or does he?
http://www.youtube.com/watch?v=9GP01KpeAUs&feature=related   Pg. 366

ANSWER THIS FOR YOURSELF:

Over the past 50 long, expensive years of prognostications and machinations, accusations and recriminations, manifestations, plain greed and especially procrastination about ALL the Wars on; Poverty, Illiteracy, AIDs, Deforestation, Overpopulation, DDT, World Famine, Terrorism. Global Terrorism, Islamic Workplace Violence,

Overseas Contingency blah, blah, Racism and Intolerance, Out-sourcing, Non-Union Shops, and the reduction of Greenhouse Gases to close the Ozone Holes, with their pontifications on Global Cooling, and then Global Warming, ("Climate Disruption" – and any CHANGE in the Environment), if it doesn't feel like Malibu or Honolulu everywhere today, with their Crowning Jewel: Selling green S&H Stamp "Carbon Credits" to save the Gaia, mother earth, and rape Independent Prosperity, in order to; Save the Farmer,

Save the Rain Forest, w/assort. Endangered Weeds,

Save the Polar Bear & Baby Seals, the Whale, the Barn Owl, red-cheeked Squirrels, Snail Darters, Newts & Frogs, Corals,

and the California Smelt, at the expense of the legal, and illegal-alien farm worker's families in southern California,

that can now starve along with the average American consumer,

as US breadbasket fertile valleys and fields go fallow, rotting by design,

with insightful help from imperious Hollywood thespians, and

Live Aid, Farm Aid, Africa Aid, Band-Aid, 9/11 Aid,

Haitian-Aid where $0.10 cent (maybe) on the dollar ever reaches the needy, but professional charlatans and dictators will always fill their pockets first, and Lemonade, (but 10-year olds now need a permit for government's cut),

....as compared to, e.g.

"Don Imus Ranch" for kids with cancer,

Rush's "Leukemia and lymphoma" telethons,

O'Reilly's charity work where 100% of proceeds are from the sale of "American-Made Only" items ....Support These Funds!

And Hannity's Summer "Freedom Alliance Concerts" for wounded warriors and College funds for: "children of soldiers" never returning home,

is where private individual's efforts, NOT Gov't., continually accomplish real, permanent and lasting change in so many lives!!!...................................

So, "What Promise Has The Democrat Party Ever Kept?" Pg. 367

And

*"What Problems Have The Democrats, the Liberals, the Progressives, the
Socialists and the Communists Ever Solved,
In Order To Earn The Right To Be Re-elected Ever, During All That Time?"*

*And How's That Anti-Capitalism, Anti-Christ, Free Love,
Dope Smoking Socialists Re-writing Our History
Work'n Out For America, and Your Wallet Today?*

At least Dr. King made some headway in one area, but he was working from
the heart for a "non-violent" higher purpose,
NOT for a government annuity, or an American Taxpayer's stimulus check!

Pet-peeves & follow-the-money bureaucrats; nice job dissecting "Ma Bell",
so that today phone booths are Decorator accessories', and at $100 per hr.
a Tech can't fix my hard-line phone or my FIOS, that Catalytic Converter
closing the Ozone Hole years ago worked-well, with the "other-shoe" Non-
Lead Gas = Clean Air? Killing DDT so Malaria could live again, good idea,
preventing Mad Cow (by gov't. inspect negligence), FDA Antibiotic-
resistant Germs thanks to Livestock feeds, Swine Flu hysteria, proliferating
Ritalin to stone our kids, age-limits for "Grand Theft Auto" & alike, teach
violent assaults and stealing cars, plus helping create obese-fat kids with
early Diabetes cause playing catch is obsolete, but placing a Bounty on
Ronald McDonald, then attacking "Oil" always a main penchant, they even
bother to "Outlaw" coconut Oil, making $6 movie popcorn taste like
sawdust, and nix school fun Bake-Sales, destroying FREE Airwaves & my
antenna TV's, and now Edison's light bulbs are antique, but breaking the
mercury coil earns felony status, what? I can list hours of green lunacies!

And bigger fish, nice job from FEMA, again, and the VA always failing, not
supplying the Troops as usual, mothballing NASA space exploration, the
scientific innovations pay for itself, but pay the Russians instead, and now
pass-out leaflets for Islam, their new purpose, hmmm. Chopping Medicare
to fund Obamacare, "Agenda 21", suing the State of Arizona & turning their
sovereignty over to those saints at the United Nations for crimes against
humanity! Gee, thanks B. Hussein Obama. And wow, thank you politicians!

Forget about everybody from the Pharaoh's to Ahmadinejad's efforts to stem global over-population, as long as it's the Jews that go first, all good! Presidents try and Presidents go, but Israel still struggles for its existence, now more than ever! And forgot our wonderful EPA compliant autos, You can't work under the hood anymore, talk about monopolies and Cartels! 18 grades of gasoline and No More "Corner Gas Stations" with, I might add smarter mechanics that weren't charging $80.00 an hour! Talk about jake!

....I could go on, but "The View" is coming-on next and I want to turn my brain off for 55 mins...Ever wonder how Cuba keeps all those Chevy's from the '50s still running strong? ...Ask Obama Motors, reinventing the wheel... I hear the Post Office will be 5 days pretty soon, and they're gearing up the Pony Express to save on Gas...wait a minute, and green compost, a bonus!

[Government - that produces nothing but inequality and heartache, can't even supply our military or build a simple fence, ineffectual, deaf, blind and dumb!.......FIRE THEM ALL, and start all over again!]

"When We start listening to international Assassin's justifying their behavior, we cease to use reason and fall prey to our own vulnerabilities.

We already have enough problems at home with our American Justice, because you just can't have enough liberal judges playing God, that continue to give deviates, pimps, pedophiles and degenerates a 2nd, and a 4th, and a 12th chance to change their ways, with low bail and early releases, suspended sentences and a 3 months' probation for raping some neighbor's child, or family member for 6 years, and then granting them yet another crack at destroying someone else's daughter's life, or inevitably killing a loving couple's little girl, even if grew to college age. .....Freedom to some today, only means:
No Rules, No Judgments, No Standards, No Accountability, No God!

And God help us, and protect your little girls, your government won't!"
...Sentryman...Oct. 8, 2010 Blog

Peace through strength!... Ronald Reagan

"The peace will not be preserved without the virtues that make victory possible in war. Peace will not be preserved by pious sentiments .... Great Heart must have his sword and armor to guard the pilgrims on their way." ...Winston Churchill

Footnote: Regional and State Employment and Unemployment Summary, Jun 18,10 United States 9.7%

Gallup Finds U.S. Unemployment at 10.1% in September

Oct 7, 2010 ...

Unemployment, as measured by Gallup without seasonal adjustment, **increased to 10.1% in September -- up sharply from 9.3% in August**

http://www.gallup.com/poll/143426/gallup-finds-unemployment-september.aspx

http://hotair.com/archives/2010/10/07/gallup-unemployment-rate-back-over-10/

WE ARE FREE FOR ONE REASON:
GOOD MEN and STRONG WOMAN DIED FOR THAT GIFT TO YOU.

You want to stay free?....FIRE THEM ALL this November. Leave a couple deserving souls, but the majority of our guys who allowed all this to come to pass, beginning with letting the DEMs and the Media select our nominee Sen. McCain, as a sacrificial lamb for us to vote for, was the "Set-Up" and just the beginning of the end for another 4 years of continued sacrifice and loss of sacred freedoms. The entire GOP went right along with that RINO-in-Chief farce. Had it been Powell, or Condoleezza, or Giuliani we certainly wouldn't have witnessed this dismantling of the greatest nation in history.
.................................."Change the Bench",.....…........... "often"!

Butchers, Bakers, Candlestick-makers serve your country in Congress and then go home to your farms and fields, the way it was meant to be.
It's Not for winning the Brass Ring and feathering your nest with deals against your employers, the "American" Taxpayer.

****On November 3rd start working on the petitions necessary to qualify and establish "Proposition 86" for the 2012 Election cycle, to rein-in the Government and finally save America, our country, our home.

If you've read my page, my blog, my book, or watched my Video, you already know I have but one purpose and desire: to keep America FREE!

ONLY one hope can pull our bacon out of this FIRE, it's to FIRE them 1st with Prop #86 and I just don't hear that idea or theme expressed, or discussed seriously from any quarter today for the fundamental purpose of securing our liberty, other than, Oh Happy Day) another much more important Proposition for voting-in "Legalized Mary/Jane in California". No, not Maria/Juan, "GRASS" which is obviously their major solution in healing America's ills according to DEM educated, DEM informed, DEM concerned, D'enlightened electorate of that bankrupt society, including I believe, originator Dude of FaceBook.

With the complacency of Julius Caesar ignoring that crazy Soothsayer, a majority of the American Electorate has the attention span of the 17-year locusts. So if You think America's problems will be solved on Election Day; ...."B-E-W-A-R-E THE 2ND OF NOVEMBER!"

"65 Million votes",
(and unsure if the Lever was pulled by 65-Mil. <u>legal, or even living voters</u>, because it's always funny that with all the criminal felons, illegals, and dead people, mixed-in to that total, they always vote: Democrats. Which might signal something even more profound to analyze on a free gov't. grant sometime, but that's another story).
These poultry 65 mil. will decided how "You and Your 300+ million" fellow neighbors will now think, and work, and live, and die, all the while paying through the nose from birth, to "beyond" death, for that privilege.
.....Like them odds?

Sure would be a shame and a national travesty if ACORN, while registering (1) person = DEMOCRAT VOTERS (25 to 75 times),
and "I can see Russia from my house", changed America forever, what world-class demagoguing might alter the Gods on Mt. Washington then!
....Feeling duped or manipulated yet?
How about just tricked, jerked around, ripped-off, played for a fool year and after year!

62%, up to 76% voted in IRAQ,
but only (1/5th of the population) in "The United States of America" voted <u>to change this nation forever and ignore the Constitution</u>.

"Those stupid, ignorant, silly, selfish, and useless, fools <u>who sat out</u>", are of the apathetic, or maybe just pathetic mindset,
<u>who allowed a Hitler ascension</u> to change Time & Fate for 75 Million DEAD!

Is that what the 2008 vote was for? Only 7,970,660 votes separated McCain from Obama. Would it be fair, OK if McCain <u>won by 8 million bogus votes</u>? Do you really think we'd have a sustained 10%, 15%, 20% unemployment, and <u>have borrowed and blown 2 or 3 Billion dollars</u> in 1-1/2 years, even if a RINO Republican was at OUR helm?................................<u>well, do'yah punk</u>?

Worse; 60,000,000 absentee ballots have already been cast for Nov. 2nd, 2010 election, and by who exactly?
...DEMs Will NOT Allow A National - ID Card.....Hmmmm,

yet, our TROOPS are "always" sent their ballots "late" so they don't even qualify, or count. Cute, who do you think the military votes for? These very people that protect yours, our very "Right To Vote", and they're aced-out!

We've heard for 10 years that Bush lost the "popular vote", and the Courts stole the election for him,
(as though the Courts would corrupt themselves for any Conservative, ya, and remember, those same Democrat precinct voting machines, Democrat run in Democrat south Florida had successfully elected Clinton TWICE, and without any malfunctioning hitch!.....Hmmm, Clinton really did win, right?), but, they never opened-up over (1-million absentee ballots in California alone), and they knew many of those were military.

Don't you think every American citizen has the Right to have their ballot opened and counted?

...Who's country is it anyway, that braver souls died for, for us!
www.youtube.com/watch?v=nmq7W_wS-uY&feature=related

Proposition-86 is the only chance to save the Republic!

God speed! ....The only one that gave you that opportunity!

SM
10/9/10 Blog

==

PILING ON

"A friend sent this to me recently and I gave it a "little-tweak",
 to *SENTRYMAN* personalize it!"

Do you remember in the early '50s & '60s when our children weren't all so (enlightened and brilliant), yet?

...Maybe one of "you was that kid" down the street,
and you can remember "just how bad things really were" way back then,

before the Age of Aquarius. *Yuk, yuk*   Pg. 372

Do you remember;

Saturday mornings you said: "see you later Mom",
and you were back home promptly for dinner and without a watch, and you
had a "ball all day", usually without any money,
and didn't sniff, or drink, or shoot, or snort,
and you didn't get molested, or kidnapped, or get hurt or disappear,
nor did You hurt anyone else or get arrested?

At school, all the girls had ugly gym uniforms?

They taught Archery in grade school, and ballroom, and the fox-trot dance
in the Gym?

It took three minutes for the TV to warm up?
1 AM the test pattern on 3 TV channels, went to snow?

A big TV with a perfect picture was $300, and the signal was FREE,
until (someone?) started screwing with the signals to lull-everyone
into spending $3000 for a TV to watch that same stuff?....duhhhh!

The radio was for entertainment, with mysteries at night,
and for listening to the World Series walking home from school?

You waited all spring for Knot-hole Day?

National baseball players signed your stuff for free?

Nobody owned a purebred dog?

When a "quarter" was a decent allowance?

Saturday afternoon's getting a "Brush-cut or Flat-top" with wax?

You'd reach into a muddy gutter for a penny?

http://www.youtube.com/watch?v=iG13xhmLxG0&feature=player_embedde
d
$.35 cent per gallon gasoline?
http://www.youtube.com/watch?v=8yMKowWlvqw&feature=player_embedd
ed

You'd flatten pennies on railroad tracks?

Your Mom wore nylons that came in two pieces?

Your Dad got the windshield cleaned, oil checked, and gas pumped, without asking, and all for free, even in the winter and every time?

You didn't pay for "air" and you got green or yellow "trading stamps", a smile, and a 'Thank You' to boot?

Laundry detergent came with free glasses, dishes, or towels hidden inside the box?

One box of "20 Mule Team Borax" could clean anything, and everything else in your home for $1.00?

Crackerjack had a "<u>real toy</u>" inside and "more" peanuts? *Big bucks now*!

It was considered a great privilege to be taken "out to dinner" to a real restaurant with your parents?

Taking a Sunday daytrip in the car with your folks, and playing: Animal, Plant, Mineral & 20 questions?

Real schools threatened to keep kids-back a grade if they failed. . .and they actually did it?

When your teacher kept you after-school you were in trouble, but not for "private sex education" tutoring?

When a '57 Chevy was everyone's dream car... to cruise, peel out, lay rubber, or watch submarine races, and people went steady?

Sporting a DA, a little sideburn, tight jeans with flipped cuffs, white T-shirt with pack of Luckys in the shoulder fold, and white socks, black sneaks?

(No belt, butt hang'n out, with your baggy boxers showing?) ...Nooooo, that's today!

No one ever asked where the car keys were, because they were always in the car, in the ignition, and the doors were never locked?

Lying on your back in the grass, with your friends, and saying things like: 'That cloud looks like a... '?

Playing baseball without adults yelling or supervising, or explaining the rules of the game, or even watching you, ever?

Stuff from the store came without safety caps, or hermetically sealed,
because no one had yet tried to poison a perfect stranger, or murder their
fellow American?

Took all summer to build the Tree House till You fell-out, and everyone
signed your cast?

And with all our futuristic innovation and progress, don't you just wish,
just once, you could slip-back to those simpler-times to savor those slower
paced, peaceful, friendlier moments of our past, we let slip away,
to share it with our children and grandchildren right now?

When being sent-down to the principal's office, wasn't as bad
as to the fate, that awaited that student when they got home?

We were basically in fear of our lives for what mom or dad
might do to us, and it wasn't because of drive-by shootings,
or drugs, and gangs, etc.
Our parents and grandparents were a much bigger threat?

But we survived, because their love was greater than the threat,
. . .as well as those summers filled with bike rides, Hula Hoops,
visits to the pool, & eating Kool-Aid sugar mix from the packet?

'Yeah, I remember that'!

*I am sharing this with you today because it ended with a
Double Dog Dare to pass it on.

Remember what a Double Dog Dare was?

Remember when the perfect age was somewhere between
'old enough to know better, and too young to care'?

Send this on to someone who can still remember;

Howdy Doody, Princess "Summer-Fall-Winter-Spring",

The Peanut Gallery, Jungle Jim, Winky Dink, Flicka,

Captain Midnight, "The Shadow Knows", Flash Gordon serials,

Sergeant Preston of the Yukon, Davey Crockett, cap & cap gun,

The Lone Ranger, Cisco Kid & Poncho: lunch box & pocket knife,

Nellie Bell, Roy and Dale, Trigger and Buttermilk, Ozzie,

The Beav, and "Father Knows Best", (and He did, a while longer!)

How Many Of These Do You Remember;
not like "Jay Walking", and never hearing about anything before?

Candy cigarettes, Chocolate cigarettes and gold coins?

Wax Coke-shaped bottles filled with colored sugar water?

Soda Pop machines that dispensed Cokes and Pepsi, 7up, grape & orange Crush, A&W, RC Colas and Hire's, Yoo Hoo and Dr. Pepper, in glass bottles, with real sugar, and a tight cap?

Soda Fountains - Ice Cream Parlors, Soda Jerks, and Coffee Shoppes with table-side Jukeboxes?

Drive-In restaurants with girls on skates?

Becker's Big Boy double USDA hamburgers that looked just like the pictures, and really tasted good?

A Large yellow colored Popcorn with coconut oil for .10 cents?

Blackjack, Clove, Cinnamon and Teaberry chewing gum?

Milk home-delivery in glass bottles,
wrapped with colored cellophane, and the cream
raised-up the cardboard stoppers in winter sitting in the box?

Newsreel, travel-log, cartoon, a short & double-feature for $0.25?

Waiting in line at the Theatre, holding hands with your Mom, or
Dad, on Saturday mornings to watch the special: 20-Cartoons?

Telephone numbers with a word prefix like..
(Ludlow, Butterfield and Yukon 2-601)?

Your neighbors listening on your Party line calls?

Shooters, aggies and clay marbles in a ring on the dirt,
Pea shooters, Slinky and Nutty Putty, belt-loop Rabbit's Foot,
Daisy Air Rifle and rolled-cap pistols?

Hi-Fi's, 78s – 33s – 45s RPM records with hole adapter?

Playing records & dancing in the basement, lights-off?

S&H Green Stamps with full catalog for redeeming?

Mimeograph paper with that odor out in the hall?

The Fort Apache Play Set, Chemistry Set, Erector Set,
Lincoln Logs (that's pre-LEGOs), and Tinker Toys?

Do You remember a time when making critical decisions
 were decided by doing; Rock, Paper, Scissors,
'eeny-meeny-miney-moe',

hand-over-fist, up a baseball bat neck and cap-the-top,

and everyone had a ball mitt, not a phone?

Mistakes were corrected by simply shouting: 'Do Over !'?

'Race issues' meant arguing about "who ran the fastest"? Pg. 377

Catching Fireflies with a quart jar
could happily occupy an entire evening?

It wasn't odd to have two or three 'Best Friends'?

Having a Weapon in School meant being caught with a
Slingshot or pea shooter?

Saturday morning TV cartoon shows lasted from 7AM till noon,
and weren't 30-minute commercials for action-figures, or video
game rip-offs?

'Oly-oly-oxen-free' made perfect sense?

Spinning around, getting dizzy, and falling down
was cause for giggles?

The Worst Embarrassment was being picked last for a team,
but you didn't die, and you still played. Everyone played?

War was a card game?

Baseball cards & a clothes pin,
or small balloons-tied around the fork in the spokes
transformed any bike into a motorcycle?

Taking drugs meant orange-flavored chewable aspirin?
And you didn't OD,
....or get shot in any Drive-By sitting on the front porch,
....or do anything extremely stupid you watched on "Jackass"!

Water balloons were the ultimate weapon?

*If you can remember most or all of these,
"You had some real fun as a kid!"*

Our country's psyche once thrived on "shared experience",
and our "collective souls" were nourished by being Americans!

Uncle Miltie, "Sid" Caesar, and Lucy,

"You're going to the moon, Alice"....

"Baby, you're the greatest"....

"a one an' a two." ....

"Oh, Rochesterrrr"....

"GOOD NIGHT, Mrs. Calabash--wherever you are!"

Red's: "Good Night & God Bless",

"Hawaiia, Hawaiia, Hawaiia".….Mister Muggs…

"Say good night, Gracie"…"Goodnight Gracie", Queen for a Day,
"I Remember Momma" and "plunk your magic twanger Froggy",

but never again: "Like sands through the hourglass,
so are the days of our lives." ...

Certainly Not with;
300+ Cable channels, HD, HP, Texting, Twitter,
Wii, cells, iBook, iPad, iSore, IOGEAR 34,000 digital photos,
 and
Up to 30,000 songs (MP3), Facebook,
 and
steal my identity and my life in a nanosecond,

and on the "www" where you can download;
"How to make a bomb", and Click here: If you hate your country,
"How to locate your victim, isolate, and rape a child"!

We've traveled many miles, and come a very long way from
burning; bras, draft cards, and a part of our souls
to share these experiences in this new reality.

Yin and Yang....Light and Shade

*Compared to this "very" moment, "right now", please tell me again, exactly; "just how bad was it again, way back when"?

Pass this on to anyone who may need a break from their 'Grown-Up' Life . . . Dude! …. I Double-Dog-Dare-Ya!

SENTRYMAN

Right VS Left….Reactionary VS Progressive
       "Nothing's New Under The Sun"

www.youtube.com/watch?v=5bDtHSAzYXI

And now back to our new reality of enlightenment, love and fairness, understanding and tolerance of all things, where everything will be regulated, governed, and "the same opportunity fits all" mandate!

So, Who are the enemies of which Presidente' Obama speaks?
Whites, Legal immigrants, Americans, all, who are not Democrats?
Anyone that disagrees with the regime and his Eminence?
So exactly who really are the enemies, of which Pres. Obama speaks?
http://www.youtube.com/watch?v=Iwt-GiNOiYU&feature=related

"Anyone" that doesn't support his vision of his new America!
http://www.youtube.com/watch?v=1YC7FXgPVWY

Who does the President of the United States represent?

Who does the President of the United States work for?

Who pays the President of the United States' salary?

Which country's Constitution did President Obama swear to defend, twice?

Bush would be impeached by the Libs & Democrats for this short sentence, but an (inclusive bipartisan bridge-builder) can say anything with impunity!

http://www.youtube.com/watch?v=gWJCjARR3rY&feature=related

Was that Racist, or just Hate-Speech we all just witnessed from our Prez?

To listen to Sean Hannity and P.J. O'Rourke today: Oct. 26, 2010, kibitzing about the same stuff I'd written in my book: FIRE THEM ALL??,
Pg. 380

two years ago, as though it was their great epiphany,
I am reminded of screaming at the radio and TV for weeks, months,
and in fact years, asking; Where have all these guys been?

And what are you really going to "suggest to help solve this disaster" with some real, practical, viable solutions, along with this daily investigative analysis.

Great for ratings, but "where's the beef," because time's run-out
for a lot of us long ago.

So, "here's exactly what you can do about it" so we can all save our collective butts, while the Obama/Social Democrat juggernaut smashes the US Constitution to bits, as these Giants of the Airways delve into their minutia of "micromanagement".

<u>I'll make it very simple</u> for those without any direction or convictions, and you supposedly "Independents" and "Fence sitters":

A. "Some" Muslims openly cheered ("without criticism" from their peers) when 9/11 happened,.....but "ALL" Democrats cheered when Obamacare happened!.....Hello?.....a passive GOP bites their tongue and zips their lip!

B. And just because those same Democrats now say: Obama Who?,
<u>Remember…Never Forget!</u>

1. Who kept the soldiers from being fully funded, subsequently extending the wars, and repeatedly forced Bush to come to Capitol Hill for our troops, hat in hand, begging?

2. Who stopped Bush from reining–in: Fanny/Freddie for years, 5xs??

3. Who wouldn't let Bush tackle Healthcare???

4. Who wouldn't let Bush tackle SSI Reform????

5. Who's been running the country and the economy since 2007, and what was the unemployment rate, GDP and the Dow before then?????

6. Who voted for the Stimulus to keep unemployment below 8% with a shovel, and the true NUMBER is never used, even by GOP??????

7. Why does every election regress into a bidding war, and a popularity contest, ignoring the greater concerns, i.e. competency?   Pg. 381

8. Why does more money in a campaign, last minute accusations, and the barrage of attack-ads influence more people to abandon their common sense, dismiss the fundamental issues, and compromise their beliefs, just to Vote-back-in the same charlatans; believing the same old promises? Like living with the drunk, an addict, or wife beater, who had dragged us to this party? "We don't have to dance with the One who-brung-us anymore".

9. How long must we all live in denial, or suffer mass Stockholm syndrome? *Does your ideology trump even your common sense?*

10. What has the Democrat Party actual ever solved in the 60 years of promises, agitation, anger, angst and control? *Answer this one?*

11. What's happened to your outrage, and indignation and love of country? *No One will protect your family, only this Constitution!*

12. *Did You answer truthfully?.....* REMEMBER........NEVER FORGET!

Let John Stossel throw away his Vote in PROTEST to the Ex-Lady of the Evening.

Don't You make the same mistake….It may be the most important Vote you have ever cast,
or maybe ever will cast in Your entire Life!......SENTRYMAN 10-27-10 Blog

Goodnight America! Braver souls will watch over us as we let down our guard to sleep, but it won't be Congress!

SENTRYMAN

DEBATE video www.youtube.com/watch?v=swFD-Ybh7dY
Remember to Click: "Pause" & restart & "Pause-stop" again to read each freeze-frame image when desired, a whole lot of images flying bye!

As DEMs distance themselves from "Obama Who;
(I'm an Independent liberal Democrat progressive, ONLY looking out for my constituents, my HOMIES"),

(though THEY were "All In", & 100% on the OBAMACARE POKER HAND: the Stimulus and Omnibus, CAP n'Tax, Taxpayer PAID Abortion for the World, and bringing GITMO to Illinois,)

Pg. 382

and NOW poised to Snooker everyone again that's NOT paying attention, numb to logic and reality, have their UNION's marching orders, or really don't care, as long as they get their Check In The Mail from Godfather Uncle Sam,

(that's the Legislative Surrogate for the American Taxpayer, since actually: WE are The Government!)

REMEMBER: OUR Legislators are but Hired Hands, run amuck, Raiding Our Cookie Jar, Our Sock Drawer, and Our Mattress Safe, when they're Not Printing Obamopoly Dollars, and Mortgaging Us-All-into-Oblivion;

We never hear this stated often enough to make the point; "Government Produces Nothing......Government Creates Nothing",

"WHAT DOES GOVERNMENT DO RIGHT,
OR EVEN WELL ENOUGH"
TO DESERVE YOUR VALUABLE VOTE AGAIN;
The Economy?,
Fannie/Fred?,
the VA?,
Infrastructure?,
SSI-?,
SSD-?,
the Border?,
Immigration?,
the Gulf?,
Obama-Motors?   http://www.youtube.com/watch?v=xx7fNQcJAjs

They can't even deliver the mail competently!
Pay Raises, No, no, they give themselves Pay Raises very well, have they ever given themselves a CUT?
...Only the People get the cuts with a Chain saw and Freddy Krueger – vote!

 Happy Halloween voters...Washington's Zombies are com'in for Us, with their eager arms extended with loving embraces again, palms up!!
http://www.sentryman.org/id18.html

**A BLOG Posted by SENTRYMAN on Sept. 9, 2010 below;

WANT YOUR COUNTRY BACK?...This may be our only chance!
God protect those brave women and men that protect us all, especially since our government won't !!

Pg. 383

Had our military been properly supplied, staffed and enthusiastically supported from Day 1, as in 1942, and not routinely obstructed by: The Left, Democrats, The Media and Hollywood, like this.......;

*(U.S. Marines "killed innocent civilians in cold blood,", John Murtha)
www.youtube.com/watch?v=cTBQW-FYEKg

www.youtube.com/watch?v=b-ZLcrOvzJM

www.youtube.com/watch?v=s-qBJwjSKA8&feature=related

*("troops just air-raiding villages and killing civilians", Sen. Obama)
www.youtube.com/watch?v=wrW4fOGIMVY

*("the war is lost" Harry Reid)
www.youtube.com/watch?v=jyDOAmJYFFA

http://www.youtube.com/watch?v=jyDOAmJYFFA

http://www.youtube.com/watch?v=rZm8j9sArdg&feature=related

http://www.youtube.com/watch?v=UP6qeBPl_HA&feature=related

*(no reason why American soldiers need to terrorize Iraqi women and children, Sen. John Kerry)
www.youtube.com/watch?v=EXaoavV1d4s

www.youtube.com/watch?v=dRjUubkhmv4&feature=related

*(in case you didn't read the memo while not-reading the Obama-Care Bill, Senator, it's a volunteer military),

......the wars would have been "quickly, successfully and victoriously" concluded years ago,
even foreign governments, and their citizens today would be on the road to Democracy, with "free enterprise and prosperity", (i.e. Japan & Germany)!

Enemies against humanity would have and should have been universally vanquished and despised, "not emulated",
and thousands more snuffed-out lives, permanent injuries and mental scars would have been saved, spared and averted,

and many, many more of our own valiant kids would be alive and at home right this minute with their loved ones enjoying the America that once was! No President, NO PRESIDENT can be successful, or popular with one hand tied behind their back, trying to protect us, and simultaneously waging a "War on the Cheap",   Pg. 384

(why respond to a "4 Alarm fire" with 2 trucks and burn up your Firemen and lose the house?...

If your Generals ask for 40,000 troops so more can go home, <u>send 70,000 troops so they all go home</u>,
but certainly Not 30,000, and piecemealed over the next year,
so your son never returns home, and just for the politic of it all !)

Nor can soldiers perform their jobs expeditiously while walking-on-egg shells, and protecting the Peace for the rest of the world they get for FREE!

<u>Hey World, who do you think pays to keep the world fed and safe?.....</u>

It's human nature not to appreciate anything one receives at no personal expense, or respect ones benefactors, and quite normal to bite the hand that feeds, but our soldiers don't have to take-it "in the back" under DEMs!

Maybe Mexicans, and the Canadians would see the world differently if they spoke German or Japanese today!.....I know the French would, and certainly not be as sanctimoniously smug, while simultaneously taking Saddam's bribes, if they eventually spoke Arabic.

Of course, they might just do that to themselves anyway, then who will they ask to help them, yet again, Ghostbusters?

I'm darn sure Germany couldn't,
nor could Canada offer its citizens FREE healthcare, if the American Taxpayers weren't indirectly footing their bills, and paying the freight to police the planet! ...How's that for simple Economics 101, children?

But, thank you England and Australia and Canada, and a very short list of other friends for assisting America and Bush in the desert, keeping the globe from being set ablaze. There's even more smoldering kindling now!

Well, so how often do you hear any of that harsh reality from our imperious Republican legislators, or from our indignant, self-righteous accusatory DEMs?...forget about the 4th Estate, they're already molder'n in the grave!!

(*Note: "Live" Video Links on My KINDLE /Click *LIVE LINKs* a couple times)

FIRE THEM ALL?? ....on Amazon.com
http://www.amazon.com/s/ref=nb_sb_noss?url=search-alias%3Ddigital-text&field-keywords=It+Was+Never+About+The+Black+Guy%2C+It+Was+About+%22That+Guy%22%21+THE+FINAL+SOLUTION...+FIRE+THEM+ALL%3F%3F

Pg. 385

"The Plan and the Final Solution to Save America for Everyone"

IQ Test: Obama Supporters
www.youtube.com/watch?v=zl0WwC9OcOl&feature=related

Some Muslim Groups Cut Young Kids Heads Open
www.youtube.com/watch?v=5bDtHSAzYXl

Obama is FOR building Ground Zero Mosque
www.youtube.com/watch?v=RaFQ7SLWnBl&feature=related

Obama Says America Muslim Nation
www.youtube.com/watch?v=wmuE-kNgeSA

Obama In Turkey "We Do Not Consider Ourselves A Christian Nation
www.youtube.com/watch?v=QIVd7YT0oWA&feature=related

OR ELSE!
Ground Zero Imam: Build the Mosque OR ELSE
www.youtube.com/watch?v=sll46-81Qkw

OR ELSE!
Obama Refuses to Wear The Flag Pin
http://www.youtube.com/watch?v=KvBpm_3kCAw&feature=player_embedded

Obama FORCED to wear the flag pin
http://www.youtube.com/watch?v=YUW1-oilDlc&feature=player_embedded

Obama Admits He Is A Muslim
http://www.youtube.com/watch?v=tCAffMSWSzY&feature=player_embedded#!

Obama Omits "Creator" from the Declaration of Independence
http://www.youtube.com/watch?v=9GP01KpeAUs&feature=related

Frances Fox Piven: "We Got Obama - that's not bad at all"
http://www.youtube.com/watch?v=DlaUFdbW8X4

Mark Levin: The Cloward Piven & Obama strategy
http://www.youtube.com/watch?v=-g6SpnTcMx8&feature=related

The End of America....The Cloward-Piven Strategy.
http://www.youtube.com/watch?v=n5xJZEY3oz0&feature=related

Rush: A Spirited Talk with President Bush 11-9-10
http://www.rushlimbaugh.com/home/daily/site_110910/content/01125111.guest.html

Decision Points: George W. Bush

http://www.amazon.com/gp/product/0307590615?ie=UTF8&tag=theofficiw0c2-20&linkCode=as2&camp=1789&creative=9325&creativeASIN=0307590615

The American President Happily Heralds Decline of US Dominance

November 9, 2010
http://www.rushlimbaugh.com/home/daily/site_110910/content/01125106.guest.html

The Times of India: Obama acknowledges decline of US dominance
http://timesofindia.indiatimes.com/india/Obama-acknowledges-decline-of-US-dominance/articleshow/6885877.cms

The New York Times – ASIA PACIFIC: Obama Visits a Nation That Knew Him as Barry
http://www.nytimes.com/2010/11/09/world/asia/09indo.html?_r=1

The Empire - On China, daylight between Schumer and Bloomberg
http://empire.wnyc.org/2010/11/on-china-daylight-between-schumer-and-bloomberg/

FIRE THEM ALL??
GOP Rep. Buyer Blasts Acting Dem Speaker: "This is why the People have...
http://www.youtube.com/watch?v=qJSnozJ4LVg&feature=player_embedded#!

RUSH: Tax Rates & Deficit Commission
http://www.rushlimbaugh.com/home/daily/site_113010/content/01125106.guest.html

Barack Obama – Why do you want to be president?
https://www.youtube.com/watch?v=JjGRIoyZrQ8&feature=related

Radical Islam is the preference for a grand finale'
http://www.youtube.com/watch?v=THICNIzMJtk&feature=related

Bodies not their own....
http://www.youtube.com/watch?v=SsExiAbCk1A&feature=related

The Whole WikiLeaks Thing Is....
http://www.youtube.com/watch?v=mB-dS2STR6s

Well Donald, tell us how you really feel....
https://www.youtube.com/watch?v=NFMDNg9VGIQ

and the Award goes to....
http://www.sentryman.org/id20.html

Bill asks if the President has any friends that aren't Leftists?
https://www.youtube.com/watch?v=BGL4PTkTOQw&feature=related

Pg. 387

"If freedom of speech is taken away, then dumb and silent we may be led, like sheep to the slaughter."
— George Washington

"I believe there are more instances of the abridgment of the freedom of the people by gradual and silent encroachments of those in power than by violent and sudden usurpations."
— James Madison

The only weapon that we have in our hands this evening is the weapon of protest. That's all."
— Martin Luther King Jr

SENTRYMAN...........truth whence came from northern skies.

The <u>God</u> Debate:
<u>http://www.youtube.com/watch?v=9V85OykSDT8&feature=related</u>

God keep the smallest among us, forbidden the light to take their first breath!
 - SENTRYMAN

Kindle 3rd Edition postscript: *Happy Memorial Day addendum...*

Think for a moment.....have I your attention?

Ever think: "If only I had _____, whatever, this or that wouldn't have happened"! (*If - Only!*)

Can we affect "any" outcome, can we change time and space, or is it completely out of our hands? Is it habit, instinct, fate, inevitable, synchronicity, and if "we're not paying attention", or if "we ignore the signs" against our better nature, *that old feeling in the pit of our stomach*; "That's the signpost up ahead—your next stop, the Twilight Zone!"......or is it "CHOICE"?

World Trade Center and 911 Connections from 1980`s Doc.
http://www.youtube.com/watch?v=siffZZvRkE0&index=21&list=PLToTG4Ur DonX9NXoBpiiwPXiepvWZeeKJ

Got'cha,
but now I really think I might have your attention, so, things-are-connected, we are all-connected, and if we don't see, or we don't act, or "go-along to just get-along", then, we are no better or safer than a loosed fishing-bobber floating aimlessly upon an endless surf; ending-up snared in someone's net, or washed-ashore in South-east Asia!

(What is he trying to say?....What is he rambling about?.....)

E.g. "If I just hadn't drank that much, hadn't gone-out, hadn't gotten into that argument, or hadn't let her leave alone!"

"If I had opened my eyes in-time, not condoned that behavior, insisted-on more from my Legislators, demanded more of my President, not turned my back on my country and the U.S. Constitution, and, had I paid "full attention" to how all of my friends were telling me "how to act", and had "just started thinking for my-self"!

James Burke: Connections, The weather and the warning!
http://www.youtube.com/watch?v=RfE8wBRelxw

http://www.youtube.com/results?search_query=james+burke+connections

If-Only President Bill Clinton had taken custody of Osama bin Laden, (either of the 2 times) he was offered to Slick Willie, instead of just chasing-skirts around the Oval Office = NO 9/11 ?

If-Only the U.N. hadn't submitted and permitted Saddam Hussein to flick-his-middle-finger at them (15 separate-sanctioned-times), by refusing their UN Inspection's supervision of his supposed "complete disposal" of those (1000's of liters of WMD materials), just as "THE U.N. had previously mandated <u>14 previous 2nd chances</u>", after another Bush and a great armada of brave "volunteer" U.S. Soldiers had already accomplished for the world, the Saudi's and Kuwaitis by finally putting Saddam back into his place = NO IRAQ WAR?

If-Only the US Sec. of State: Hillary Clinton had "answered that 3AM emergency phone call from Africa she'd promised her Countrymen many times, or
if-ONLY our own President Barack Hussein Obama had "Called-In-The-Calvary" to rescue our desperate fighting men, as he'd sworn an oath to do;
(During Real Time Were Immediately Ordered To "STAND-DOWN" and Not-To-Assist *Christopher Stevens* Our Ambassador, While He Was Being Attacked and Overrun By Unknown Professional Hostile Forces, our-braver-men ignored that "chicken-$#!& SNAFU Order", to risk their own lives by successfully still saving approximately 20 other additional Outpost Personnel from their certain DEATH that night in Benghazi, before they, themselves being (abandoned by their Commander-in-Chief Pres. BHO and their boss Hillary Rodham Clinton, and died) some 7 hours later): WHO was instead thinking about HIS re-election fund-raiser the next morning, while packing HIS suits for Vegas = Hussein would be a Hero too, <u>instead</u>?

If-Only Barack had kept at least the (1) promise about overhauling the VA, just as a "Test-case", and a simple "Object Lesson" of his great personal Healthcare prowess and expertise, then (10s, of probably 100s) of brave U.S. Military Service Veterans = would be celebrating this Memorial Day weekend with their grandchildren,
instead of becoming "bitter-sweet memories" for their families who were setting an empty-plate for THEM at their holiday picnic table?

If-Only Barry had stood-up like "every other US President" for the usually prescribed "normal sanctions and status protocols" when exiting Iraq and Afghanistan in Victory, we'd have a secured-presents, plus a growing Democracy in each country as a Legacy for the US and the Allied free-world country's blood and treasure donated-Freely to them, but NOW, ONLY a momentarily-Freed People!

But instead now, what "the fates" will bring our weaker unstable-world in this greatly shortened uncertain future as again our brave volunteer women and men are shot in-the-back while hastily readying to return home to Barack's Peace-In-Our-Time,

with (the 3rd Joker in the deck) Iran of this 3-legged stool, rapidly sawing-off the 3rd leg of "Hope" in this (3-on-a-match) region, and giving America their (3rd finger salute) this holiday weekend, yet once again and not just for the 3rd time either.....(3rd times the charm or 3 strikes and you're out? Not with Hussein Obama!) This most probably will denote the demise and end of Israel and the Jewish people; if that wasn't the real plan all along. Unfortunately too, for these "vanquished foes", who would most-assuredly have ended-up like 2 other defeated-foes of American's strength and generosity in bye-gone days: Germany and Japan, NOPE, too bad = stay in the 8th century if that serves your purposes and enslaved people!

If-Only our government had at least done their usual "inept cursory-job" in Vetting our current President, prior to his anointment = "what would America look like today" with a McCain, or a Romney, or even a Hillary, and our once lofty position on the world stage and honored place in history?

.....we sure wouldn't be scrambling the roof for the last Chopper-OUT!

CONNECTIONs = Pay ATTENTION,
follow the U.S. Constitution, and demand the same of the Democrat party!
There is no party tonight, just our Americans thinking about better days.

May 24th 2014
S.

...and buy a Poppy from that man standing in the sun, in front of your grocery store this weekend, and say: "Thank you for your service"!
.....If only!

Kindle BACK COVER

After 235 years in America, shouldn't the Supreme Court's undeniably perceived difference between "right and wrong" be greater than a "4 to 5" opinion?... A revolution has started and it's 1938 all over again; Peace In Our Time? ...You're not listening, again! ...Time has run out! ...The only hope: Prop. 86! ...My book offers ideas outside the mainstream, which can restore the economy & jobs, solutions for a renegade government, and confronts terrorism. "America's liberty wasn't forged in the same furnace as the Samurai and Damascus blades; it was tempered by an idea: All men only united and equal under God can help each-other stay free!" This book analyzes, examines, challenges and exposes "all who are unwilling" to play fairly and by the Rules, and those who DO NOT obey or hold sacred the Constitution of the U.S. of A, I humbly advise with some good old fashioned Common Sense. I attempt to enlighten those perpe-traitors with rational debate and honest opinion tempered by time; yet with a fundamental Faith in the Human Spirit; To Do Good, and To Do No Harm! And since Heaven helps those that "Do", We must still help those who Can't, but Not those that Don't, who Rule and Won't FREE their people to realize who they wish to be. We too must recognize, with deep respect ALL those that choose to live their lives by the moral "Golden Rule"!..... 		EM - SENTRYMAN There but for the Grace Of GOD go we!........

This treatise advocates that any action; implied, suggested, intended or demanded, be conducted and waged by NON-VIOLENT means, and with-in the limits of the Laws of the United States of America.

In closing: a Special "Thank You" To The Ones That Mean The Most!

On behalf of all the named & unnamed persons mentioned in this book, who have unfortunately and continually dishonored, or are reticent to pay due respect to give rightful acknowledgment for the sacrifices by those that came before us, a Special "Thank You" to the ones that mean the most! Those who put their "personal lives on-hold" to protect us all, to those who donated their professional careers to watch over us, and especially to the families of those that never came back, who give and gave full measure of themselves selflessly for fellow countrymen and countrywomen; those brave women and men of the U.S. Armed Forces!

Thank You To Those That Watch And Wait…..
Thank You To Those That Stave Off The Hate…..
Thank You To Those That Stand Through The Night…
Thank You To Those That Never Abandon The Fight…..
Thank You To Those That Stay And Serve A Third Tour….
 …..When Leaving The 2nd Their Own Lives They'd Secure….
Thank You To Those That Protect Brothers Protecting Our Sons….
Thank You To Those That Always Remain Till The Mission Is Done….
Thank You To The Fallen, …For Our Lives and Our Daily Bread,………
Thank You To The Fallen, …Homage To Your Sacrifice: Freedom Never Dead,…
Better Men Than We, That Guard As Peter; Upon This Rock,
May He Watch Over You As You Shepherd Your Flock!

"Thank You" Can Never, Will Never Be Enough!		S. 4-6-2010